EVERYMAN'S ENGLAND

For several years the author has been editor of the British Tourist Authority's monthly travel and feature magazine *In Britain*, which is primarily aimed at overseas visitors to this country but has a substantial following at home. He particularly wishes to thank the BTA for their kind co-operation in making available the black-and-white photographs in this book from their excellent library.

The colour photographs are from the library of the late Eric Rowell and are reproduced by kind permission of the copyright owner, Mrs D. Rowell.

EVERYMAN'S ENGLAND

Bryn Frank

1817

HARPER & ROW, PUBLISHERS, New York

Cambridge, Philadelphia, San Francisco,
London, Mexico City, São Paulo, Sydney

FIRST U.S. EDITION

ISBN: 0-06-015361-X

LIBRARY OF CONGRESS CATALOG CARD NUMBER: 84-47368

Contents

I

II

III

List of Colour Photographs

List of Maps

Preface

I was curious from an early age about those odd and unregarded corners of England that rarely get into the guide books. I am familiar with corners of moorland in counties that are beyond most people's ken ('What do you mean, Cleveland?') and strangers en route for exotic destinations ask my advice: 'I believe you can recommend a good hotel in Runcorn.' I have dished out information about provincial Indian restaurants and dug up deserted sandy coves for friends who have to take their holidays in the height of August.

In no respect, however, is this book a definitive guide. Any country house buff or hill walker who attempts to use it as an essential companion will end up flinging it in frustration to the back of the car, and cursing my name. Any local councillor who would judge me by glancing at the index can save himself the trouble: his town is probably not even mentioned. Some whole counties will cry 'Stinking fish' while others, I hope, will be flattered by the attention they get. But for the ordinary traveller it might just spark off some ideas, and for the armchair traveller it might be the stuff that future plans or nostalgic dreams are made of.

Most of it is loosely – but loosely – based on an anti-clockwise journey through England, and is an amalgam of several journeys, sometimes recollected in tranquillity, sometimes written up over a plate of biriani-of-old-England in a one-horse town, with the sun setting over the industrial estate and the only reasonable looking guest house within a radius of ten miles about to lock its doors for the night.

Most of it derives from an England viewed from the windscreen of a car. Some of it, like a few famous people, was conceived on the back of a bus. Sometimes I even walked, and when I could I took the train: surely still, at its best, the most civilised way to travel. Most of my impressions were personal, but some were coloured by the views of back-of-beyond garage mechanics (mechanical breakdowns do wonders for breaking down social barriers) and loquacious antique shop owners ('You're the first person who's been in here for a week') who were never quite certain whether or not I would buy something. And just occasionally I did.

There are still waspish and jaded books to be written about England, which is not a difficult option, and Mrs Cholmondeley's coffee table shows there is a market for rose-coloured spectacles. Hopefully this comes over as neither jaded nor rosy. If it has to be categorised at all it is probably 'off beat'. Not always deliberately. It is just that in both tourist honeypots and tucked away places I have always preferred to be around at odd times or unlikely seasons of the year. Falmouth in March does not leave me cold, and I am a sucker for the back streets of Stoke-on-Trent on quiet Sunday afternoons. I will take Anne Hathaway's Cottage in January but leave well alone in August. In these pages I have also taken a sidelong glance at how England turned out the way it did, and at some of the mysteries and legends that invest every other square mile of the country. I have tried to encapsulate some of the unflagging appeal of stately homes and the romance of castles. I have also tried to convince southerners that there is life north of Watford and northerners that they do not have the monopoly of native wit and an ability to make strangers feel at home.

I would have got nowhere (literally) without the patience and hard work of Elaine Robertson, who helped prepare the manuscript. My thanks are also due not only to the BTA photographic library but also to Dee Rowell for allowing me to choose from the photographic library of her late husband, Eric.

Most of all, without the encouragement and understanding of my wife Carole, and my children Nicholas and Rachel, to whom I was too often an absentee husband and father, I would probably have given up somewhere near Northampton and gone home to watch the telly. . . .

Bryn Frank

Introduction

The 'idea of England' travels well. Expatriates particularly miss the English sense of humour, and I suspect that they get just as nostalgic about the weather. Not, however, that it rains as much as they think: a Fleet Street journalist of my acquaintance, who lives near Regent's Park and walks to work, says the average number of days on which she has got wet, calculated over a decade, is twelve a year. Not all of them will admit it, but I believe many exiles secretly hanker after those November fogs that muffle the sound of traffic in big cities, or the lightning that illuminates bruised skies on summer afternoons, or snowstorms that mean you get stuck in country pubs after closing time.

It is hard to convince publishers of glossy calendars of the fact, but perpetual blue skies are unnecessary to sell the idea of England. Certainly I have enjoyed lazy hours on the edge of Lincolnshire's cornfields and gazed up into what Tennyson called 'yonder living blue'. And I have chugged shirtless up the River Fal in Cornwall on a summer evening on an excursion boat, turned lobster pink and glowed as if I were radioactive. But most of my nostalgia trips seem to involve a bit of real weather. Take Ilkley Moor, in Yorkshire. I have wilted there among the bracken during one of those heatwaves that meteorologists tell us are rare in England but which seem to come round quite regularly. I much preferred the place as night began to fall and Ilkley's street lamps came on, or, just as nice, on one of those days when rain has taken over the town like an army of occupation, driving the population indoors but leaving only hikers in their incongruously bright anoraks mooching disconsolately among the dark stone buildings. It is not, of course, just a matter of personal comfort, for the shaping of England and most of the nicest characteristics of the countryside are largely due to the effects of weather in all its forms. It has created caves, marshes, deepened river gorges; it has formed watermeadows, smoothed sandstone, pockmarked limestone, widened lakes, rendered farmland green and prosperous, cloaked hills in trees, made most of the country not just habitable but a pleasure to live in.

I like weather that fights back a bit, and I dislike the physical manifestations of summer: flies that alight on your skin as if it was toast spread with honey, insect bites that flare up on your flesh and linger for a fortnight, the seat of the car that sticks to your clothes like spilt Coca Cola, the airless, suffocating, sleepless nights. In winter, in the country, the town dweller at least notices more. The sharper air concentrates the mind. Perhaps there really is more to see: flocks of starlings against a 3 pm sunset like a handful of currants flung into the air, a stoat that scuttles across the road in front of you like a supercharged clockwork mouse, a pheasant that lethargically takes flight from behind a threadbare winter hedge.

Bleak and windswept moorland looms large in my own home thoughts from abroad, but so do cool and sun-dappled forests and woods, especially the ones you find among little valleys tucked away within the Kentish Weald: where the smell of woodsmoke on an autumn afternoon mingles with the earthy and pungent aroma of tree fungus, and where the jolly woodman whose axe blows against the trunk of a silver birch echo across the hillside turns out to be a London bank manager enjoying his weekend off.

Living on an island is supposed to make bank managers, and anybody else, more in tune with the world. The idea that Englishmen, notwithstanding their Celtic neighbours, are an island people, might confuse a Brummie, since he is so far from the sea, but the combination of our insular status and the vagaries of the seasons may account for some of our national characteristics. This will inevitably seem self-congratulatory, but the English *are* tolerant. As long as nobody else's dog pees in their back garden, they will put up with all sorts of bizarre behaviour down their street. As long as they get home at night they don't worry overmuch about whether their trains actually run on time.

The English do seem to be well organised within a comparatively small space, which is not to say that England is anything like as crowded as some people think. In their way, spring, summer, autumn and winter bring Geordies and Liverpudleans as close to nature as the ever-shifting tides that remind Orcadians who is really boss. Salford on a wet day in February may not inspire many poets (though it did all right for L. S. Lowry), and Sir John Betjeman may still find it hard to love Slough; contraflow systems on the M6 on a hot August Bank Holiday Monday may cause Thomas Telford to turn in his grave, and it is not so much the chips with everything that would now upset Arnold Wesker, literally as well as figuratively, as the hamburgers that come with the chips. In spite of such things, however, England is a very civilised place indeed. It is identifiable, tangible, and altogether worth writing home about.

I once worked temporarily for a travel agent and was prevailed upon to accompany an elderly farmer from Ohio, a second-generation American called Sam, on a nostalgic last trip to England. The fact that he has been back several times since then is a tribute less to my skill as a guide than to his unexpected longevity. He had a very precise list of the things he wanted to do. He absolutely had to fulfil a long-standing ambition and travel on a canal boat, and to go to the races. He wanted to be accompanied to a village cricket match and to a funfair. He wanted to travel on a steam train and to go on a picnic, and, as he was not going to pass this way again, and his son had been a student there, he absolutely had to go punting on the river at Cambridge.

Those two weeks or so during which Sam and I travelled together provided me with the raw material for off-duty weekends to last decades, and the stuff of dreams of England that were to get me by in the tropics and the deserts of Western Australia. I had never before even set foot on a canal boat, nor, since school, sat through a cricket match. I had not been to the races since a charabanc outing to the Derby during which I saw a lot of people but no horses, nor been to a fair since I was fifteen and a gipsy had cursed me for cheating on the roll-a-penny-down-the-chute stall. (I had placed a coin much too neatly to be true on the sixpenny square, avoiding the black lines, and won nothing except a nasty fright for my pains.) And as for picnics, for years I had preferred flock-walled Indian restaurants and four-star hotels. Fish and chips, at least, I knew about because I have roots in the north-east of England, which claims to do a better cod and twenty penn'orth of chips than anywhere else in the country.

The man from the tourist board arranged for us to meet a canal boat owner. It could only have been the owner, for a holidaymaker would not have been watering his garden – a well nurtured, carefully tended vegetable and flower garden running the whole length of the sixty-foot-long boat. For three years, he said, he had lived alone on the boat, and had covered most of the country at an average of three miles an hour.

We spent three days with him, mainly on the Worcester and Birmingham canal, sometimes threading our way through pastoral green backwaters, sometimes rather surreptitiously behind factories, between warehouses, past skyscrapers. I said it must be a lonely life. 'Not at all,' he insisted, 'there is always somebody around to tell me where the Chinese takeaway is, or where I can find a launderette or a supermarket, and, like tramps, you tend to get the very best local knowledge and practical information from other permanent boatmen.'

We found our cricket match courtesy of an old schoolfriend. It has been pithily pointed out that five-day international Test matches can last a total of thirty hours and not produce a result. Real cricket fans will, of course, say that such details are irrelevant. Village cricket, however, is not only more accessible for the uninitiated but much less likely to end in a draw. And with a pint of scrumpy inside him, the shade of a chestnut tree and the sight of fifteen flannelled fools – that is, including two umpires – Sam did not really care what the rules were. 'If my friends could see me now,' he chuckled, his bony, pink knees protruding from his long shorts, totally unreminiscent of Shirley MacLaine.

What I had not bargained for was that I would be expected to play. The match I had arranged for us to see was in a Kent village in which both sides were composed mainly of solicitors and chartered accountants of my vague acquaintance. Only the village blacksmith seemed conspicuous by his absence. They rang me up the evening before we were due to go down. It was all too ominously like *England, their England*. 'We hope you don't mind,' they said, 'but we've said you wouldn't mind making up for somebody who can't play. Our usual chap can't make it because his wife has left him and he's gone to get her back.' To tell the truth, I was more concerned about getting hold of the right clothes than the ordeal of playing. The white sweater and shirt I could manage, and my plimsolls (boots were quite out of the question) I could at least whiten up. The trousers eventually had to come from somebody's attic, however, though they did not actually flap around my ankles too conspicuously. In the end it was all right. The eleventh man discovered his wife was merely upset because she was tired of washing up in the pavilion every Sunday, and I became twelfth man by default, and was not called upon to play. Thus, in the comfort of our deckchairs, half watching the match, Sam and I discovered that the sounds of cricket are every bit as nostalgic as the sights: the tinkle of teacups from the pavilion (eleventh man's wife was not on duty), the humming of bees, snatches of half-heard conversation from two deckchairs away, the sharp crack of bat against ball, the strangled cry of 'Howzzat' from the fielders.

Cricket is an unselfconscious link with England's past, and if, pint glass in hand, the spectators at Hambledon, in Hampshire, do not know that during the second half of the eighteenth century this village regularly took on the rest of England for stakes that would be today's equivalent of tens of thousands of pounds, it is not important. Even two hundred years before that there are records of a form of cricket having been played by schoolboys in Guildford, though even in Surrey and Hampshire cricket is probably never taken quite so seriously as it is in Yorkshire, where people still remember that one hamlet, Lascelles Hall, once had seven players in a Yorkshire eleven. Sunday afternoon drivers, incidentally, may need to take care in certain locations: cricket played on the green at Lyndhurst, in Hampshire, may cause balls to land on the Southampton to Bournemouth road, and in a village called No Man's Land, the county boundary of Hampshire passes through the middle of the pitch. As cricket commentator and writer John Arlott, now exiled in cricket-less Alderney, among the Channel Islands, once pointed out, a batsman may be caught in Wiltshire from a ball bowled in Wiltshire, without leaving Hampshire.

We found our fair, in Norwich, and I was surprisingly easily persuaded to waste the whole evening there. The acrid smell of grilling hamburgers, cheap teenage perfume and candyfloss is a heady combination, even if anybody over thirty feels like a grandfather. We must have made an incongruous couple as we traipsed through mud fast beginning to resemble Flanders' fields. Sam did have the advantage over most of the people there in that he seemed to know an awful lot about fairgrounds. It turned out that his grandfather had operated the wall of death at Nottingham Goose Fair for twenty years or more before the last war. Apparently most fairs originated in the Middle Ages and were a focal point for trade. Having a fair could be so important economically that local people would petition the king for a charter to hold one, and could pay through the nose for the privilege: Charles I took £400 (worth perhaps £40,000 today) from the people of Derby before he would grant their petition. The Goose Fair at which Sam's grandfather had worked claimed to be the biggest in the country. It was once the centre of a huge catchment area for smallholders and large farmers breeding geese, and they were walked to Nottingham for upwards of 150 miles, their feet shod in a mixture of sand and tar. There are no geese now, though there is quite a lot of goosing.

We got our fish and chips that same evening, but obviously not the way Sam expected them. The fish and chip shop was next door to a Chinese takeaway, and was run by the same owner, from Taiwan. In his way, though, he was quite a traditionalist: he wrapped up our Yarmouth cod in pages of the *News of the World*, and he sold bottles of pop. Sam and I went back to the car and shared a lukewarm bottle of gassy dandelion and burdock.

We went punting on the River Cam, and such was Sam's single-mindedness that he hardly glanced at that city-within-a-university. We made straight for Scudamores, where body-builders in tee shirts and faded jeans dole out punts like over-worked Charons. We both had a go and neither of us fell in, although even such a dramatic event as falling into the river here is usually quite a low-key affair: much flailing of arms and the occasional pirouette may give the passer-by cause for contemplation, but harm is rarely done. Unlike the Norfolk Broads, which unhappily claim on average half a dozen drownings a year, the Cam is innocent stuff: about the worst thing you can do is to damage your punt and lose your deposit. Sam pronounced that it was by far the best way to see the Backs, especially as one is admired and envied by assembled hundreds of language school students and Japanese rubber-neckers who, at the hint of a pale sun over the pinnacles of King's College Chapel, will prostrate themselves on the grassy river bank. After a bit of trial and error we quickly discovered the golden rule, which is to look as if you mean to do what you are doing even if you are doing it wrong.

And we went to the races. Happily, it was Goodwood week, and I was saved the indignity of Ladies' Day at Ascot, which is what he had in mind at first: too many women, with cheeks of porcelain and voices of tin, more concerned with what Jonquil did for his holidays and when Antonia is Coming Out than with who is going to win the three-thirty. I had, however, been warned off racecourse food, even at Glorious Goodwood, which is how we picked up the makings of a picnic in Haslemere and tucked into it on the downs. We were lucky enough to find a shop that sold Real Food: that is, pork pies with aspic in them, ham off the bone, enhanced by a crispy black skin I took to be baked-on honey, cold roast chicken that was white and not pink. We bought some home-made rolls too, and some crumbly mince slices. The cottage-loaf-shaped lady who sold them to us turned out to be an enthusiastic Haslemere Festival-goer and a member of the church choir to boot. She seemed to be well up on religious connotations and gastronomic anecdotes, for she told us that mince pies were once savoury pasties made of exotic spices, and baked in an oblong shape said to resemble the manger at Bethlehem. They were abjured by Puritans on the grounds that this was part of a Papist plot.

We ate the remains of our feast on Trundle Hill, from which hoi polloi get a reasonable view of the races without paying over the odds. The climb was steep, but not as steep as the price of Bollinger and Pacific prawns. (We overheard somebody who *had* pushed the boat out complain, 'You'd think that at these prices they would chill the damn glasses.') Unlike Royal Ascot, Goodwood is not a place where you have to mind your p's and q's, though you might have to queue to pee. People are more concerned about whether Lester is liable to cop a seven day suspension than whether the Earl of March is in the crowd that afternoon. It is, rather, a garden party writ large, a hedonistic feast with top class horses and jockeys amid the scented Downs, under a sun that – if you are lucky – is sufficiently warm and soporific to make the nastier manifestations of the twentieth century seem a long way away.

Sam's steam trains were not difficult to find. Like the thatcher who seemed only a few years ago to be about to disappear into the history books, the fireman and the brass-hatted station master have made an unlikely comeback. There seem to be more full-sized steam trains puffing around England than there are train sets in Hamleys. We wandered through England as in a Doctor Who time warp. We took in the Keighley and Worth Valley railway, the North Norfolk railway, the Tenterden Railway in Kent, and others, and particularly enjoyed (an unfashionable one this) the Nene Valley Railway, just a five-minute drive from the age-old Haycock Inn, just off the A1 near Peterborough. The Nene Valley Railway brings you slap bang into the 1920s and '30s. But it has to be admitted it is somewhat un-English. Half close your eyes, and depending on which rolling stock you are travelling in, you could be part of some Ruritanian spy drama. Or, under blue East Anglian skies, the arable farms you judder through could be somewhere in Russia or Poland. That illusion will be shattered of course when you reach the end of the line, amid a Milton Keynesian landscape of flyovers and cleverly landscaped wasteland. We also liked the Bluebell Railway. Very Southern Region in ambience, with its dark-green carriages and grey or blue upholstery, it is a Sussex institution, and even people who don't travel up and down the line (What's the point of going all that way', said one woman on the platform, 'when you've only got to come back again?') mill around the station buildings to watch engines being shunted into position, their pistons a seething mass of steel and grease, surely red-hot to the touch, lethal, gleaming and awe-inspiring. All of it wreathed about with clouds of steam that would not disgrace a Turkish bath.

Despite all this, however, my preference is for 'real' railways, that is to say the miraculously surviving British Rail branch lines, still by some oversight part of the dwindling rail network. Like the diesel-fed link between Middlesbrough and Whitby, in Yorkshire. My visitor was not impressed by the glorified omnibus the train turned out to resemble, but the journey left its mark. The two-coach train was all but full when it drew into Middlesbrough's sun-lit, red-brick station, half of it full of beer-quaffing sea anglers. Most of them were youths but two appeared to be girls, who spent most of the next hour and a half covered with most of the youths for all the world like mating frogs. The train thinned out quickly as it stopped at every lampost and tree between Middlesbrough and Great Ayton, but by the time it threaded its way through the Cleveland Hills there were only half a dozen passengers. The country here may be a far cry from the primeval wasteland of Ribblehead and Wild Boar Fell which you can or could see from the Settle to Carlisle railway, but it is impressive all the same. I was reminded by the train's noisy progress over clattering metal bridges and round steep hills that peter out into riverbanks studded with wild flowers of the glorified ghost train at the Norwich fair.

But on the whole, except for arterial routes served by sleek, high-speed Inter-City expresses we are having to learn to do without trains. Fortunately, I not only enjoy driving, but actually like motorways. Not that I have pretensions to outlandish driving skills. I have never entered a rally, and I am no good at motorised treasure hunts. What I can and will do is drive for hours at a time the length and breadth of England, solaced by BBC radio when the going gets suburban or arterial.

Inevitably, then, most of this book was written from the driver's point of view. Sometimes I drove dutifully, sometimes I felt as if I could have gone on for ever. Like the weekend just before one Christmas during which I travelled from near the Welsh border across the midriff of England to Norfolk. I drove through Ledbury in mid-afternoon, just as the naked lightbulbs illuminating open-fronted greengrocers shops were beginning to make some impact on the gathering gloom. There was not much more light the following morning. The mist lingered until noon, and the Worcestershire countryside was as colourless and abstract as a pencil sketch. After midday, as I travelled through Northamptonshire, a pale sun picked out a surprising amount of colour from red brick and ironstone, and near Oundle I stopped to watch the bruised clouds of a gathering storm behind a red brick farm and a stone church: pale gold, fiery red, bright green, purple skies. If it had been a child's painting you would have dismissed it as unreal. Later the same day I reached the fen country, where farms are like islands in the middle of a sea of fertile black earth, where tractors stand as if they have been abandoned. Signs outside pubs say 'No van dwellers'. Straight roads run close to high dykes, and you wonder what is on the other side. It is even stranger at night: distant lights in lonely buildings wink like ships at sea.

The North Norfolk coast was just a night in a bed with nylon sheets and an underdone bacon-and-egg-breakfast away, but already I felt as if I had reached the end of the world. At such times, between dusk and dark, you could be convinced that England is huge – especially when the countryside is quiet and there are no traffic sounds. There was nothing to remind me of the twentieth century, and I could have been standing there 200 or 500 years before. (Even 100 years ago, life was more silent: the clatter of horses' hooves in a stable yard was a cacophony, noise pollution was a steam train fussing over a nearby bridge, the sound of footsteps along a country lane at an unusual time of day was an event. A parish was a world to itself, and all human life was there.)

Generally during the course of my travels I had the best of both worlds. I was able to potter around the parish the way an Inter-City traveller probably never would, but I could also climb into my car and drive off towards the setting sun. Sometimes I would delay my departure until the sun had set, until that point at which it was a toss-up whether to put the headlights on. That is when England comes under a spell – the town as well as the countryside, when harsh modern buildings assume warmth and subtlety by the light of street lamps. Even the City of London, floodlit, is a beauty: nearly deserted streets, three-hundred-year-old churches inconveniently cheek-by-jowl with banks and building societies, a lone taxi going home, a security guard taking the air.

Once on the edge of Dartmoor, just as nightfall was past the point of no return, I spotted a barn owl perched on a Forest Commission fence, wraith-like, its chest white in the gathering gloom. But I had disturbed it, and it floated away soundlessly into the depths of the forest. By night I could imagine it to be the spirit of some tortured soul, by day it would have been worth a second but probably not a third glance.

The main thing, I suppose, is not to take everyday things for granted. In its way, a suburban street is as interesting as Anne Hathaway's cottage garden. A boy scout fête can turn out to be more entertaining than the most sophisticated county show. The tap room of somebody's local in Stoke-on-Trent or the public bar of a Victorian monstrosity in Whitechapel on amateur night can produce just as enjoyable an evening as the most exquisitely thatched and brassy inn in rural Devon. A trip to the mudflats of south-east Essex may make a nice change from some too-perfect-to-be-true garden owned by the National Trust.

I

Map 1 Eastern England

2

1. Essex: so near but so far

Epping Forest; Dunmow and the Black Chapel;
Saffron Walden; some villages-on-the-edge-of-the-world;
Burnham-on-Crouch

People who have a guarded respect for bosky Bucks and stockbroker-belt Surrey tend to be very rude about Essex. 'Ugh, that A12,' they shudder. Dagenham strikes fear into the hearts of well-bred young ladies from Kensington, and, well, Canvey Island is beyond the pale. How then to reassure open-minded travellers that Essex is a county of great charm?

For a start, try going in the back way, via Epping Forest. Take a tube or a bus (still red, even out there), to Theydon Bois, and walk up the hill and into the woods: I have done it on an August Bank Holiday Monday, and within a hundred yards been enclosed by treescapes in which Hansel and Gretel would have felt at home. Nice places, indeed, as somebody once said in my hearing on top of a double-decker bus in Loughton, for a really juicy murder. In the 1870s it looked as if Epping Forest would be completely absorbed into the ever-swelling London metropolis. But in the nick of time the Corporation of London won a High Court action against the Lords of the Manors who had illegally appropriated parts of the forest, and in 1878, there was passed an Epping Forest Act guaranteeing the forest's preservation for perpetuity as public domain. The forest was dedicated by Queen Victoria in 1882. On a memorable day she travelled from Windsor to Chingford by train and then in her carriage towards High Beech in the very heart of the forest to the accompaniment of military bands and, it seemed, half the population of East London. She was in good company, for there is a local tradition that Henry VIII picnicked under one of the forest's great beech trees at High Beech, listening out for the cannon fired in the Tower of London to signify that Anne Boleyn had been executed. There are other royal connections, for Elizabeth I frequently transplanted her whole court out to the hunting lodge that was built especially for her, and still stands. Looking like a spectacularly preserved or restored roadside pub, this timber framed and plaster building is open to the public. It is said to be here that Elizabeth heard of Sir Francis Drake's victory over the Spanish Armada, and legend says that with whoops of joy she rode her horse up the fifteen-foot-wide staircase made of oak to the uppermost storey of the building.

On a summer afternoon in Epping Forest you could be in the depths of rural Sussex. Traffic and aircraft noise is at an absolute minimum because of the quietening effect of masses of trees. There are none of the functional conifers grown in most of England's forests: only deciduous trees are permitted, and they too must be of 'sturdy stock'. Deer still populate the forest, but the herd of so-called fallow deer, which are actually dark brown, is kept to about sixty. Those deer, incidentally, have found ways of overcoming the time-honoured method whereby they can be corralled without fences where main roads pass into the forest—the cattle grids apparently designed to prevent animals with cloven hoofs passing over have been negotiated by deer lying down and sliding over on their backs.

Of course, there are people who will quibble and say that Epping and Epping Forest really belong to London. Poor Essex: they also carp about Constable Country, which straddles the border between Essex and Suffolk, but Dedham, every flint of whose great church Constable sketched and painted, is emphatically in Essex, and Flatford Mill is a matter of yards from the county boundary. So is one of the prettiest villages I know that is within a couple of hours' drive of London, which is Stratford St Mary. It is just a pity that traffic on the four-lane A12 thunders just a few yards away. The hay wain would not stand a chance if it tried to cross.

The best of Essex, however, probably lies amid the prosperous farmland between Chelmsford and Dunmow, or close to the easternmost edge of the county, where marshy, pale green countryside peters out into the grey North Sea. It lies in the village of Pleshey, for example, all hollyhocks and dormers, hard by the remains of a once-great Norman Castle (history teachers will say 'Never heard of it'); or by the Black Chapel – nothing to do with black magic, but perpetuating the memory of the Black Friars – in the middle of nowhere but conveniently close to a smoky and low-ceilinged pub that used, it is said, to be connected to the chapel by a secret underground passage.

Part of Pleshey Castle, Essex. The great mound on which a Norman castle once stood completely dominates the pretty village, giving it an enclosed, hidden-away feeling.

Hereabouts, perhaps thirty miles from London, you could be a hundred miles away. As in rural Suffolk, where you expect to find such things because they are chic, some cottages are painted candy-floss pink. Cottages have front gardens full of cabbages, brought on as proudly as if they were dahlias or sweet peas. Cats slink along grass verges but turn some distance away to look at you to make sure they are not missing anything, and pheasants peck around distractedly in the fields beyond like people who have lost a contact lens.

Just a few miles to the north of the Black Chapel lies Dunmow, the best of which (though almost all of it is pretty and unassuming) is probably the bit that lies off the High Street towards Finchingfield. There is a spectacularly old-fashioned and aromatic grocer's shop, the kind where bare boards sound under your feet as you walk through the shop to investigate, say, some brand of pickles you have not seen before and where you expect a family of Beatrix Potter mice to scamper about when the shop is closed. Certainly you pay more than you do at the Co-op, and only wealthy local dowagers or the nouveau riche buy their weekly groceries in one go at such a place. Next door but two there is an antique shop, and beyond that an off-licence that is more remarkable for its French vintages from obscure vineyards than for its special offers on Party-Fours.

I like pecking around Saffron Walden, which is further to the north. It is said that Dick Turpin began his chequered career selling cattle in the market place here. That was in the 1730s, when the market square had already been licensed for trade for about five hundred years. Hereabouts such aeons are not regarded as remarkable: it is not unknown for gardeners to strike (literally) upon Saxon jewellery and paraphernalia in among their cabbages and shallots, and picking up Roman coins hardly earns them a free pint of Greene King in their local pub. Saffron Walden wears its history lightly. Samuel Pepys reported sleeping in the Hoops Pub, and 'being disturbed by a buxom wench' – though in what sense he meant disturbed is not immediately clear. This part of Essex was right in the line of the Danish invasion of about AD 800, though the Danes were unlucky enough to come up against Walden settlers called Angles who, while embracing Christianity, did not adhere to twentieth century Christian principles, and took satisfaction in splaying dead Danes' skins over the doors of local churches. The full and melodic name of the town derives from the increasing importance, mainly during the sixteenth century, of the growth of saffron, which even today is such a rare commodity that it fetches in the region of £1,000 per pound. As early as 1444, saffron was a taxable commodity, much in demand for medicine, cooking and dyeing, and when Henry VIII granted the town charter in 1514, saffron flowers appeared in the official coat of arms. About 30,000 blossoms, or heads, of crocuses were needed to produce just one pound of dried saffron, so each intensively cultivated acre yielded between seven and nine pounds of the precious substance. Queen Elizabeth I received a saffron cake in 1571 during a visit here, as did Charles I and George III. The crocus, incidentally, produces purple flowers, but was used as a yellow dye for cloth. Saffron is no longer produced here and all Britain's is imported. Saffron Walden is also famous for its pargetting, that tradition of superimposing decorative plasterwork on the walls of buildings.

Saffron Walden does at least have the reputation of being pretty, even if very few people, unless they get lost looking for the great Elizabethan house at Audley End, actually go there. The flat and marshy countryside a few miles to the north of Southend

Above and right: Saffron Walden, Essex, is just on the edge of commuter country, and belongs more to half-forgotten, rural Essex than the metropolis. It is a period piece, but not 'precious'.

is a better example of just how 'unknown' some of the pleasantest and yet comparatively accessible parts of the county can be. In clear conditions it is possible to see the tower blocks of Southend, but this does not detract from chestnut-tree shaded and white-weatherboarded villages, or the calm grey waters of the wide River Crouch that are viewed best, perhaps, from a grassy knoll next to some five-hundred-year-old flint-knapped parish church, or from the eeriness of deep, muddy inlets near Foulness Island. Perhaps because of the proximity of workaday Southend, the villages or hamlets of Canewdon, Rochford and Paglesham (the latter's two parts are joined by a footpath across rich farmland as well as by a more circuitous road) have always been overlooked even by day trippers from London, especially by Sunday drivers who are more familiar with the cockle stalls and seafront of Southend itself. Yet the cosy, low-ceilinged pubs in and between these villages are well within the scope of an evening jaunt from London.

Across the River Crouch from Paglesham and Canewdon lies Burnham. To many outsiders it may be the end of the world, but it is at least known to many weekend sailors who make it to Burnham-on-Crouch, the best known yachting resort in easy reach of London. Yachtsmen at least have discovered that Essex is not just a place you go through to get to Suffolk. If you approach Burnham by road, it hardly gives the impression of being a river town, which is what it is. You could almost pay a visit

Southend used to be London-by-the-sea. Then people began to take their
day trips and holidays in more exotic places and it became mainly a
glass-and-concrete commercial centre. There is still a haunting beauty, an
ozone tonic for city dwellers.

without even knowing that it is on the Crouch. It minds its own business, which is
chandlery, yacht building and repairing. The acid test, as it always is, is that you get the
best view of Burnham from the water. It is a genteel backwater now, but was not always,
its former prosperity indicated by the elegance of its bow-windowed Georgian and
Regency houses, dating back to the time coasters from Hull and Newcastle moored
here, and when there was a busy oyster industry. In the unlikely event that you think

south-east Essex is not for you, that the solitude is likely to be too oppressive, visit Burnham during Burnham Week. This is the East Anglian equivalent of Cowes Week, when the day sailors and the fibre-glass men, the yellow oilskin and the blue jersey men, finally get their chance to put landlubbers to shame.

Sailors do have it best sometimes. If only landlubbers could travel up the coast into Suffolk, through brash Clacton and genteel Frinton, this side of England would make more sense. By road it is a frustrating business, and means taking on Colchester and at least the outskirts of Ipswich. A new bridge over the Orwell river, beyond which you can take the back way to Woodbridge and the Suffolk coast, does of course help, though the great pity is that you cannot see the river as you cross the bridge because the parapets are too high.

Burnham-on-Crouch, Essex, has that edge-of-the-world air about it that applies to so much of south-east Essex. All around is flattish, windswept country, and to the east the great and relentless North Sea.

2. East Anglia: keeping a low profile

Constable country; Ipswich and Felixstowe;
the North Sea coast; Bury St Edmunds;
Newmarket and the western approaches;
Cromer; the Broads; Cambridge and the Fens;
Ely; Huntingdonshire

No part of Suffolk is more than five hundred feet above sea level, but many of its pastel painted and half-timbered villages are tucked away in wooded hollows, and there are peaks and troughs. It has come into its own in the last twenty years – if coming into its own has anything to do with being discovered by weekend cottagers from Hampstead and Wimbledon. Noel Coward was wrong about Suffolk's northerly neighbour ('Very flat, Norfolk') and people who declare that anyone bred on northern England's rugged moors and Scotland's crags will find Suffolk unsympathetic are usually wrong too. It is not just the seafront entertainment at Lowestoft and Felixstowe, nor even what are reputed to be the best fish-and-chip shops in England, that bring people here, but, among other pleasures, the prospect of combining a traditional seaside holiday with excursions into the soft and undulating hinterland.

The county divides conveniently into two halves: east and west Suffolk. Until those traumatic days of 1974, when old loyalties were turned upside down, and counties had their boundaries moved backwards and forwards as if in the control of the occupying forces in Europe in 1945, there was a county seat for East Suffolk and a county seat for West Suffolk: respectively, Ipswich and Bury St Edmunds. Now Ipswich is king. But the two sides of the county are very different. The east is generally flatter and windier, with ready access to a part-shingly, part-sandy seaside that some people would call an acquired taste, and is therefore doubly agreeable for those who seek it out. The west of the county is more reminiscent of rural Herefordshire or Worcestershire, though, of course, it is really nothing like either of them.

The Suffolk–Essex border is, well, good in parts. Very good if you strike it right: all watermeadows and lazy riverscapes. Dedham belongs to Essex, not Suffolk, but Essex people seem willing to allow that and other parts of Constable country to be taken as Suffolk. Constable was especially fond of Dedham church tower, and would sometimes cheat about its location in order to include it in his paintings. This is 'inch of land and mile of sky' country in which the River Stour winds modestly between banks of rush and reed, cowparsley and meadowsweet. Fewer of Constable's landscapes were actually painted here than most people assume, but sketches or paintings inspired by or executed in Dedham Vale do include 'The Hay Wain', 'Barges on the Stour', 'Cottages on the Stour', 'Boatbuilding near Flatford Mill', and several studies of the mill itself.

Flatford Mill suffers inexplicably from invasion by gangs of motor cyclists, but on one of those days when not many people are around, when the leaves of the trees above the lane leading down to the mill are rich and green, and when the sun sparkles on Willy Lott's Cottage, you will know why painters and photographers rave about it.

Constable enjoyed some early commercial successes in London, imitating fashionable painters of the period, but it wasn't long before he found his way back to Suffolk. 'I shall return to Bergholt', he said, 'where I shall endeavour to get a pure and unaffected manner of representing the scenes that may employ me. There is room enough for a natural painter.' Constable's father once owned Flatford Mill, and the mill was first portrayed in 'The Hay Wain' – first exhibited, incidentally, at the Paris Salon in 1821.

Ipswich is just up the road from Constable's former beat, via the fast, dual-carriageway A12 if you are in a hurry, or the more serpentine A137 if you are not. So many of the county towns I have come across are at odds with what we expect them to be, which is to reflect in miniature the popular image of the county. And though it has a bit of a maritime flavour still, with coasters on the muddy River Orwell, Ipswich does not seem to belong to Suffolk at all. The docks were hollowed out of the gravelly river to make it easier for shipping and local tradesmen, but there was a limit to what could be achieved. Once, in Bury St Edmunds, I met a man who had lost a fortune in contracting to remove the silt for the local council. (It was a terrific gamble, and he lost.)

In the sixteenth century, this was where the wool woven into marketable cloth in Lavenham, Hadleigh, Kersey and other points west, was shipped out to a waiting world. On crowded, traffic-snarling days, Ipswich is not charming. If it is a matter of take it or leave it, you will probably leave it. Yet Ipswich is not, as somebody once said, just a load of bricks that fell off a lorry on the way from London to Norwich, but quite an exciting community. On certain days it is whiffy with yeast from the Tolly Cobbold brewery, and even if you don't like that, it is a small price to pay for the town's architectural flourishes and a surprising number of antique shops and bookshops that can yield treasures you might not find, say, in more self-conscious Lavenham.

Ipswich has no fewer than ten churches. Not as many as Norwich, but still not bad going. These have lived so long with the hustle and bustle of people more concerned with the price of cabbages or where to buy formica while a cheap offer lasts than whose tomb lies where or when the flints were knapped, that they now let it all wash over them. But when you start to think there is no more to Ipswich than those churches and a nice bit of Victorian dockland that looks as if some developer is going to have a go at it very soon, you find there are other little pockets of the past that make up for the straggly outskirts and the nightmarish inner ring road that carries the A12 traffic to the west of the town (though that sparkling new road bridge over the River Orwell means that traffic between London and Felixstowe spares many vehicles from the town centre; and the feeling is mutual). There is, for example, the Ancient House whose exterior pargetting, or decorative plasterwork, is as good as anything in Saffron Walden – which is famous for it. There is, too, Christchurch Mansion, a wooded park where chestnut and lime trees offer office girls lunchtime shade while they investigate their sandwiches. Like most municipally owned old houses, Christchurch Mansion is generally totally neglected by the local people, but it is a gem. Mainly Tudor, with some Victorian additions, the house was once the town home of Felix Cobbold, who presented it to Ipswich in recognition of the town's devotion to his beer.

Unmoved by the fact that Felixstowe people are traditionally very rude about them, the inhabitants of Ipswich regularly travel 'down the road' to their very convenient seaside resort, just eleven miles away. If you go to Felixstowe, you could do worse than to arrive at dusk, to get a nostalgic kick out of the fairy lights on the slightly raffish pier and the antics of the stallholders and the teenyboppers at the big permanent funfair at the southern end of the seafront. If you come only for the evening, however, you'll miss the chance of a ride along the front in an open-top bus and your children will miss out on the miniature railway.

Like all the traditional seaside resorts that grew up in the last few years of Queen Victoria's reign, Felixstowe has retained a degree of elegance, despite the effect of its quite recent development as a major and prosperous container and ferry port. In fact, you could, in an expansive mood over a glass of East Anglia's very own Adnams ale, declare that Felixstowe has everything: fun and games – by which I don't mean dirty weekends, though I suppose Felixstowe's nice crop of smaller Victorian and Edwardian hotels has seen quite a lot of Mr and Mrs Smiths, a beach that, though shingly, does have substantial patches of sand, and a breezy edge-of-the-world quarter at Felixstowe-ferry, where there are passenger boats to the far side of the River Deben.

All that is on the far side of the bracing sea-side golf course and, for the moderately energetic, at the end of a healthy constitutional along the seafront. On this side of town, of course, you have to do without the kiosks, the teashops, the rock-and-souvenir emporia, though there is a good workaday pub and you can buy freshly landed North Sea fish, which they will gut for you if you ask nicely. The walk to Felixstoweferry will take you past a Martello Tower, one of many built around the east coast in about 1810–12 as protection against a threatened Napoleonic invasion. It is now a private house. Though it will hardly concern the average visitor, Felixstowe began as a Roman fort whose ruins – due to continual coastal erosion – lie beneath the ever-encroaching sea. It wasn't until the end of the nineteenth century that it was rediscovered, and builders and entrepreneurs moved in to capitalise, comparatively late, on the great Victorian vogue for seaside holidays.

The older, residential part of the town has a slightly faded flavour, a little bit shabby-genteel. But it tries hard, especially with the sub-tropical floral gardens next to the seafront Spa Pavilion that hosts live shows and has nearly all the salty and invigorating atmosphere of an end-of-the-pier theatre. The Spa drama festival is popular with bit-part actors: they can go swimming when their bit is finished.

Both east and west Suffolk are easy to encompass from Ipswich. In concentrating on the east, drive via the A12 to Woodbridge. From there, up to Orford and then, negotiating the River Alde via Snape, to Aldeburgh.

Though it has a couple of substantial Victorian or Edwardian hotels sternly facing the North Sea and not flinching, Aldeburgh is not particularly known for gastronomic excellence. You will not, however, go hungry. The fish and chips can be superb, and you can buy smoked salmon here too. And if you choose your moment right, you can pick up fresh crabs, and even occasionally a lobster, from a wizened fisherman in his blue jersey on the shingly beach itself, and in at least one of the town's low-ceilinged pubs, more used to keeping the autumn, winter and spring cold out than entertaining summer visitors, you can get fish pie, shrimps on toast and home-made soups. People

Orford, Suffolk, seen from its castle. From the comfortably enclosed village
square you would hardly know that the marshes and the North Sea are
close at hand.

used to the fleshpots of Barbados do not ignore Aldeburgh, but they do not come here
looking for the same things, and know what they are in for: a fresh east wind that makes
them glad of their sheepskin coats, and the log fire in the hotel bar, the crunch of shingle
underfoot as they stumble across the beach for a closer look at Aldeburgh's
bright-red-and-blue lifeboat, a totally unexpected cinema, a winter musical weekend in
the Brudenell Hotel at the far end of the little town. The Moot Hall that trebles as
tourist office, museum and town hall used to be well inland. Now it is all but on the
beach, separated from the sea by just a patch of greensward. The culture oozes out of
every Victorian eave, from round the corner of every little backstreet. It is, after all, the
chief coastal encounter of the Aldeburgh Festival. Benjamin Britten based his opera
'Peter Grimes' on a character from a poem by George Crabbe, described in the parish
church that bears his memorial as 'the poet of nature and truth'. George Crabbe wrote
about a tough, uncompromising, unpleasant rural life that is at odds with the Aldeburgh
we know today, with its delicate pastel-coloured, balconied Edwardian seafront houses,
never better than when the evening sun strikes across their bow windows, and picks up
details that you miss during the day.

The Aldeburgh Festival is said to have split the town in two. Local fishermen did
not think a lot of the musicians taking constitutionals along the front, and visitors,

though they did buy crabs and cod to take back home, hardly spoke the same language as the men gutting their catch on the beach. Things changed a bit when the fishermen realised they could sell their little old seafront cottages for tens of thousand of pounds, and settle for more modest Victorian dwellings or move a bit inland.

The sets for the first production of 'Peter Grimes' were based on the Moot Hall and the green separating it from the North Sea, and in the very ordinary-looking Jubilee Hall in Crabbe Street, many of Britten's first performances were held. The Aldeburgh Festival has now been held annually for thirty-six years, and the Maltings concert hall at Snape has the distinction of being the only one in Britain to have been formally opened twice – on both occasions by the Queen. Two years after the first opening of the Festival in 1967 it was destroyed by fire. Only one day's performances were cancelled, and with true British phlegm, Mozart's 'Idomeneo' was transported hook, line and scenery to Blythburgh church, just inland. The whole thing was rebuilt in nine or ten months, in time for the 1970 Festival.

I went one blustery February to a music weekend in one of the big hotels, in which two then virtually unknown young string quartets, the Coull and the Bochmann, played Mozart and Mendelssohn against (during the daytime recitals at least) the background of a heaving grey North Sea. An incident early on the first day brought home some of the advantages young musicians have over old-timers. As instruments and scores were being unloaded, a gust of wind caught most of the paperwork and bowled it along the High Street. It was only due to the athletic prowess of two fiddle players and a lanky cellist that any of it was scooped up before it reached the sea. As they pointed out later that evening: 'It would have been very nice to have had the Amadeus, but if the same thing had happened to them they would have had to abandon the published programme.'

From Aldeburgh, drive via the tucked-away pink-washed village of Westleton to Dunwich, Walberswick and Southwold, with a detour to Framlingham so as not to miss that exceptional small town, or come back to Ipswich via Yoxford, Framlingham, en route for Debenham, Grundisburgh and Woodbridge.

Dunwich is worth seeing, more for what is not there than what is. The road to Dunwich across heathland in the hands of the National Trust and the Forestry Commission suggests that there is something worthwhile at the end, though you are never really prepared for something so strange. You do need to bring your imagination along with your windbreak and your sandwiches. But you can leave your bucket and spade behind, for this steeply shelving beach is composed of shingle. This was once a thriving medieval city, with several churches, and a fish and vegetable market where there now is a car park. The windy marshes just to the west and north of where you now buy fresh-caught cod direct from the fishermen on the beach were once outlying reaches of the town. What brings the coastal erosion home most of all is the climb up to the last remaining headstone in what used to be a crowded churchyard. The church has gone, and so have the rest of the graves. It is a poignant place from which to gaze into the grey waters of the North Sea, and wonder if there is anything in the old superstition that you can hear the sound, on certain winter nights, of submerged church bells ringing under the waves. Not all the coastal erosion was gradual. On one dramatic night, 14 January 1328, the harbour disappeared into the sea, the victim of tidal drift, of the constant scouring motion of the sea along the coast.

Walberswick is Southwold's twin, but Southwold is a genteel resort that suits people who, in retirement, like the sting of the spray in their face. Walberswick is closer to nature: weekend painters come here to get away from it all and rent one of the old net-houses close to the muddy and elusive shore line. It is a world of dunes and mudflats: a bit of a sandy beach, a few houses around the village green where roses around the door look more like nature taking over than the lifetime's work of a dedicated gardener, close enough to the sea even if you don't see much of it. Over a thousand acres of heathland, wood and marsh near Walberswick are now a nature reserve. Much of the heathland used to be criss-crossed by sheep walks and the old Southwold railway ran here, though it disappeared before Beeching. Southwold has some neatly cropped greens, fanned by sea breezes, a famous inland lighthouse, and the stubby end of what was once a fully fledged pier. It is an all-year-round place that is just as appealing in the winter months, when the water lashes the prom and slams on to the shingle, as in the summer, when people tend to have their overcoats handy even if the wind has dropped and the sky is cloudless.

If you return to the A12 from Southwold and are not seduced by the wooded and sun-dappled road, enticingly cool on a hot summer's day, that runs off at right angles westwards towards Beccles, you quickly come to Blythburgh. The village is nothing special, though the Dutch roof of the White Hart pub is distinctive (and they serve Adnams' own ale), but it is Blythburgh church that counts, overlooking the marshes between the main road and Walberswick. I have long admired the church on its grassy promontory. It seems to stand alone, hardly indicating to the casual passer-by that little cottages and a substantial vicarage are close at hand. I like it in all weathers and at all times of the day, but best of all by far for me is at dusk in November or December, when a light burns inside the church like a beacon and when, if there are any streaks of light left in the winter sky, just the outline of roofs and tall trees is visible.

Framlingham Castle dominates its little town, but it is not the only thing worth seeing. Visit the castle of course; walk around it, above the surrounding lush green fields on the safe though *seemingly* precarious walkway and mug up the essentials of its history. The castle was given by Henry I to Roger Bigod. It had a chequered history, and at one point it belonged to Pembroke College, Cambridge. It has always been a bit of a white elephant. But do leave time too for meandering around the adjacent church and peeping into or browsing around the antique shops in or off the market square, or just admiring the Georgian style of the houses. There is hardly anything to spoil this little place unless you do what I did on my first visit here, and have a puncture in the very centre.

The plague reached Framlingham in 1666, a year after it broke out in London, which was about par for the course in terms of the speed at which the virus travelled. It is recorded that at the time the market square was covered in grass. Framlingham was the birthplace of Oliver Cromwell's 'Parliamentary Visitor' for Suffolk, William Dowsing, who was the acknowledged expert at destroying ancient churches. He is reputed to have been responsible for knocking down in excess of a thousand, about two hundred of which he did personally. He seems to have been about as amicable and engaging as Himmler.

Debenham is a large village on the River Deben that flows past Woodbridge and thence, in a course wide enough to delight yachtsmen, almost a further ten miles out to

Framlingham, Suffolk. The castle is exceptional enough, but the little town
is worth a long detour for its own sake. There is scarcely any
through-traffic.

the sea at Felixstoweferry. It is full of antique shops, but not quite the type that, all Georgian silver and buffed mahogany, frighten you off with their prices. They are of the country auction sort, with carved stone bird baths and, if you should be badly in need of one, an old haycart, an ancient scythe, or a sewing machine. You are more likely to find a seed and pet food shop next to a bric-à-brac shop than a smart boutique or a building society office. This is almost west Suffolk in mood, but not quite. It is quite high-lying and if you imagine you can smell the sea it is probably imagination – but not necessarily, for this is only fifteen miles as the crow flies from Orford and the desolate country immediately to the south of Orford around Hollesley Bay, a classic no man's land in a county that, for all its recent popularity, keeps most of its secrets to itself, and, at a rough estimate, has another century or two to go before it is so familiar that it can be treated with any degree of contempt.

Woodbridge is one of the best-kept secrets in England. It is exquisite. I have never met anybody who has not been captivated by it. It is all red brick, pantiles and flint. There are workaday building societies, but there are antique shops big enough to house half a dozen Tudor refectory tables at once. There is a branch of Woolworths that has scarcely changed outwardly since the 1920s; there are teashops, picture galleries, trendy fishmongers, second-hand bookshops and, down near the quay, a chandler's. If you as much as lick your lips on a blustery day, you can taste the maritime flavour; there are

more yachts than cars, and the up platform of the railway station has the best outlook –
of mudflats when the tide is low, of ocean-going beauties when it is high. Oh, and there's
also the low hill where in 1939 they happened across the fabulous Sutton Hoo treasure.

To all intents and purposes Bury St Edmunds, now the *unofficial* capital of west
Suffolk, is a Georgian market town – its grandeur much enhanced by the squat-towered
St Mary's Church, and the remains of a once great abbey that, hundreds of years ago,
used to be bracketed with St Peter's in Rome and Cologne Cathedral as one of the
highest points of Christendom. In 1479 its measurements were recorded at over 500 feet
long. It had a west front of nearly 250 feet and a nave over 80 feet wide.

But even the Georgian part of the town is just a front, for secular Bury is much older.
I especially like the fact that from several points within it you can look out and see
cornfields shimmering in the breeze. Over three hundred years ago Daniel Defoe
described the town as 'famed for its pleasant situation and wholesome air'. In spite of
the busy market and the charms of the market square, this is still a place going about its
business and not trying too hard. So red buses trundle unceremoniously past the
elegant eighteenth-century Corn Exchange and past shops whose bow-fronted
windows would not disgrace the more chic corners of Bath or Cheltenham. And the
ivy-covered Angel Hotel, where Charles Dickens really did stay, is not too proud to
offer good-value bar lunches and to tempt outsiders with the prospect of special
weekend packages. This is, incidentally, not just Greene King country, but the actual
source of that much-prized beer.

You will know there is a brewery here when, as in Ipswich, you pick up the slightly
sickening scent of the malting process. This does not seem to bother local people, since
Bury is gradually growing in size. They seem to be loyal to Bury as a shopping centre,
even though there are easy roads hereabouts to take them to bigger conurbations and
smarter shopping precincts, where they might save a few pennies here and there.

Just a few minutes' drive west of Bury St Edmunds is Newmarket. The best view of
what makes this exceptional town tick is to be had from the Devil's Dyke, an
eight-mile-long Bronze Age fortification from whose readily accessible top you can
observe the comings and goings on Newmarket Heath. Mainly, that is horses coming
and horses going. If you can read a local plan or Ordnance Survey map, you will work
out that the Devil's Dyke crosses Newmarket Heath roughly from north-west to
south-east, and forms a barrier between the two great racecourses: the Rowley Mile and
the July Course.

Do not, of course, attempt to see Newmarket-proper, as opposed to Newmarket
races, on the day of a meeting, and do not attempt to find accommodation then, not even
in the capacious Rutland Arms, which stands close to and is built in a similar style to the
roughly 225-year-old Jockey Club, home of the great and good who determine the rules
of racing, and are the final arbiters of what happens in the industry. There are about
2,000 horses in training at Newmarket at any one time, and perhaps 1,200 of these will
be taking exercise on the surrounding heaths on any day. You will have to get up early to
see them in full flight, or you might just settle for waiting in a line of traffic as they return
to their stables after morning gallops, crossing the road for all the world like a Sunday
School outing returning home after a tiring day.

Incidentally, still in existence at the Rutland Arms is a special bed built to
accommodate the father of the present Aga Khan, a man of substantial girth. Also inside

the hotel is a painting which commemorates an event that must have been the talk of Newmarket for years: during the reign of George II, the Earl of Oxford arrived at speed in the courtyard of the Rutland Arms in a coach driven by four trained stags. The Essex Hounds, who happened to be being exercised nearby, picked up the scent of the animals and pursued the coach all the way along the High Street and into the yard. An ostler, quick off the mark, managed to shut out all of the hounds except one.

You could not make any mistake about being in a racing town, because the streets are peopled with wiry old men who seem to be a foot shorter than anybody else, and their influence even extends to the pubs, where some bars are set at a height that is uncomfortable for ordinary mortals. The county border actually passes through Newmarket railway station. One platform is in Cambridgeshire, the other in Suffolk. And though few people may intentionally approach Suffolk this way, it being a low-key, low-lying and almost fenny part of England, it is a pleasantly smooth transition.

A better place from which to explore west Suffolk is Hadleigh, about half an hour's drive south-west of Ipswich. It is a fine example of a market town going about its business, and coping with modern traffic without detriment to the medieval layout of its streets and its pastel-washed, half-timbered houses, its elaborate pargetting, its bright pantiled roofscapes. There is an industrial estate, but it is tucked away well out of the town centre. The fifteenth-century Guildhall dates from the time that Hadleigh, like most of the county, enjoyed great prosperity because of the wool trade. The interior had already been restored by the end of the eighteenth century.

From Hadleigh, it is an easy drive (cycling is a possibility too) through lanes half submerged by meadowsweet to two rare beauties: Kersey and Lavenham. If you were to stay for a bargain weekend at the Swan, a sprawling half-timbered hotel that incorporates the sixteenth-century Wool Hall, just a matter of yards downhill from the medieval Guildhall that overlooks the market place, you might appreciate that peculiar contrast between the day-trippers' Lavenham, and what the place is like after hours. But I suppose this is true of almost anywhere, when, on a summer afternoon and early evening, offices and shops empty at around five-thirty, leaving the centre of the place to you and any stray cats and dogs. It may not be the time to attempt to pop into the chemist's to buy the camera film you forgot to pick up earlier in the day but it has its advantages.

Lavenham's church, St Peter and St Paul, is not in the heart of the small town, but on the edge. Richly endowed, its greatest benefactor was the local wool merchant Thomas de Vere, whose house in Water Street is preserved virtually intact. Water Street, incidentally, incorporates Lavenham's oldest houses, dating from around 1400. Sometimes Suffolk houses as old as this are in an acute state of disrepair – always apparently being rescued in the nick of time – but if you see them with their sides and innards exposed to the elements, perhaps during restoration, you can enjoy a quick lesson in how dwellings were built up to five hundred years ago.

The wattle and daub construction, consisting of mud and cow-dung interlaced with criss-crossed willow slats, may look primitive, but could put many modern buildings to shame. On to this would be superimposed plaster and on top of that perhaps the traditional pink Suffolk wash that is said to have been created by mixing pigs' blood with whitewash. This was always a pig-producing county, and according to the customs of the time, nothing was ever wasted.

Lavenham has one foot in the past – embalmed, some would say – the other in the present, and the medieval Guildhall, once the meeting place of the Guild of Corpus Christi, contains not only a local history museum, but is used for barn dances, discos, as a lecture hall or a scout hut. Lavenham has more than its share of antique shops. Not the place to find a bargain, perhaps, but maybe the source of your own little bit of history to take home. ('Instant Ancestors' somebody remarked once, when I returned from a country auction with a slightly pockmarked portrait of some dark lady of the bonnets.)

Kersey is built on a hill, and to see it properly – that is to walk from one extreme to the other – does involve starting off or finishing at the perfect flint-knapped church, with its bright-blue-faced clock, at the top of Kersey's steep hill. Then it will mean walking across the watersplash where ducks are so well fed that they will usually ignore what you throw to them if other tourists have been there before you, and then up to the opposite end of the village past overhanging, two-storeyed, pastel-coloured or darker half-timbered houses. I have in front of me a photograph of Kersey taken in the very early 1930s, and it is virtually unchanged – a small thing to say in praise of a place that is around five hundred years old, but remember that most alterations, except what the Victorians did with half-timbered houses, which was mainly to plaster them over, have been wrought during the last fifty or so years. All that changes is the amount of water that flows through the ford. If you are lucky, you will find just enough to keep the ducks afloat, including some of the more exotic Chinese variety, and to allow children to splash through without the stream actually coming over the tops of their wellies.

If you call on Lavenham second, instead of first, it is too short a journey to Long Melford for that long and straggling village to be ignored. Here, too, there is a huge, many-windowed church that would easily pass as a cathedral if it were anywhere else but rural Suffolk, where such places are nearly ten a penny. The Church of Holy Trinity was built on the ruins of a Roman temple, and the stained glass alone brings people who know what they are looking for from many miles around. It includes the unique Rabbit Window, depicting three rabbits linked by their ears, said to symbolise the Trinity. Within a picnic basket's throw of the large, roughly triangular green overlooked by the church, is Kentwell Hall, dating from 1564, surrounded by a moat. It is a place that has captured the imagination of half of eastern England, not to mention several film companies, all because of the work put in by a dedicated husband and wife who have devoted a dozen years or more to its restoration, or rather, its rescue. In the other direction, within sight of the church, is Long Melford Hall, a turreted Tudor house that is not just good to look at, but contains priceless treasures.

Long Melford's main street, if it were chopped up and cut into different sections branching off at different angles, could amount to a substantial town: there are restaurants, pubs, places to park, shops used by local people and not just for the amusement of browsing tourists.

From Long Melford, it is just a few minutes' drive along slightly tortuous lanes to Cavendish and Clare. Cavendish is something of a Suffolk cliché, on account of Hyde Park Cottages, a right-angled row of pink almshouses hard by the parish church. Perhaps less self-conscious is the tiny town – just too large to be a village – of Clare, where there is much pargetting, tea shops, low-ceilinged pubs, and a country park virtually in the centre of town which adds more than a dash of greenery to as nice a selection of medieval pink-and-white houses as you will find this side of Lavenham. Bury St Edmunds lies a few miles north-east of Clare, from where the A45 dual carriageway brings one within less than forty-five minutes back to Ipswich.

Almost due north of Bury St Edmunds lies one of England's most sparsely inhabited regions, especially if you do not take into account the massive American Air Force bases that in themselves represent major conurbations. Not that the casual driver who passes through this pine-studded, scrubby and sandy landscape would necessarily realise that it is under-populated. Many of them will simply know it as convenient picnic country roughly midway between outer London and the North Norfolk coast, especially as they have grown used to the trestle-style picnic tables placed sympathetically by local authorities and the Forestry Commission between the trees near the A11.

Those trees make a very effective acoustic screen and you do not need to walk far, for example, into Thetford Chase to escape the sound of traffic completely. This is the biggest forest in southern England. Composed mainly of Scots and Corsican pines, it was planted during the 1920s, when agriculture on the barren heath was given up as a bad job. (Things became so desperate that some farmers were reduced to breeding rabbits for their pelts. It was at this time that rabbit fur, or coney, became more popular than ever before or since.)

Because the ground never rises above approximately 180 feet, it is hard for the average visitor to appreciate how big the forest really is. Short, that is, of climbing a fire lookout tower. Probably the best point from which to see the forest spread out over a large stretch of East Anglia is Gallows Hill on the main Thetford to Kings Lynn road, about a mile north of Thetford itself. Thetford is actually in Norfolk, though it feels like a no man's land: neither Suffolk nor Norfolk. The best of Norfolk is well to the north, though the soft 'middle bit' is not at all bad.

There are precious few corners of England left where no tourist treads. So for the greater part of the population of, say, the Midlands and London, Norfolk is firstly the Broads, secondly the sandy, pine-dotted North Norfolk coast. But, of course, there is more to Norfolk than that. More too than the weekend cottage country that parts of the county have become, and more too even than the city of Norwich itself, despite its superb and much-vaunted open-air market, or the cathedral with an elegant spire that by virtue of the surrounding flattish country can be seen for such a long way, or the pedestrian precinct that showed so many other cities the way.

Norfolk is not one of those counties which claims to have everything for the delectation of visitors, but there is enough to sustain a couple of those fortnightly holidays that used to be all the rage when Cromer was built in Edwardian days and, much later, when permission was first sought to create those famous caravan parks at Sheringham and elsewhere along the coast. There are enough stately homes to make a weekend tour, and enough antique shops with a leavening of ordinary bric-à-brac, if not quite junk, to make up an antique-hunting weekend.

I have always been fond of Cromer, which stands a crucial test: it is as nice out of season as it is in high summer. It is self-contained, with its back to the sea. In winter the centre of town seems dominated by the huge church, and as early as nine in the evening

Cottage at Burnham Market, Norfolk: the English eccentric is not dead.

the streets are deserted, but a pub with fairy lights and the muffled sound of country and western music add a sign of life. Junk shops have surprisingly good selections of inexpensive maritime views and old photographs, and one has a stack of Oxford frames and some redundant stained-glass windows. The brightest lights of all belong to the fish and chip stall, empty of customers but with several assistants chatting behind the stainless steel and plastic counter. In a shop window are postcard-sized advertisements about local dramatic society productions and an announcement that potato and mushroom pickers are required. Another offers the services of 'an active pensioner for gardening or similar'. On the seafront itself, the pier is still lit, but its CLOSED sign is the most brightly illuminated of all. There is enough electric light to pick up white horses under the prom. I seem to experience England in extremes of climate. I remember travelling along the North Norfolk coast in another mid-winter (but a damp and dreary mid-winter, not a crisp and icy one) and on a rainswept night deciding at Sheringham that enough was enough. I settled for a deserted seafront hotel that for some inexplicable reason had stayed open instead of closing in late October for the season. I was too late for dinner and had to make do with cod and twenty penn'orth at Mac's Fish Bar. Even in the High Street I was finding the weather uncomfortable and I did not neglect to spare a thought for the men who had landed the fish. The following day only just dawned: it was porridge-grey, and though the sun seemed intent on rising it apparently had the sense to go back to bed. It had stopped raining but piles of manure in a layby were still weeping on to the tarmac. At such times you appreciate the banks of trees that protect the tightly knit red-brick and flint villages from the wind that blows across the marshes.

Along the coastal road between Kelling and Blakeney the landward side is all hillocky farmland, dotted with copses and cattle. On the seaward side, beyond banks of gorse, are mudflats. Most of the time you hardly see the sea, just the line of the dunes. At Salthouse, near Kelling, you can buy shrimps and kippers in the Post Office-cum-general store. A chalked notice on a blackboard outside the Dun Cow offers 'bait lug, sand eels, peeler crabs, squid'. One or two lanes are marked 'to the beach'.

Unfortunately for Norwich's hotels the county capital is just a little bit too far away from the coast (which attracts almost as many people as the Broads) for its hotels to be much used by the bucket-and-spade brigade. And although Norwich actually is accessible by motor cruiser and yacht, by definition people holidaying on the Broads bring their own accommodation with them. It is a clever blend, generally, of ancient and modern. Too many churches, perhaps, which has meant that several are redundant and suffer the indignities of being used as furniture stores, but anyway they have always played second or thirty-second fiddle to the great cathedral. The effort it takes to clamber up to Norwich's square Castle Keep, high on its mound, comes as a surprise to people who think that Norfolk is 'very flat'. If you do make the effort you will be offered a view into the city which is not only fun but will help you get orientated.

Norwich was and is an inland port, and the open-air market that has existed here since before the Normans came and built their castle, depended partly on goods brought here by those distinctive wherries, one or two of which you might just spot on the Broads. For via the River Yare, Norwich has links with the North Sea and the ports of Northern Europe. The fortunes of Norwich and Norfolk really took off during the fourteenth century when Flemish weavers came here, and the great worsted weaving

Pulls Ferry, Norwich, Norfolk, has not seen any ferry proper since 1939
but, being just a stroll from the cathedral precincts, is one of the most
tranquil corners of this increasingly busy city.

industry (there is still a small village outside the city called Worsted) thrived for three hundred years or more, turning Norwich into the second city in the land – a title that Birmingham has since claimed.

Even better, for people trying to turn an honest, or dishonest, penny, Norwich lies right on the pilgrim route to Walsingham, four miles inland from Wells-next-the-Sea. The story goes that a vision of the Virgin Mary appeared in Walsingham to a Saxon woman, in which she commanded a replica of the Nazareth House, in which the Annunciation took place, to be built. Slim grounds perhaps for what became the main place of Catholic pilgrimage in the southern half of England, but a catalyst all the same. The pilgrims en route for Walsingham helped to endow Norwich's nine-hundred-year-old cathedral, whose spire, incidentally, is second in height only to that of Salisbury.

Unlike many holidaymakers in Norfolk, I first saw the Broads as a landlubber and not as a sailor. I was taken on a Saturday afternoon excursion to Ranworth Church, ostensibly to see the famous medieval decorative rood screens. But my guide, an embarrassingly energetic septuagenarian, insisted that we climb the church tower, and chuckled quietly to himself with anticipation, for he knew I would be impressed. From the top I could just make out a line of low hills about five miles away. In between was flat, pale-green marshland dotted with black-and-white cattle and squat, disused brick windmills.

Between Ranworth Broad itself, whose sparkling and largely unpolluted water laps only twenty or thirty yards from the church walls, a thick and bush-like undergrowth with closely packed small trees created a barrier into which just a few houseboat-lined waterways made placid inroads.

You can climb almost any church tower in Broadland and be rewarded, if not with vertigo or a heart attack, then with a predictable but tranquil panorama of slow rivers snaking towards the chill North Sea, of secret, scrubby and little-frequented woodlands, or red-pantiled, red-brick farmsteads with tidy houses and outbuildings. The walls of Norfolk's churches and ancient barns, and Ranworth is no exception, contain much more colour than you would believe from a distance: flecked with wood-pigeon blue and egg-shell cream and pearl-barley grey and, sometimes, where it has been repaired, bits of red brick. When these colours are picked out even by the palest shaft of sunlight or, even better, by sunlight following a shower of rain, they positively glow.

Quite how the Norfolk Broads were formed is disputed, but it is probable that most of them were created by peat workings from the thirteenth century onwards. And some say earlier than that. The Broads have become so popular that conservationists are up in arms about the effect such a concentration of people in yachting caps and sou'westers is having on this delicate filigree of waterways north and north-west of Norwich. More critical is the determination of farmers whose land borders the Broads to drain the marshland on which cattle graze so picturesquely: this would substantially alter the character of the region.

The watery and misshapen spider's web that is the Broads has a natural bottleneck at Great Yarmouth, where cruisers pass via the dramatically tidal River Yare into the most northerly and the most popular Broadscape, within which are a number of famous tourist honeypots (most of them as easily accessible by road as by boat). They include Wroxham, Horning and Hickling. Passing through Yarmouth, which is roughly at the centrepoint of the boomerang-shaped network, is the Broadland equivalent of hiring a canal longboat and passing from peaceful unspectacular farmland into the backyards of Manchester and Birmingham. Yarmouth's marker buoys and signs telling you not to venture into the stretch of the River Yare that leads to the North Sea contrast with the reedy marshlands that are more typical of the region.

I have a greater fondness for the Suffolk side of the Broads, where, on the Waveney or the Bure, you find fewer boats because most people prefer the longer and more challenging journey up to the north. It is possible to get away from the madding crowd, even in the popular places, but a Broads holiday is basically for the gregarious. The sight of a lone, self-contained craft moored out in the wilds at sunset is all the more poignant because people cling together at night in little colonies, and borrow cups of sugar or paperbacks by Uffa Fox and Thor Heyerdahl from each other, or, as if they are old salts, discuss the tides at Breydon Water. Or else they stand, beer glasses in hand, by riverside pubs, and watch greenhorns who are even worse at mooring their boats than I was. You can usually spot first-timers, because they shout a lot and often fall in the water. Or like Billy the Kid, who had a notch on his gun for every man killed, they have a dent on the bow of their cruiser for every iron jetty or marker post they have hit at speed.

Perhaps the best thing about a Broads holiday is your chance to get into village backwaters and pub gardens and lanes leading to untended churchyards not normally

discovered by road. Having eventually done it both ways, I would say the church at
Ranworth, for example, is best approached by water. And it is really the only way to get
to the remote hamlet of Berney Arms, which consists just of a pub, a railway halt and an
old windmill, scarcely accessible by road. From the station you can take the short train
journey by diesel multiple unit to Yarmouth. So, on a nice day, children can have the
best of both worlds: in the morning they can fish for tiddlers off their boat, or feed the
voracious Broadland swans, and in the afternoon they can go to the seaside for donkey
rides and amusement arcades.

One of the unexpected pleasures of a few days pottering around the Broads (the
village of Potter Heigham is suitably, though unintentionally, named) is getting to
recognise the names of some of the boats. So the sleek 'Amber Gem' ('the sliding
sun-roof over stateroom and wide windows gives panoramic views' says the Blakes
brochure) that you first meet at Reedham, turns up outside The Swan at Horning the
following day, and the more venerable 'Ferry Privateer' ('one-piece sliding bridge,
ample ventilation and excellent visibility') that you follow across wide, choppy Breydon
Water, turns up that evening at the man-made mooring at Beccles, on the windswept
River Waveney, just over the Suffolk border. Sailing on the Broads, however, remains
much more chic than trundling about in a cruiser, and sailors who favour Cowes have
been known to speak quite respectfully of Broads yachtsmen, saying that if you can sail
on the Broads, you can sail anywhere.

The character of the Broads changes mile for mile more markedly than the
countryside of mid- and east Norfolk. There is Breydon Water, three miles from the
mouth of the River Yare, which is a tidal lake, almost four miles long that, though
shallow, has clearly marked navigation channels. At low tide its shining mudflats are
spectacular. There is the Berney Arms, the first safe mooring south of Yarmouth, whose
windmill dates from 1870, and is over seventy feet high. From the banks you may see
small ocean-going merchant ships of several hundred tons. There is Reedham, famous
for its chain-operated car ferry and, incidentally, for its nearby taxidermist and novelty
manufacturer known as Pettit's Rural Industries. The showrooms here are open, and
factory tours can be made. There is Norwich itself, accessible right into its heart by
boat, though that is not the prettiest approach to the city, and Acle, a small town with
lots of boatyards, remembered locally for the public execution site which was here:
wherry (Broads sailing craft) crews used to complain that decomposing bodies
suspended in the arches of the river got in their way. Then there is Horning, a large
village or small town with a lot of commercial development, a couple of hotels and some
guesthouses with several inns and restaurants. This is one of the best places for people
who are car-bound to taste something of the flavour of the Broads. I have a fondness for
Salhouse Broad, a well-wooded reach beyond Horning much used by sailors, and for
Wroxham, the unofficial capital of the Broads, with over twenty boatyards, many shops,
chandlers – and one shop that claims to be the largest village shop in Britain. It is at
Wroxham, incidentally, that the highly successful consortium of private boat owners,
Blakes, has its headquarters.

There is Potter Heigham, with lots of holiday bungalows, boatyards, and a bridge so
low that, on leafing through Broads cruiser hire brochures, you will seen many a
warning that such and such a craft 'will not go under Potter Heigham bridge'. It is even
necessary for other craft to take pilots on board to steer through the only arch of the

medieval bridge that will allow them through. The experience is heightened further by the fact that speed has to be maintained to keep up steerage way. Hickling Broad, the largest of all the Broads, is shallow but is readily accessible to cruiser craft. A 1300-acre nature reserve, with many examples of wildlife to see and perfect Broadland countryside, makes this into an essential place to visit. This part of the Broads, by the way, was associated with smuggling in the eighteenth century: goods came in from Yarmouth and were stored until appropriate times for them to be slipped into Norwich.

Yet for all these famous places it is one little detail that stays in my mind. I found myself a couple of miles from Wroxham, but in a spot that could be twenty miles from anywhere. I walked on down the lane past the church and away from the road, and came to the sluggish backwater of the Broad. Nothing much moved except a couple of swans foraging among the creeks. Out of sight, beyond a belt of scrubby trees, I heard the noise of wild geese ascending, the sound of their wings like somebody shaking out a blanket. I lingered until dusk, and the cries of waterfowl became more insistent, their shrieks like an old crone shouting obscenities at dead of night. It is a haunting place, and better for your peace of mind than a couple of tranquillisers.

As if not content with those Broads, the spectacular beaches, the best crop of country and city churches in England, and all that fish and wildfowl, Norfolk even has some of the Fen Country to its credit. But Cambridgeshire and Lincolnshire have divided the best spoils of this rich and prosperous, if literally low-key, corner of eastern England between themselves. People say the fens are flat and boring. Or at least they do if they have never had time to kill en route, say, between Peterborough and Boston, on a chilly day and been the only customer in a lonely pub whose bright coal fire costs the landlord more by the hour than he can earn from your two pints of Greene King. If you are lucky he will entertain you with true tales of how there are more Rolls-Royces among the farming population of the Fen Country than anywhere else within Britain, or more fanciful ones about why you should never marry a woman from the fens, as it is likely she will turn out on your wedding night (they are traditionalists here) to have webbed feet.

At a warmer time of year, any hamlet will seem all the more dark, leafy and protective, its summertime chestnut trees all the more lush because the land on all sides is as flat and about as green as a faded billiard table. 'Flat and boring' is people's reaction only if they have never found an almost shamefully sensuous coolness on a sultry Fenland day in which only an occasional puffy cloud rides the sky like a Spanish galleon and larks are trilling like kite-tails, in one of those cathedral-like churches with spires that go closer to the stratosphere than anywhere else in the country, and serve to emphasise its remoteness.

I would stick my neck out and call The Fens the best-kept secret in Britain. There are good reasons for its apparent isolation and self-sufficiency, for the loneliness of its villages, and even some of the major towns, makes most of Suffolk and Norfolk look positively metropolitan. And that is saying something, for the whole of East Anglia has retained much of its secrecy ever since the Magna Carta was drawn up in Bury St Edmunds in Suffolk because it was well out of reach of interfering monarchs – being at least three days' ride across dangerous country. The main reason Hereward the Wake could stand out at Ely (the name means 'eel island') for so long against the Norman invaders is that the land all around was more like an inland sea than solid earth, and even during this century, farmers in parts of Cambridgeshire and Lincolnshire went out in rowing boats (called skerries) to milk their cattle. It does not do for drivers to assume too many river crossings, and a road map will remind them of the legacy of the country: Waterbeach, Dry Drayton, Landbeach, Gedney Marsh, Ten Mile Bank, are just a few Fenland places that come to mind.

The Fens are like an enormous draining board guiding the trickles from dishes washed in rain from the Lincolnshire Wolds and the heavily forested hills that are, incidentally, a part of that county as secret and little known as the fens themselves. The rivers Nene, Welland and Ouse slink into that vast sandy, silty sink, but aside from them the drains that criss-cross the Fen Country have long had a dual purpose, being excellent waterways.

If we bring this little known corner of England that roughly occupies a couple of thousand square miles within an oblong shape of country bordered by Wainfleet, Sleaford, Bourne, Peterborough, Huntingdon, Mildenhall and King's Lynn, and add to it the most underrated of all the seasons, you have a powerful combination: winter in the fens. Then the country is taken over by the elements, just as completely as if this was some beetling, spray-tossed headland on the Yorkshire coast. But it is a joint assault by nature and the elements, and only man in his anorak and wellies, and his nice warm car, is an intruder. Frosty mornings in the fens are like the beginning of the world. Silence envelops you like a blanket. The mist mitigates any ugliness. It even flatters those functional black barns with pantiled roofs that stand on green islands in the middle of black-earthed seas that represent the most fertile farmland in Europe. The Lincolnshire or Cambridgeshire fens in winter echo to the 'paff-paff' of shotguns and the country's strange intensity was underlined for me by the solitary figure of the coarse fisherman I observed one January afternoon on the banks of the Great Ouse, hunched immovable on his canvas stool among the rushes of the river bank.

A cock-pheasant is like something out of a medieval painting seen against frost-rimed fields. Rooks agitate among the high trees, the chocolatey-brown earth (milk *and* plain!) is not boring, but sets off to advantage those horizon-stealing churches. When there is frost after rain, particularly at dusk, the countryside is as quiet as the grave, and when it does get dark its bleakness is emphasised by the distant winking of yellow lights from an isolated farmhouse. Because there is no wind you can stop and listen to that rare luxury, the sound of absolute silence, but if you step on an iced-over puddle, it cracks frighteningly, like a car's windscreen hit by a stone. When the wind does blow, however, it is the real scourge. I have sat in a heavily misted-up window seat in a café in Wisbech, unwilling to leave the soporific warmth and face the icy weather, and watched people outside in the street bent like boomerangs against the wind. Then I had to press on towards Boston, and saw telephone wires hanging like violin strings after being broken in the teeth of a gale, and watched policemen with breakdown vehicles hauling a car from the iced-over waters of a dyke where it had been blown from an unfenced and treacherous road.

One of the more agreeable things about the fens 'out of season' is that both Cambridge and Ely, two of the Fenland places that are worth a long detour, are at their most intimate and accessible then. Mists that last all day can be part of Cambridge's winter scene and, if you venture along the towpath of the Granta, watch out for heavily scarfed cyclists reeling dreamlike out of the frozen fog en route for a dissertation in some blissfully overheated lecture room. On some days in December and January, students who cannot see all the way across Trinity Great Court because of a rapidly descending grey mist are thinking by three in the afternoon of crumpets toasted in front of cheery gas fires.

The Fen Country in high summer is a different proposition. In its way, the land is as eerie in August as in January. It is less forbidding, but it is soporific and enervating, and on a hot day you might be walking or driving between rich cornfields and the banks of sluggish waterways, as if under an airless glass bowl. If the winter is daunting, so, in its way, is spring and summer. Around Spalding at least, it is unreal. Thousands of acres of tulips and other bulbs are grown here as seriously and scientifically as if they were cabbages or carrots. In high summer, except for the trailing larks, there is little birdsong, though you might just pick up the yellowhammer's 'little bit o' bread and no cheese' in some hedge. The almost ripening wheat is reddish-gold, barley-sugar brown, butterscotch yellow. Though fingernail-red poppies pick up what little breeze there is, there is little movement: this is the lull before the hustle and bustle of the harvest. The talk in the brown-stained taprooms of the village pubs is mainly of this harvest. Darkly punctuated by copses of oak and sycamore, sometimes with a wraithlike dead elm, the yellow fields ripple in anything like a sharp breeze as if they were water. Public footpaths on the edges of fields become obscured by the lush crop, and intrepid or stubborn hikers sometimes lose their way, standing waist-deep and bewildered on the edge of wheatfields like 'Ruth, sick for home', standing 'in tears amid the alien corn'.

It was during the heat of such a summer day, on a Sunday afternoon, that, apropos nothing in particular, I discovered Wainfleet All Saints. The parish church clock struck two as I stood in the market square. Nothing moved except a marmalade cat that slunk further into what shadow there was; the peeling green paintwork of a shuttered hardware and ironmonger's store seemed to blister in the sun, and in the window of the Co-op, faded packets of soap powder faded a little more. I walked the few yards to the railway station, and from the deserted platform, through the heat-haze, I could make out the distant shape of Boston Stump across a prairie of ochre-coloured wheat dotted with poppies like flecks of blood.

To my mind, Boston is one of the Fenland 'musts'. So are Ely Cathedral, Cambridge, the 'Brinks' at Wisbech, the other-worldly, concrete, no man's land of the River Nene's outfall to the North Sea, the Nature Conservancy's Wicken Fen, unchanged for centuries, the subtly beautiful railway journey between Boston, Wainfleet and Skegness, and the superb parish churches of Grantham, Donington, Heckington.

I have seen Ely Cathedral early on uneventful weekday mornings when it seemed indecent not to be at work behind a desk, when only the verger and an old man in a raincoat who was looking after the bookstore gave the place any sign of life; and I have seen it on a carnival day when that half of the town's population that is not taking part in the parade is standing several deep in the streets and watching it go by. Even in high summer the inside of the cathedral is cool; people soon learn to gravitate to its pleasantly sunless interior. They emerge from the human-sized entrance door into the street, rubbing necks stiff from gazing up into the cathedral roof. I have also seen it on a cold

Even two decades ago, a building such as this, in Boston, Lincolnshire,
might have been in danger of extinction. But nowadays its continued
existence is probably assured.

Wicken Fen, Cambridgeshire, seems hardly to belong to the twentieth
century. It is bleak, primeval and eerie. (*Photo: Richard Muir*)

winter afternoon, when the surrounding fens are wreathed in mist, and shopkeepers
wonder if they can get away with closing early, and the verger is comfortably ensconced
in front of a coal fire having his tea. What little light there is comes palely through the
famous octagon that houses a pinnacled and fretted 'lantern'. The dead seem to settle
comfortably into their tombs and the events that have troubled the world in getting on
for a thousand years of the cathedral's existence seem to have no real significance.

For all the talk about Fenland church spires, Ely – the best church of all in the fens, and perhaps the best in the country – has no spire. Neither does it have much in the way of flying buttresses, nor tall clerestory windows: it has been described as 'disquietingly unEnglish'. In fact, it is not nearly as attractive from the outside (being more reminiscent of some fanciful Bavarian castle) as inside. It is basically a Norman church of the late eleventh and twelfth centuries, with substantial additions from the early English style of the thirteenth century. But it cannot be pigeonholed as neatly as that, for you will find the Choir and Lady Chapel in the decorative style of the fourteenth century, and two Perpendicular chantry chapels dating respectively from 1524 and 1550: slap-bang in the middle of the Renaissance. The Norman nave is no less than 248 feet long, and the simple geometry of this earliest of Gothic designs has been treated to every possible permutation. Even the great fat pillars are arranged in three separate storeys, clambering intricately towards the remote roof. Medieval architects and stonemasons achieved things that today, six or seven hundred years later, would be regarded as very tricky indeed, and that was without the aid of any sophisticated machinery, calculators or lifting gear.

There are no illustrious kings or queens to be found among Ely's dead. Most memorials are of noblemen and bishops, or clerics, as well as quite a few ordinary Ely people. They would go a long way to find a more impressive resting place. They are entombed on an island in a strangely beautiful sea. But the cathedral completely dominates the place – something you see best if you climb to the top of the Norman west tower: every morning and afternoon a conducted party is taken up as if to the top of the Matterhorn. From the top of the tower on anything like a fine day you can see the Cambridge colleges to the south; in the opposite direction the North Sea; to the east the headquarters of the racing world, Newmarket, and, directly below, a scale model of a market town, with boys from the King's School dawdling between lessons, townspeople shopping and scurrying in front of cars weaving through streets laid out when the horse and cart was a threat to road safety. Mundane shopfronts are punctuated by monastic gateways. Beyond the city the straight Fenland roads are threaded by lorries transporting a few more hundredweight of potatoes, broad beans, and washed carrots the colour of marigolds.

I once cycled all the way from Ely to Cambridge. Athletes may smile sardonically at 'all the way', but they have probably never experienced the effect of Force 10 winds blowing straight from the Urals, forcing you in every direction except the one you want to go. Not for nothing did this used to be windmill country. Cambridge was first developed by the Romans because it was one of the few comparatively dry places in marshy and dangerous East Anglia. Nevertheless it long retained a sense of mystery and remoteness from the rest of England: in the Middle Ages, ill-fed academics lived lives even more uncomfortable than those of monks, amid a backward and often hostile population. But the Romans found the geographical location excellent, for there was a network of Fenland rivers by which they could transport troops and building stone, as well as the wildfowl and fresh fish, especially eels, which abounded among the marshes and for which the fens soon became known. The settlement was improved and extended by the Saxons, and there is an outstanding example of the Saxon period in St Bene't's Church (originally St Benedict's) only about fifty yards from King's College Chapel. Unfortunately it goes unnoticed by most visitors.

No one knows exactly why a university began here, though *how* is better recorded.

The 'lantern', Ely Cathedral. When the last light fades from the fenland
sky the starkly beautiful interior of the cathedral seems not quite to belong
to this world: agnostics may have second thoughts.

In 1209, it is said, there was a breakaway group of students from Oxford. For some reason they came to Cambridge, though it was seventy-five years before they built their first college – Peterhouse. This fairly small and intimate college therefore has three claims to fame. It is the oldest of the university's thirty-one colleges; it is said by undergraduates to serve the best food; and it is the first college that visitors see if they arrive by road from London – or if a taxi from the station takes that route – standing, as it does, a few yards north of the Fitzwilliam Museum, on Trumpington Street.

The only thing that really divides graduates of Oxford and Cambridge is the question of which is the more beautiful city. That will never be resolved, but it has been said that Oxford is a university within a city and Cambridge is a city within a university, and Cambridge, which is somewhat smaller in terms of population (103,000 as opposed to Oxford's 117,000) is certainly much easier for the visitor to grasp in its entirety. Except for the outlying colleges of Churchill, Robinson, Fitzwilliam, New Hall and – two miles out of town – Girton, all the colleges can be encompassed on foot, inside and out, well within a day. (The remoteness of Girton – no longer, to the chagrin of some bluestockings, for women only – is brought home during the winter months by the sight in the city centre of bicycles ridden by cold girls with blue knees.)

Being an exceptionally well-endowed city (in the financial sense), Cambridge has always had a regular injection of new buildings, from the sternly neo-classical Fitzwilliam Museum to the Venetian palace that is the old Addenbrookes Hospital, to the contemporary Robinson College, or the even more daring New Hall on the road to Girton. The Fitzwilliam Museum has always kept a low profile, as if to keep back the astonishing world of beauty that lies in its portals from all but the most enterprising visitor. It is unnoticed by the greater mass of the townspeople, and unvisited by generations of undergraduates. It is highly admired for its Egyptian, Greek and Roman antiquities, its eighteenth century English paintings, its medieval illuminated manuscripts, its Elizabethan miniatures, its Japanese and modern prints, and perhaps most important of all, the collection of William Blake's work. On quiet Saturday afternoons, however, university students are far more likely to be out on punts, or cycling around the low-profile Gog Magog hills, than mooching around the Fitzwilliam. Their cycle trips probably have a more nostalgic value for them than the legendary May Balls, and the murky aftermath in which tradition dictates people should punt to Grantchester after breakfast. Unless they are very lucky, they will find the dawn does not really break, but that the cloud diminishes a couple of shades from pitch-black to grey.

Energetic students are inclined to cycle into what used to be Huntingdonshire, though that is now part of Cambridgeshire. Of all the counties affected by the famous boundary changes of 1974, Huntingdonshire was the one which seemed to make the least fuss about its change of status and 'loss of identity'. It used to be the second smallest county in England after Rutland, which was another one to be absorbed into a larger county. The A1 road ran right through it, which meant that people technically saw something of the place, but usually sped past flattish farmland and willow-fringed rivers without really absorbing anything at all. It was always hard to categorise, because of the way it fell between East Anglia and the East Midlands. The nature of the farmland really gives the clue, however: Huntingdon is on the edge of the fens, and although the western half of this former county is soft, pale green and pleasantly undulating, it is the east side that is closest to the truth.

Huntingdon has its own St Ives, and although this will hardly compare among the tourist brochures with the much more famous Cornish one, it is not to be entirely overlooked. A pleasant tour of this part of the country might start, say, from Cambridge, and take you westwards via tranquil Hemingford Grey, St Ives, and then towards Grafham Water, then St Neots, and finally back to Cambridge. Being at the head of the River Ouse, more of a natural waterway then than now, St Ives was an important medieval market, and still deals in cattle, sheep and pigs, twice weekly. Barges from northern Europe travelled here, and a miniature quay still stands where it has done for hundreds of years. St Neots, also on the River Ouse, had a similar role, and enjoyed the same kind of prosperity. Its fifteenth-century church is known to some guidebook writers as the Cathedral of Huntingdonshire, and the whole of Brook Street was once a line of wharves and warehouses, being just off the Great North Road. St Neots also did well during the coaching era, though not so well when the railway came. This caused the demise of the river as an arterial trading route, and between the wars the huge paper mill, the iron foundry, and even, surprisingly, the brewery (usually able to withstand recession) went through bad times. St Neots is a London overspill town, but not unpleasant for all that, and its huge market place with the mainly two- and

Hemingford Grey and the River Ouse, Cambridgeshire. Until 1974 this was part of Huntingdonshire, and the merger was very much to Cambridge's advantage.

three-storeyed houses, pubs and shops around it allows enough sky to be visible to do away with that slightly claustrophobic impression some old towns convey.

Not especially strong in stately homes, castles and abbeys, this part of Cambridgeshire does at least have the advantage of Houghton Mill, a seventeenth-century structure on the Great Ouse that is now a youth hostel, and Ramsey Abbey, on the very edge of the fens, which was a Benedictine foundation dating back about a thousand years. As you stroll among the overgrown tombstones of the Abbey, you literally look across a low churchyard wall to lush pastureland dotted with small trees that begins to suggest the flatlands of Lincolnshire. Now that it has, perhaps in the nick of time, diverted all the heavy traffic, Huntingdon has managed to maintain a town centre that, even dominated by the familiar fronts of the all-England chain stores, has some character. One of the best buildings is the Cromwell Museum, originally a school which Cromwell and, a generation later, Samuel Pepys both attended. All Saints Church, rising up handsomely from the edge of the Market Square, is Norman, and the George Hotel and Falcon Inn are good eighteenth-century coaching inns. Outside the town is a stately home proper, Hinchingbrooke House, a fine Tudor building which, although Oliver himself had little connection with it, was the family seat of the Cromwells. It almost came to Oliver Cromwell, but his uncle (another Oliver) sold it before Oliver could claim his inheritance.

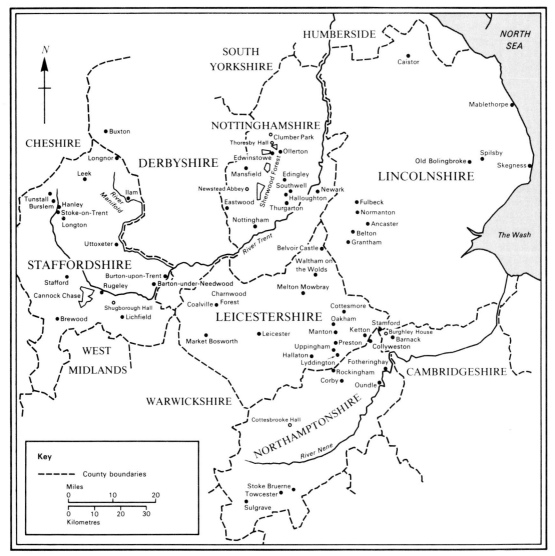

Map 2 The Midlands

3. The Midlands:
the light under the bushel

Rutland – gone but not forgotten; Leicestershire,
Northamptonshire, Staffordshire, Nottinghamshire;
Lincolnshire: an inch of land and a mile of sky

There is hardly a square yard of England that is uncharted, scarcely a village or field that has not figured in some topographical survey or first-hand motoring itinerary. Any attempt to identify corners of the country that are unknown or off-beat will raise the cry from Burton-upon-Trent or Newark 'Well, it's not unknown to me' or 'It may be off your beat, mate, but it's not off mine!' But just watch the eyes of people who claim to know their way around Northamptonshire glaze over when you mention Rockingham. Just ask a bevy of commercial travellers in any saloon bar in Lincoln if they have ever been to Caistor and observe their blank looks.

Australia's Western Desert may be awe-inspiring and America's Deep South lush, nostalgic and full of faded elegance and picturesque poverty. But the number of good things tucked away in the nooks and crannies of England's landscape is apparently inexhaustible. I have heard New Zealanders say they get claustrophobic here, but it is not really overcrowded. More a matter, perhaps, of every acre being used to somebody's advantage, every village and hamlet preened and the best of it preserved. The England which people tend to like best is reminiscent of a country park in the hands of an architect who has a good sense of history. Perhaps after all. England *is* a garden or, rather, a Secret Garden.

The happiest American tourist I remember meeting was from Boise, Idaho, who had gone looking for George Washington's ancestral home at Sulgrave, in Northamptonshire. He found it easily enough but then turned the wrong way. Instead of arriving in the Cotswolds, he struck northwards into the Midlands. Not the West Midlands, which he might have found disconcerting, but the East Midlands, which to my mind is the best of unsung England: Leicestershire (including what was Rutland), Northamptonshire, Lincolnshire and much of Nottinghamshire are low-key and unregarded beauties born to blush unseen by nine-tenths of travellers. Of course, my friend realised his mistake before he had gone too many miles. 'What the hell, I thought. It was just great anyway. I decided to do the Cotswolds some other time and carried on to my cousins in Nottinghamshire.'

You do not have to be an American, however, to enjoy Sulgrave. It is a perfect example in its own right of a sixteenth-century manor house, beautifully maintained, all gleaming copper and oak furniture. For atmosphere, see it on an autumn afternoon, as the light begins to fade, and afterwards have tea in the thatched house across the road.

Spalding, Lincolnshire, is better known for its bulb fields than its Georgian architecture, but these houses on the banks of the River Welland would not disgrace Cheltenham or Bath.

The Romans colonised what is now Northamptonshire, and created Watling Street. This eventually became the A5, running more or less parallel with what is now England's first motorway. And several of the country's most memorable places grew up simply because they happened to be useful feeding and watering points en route for something else. In Towcester, for example, when the coaching era was at its peak in the first decade of the nineteenth century, there were no fewer than twenty inns along the main street. Several still exist, among them the Saracen's Head.

It is not just that Northamptonshire's prevailing stone looks good and has always been readily accessible, but also because of what could be done with it: those decorative church spires, those carved entrance gates gracing dozens of little stately homes hidden behind high hedges and banks of trees. My abiding impression of this much underrated county is of lushness and darkness. The greens are heavy and rich, the stone of the houses is orange or brown, the canals that dissect the county (the Grand Union is the most prominent of them all) are grey on overcast days, but startlingly blue when the sun shines. If canals appeal, visit Stoke Bruerne, spiritual home of the British Waterways network. Just south of the Blisworth Canal Tunnel, one of the longest on the whole spider's web of English canals, you will find an old warehouse and mill that are now a museum and a magnet for anybody who appreciates the charm of canal boat travel.

Leicestershire, on the other hand, I tend to associate with the pleasure of exploring the busy streets of any one of half a dozen small market towns on a sharp autumn afternoon at dusk, when brightly lit butchers' shops are hung with local game and wildfowl. Or with the taste of a glass of locally brewed beer in the wood-panelled bar of a pub that might have seen service as a coaching inn over two hundred years ago.

If you travel due north on the A1 you will just clip the north-east corner of what used to be Rutland, not far from a big Royal Air Force base near Cottesmore, about two hours away from London. Adjoining what was Rutland on its western edge, Leicestershire lies astride the M1 motorway, which slices it in two. There seems to be little to write home about but even a detour of ten miles will correct that first impression.

In high summer, even at weekends, you can count on having large chunks of rural parts of the county to yourself. Like the leafy country lanes that branch off the high-lying roads linking the prosperous single-street towns and villages of the Leicestershire Wolds and the north-east side of Leicestershire – Waltham on the Wolds among them – which take you down into wide sweeping valleys enveloping farm-houses and mansions, built during the great wool-producing prosperity of the sixteenth century, of rich limestone that glows like old gold. Such places are thus sheltered from the chill winter wind that blows across this limestone plateau. On a summer evening, perhaps in a mixed woodland of elm, ash and especially oak, in a place that you seem to share only with blackbirds, stoats and half-glimpsed foxes, you might be convinced that this is the essence of the English rural scene.

Despite the off-beat nature of much of the county, some places do figure in all the basic guide books, several with a tag that cannot be shaken off. There's Melton Mowbray, whence first came the pork pie that expatriates dream of, and which is still famous for the fox hunting that most people love to hate, and Market Bosworth, where Richard III, Shakespeare's villain but other people's hero, relinquished the English crown on which he had had so short a hold. (From here Henry VII rode in triumph the ten miles to Leicester with Richard's body across the crupper of his horse 'all bespattered of mire and filth . . . naked of all clothing'.)

Belvoir Castle (pronounced 'Beever') also has a reputation, but a much grander one. It stands at Leicestershire's extreme north-east edge, high up on a thickly-wooded escarpment overlooking the plains of Lincolnshire. Some say it is here that Stilton cheese originated – created, it is unreliably reported, by a Mrs Stilton, who worked as one of the cooks in the Duke of Rutland's household. The true origins of the cheese – the name of which is now protected by law, which means that what is called Stilton must be made only in Leicestershire and a handful of places in neighbouring counties – are actually unknown. Belvoir is a child's cardboard castle made real. Incredibly intricate, it is like a cross between something out of *Jack and the Beanstalk* and Windsor Castle. If ever you dreamt you dwelt in marble halls, this is the dream come true.

Belvoir is in sight of Nottinghamshire, which is at the opposite end of the Leicestershire spectrum from what used to be Rutland. My favourite part of that now defunct county has always been around Uppingham, including the villages of Manton and Preston and, on the road to the industrial Northamptonshire town of Corby, the village of Lyddington. This is a straggling community which, if you approach it from the Uppingham end, only gradually reveals the treasures of its domestic architecture, the highspot being the Bede House. This was once a bishop's palace, and here, it is said, Henry VIII stayed while on a personal tax-gathering expedition late in his reign.

An unsuspecting stranger might come across Lyddington if he happens to lose his way near Rockingham, over the Northamptonshire border, but it would be a lucky traveller indeed who stumbles across Manton. Like so many of Britain's nicest topographical finds it is tucked away off the beaten track, down a lane at right angles to the main road – in this case the A6003 Uppingham to Oakham road. There is a pub with a grey thatch and, close by, a grander house of three storeys, probably built in the early 1800s. Then an ironstone terrace of what were once workmen's cottages but now fetch tens of thousands of pounds each as weekend retreats for Leicester businessmen. And then the thirteenth-century church – with an appearance unique to the county, for it has a double bell-gable, like an archway with bells hung from it – giving the church at first glance a strange, half-ruined appearance.

Rutland used to be moved around as in a game of pass-the-parcel, usually as a gift from a king or a queen to a favourite kinsman. Edward the Confessor granted it to Queen Emma, King John gave it to Queen Isabella. It also claims never to have had a battle or even a skirmish on its soil, and it has always been a bit of a backwater. Industry never really took off, though they did quarry the limestone at Ketton, for example, some of which went to build the Tower of London. Churches and villages tend to be on a small scale, and even Oakham, once the county town, has the look of a film set.

Oakham Castle is a rare example of Norman domestic architecture. Assize courts were held here twice a year when Rutland was officially a county. The hall is hung with horseshoes, and the tradition goes that every time a peer passes through Oakham on a formal occasion, he presents a horseshoe to the castle. If he refuses, local people are said to be entitled to demand a horseshoe from him or his entourage. Most of the best of Oakham is off the High Street, but not far off: except, that is, for the superb modern museum of local crafts and bygones, which lies on the main road at the eastern end of the town. My preference, however, is generally for takeaway antiquities: down one side-street I found two antique shops close together, and for a total of £4 I bought a not too moth-eaten fox's head, a brass pipe rack, though I do not smoke, and a kitsch but attractive piece of porcelain made in the form of an envelope. It even bore a postmark: Stoke-on-Trent 1888.

They used to swear that the chef at the Falcon Hotel, Uppingham, put Ruddles beer into his steak and kidney pie. Since Ruddles have several times won awards for producing the best cask-conditioned draught beer in England, it is not surprising that people make a special journey here. Just outside the hotel is the town's tiny market square, almost too small to be taken seriously. In a corner of the gingerbread-coloured market place is an antique shop where they do not mind if people who could never afford to buy any of the items for sale browse around.

These sleepy hamlets and small towns of Rutland and the Wolds country of eastern Leicestershire are very different from the rural and semi-rural ones of the country beyond Leicester itself, which tend to take on the character of Nottinghamshire and Derbyshire. There, near to or right among the coalfields, red-brick houses predominate, with the best nineteenth-century buildings typically finished off in white paint, with slate roofs rather than stone tiles. The coalfields are in a fairly confined area, but they are none the less a vital part of Leicestershire's very apparent economic prosperity: neon-lit plush pubs and steak bars, new cars, architect-designed surburban houses. People here tend to look north and west for their weekend jaunts rather than eastwards to the Wolds or to Lincolnshire. They travel to the heathland and the pubs of the Charnwood Forest for country walks, and for fishing in the big reservoirs contained there. If they roam farther afield they go to the Dukeries and Sherwood Forest in Nottinghamshire, rather than the slightly eerie, other-worldly Lincolnshire fen country.

On Saturday nights they drive out to roadside restaurants and inns, where the dominant motif in the decor will, whatever side of Leicester the place is on, be fox hunting. It is a recurring theme that does not really become offensive, for it shows off a local pride in some distinctive traditions that happen to be delightful to most tourists, and also tangible. For you really *can* get to see a fox hunt if you are in the area. Any local paper will carry the time and venue of half a dozen meets.

I am inordinately fond of provincial cities. Nottingham, Newcastle, Liverpool, Northampton have more character than they are normally given credit for. And so does Leicester. There is a vast covered market that has all the razzamatazz of a medieval fair and a smart shopping precinct as good as any in a major city like Manchester. The covered market brings a flavour of Calcutta to Leicester that seems to me to inject a special zest for life into the city. Here you have direct contact with part of Leicester's considerable Asian community. There are still several cinemas, too, a repertory theatre – and even nightclubs.

Behind the shopping streets there is still some evidence of Leicestershire's past, especially in the impressive St Mary de Castro Church, the medieval Guildhall, and the eighteenth-century buildings in Friar Lane and New Street. There is a cathedral, too, though it has only been a cathedral-proper since the 1920s and was enthusiastically restored in Victorian times. But it would be true to say that these places provide a breathing space from the buzz of city life rather than a particularly well-preserved medieval idiom.

But for all its energy and prosperity Leicester seems untypical of its county. Other impressions stick in the mind and render Leicestershire a lot more memorable than the average all-England guide-book might suggest: a day in high summer on the Leicestershire Wolds, amid a scene more reminiscent of Van Gogh than Constable – a brilliant-blue sky, lanes bordered by huge green oaks, yellow-stone farmhouses; or browsing in an antique shop in Uppingham's tiny marketplace on a winter afternoon, just as a frost begins to form on the brown fields beyond the town; or taking it gently while early morning mist lingers in the small valleys well hidden from the main roads, just hinted at perhaps by the quickly glimpsed stone-tiled roof of a farm or a red-brick pub with the unmistakable dash of colour as a post office van goes past it, then disappears down a hill; or the Meccano-look of distant pitheads and factory chimneys in a low partly-wooded valley near Coalville.

Parts of rural Northamptonshire seem almost deserted. And if you drive on a weekday morning to lonely Fotheringhay, near Oundle, you need not be surprised to see nothing

Chipping Warden, Northamptonshire. People who are already in the know might just prefer Northamptonshire's mellow limestone villages to those of the Cotswolds.

more on the roads than an old man on a bike with flowers from his allotment, or, if it is a *really* busy day, a post office van and a butcher's boy.

Richard III was born at Fotheringhay, but it is Mary Queen of Scots who is most closely associated with the village. The church, with a fine and elaborate fifteenth-century tower that seems higher than it is because of the comparatively flat surrounding country, overlooks the placid River Nene as it meanders through fertile water meadows. The castle where Mary was beheaded is long gone, but the stone bridge over which her coffin would have passed by torchlight in the small hours of the morning of 8 February 1587 is still there. And in Oundle, a well-preserved stone-built community with a famous public school, is the Talbot Inn, which is particularly proud of the oak staircase that came from Fotheringhay Castle and which would certainly have been used by Mary herself. There is an imprint of a ring on the balustrade that is said to have been made by her own hand.

Contemporary historians reported that Mary's rheumatism was aggravated by her sojourn at cold and clammy Fotheringhay. The morning mist across the fields which one is recommended to negotiate for the best camera-views of the parish church may be pleasant enough after a good English breakfast at the Talbot, but when Mary was there four hundred years ago it must indeed have been a depressing place.

Northamptonshire has been called a county of squires and spires, and the horizon really is liberally dotted with churches. Oundle, which has one or two spires itself, lies

Fotheringhay Church, near Oundle. Northamptonshire, has been described
as a mini-cathedral. It is one of England's finest parish churches, and is
complemented by a tree-shaded, tranquil, limestone village.

Rockingham, Northamptonshire. Like so much of the county, the village
and the great castle that dominates it are off the average tourist beat.

within a protective loop of the River Nene. The school was founded over four hundred
years ago, and among the lessons it used to provide for its pupils were courses in
bee-keeping, and the brewing of ale. Jane Austen is supposed to have had romantic-
looking Cottesbrooke Hall in mind when she wrote *Mansfield Park*, and Charles
Dickens wrote most of *Bleak House* during frequent visits as a friend of the family to
Rockingham Castle, right on Northamptonshire's Leicestershire border. Not that
there's anything bleak about this homeliest of Britain's historic castles – except perhaps
in mid-winter, when the fabulous views from its terraces over several counties are
obscured by mist or rain.

Both Dickens and Jane Austen, though, were itinerant figures. The casual reader of
guide books might wonder if there was any town in the south of England where one of
them didn't finish off a chapter, or rush off a few letters to catch the post. The
nineteenth-century poet John Clare, on the other hand, belongs as much to
Northamptonshire as Wordsworth does to the Lakes. Clare's birthplace – and his home
for much of his life – at Helpston, now lies just outside the county boundary, however.
The cottage, even in its prettied-up state, is worth a look. And so is the Blue Bell Inn
next door. Clare knew it well.

Clare is out of favour at the moment, though that is probably just fashion. In a
television dramatisation of his life and work some years ago, he was portrayed as

something close to a simpering idiot. His poetry was played down, and it is still his reputation as a long-term inmate of Northampton asylum that is best remembered. Actually, he wrote some of his best work there. It doesn't need a very long acquaintance with Clare's work, however, to appreciate that his rather mournful spirit still haunts the tracks and by-roads over Northamptonshire's rolling hills that always seem to be much higher and more remote than they actually are.

Arthur Hewitt is hardly in the same class as John Clare. But a little book he wrote, that I discovered in Oundle, in one of those shops that would like to think of themselves as antique shops but can't bring themselves to throw away fifty years' worth of accumulated bric-à-brac, has a lot of the old flavour of the county. It is entitled *Oundle Reminiscences*, 'The little town', says Mr Hewitt, 'has seen many changes.' He remembers some of the names he knew when he was young: 'We now have a Bull, a Hogg and a Cook, but it is a long time since we had a Brawn, Bacon and Fry. We used to have plenty of Steers, and some Trotters . . . We still have a Church, Chapel, Monk, Viccars, Bells, Chaplin and Priest. Sexton, Parsons, Deacons, Friars and a Pope used to live here.'

They sell tripe and chips in the fish shops in Longton, Staffordshire. That piece of information is not news to people who live in the Potteries, but it will be useful for strangers who witness the unaccustomed sight of a cow's stomach-lining lying on cold marble slabs, for all the world like a hairy, wet blanket. I was undaunted by the reputation of the Potteries as a Victorian stew without charm either in its buildings or among its people, relieved only slightly in its impact on the world at large by the ever readable Arnold Bennett's *Five Towns*, which are really six. They say he omitted ever to mention Fenton because of disagreements with a landlady who came from there. The other towns that make up the famous six are Tunstall, Burslem, Hanley, Longton, and Stoke-on-Trent itself. They don't like to be lumped together as the city of Stoke-on-Trent, so tread carefully, and if you have to refer to them generically, afford them a degree of individuality. Bennett's books and plays are peopled with portly bankers and thrusting young entrepreneurs grabbing their share of the tremendous wealth that was first generated here at the end of the eighteenth century. Enough remains of Edwardian Stoke for a figure out of a Bennett novel or play to be able to pass muster even in the late 1970s, complete with pinstripes, paunch, watch and chain, outside the Grand Hotel in Hanley.

This relationship with the five (or rather six) towns of his birth veered more towards hate than love-hate, and he preferred to set his early stories in London rather than Staffordshire. Later, he relented, and in *Clayhanger* he reveals that he saw in the industrial landscape a certain beauty that had originally eluded him. 'In the wreathing mist of the Caldon Bar Iron Works there was a yellow gleam that even the capricious sunlight could not kill, and then two rivers of fire sprang from the gleam, and rained in a thousand delicate and lovely hues, down the side of a mountain of refuse.' Redevelopment is sufficiently cautious for some fine architectural details to remain, as well as some of the original factories.

The Potteries proper cover an area about twelve miles long and three or four miles wide. Of course, they would have spread further than that but for a subtle but unavoidable ring of hills that keeps the six towns in check. Several factors combined to turn the Potteries into what they were. There was coal in this part of the Trent Valley, quite near the surface too, and a seam of clay: both minerals are essential to the making of pottery, and Stoke-on-Trent got off to a very good start. Ironically, it was Fenton, the pottery town that Bennett chose to ignore, that first became known as the source of fine china. And at the very beginning of the nineteenth century, at the time of the Battle of Waterloo, Fenton china enjoyed great prestige. Longton is the least inspiring of all the pottery towns, but traditionally it produced the finest-quality porcelain. It is the southernmost of the Six Towns.

It was all quite simple really. Many Potters, a rather grand name considering that many craftsmen who rejoiced in the name were actually displaced labourers who didn't have much idea of what they were about, set up or hired or borrowed one of those now not quite so familiar bottle kilns that used to give the Potteries a fairytale look, dug some clay out of a field, shaped it and fired it. (J. B. Priestley described some of these in 1933: 'A fantastic collection of narrow-necked jars or bottles peeping above the house tops on every side, looking as if giant Biblical characters, after a search for oil or wine, had popped them there, among the dwarf streets.')

People actually took clay from the roads, hence the term 'pothole'. Gradually a very localised cottage industry became transformed, at its highest level at least, into a fine art. As the legend on the monument to Josiah Wedgwood in Stoke parish church says, they 'converted a rude and inconsiderable manufactury into an elegant art'. The Wedgwood works have been displaced to Barlaston, which really is effectively the seventh town, four miles to the south. In a fine five-hundred-acre park, many Wedgwood employees live as well as work. There are tours of the works, and although most visitors go in conducted parties, individuals can also turn up informally. In contrast the city's art gallery and museum, which happens to be in Hanley, has a nice municipal air about it.

In 1971 a local manufacturer of pottery tiles thought it would be a good idea to find a typical nineteenth-century pottery before it disappeared and to recreate the original as far as possible. But he went one better, and fostered the idea of getting real potters to reproduce pottery artefacts exactly the same way as they had done all through the Victorian age and before. Here, at the Gladstone Pottery Museum, there are four bottle kilns placed around open yards and two-storeyed warehouses: all in a curious architectural style that is entirely Stoke's own and refreshing for all that. The function of the kilns dictated their shape. They needed to have an outlet, but the heat was so intense it had to be spread evenly around the available space. On the other hand, the outlet to preserve that heat had to be as small as possible.

Stoke-on-Trent affords very easy access to some of England's most unlikely but pleasant countryside. You can easily drive to Buxton and the Derbyshire High Peak, via underrated Leek, which itself is full of rare Victorian semi-industrial architecture, and with a tough, independent air of its own. There's quite enough in Staffordshire, contrary to most people's expectations, to please any chocolate-box photographer: he will do well to visit Lichfield, Brewood, Barton-under-Needwood, Ilam and Longnor. He will neglect the Potteries, however, only at the risk of giving an unbalanced picture of this medium-sized landlocked county that is geographically part of the Midlands but

The Gladstone Pottery Museum, Longton, Staffordshire. It was saved
from extinction in the nick of time, and is a moving and tangible link with
England's industrial heritage.

has more of a North Country feel about it – especially in its industrial belt and on the high, chilly moors above Dovedale, close to the Derbyshire border.

Lichfield lies at the opposite end of the county, almost within walking distance of Warwickshire and Leicestershire, but it could be hundreds of miles away from the Six Towns. If the Potteries have their roots in the grime and sweat of the Victorian industrial age, the heart of Lichfield, its market place, a couple of its fine hotels (once coaching inns), and its cathedral close, belong very much to the eighteenth century. The four-storeyed house where Dr Johnson was born, on the edge of the market square and close to a lugubrious statue of himself, is a museum. The rooms are tiny and the large Doctor, with Boswell, must almost have filled whichever one they were in. Simply climbing the stairs should have kept them fit. Among other occasions, it is recorded that James Boswell called there on 23 March 1776: 'After dinner I visited his house. A beautiful, gentle sweet maid showed me to one of the garret rooms. I kissed her, and she curtseyed.' A nice insight into eighteenth-century manners, though Boswell probably made further assignations with the young woman.

From the top floor of the house you can see the grey slate and red tile roofs of old Lichfield and the three gaunt spires of Lichfield Cathedral that in local guide books are known as 'The Ladies of the Vale'. The cathedral is famous for two reasons: the quality of evensong is outstandingly good, and the west front is a rare example of intricate decoration, like a Midlands version of the west front of Rouen Cathedral. I have visited Lichfield Cathedral in summer and winter. In summer it is pleasantly cool and dark, little frequented in comparison with the major league that is composed of the Canterburys, the Winchesters, the Salisburys. In winter, by contrast, the blue-and-yellow stained-glass windows of the Lady Chapel pick up what light there is, and at four o'clock on a quiet November afternoon, when you have the place to yourself, it is quiet and moving. From the top storey of one of Lichfield's hotels I watched the sun setting over the eastern extremes of Cannock Chase – twenty-six square miles of woodland and scrub, bracken and silver birch. Coal mines and other heavy industrial plants are even now gnawing away at the edges of Cannock Chase – there's hardly a road of any size that skirts it or crosses it from which you don't see an industrial skyline.

Perhaps the best side of Cannock Chase is the far north-west corner, near Milford. The chief prize here, apart from a 'leisure drive' between Rugeley and Stafford that goes past the edge of the Shugborough estate, is Shugborough itself, ancestral home of the Earls of Lichfield. A complete village was pulled down in the eighteenth century and re-sited to make the estate perfect. The park and the museum, which is partly centred round the old stable block and the brewhouse, are accessible to the public almost all year round.

All the small towns and villages south of the A5 at this point owe a lot to Shropshire, whose border is only a couple of miles away, or even nearer in the case of Weston Park: the county boundary actually runs through the grounds of the great 1670 house. The postal address is Shifnal, Shropshire, but the house itself lies in Staffordshire. As you get closer to the border some of the farmhouses take on the half-timbered black-and-white look that is typical of rural Shropshire buildings (in this rich green landscape, black-and-white cattle complement the houses).

This is the sort of thing that happens in a land-locked county; the edges take on some of the characteristics of their neighbours. It is just as true of that north-eastern part of

Staffordshire which belongs to the Peak District. I doubt if many visitors to the Peak District National Park stray over into Staffordshire, which is a pity because this part of the county is lonely and surprisingly wild. It has all the dramatic beauty of the Durham–Northumberland border, but is no great distance for romantically inclined southerners who want a breath of chill moorland air. The village of Longnor, for example, is as remote as a moorland farm: I even saw a sheepdog lying outside the sweetshop, half asleep in the spring sunshine. The houses and the church are of as solid a grey stone as any in North Yorkshire.

If Longnor is a nice North Country touch in a windy no man's land of moors and limestone, Ilam is an oasis beside the River Manifold. The great Gothic hall by the river has seen better days: only part of the 1820s building remains, and is now a youth hostel – one of the biggest and certainly one of the best-situated in the country. The tiny church in the grounds is actually medieval, but it was so heavily restored after the hall was built that it looks entirely Victorian. The whole scene is like a line drawing from an old edition of a Gothic novel come to life.

Leek and Uttoxeter are handy jumping-off points for the moors, and they are well worth a couple of hours' exploration. Leek is more of an industrial town than a market town, but it is still very attractive, rather hilly, with a good mixture of eighteenth- and nineteenth-century architectural styles around its cobbled market-place, with the Victorian parish church looking on. It's good for shopping, too – if you like pottering around gunsmiths, pet-food and seedstores, junk and bric-à-brac shops, and – for this is Izaak Walton country (his cottage at Shallowford is open to the public) – fishing tackle suppliers. Dr Johnson's father had a bookstall at Uttoxeter, but Johnson refused as a young man to help him in the business. This troubled his conscience when he was older, for he records that he stood in atonement for an hour, in pouring rain, in Uttoxeter market place. There is a racecourse for National Hunt meetings on the outskirts of the town – the only fully-fledged racecourse in the county.

Serious beer drinkers at least know Burton upon Trent. In the thirteenth century a monk at Burton Abbey is supposed to have discovered that the water produced good ale. Burton's beer was once exported to Russia where it was known as *Piva Burtonski* and their India Pale Ale was produced for the British in India. A consignment shipwrecked off the English coast was salvaged and sold in Britain: it became a national drink and at one point ninety per cent of the working population of Burton were employed in the brewery business.

I cannot think of a better image to sum up the character of rural Nottinghamshire than the one that has stayed in my mind ever since I visited Newstead Abbey. I approached this strange, brooding place, which really does look like the exact cross between the ruined abbey and the grand private home that it was, along a narrow road bordered by rhododendrons. That was impressive enough. On leaving the abbey I took a wrong turning, crossed over a waterfall, and ended up lost in the shunting yard of a colliery, its pit-head gear bluntly emphasising that coal means more to Nottinghamshire in practical terms than Lord Byron ever did. Newstead was once Lord Byron's home, though he sold it to get out of debt. Even so, it is most closely associated with him, and he is still something of a local hero. At Southwell, only half an hour's drive from

Newstead, I was reminded by the newsagent that Byron had a girlfriend or two here and belonged to a local amateur dramatic society.

I stayed at the Saracen's Head. This is highly recommended, being that ideal combination of cosy, timbered historical charm and all mod cons. Byron was a visitor too, and he wrote a ditty on hearing of the death of a fellow customer from over-indulgence in the grape:

> John Adam was here, of the Parish of Southwell
> A carrier who carried his can to his mouth well;
> He carried so much and he carried so fast
> He could carry no more so was carried at last.

If this doesn't tell us much about Byron's poetic skills it does at least tell us how the name of the town should be pronounced: only outsiders – including a lot of racegoers who come here for National Hunt racing during the winter months – betray their ignorance by calling it Suth'll. Southwell is a modest little market town that is really just a busy street at right angles to the Minster. Some people have called Southwell Minster the most beautiful church in the country. James I was impressed by it on his way south from Scotland to be crowned. 'Vara weel,' he is reported to have said, 'by my blude this kirk shall justle with York or Durham or any other kirk in Christendom.' There is even a row of perfectly proportioned Georgian houses across the road from the Minster, which enhances its beauty. Not quite a 'cathedral close', but not far off.

Of all the things that appeal to me about the Midlands counties, it is the undiscovered landscapes and villages that I like most. Here in Nottinghamshire I think of the Dukeries, those vast country estates on the edge of the industrial cities, of Sherwood Forest, of the upland Wolds on the Leicestershire border – where a height above sea-level of two hundred feet makes you feel – in more ways than one – on top of the world.

If you stay in Southwell, I recommend an hour or two exploring the villages and the lanes around Edingley, Thurgarton, Halloughton, Normanton. The red brick of which most houses and farm buildings are constructed may not be the most exciting of all building material, but see it with the late afternoon sun lighting it as if with an inner fire, and it puts flint or limestone into the shade. Thus the predominant colours of this quiet corner of the county are rich green from the pasture and dark red from the villages and scattered houses.

East of Southwell, and right on the Lincolnshire border, Newark Castle marks the place where King John died in 1216. While some impressively ruined castles have fallen down because of neglect or dry rot, Newark really has seen some action. It was ruined during the Civil War, as the town refused to submit to Cromwell and withstood three sieges.

Once you negotiate the bypass which cleverly saves Newark from the worst ravages of cars and lorries you will discover a pleasant market town that is inward-looking and medieval in atmosphere. I was impressed by the 'Bacon Shop' – it seemed to sell more blended teas and regional cheeses than bacon, actually – on the corner of the market-place, and the china and book stalls in the huge market square. Newark church is rather tucked away, and you come up to it rather unexpectedly. It is delicately detailed, inside and out.

Newark has one foot in the fens, and it could almost belong to Lincolnshire. But if I could have a present of a hundred acres of Nottinghamshire I would choose a piece of Clumber Park, north of Nottingham and Sherwood Forest. Clumber, which belongs to the Dukeries, is close to the everyday world of fast roads and housing estates but so easily accessible that it seems like a pre-packaged, instant-eighteenth-century-landscape. It has just about everything a city-dweller would want: a sprawling birch forest, rolling heaths, a tranquil lake with flying-squads of ducks. Clumber House no longer exists, though its strange, gaunt, black chapel is there. This looks as if it would be more at home in the middle of a city, but it is all the more effective in this pleasant, silent setting.

The greatest Victorian country house in the Midlands, Thoresby Hall, is a few miles south of Clumber, and it is almost as incongruous. One of the few herds of deer in the Dukeries can often be seen by visitors to pseudo-medieval Thoresby, and they make a soft contrast to the high, grand building whose rooms no one, it is reported, has ever counted.

Thoresby lies on the edge of Sherwood Forest, which is the place most people would associate with Nottinghamshire, and is a huge tract of forest and heathland, unchanged for hundreds of years, to the south of the Dukeries. It makes a back garden for the industrial towns of Mansfield, Ollerton and Nottingham itself – and some back garden it is. Alas, it has been reported that the famous 'Major Oak' that Robin Hood is said to have sheltered inside is, after all, only four hundred years old, and not nine hundred. A dozen people can stand together in its partly hollowed-out trunk. Edwinstowe is the nearest village; a visitors' centre has been completed near here, and some idea of the popularity of the place can be had from the number of restaurants and pubs.

Sherwood Forest makes up in fame what it lacks in acres. For this breathing space in the heart of the industrial Midlands is nowhere near as big as the New Forest and would be absorbed a hundred times over by Northumberland's Kielder Forest. Daniel Defoe was able to write, even in about 1700, 'Tis now given up to waste and Robin Hood would hardly find shelter for one week.' In fact ecologists would say that Defoe complained too loudly, for the real decline set in during the nineteenth and early twentieth centuries. Through bad management Sherwood Forest was allowed to go as close to rack and ruin as possible, added to which the Robin Hood legend that brought hundreds of thousands of visitors here hardly allowed the forest to regenerate itself. Things are more organised today, and the third of a million people who visit the Sherwood Forest Country Park every year have helped to turn this into a slightly antiseptic but still worthwhile tourist attraction.

Of the events and the people associated with the Dukeries none was more bizarre than the Duke of Portland, an eccentric recluse whose obsession at his home in Welbeck Abbey was to burrow and build underground like a mole crossed with an architect. He built a suite of rooms lit by 1,100 gas jets, then a ballroom which actually began as a chapel, and a miniature railway designed to convey the food and drink from the kitchens in the main house for underground banquets.

Not many visitors make it to 'Lawrence Country'. It is much more elusive than other places to which a lot of people make literary pilgrimages, like Brontë country in Yorkshire, or Hardy country in Dorset, but it is there all the same. *The White Peacock*

In this house at Eastwood, Nottinghamshire, D. H. Lawrence was born on
11 September 1885.

and *Sons and Lovers* both contain scenes closely based on Eastwood life and
surroundings, and though Lawrence had little affection for the area he could never quite
escape it. The back-to-back miners' houses and red roofs and stark pit-head gear of
D. H. Lawrence's home town still exist here at Eastwood, though these are likely in a
very few years to be few and far between and of curiosity value only.

Waste not, want not: houses built into the ruins of the twelfth-century
abbey walls at Bury St Edmunds, Suffolk.

Pargetting par excellence: the Ancient House, Clare, Suffolk. Such
decorative plasterwork is an East Anglian speciality.

King's College Chapel, Cambridge, from the top of Great St Mary's
Church tower. In the right foreground is the Senate House.

Rhapsody in sandstone and red brick. The three spires of Lichfield
Cathedral, Staffordshire, are known as 'the ladies of the vale'.

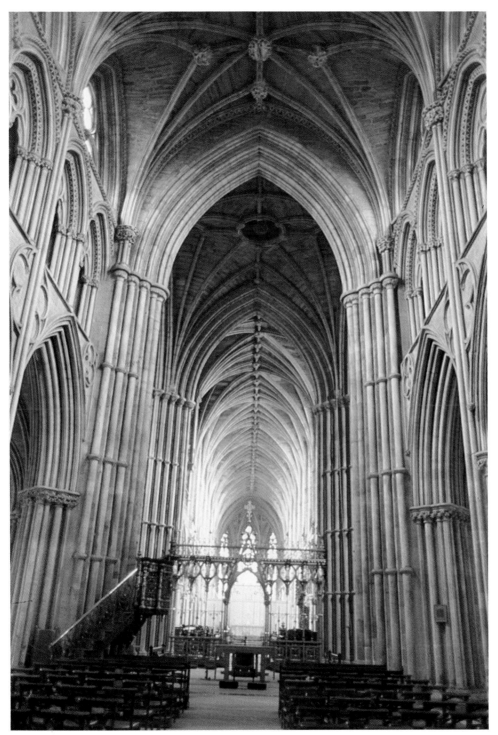

The soaring interior of Lichfield Cathedral, though much restored,
contains some of the best Early English and Decorated work in the
country.

Classic limestone country: a corner of Ketton, in what used to be Rutland but is now Leicestershire. The roofs of most cottages are of slate from nearby Collyweston, and the very pretty parish church of St Mary is of Barnack stone.

Thwaite, North Yorkshire. In this, as in so many Swaledale villages and hamlets, the cottages and farms seem to spring directly from the landscape. Not a hair is out of place.

Winterscape among the Pennines, between Alston, Cumbria and Stanhope, County Durham.

Much of my life is spent ferreting around provincial towns and cities. Nottingham is one of my favourite places. I like the way it belongs neither to the North nor the Midlands, and the fact that either sentiment or expediency has caused a lot of old Victorian shopfronts and pubs to remain alongside new shopping precincts – notable among these are the Victorian Centre, a space-age, all-in-one, air-conditioned shoppers' paradise. I also like the way one or two Victorian mills (not counting the old lace-market, which is deliberately preserved) remain in or near the city centre. I like the tough, matter-of-fact flavour they impart. The same goes for the industrial landscape views from the castle ramparts.

Nottingham Castle would not appeal to small boys – there are no battlements, no cannon, though there are underground caves in the great rock the castle stands on, and a statue of Robin Hood at its base. The castle is quite close to the city centre and, with the proximity of a famous old inn called Ye Olde Trip to Jerusalem as an added incentive (it is built into the castle rock, and they say it was patronised by the Crusaders), it attracts many thousands of visitors.

The proverbial border between the north and south of England first sees the light of day on Mow Cop, a 1,000-foot high hill on which the Primitive Methodist church was born. It is on Biddulph Moor, in north Staffordshire and it was here that Hugh Bourne, a local carpenter, held revivalist meetings in 1807. Since it flows from north to south through the Potteries, it is very hard to come to terms with the Trent as the true and only border, but most people will know what you mean. It is really only when it gets beyond the Potteries, well south of Stone (not a bad market town in its own right, by the way), and swings south of Rugeley, then up to Burton upon Trent en route for Nottingham, that the river starts to look like that famous dividing line. Nottingham people, however, never quite commit themselves to being northerners or southerners, and maintain a diplomatic neutrality.

As it flows through the Potteries, the Trent is hardly that unassuming and surprisingly narrow serpent that meanders through the paddocks of rural Staffordshire, well known incidentally at this stage of its development to Izaak Walton, who wrote *The Compleat Angler* at the age of sixty and whose cottage at Shallowford, on a tributary of the Trent, is now an angling museum. But even in the Potteries, Trent is not as black and oily as tradition would suggest: the great clean-up is well under way.

Nottingham does not make a lot of its river, though the city only really developed because there was a handy river crossing here. This was Trent Bridge, whose cricket pitch reputedly is a fast bowler's delight. It is better to see the river from Newark-on-Trent, where there are enough river craft to make the stroll to the banks worthwhile, and Newark will return the compliment if you are in a hired canal or river boat and decide to see something of the town. The outskirts are depressing, but the cobbled market square, whether or not the awnings are up and there is a market in progress, is one of my favourite workaday places. From here the river runs due north again into the Humber.

Nottingham was always an important trade centre – it still makes lace, though less and less by hand – especially in the great late-eighteenth and early-nineteenth-century coaching days. The stage coaches would set off from the Swan With Two Necks Inn in

The River Trent and Trent Bridge, Nottingham. The city does not belong
quite to the North nor quite to the Midlands. It is independent and full of
character.

London every Monday and Thursday morning and, after an overnight halt at
Northampton, would arrive at the Blackamoor's Head in Nottingham the following
evening. 'If', as the operators said, 'God permits . . .'

Newark is on the Nottinghamshire border, and looks across to Lincolnshire. You can
see the spire of Newark's parish church from the high escarpment at the northerly end
of Lincolnshire's rolling wolds, so reminiscent of Sussex's South Downs. The
occasionally heavily wooded, chalky uplands that dominate the central part of
Lincolnshire like vertebrae were the home and inspiration of one of England's greatest
poets. But of all the officially designated Areas of Outstanding Natural Beauty it is
surprisingly little known. This is doubly remarkable when you consider that the
Lincolnshire coast at Skegness and Mablethorpe, which Tennyson also wrote about
long before it became a popular resort, is so famous. This countryside of marvellous,
rolling views, hamlets that are often just sprawling farmsteads of red brick or pale grey
limestone, of clumps of trees on bare hills that seem higher than they are, covers roughly

thirty miles from north (near Caistor) to south (near Spilsby), and is between five and ten miles wide.

I remember looking for Old Bolingbroke Castle, on the edge of the Lincolnshire Wolds, at about nine o'clock one January morning. Early morning mist still hung over the fields like a surfeit of smoke wreathing around an amateur production of Macbeth. The next time I saw the village it was after dark, when I was en route to visit friends in the village pub. I drove up the slight incline on top of which the village and the castle ruins stand. The full moon riding across the cloud-scudded sky threw enough light behind copses and farm buildings to raise ghosts.

The southerly and western edges of Lincolnshire are much better known, and people who know Stamford would hardly call it off-beat. But the bypass that took the A1 trunk road from London to Edinburgh well away from this almost-perfect stone built town on the River Welland, and has rendered it quieter during the last few years than it had been for the previous two hundred, has also hidden the place from the gaze of the unsuspecting outsider. The fame of one of the finest buildings in the town – and that is saying something, because this is an almost incomparable collection of elegant stone houses and churches – has spread far and wide. This is the George, one of the best examples of a largely eighteenth-century coaching inn in the country.

Stamford owed its original prosperity as an important trading centre to its geographical position. To the east were the fens, whence came fish (particularly large eels, which were much more highly regarded in the Middle Ages than today) and wildfowl, and to the west were the great wool-producing grasslands. Europe was not far away by sea, and London was a couple of days' trip by wagon, along comparatively safe roads. The church was strong, and medieval schools were so good that the expanding universities of Oxford and Cambridge were afraid that Stamford would become a rival. The parish churches that make such an attractive skyline when one sees the town from the meadows beside the Welland add extra interest to walk through Stamford. It has always had everything going for it. Its position meant that it was an important coaching stop, which is why the George and other inns exist (the original waiting rooms for coach passengers can still be seen at the George, in whose cobbled yard a team of horses could be changed in sixty seconds). By a curious personal link with eighteenth-century history, I first got to know Stamford because the long-distance coaches, which I travelled on for teenage holidays to the north of England, used to stop there for food, drink and diesel oil. 'Ladies and gentlemen, you have an hour and a half' – a nice throwback to the Georgian era, and a custom that Queen Victoria, who hated eating and drinking in transit, would have thoroughly approved.

Stamford was also given a big financial and political boost when, between 1560 and 1587, Lord Burghley, Queen Elizabeth's Secretary of State, had a palatial mansion built on the edge of the town. Burghley House, annual venue of the Burghley Horse Trials, is open to the public. It has, however, had a chequered geography. Until a few years ago it was in Northamptonshire, but this became the Soke of Peterborough, which was then absorbed into Huntingdonshire, which in turn (in 1974) became part of Cambridgeshire.

When it comes to dominant counties, however, there is none that can touch Yorkshire. It has always put Lincolnshire into the shade, and it is more a matter of charisma than size.

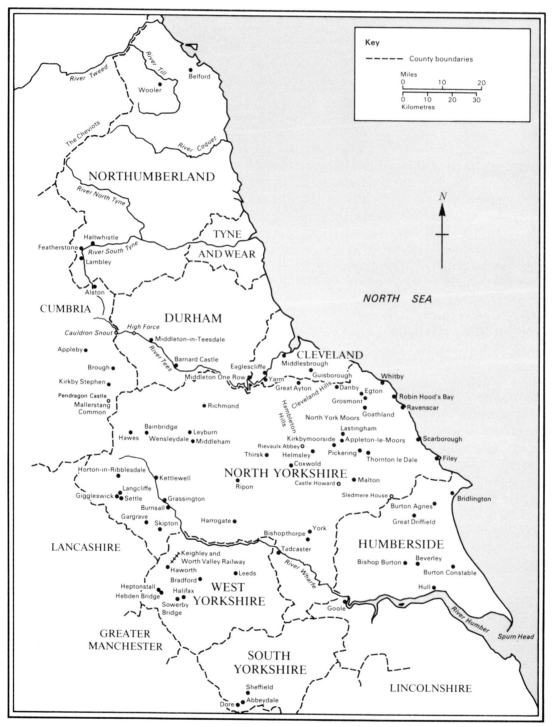

Map 3 North-East England

4. Yorkshire: up hill and down dale

The pleasures of Hull; Helmsley;
the North York Moors and the Dales;
the seaside and the industrial heartland;
Cleveland and the Durham border

Seasoned travellers in Yorkshire may have heard that 'apple pie wi'out the cheese is like a kiss wi'out the squeeze'. But only the more sophisticated among them will know that *the* cheese to serve with apple pie ('deep dish', in pizza parlour parlance, is best) is Wensleydale. Most people know something about Yorkshire's role in the Wars of the Roses, but get confused about which rose Yorkshire wore: for the record, it was white. And they naturally expect to be served Yorkshire pudding the right way, that is, all puffed up and crispy on top, but are surprised that there is a hotel in Harrogate that serves it *twelve* different ways, sweet and savoury, and even more surprised that there is a Chinese takeaway in Leeds that sells Yorkshire pud alongside the chop suey.

Apple pie, Yorkshire pudding and the white rose that crops up outside elegant restaurants and mundane filling stations are just tip-of-the-iceberg manifestations of Yorkshire tourist appeal. Lancastrians will not like this, but Yorkshire is closer to bursting at the seams with infectious energy and has more places of tourist interest than any other county in the north of England. If, that is, we think of Yorkshire as one single county rather than an amorphous quintet of them. The county boundaries were redrawn in 1974 and Yorkshire now consists of Humberside, South Yorkshire, West Yorkshire, North Yorkshire and Cleveland. Feelings run especially high about Humberside. The very word is taboo in certain company. Outsiders may think the word is quite acceptable, since it appertains to a great and proud river, but many Yorkshiremen will go pale. You might even be asked to leave the pub – especially in Hull – which would be a pity, as Hull has some fascinating ones. Beware, however, the professional Yorkshireman. Michael Parkinson may be the most popular chat-show host in the history of British television, but his obsession with Barnsley (in South Yorkshire) and the Yorkshire county cricket team has been known to drive desperate viewers into the bosom of arch-rival Russell Harty, who derives from the other side of the Pennines – namely Blackburn.

If James Herriot had not existed, the Yorkshire and Humberside Tourist Board might have invented him. His books, sold in their millions, have popularised the windswept moors and the deserted dales in a way that no end of brochures and glossy promotional films could have done. Herriot lives near Thirsk ('Darrowby' in the books) but does not thank people for arriving with their autograph books at his surgery – for he is a practising vet who has, it was reported in 1983, finally given up the (for him) extravagantly lucrative world of writing for a return to ministering to, say, a cow with a collapsed uterus or mongrels run over and all but given up for lost. The Yorkshire

Herriot portrays is beautiful but primitive. It belongs to the late 1930s. But you might think, as you struggle to extricate yourself from a snowdrift up on the fells or ponder the meaning of life in the corner of a Skipton snug bar over a glass of Theakston's ale, that nothing has really changed.

I have travelled over Yorkshire's whaleback hills in all weathers, when you could look down over, say, Burnsall, near Kettlewell, and see so clearly that from half a mile away, especially after a sharp shower of rain, you knew what kind of dog it was trotting alongside its owner who was sensibly riding a bicycle; and also when, over Buttertubs Pass, between Bainbridge and Hawes, it was so foggy you felt that a few more yards would pitch you over a precipice to certain death and a dour North Yorkshire funeral among the hill farmers.

A distant view of Burnsall, North Yorkshire. When you get there the village is as pretty as it is from the surrounding hills.

Summer is when most visitors arrive, naturally, but it is a deception. Those balmy afternoons watching village cricket at Leyburn, those midday paddles the children enjoy at Thornton Dale, on the road from Malton to Scarborough, those shirtless (and insect-bitten) hikes up into the parched brown hills above Helmsley, have caused many an expatriate Leeds or Sheffield man, who thought he had left Yorkshire for good, to buy a cottage in the hills, only to regret it when the snows came. The hills make

Yorkshire seem even vaster than it is: you can, foolishly perhaps, encompass Lincolnshire in an hour or two in a fast car and pigeonhole that county. Yorkshire defies such simple categorisation – you cannot take it for granted. Naturally, it is the inconsequential details that stay in the mind: the ticking of a grandfather clock in the parlour of a pub at Oswaldkirk, near Helmsley; the sight of a thin covering of snow early on an April morning from the window of a bed-and-breakfast-only hotel on the edge of the Hambleton Hills.

If Yorkshire declared independence, Hull and the rest of Humberside would probably secede too. The flat fields of what were, before 1974, the East Riding, may not seem to have much in common with the bare brown moors among Helmsley in North Yorkshire, nor the green, limestone dales much further to the west, but people in Hull still think of themselves as 'Yorkshire folk'. There are further complications for the unwary traveller, for North Humberside – an unofficial division – will have no truck with South Humberside. The former was part of the old East Riding, the latter used to belong to Lincolnshire. The terrain may be dramatically different between the canal-scape and the Victorian red brick of Goole on the backs of the Humber and the most northerly reaches of the county around Richmond, but you will find character-istics of speech and personality that unite the county.

Yorkshire is full of superlatives: more stately homes to the square mile than any other part of England, towns and villages that are milestones of history, castles and abbeys scattered like farmhouses. People are not coy about the castles, which makes visiting them much nicer. So if you go to Middleham, whose castle was built by Richard III, you will see no 'castle tearooms' or 'Richard III Garage'. Yorkshire traditionally has more acres to its credit than letters in the Bible – that is about four million. Nearly every one of them – acres that is – is worth treading. I like the eastern half of the M62 motorway via which you travel to Hull from the west – a kind of no man's land, uncluttered by service areas – between the A1 and the point where, under dizzy-making wide skies, the motorway gives up the ghost. In fact, it is my favourite part of the whole motorway network. I even like Goole – with its Meccano-set dockside cranes – though not as much as Hull.

It will not be to everybody's taste, but Goole conceals a lot of interesting things behind its rather functional red-brick façade. Much of the best of the town dates from the early part of Queen Victoria's reign when, a few years after the opening of the Goole canal, there was a lot of activity here. The docks are still busy: they are famous for their canal trains of coal from the Yorkshire coalfields, with pans known as Tom Puddings that are hoisted on to waiting coasters. These, as well as the trains themselves, hold drivers up: they have to wait for swing bridges to open. All this despite the fact that Goole is almost fifty miles from the sea. It is surrounded by green fields, and you can see the cranes from many miles away. It's a down-to-earth place, with a nightclub tucked away behind a butcher's shop, Polish seamen in donkey jackets whose footsteps echo on metallic gangplanks at dead of night.

In common with perhaps a couple of dozen English cities Hull (or Kingston upon Hull, as it has sometimes been called since Edward I bought the land it was built on) belies its plain and workaday reputation and throbs with life. People who are misled by the city's popular image are missing a lot. Even though the ferry that chugged between Hull and New Holland, on the south side of the Humber, which used to be one of the most glorious unsung delights in the north of England, was banished to oblivion after the opening of the spectacular Humber Bridge, there is a lot to see. One of the great advantages of the ferry that used to turn such a mundane thing as crossing a big river into a blustery voyage of discovery was that it took you right into the heart of the old docks, a windy-cornered, thickly-pubbed, seagull-screaming city fringe that few people find by chance today. This part of the city was almost razed to the ground by enemy bombing during the war, but much of what remained and survived the ravages of the property developer is being restored.

A lane known as 'The Land O' Green Ginger' may not quite be the romantic place it sounds, though it did once run between warehouses full of exotic spices brought into Hull by sailing ships from the East Indies, but if you walk down the High Street, parallel with the River Hull that runs at right angles into the Humber, you will find a beautifully converted warehouse – now flats – that dates from the eighteenth century, and the elegant, red-brick, many-roomed Wilberforce Museum, where the anti-slavery campaigner was born in 1759. This is one of the best small museums I have found in all my travels around Britain. Nearby are well preserved Georgian merchants' houses, notably Maister's House, a Palladian Mansion of 1743 that would not disgrace the City of Bath. Almost opposite is the transport and archeology museum, which contains – another trick Hull has up its sleeve – one of the best Roman mosaics in Britain.

The commercial centre of Hull, which is only a sailor's Saturday night lurch from the pleasures described above, has its share of soulless modern architecture, much relieved, however, by the city's unusually wide streets. These, coupled with the rather gaunt, high, solid-looking buildings that dominate the city centre – especially around the many-flowered Queen's Gardens that cover what was the city's first dock, of 1778 – give Hull a more than faintly Baltic air. If you confine your visit to Hull to the railway terminus and stay in the adjacent Royal Station Hotel that retains the high ceilings and faded elegance of the Victorian age, or if you drive from the end of that pleasantly underused M62 motorway that links Hull so quickly and neatly with the M1 and the A1 and don't venture into the city centre at all, then you might just miss Hull's nautical connections. Otherwise, there are constant reminders. Even if you are recommended to try one of Hull's most famous pubs, the Black Boy, it may not be pointed out to you that the name comes from the cargoes of African slaves that much of Hull's early wealth was founded on. Some sage may also suggest that the name derives from Charles II's nickname: the king was exceptionally swarthy and *some* Black Boys are indeed named after him. Or you might notice young men in the uniform of Merchant Navy Cadets. They will almost certainly be students at the Navigation School at Trinity House, which is the oldest school of its kind in the world, having been founded in 1789.

Try also to see the Maritime Museum, converted from the Victorian Docks Office, and the Ferens Art Gallery, which is remarkable for the number of fine marine paintings in its collection. So far, it contains no paintings of the Humber Bridge – but it can only be a matter of time. For this, the longest single-span suspension bridge in the world, and perhaps the most beautiful, is bringing thousands of people to Hull just so they can say that they have seen it. Though Hull has long enjoyed that M62 motorway link, and it was not really any hardship to go north and turn right off the M1 or the A1, or come south and turn left, you can now cross South Humberside and travel over the great river in a manner not quite as nostalgic and charming as by a ferry long overdue for the scrap heap, but in great style. It is also worth £2 per car just for the trip over the bridge and back. Try it during a morning when the sun sparkles on the water and there is a mist over the estuary to the east, or on a summer evening when the light is like apple juice and visibility is perfect.

Hull is no pale shadow of what it once was but a working port, and luxurious car ferries run from here to Scandinavia. Among other advantages, a bonus for the ferry passenger, is a close encounter with Spurn Head, an elusive, shifting finger of land that points crookedly into the Humber estuary. It is unashamedly fickle. Every day it moves a few inches, a foot, a few inches again, and they say that within the space of a hundred years it adopts a completely new position. It is an insubstantial half-land, half-sea of sand and shingle. Probably the best way to see it at reasonably close quarters is to take a DFDS/Tor Lines ferry from Hull to Gothenberg. In doing so, you can wave hello to Spurn Head's tiny population.

I am constantly drawn to the eastern side of the county, to that stretch of country bordered roughly by Beverley, Great Driffield and Bridlington. Give it a miss and you won't know what you are missing: mainly, a trio of stately homes – Burton Constable, Burton Agnes and Sledmere House – that are almost never overrun with visitors, but between them encapsulate the best of how the other one per cent used to live. I also remember pottering around little red-brick Lund, which is unregarded but exquisite, among fertile farmland (there are two pictures on the sign outside the Wellington Inn: one shows the Iron Duke as a young man, the other as he was in later years); and Bishop Burton, an unlikely oasis of great oaks and chestnuts around a crescent-shaped village pond, but unfortunately along the main road from Beverley to York.

I have visited York long enough to stay overnight perhaps a dozen times. It was always done intentionally, but it might have been accidental. For all roads, except the A1 and the motorway-proper, lead here, certainly within Yorkshire itself: from the wide-skied North Sea edge of the East Riding (Humberside to some), from the strangely appealing no man's land of the M62 motorway, from the scrubby heights of the Howardian hills due north, from Ripon and Harrogate, beyond which lie the Dales – another face of Yorkshire.

From the A1, if you approach the city from the south of England, you can pick up the A64 through Tadcaster past the approach to Bishopthorpe – a delightful village, incidentally, which is untroubled by much traffic and which peters out, in a way I especially like, into open country. This way you see the racecourse before the city. If it were not for the racecourse, many people who count themselves among York's admirers would never have come here at all. It ranks with the best-looking handful of courses in England, on a par with Goodwood's rolling greensward and Lingfield's pretty, well-tended paddocks and flowers. Viewing is nearly as good as at Sandown, which is saying something, and the atmosphere tends to be tough and light-hearted at the same time.

Win or lose at the races, York is perhaps the least disappointing 'historic' city in the country. The way it has preserved the best of its Roman and medieval past, nicely seasoned with echoes of the industrial revolution (just take a train from the marvellous high-vaulted railway station for a taste of that), is nothing less than superb. And if the tangle of medieval streets called The Shambles is almost invariably busy with human traffic, then that too has a degree of authenticity. I have a special fondness for this quarter of the city after dark, when judicious floodlighting picks out architectural details that get missed in the cold light of day. Nor do the pizzerias and the French bistros, that are especially welcoming on cold autumn nights, jar: medieval York, after all, was also a cosmopolitan place.

The railway museum cuts mere mortals down to size. Unimpeded by station platforms you are knee-high-to-a-piston-rod as you root among leviathans of the Iron Age in their great engine shed. On specially built walkways you can peer into locomotive cabs and, most titillating of all, into the plush interiors of carriages once occupied by Queen Victoria. There are, however, no restaurant cars: Her Majesty refused to dine (or breakfast, or lunch) other than in conventional station hotels or restaurants. Later Royal trains – or at least parts of them – are also present and very correct.

York is worth a fortnight of anybody's life, but some people on a grand tour give it just an afternoon, which at least allows time for a token acquaintance with 'the big three': the Minster, the Railway Museum and the Castle Museum. For you will see the medieval walls from the railway station approach, and the old city, including The Shambles, en route for the Minster.

A country bus driver, based in York, pauses during his afternoon shift.

The Castle Museum is housed in what was once York's Women's Prison and the adjoining former Debtor's Prison. It is astonishing – one of those museums that nobody gets bored in. You will go a long way to see a better selection of bygones, reconstructed street scenes and domestic interiors. There is the façade of a hotel as it was in the 1840s, a garage of the 1930s, a sweetshop the Victorians would recognise, a post office of the same period and Dick Turpin's cell, exactly as he would have known it the night before his execution here in 1739.

I used to wonder whether I would ever see York Minster unadorned by scaffolding, because my first visits to the city were all made between 1967 and 1972, when much of the exterior of York Minster was being restored. When a massive programme of renovation and cleaning, undertaken at the same time as essential repairs to the 20,000 ton central lantern tower, had been completed, and the scaffolding removed, there was revealed to the people of this lovely and well-cared-for city a cathedral in honey-coloured stone that was almost exactly as it looked in the fifteenth century.

The great Gothic Minster has watched over every episode in York's turbulent history, though at least three times in its existence it was in danger of being consumed by fire – in 1829 by an arsonist who objected to the worldly ways of priests, in 1840, and again in 1972. Even before the present building was begun there was a wooden church on the site. Plans for its replacement by a stone building were put in hand in 633 by Edwin, King of Northumbria, a Christian convert, though he was killed in battle and never saw it completed. Before that, the spot where the Minster stands had been a Roman military headquarters (close by, in the cellars of the Treasurer's House, there are persistent ghost stories concerning Roman legionnaires), and a number of Roman remains that are now incorporated in the fabric of the Minster have been excavated.

Much of the stonework, both on the exterior and inside the Minster, reflects the glory of Yorkshire's stonemasons over hundreds of years, and it is said that some of the superb collection of medieval stained glass, the best in England, and especially the thirteenth-century Five Sisters Window, was part of the inspiration of Sir Basil Spence when he was drawing up plans for modern Coventry Cathedral. The Minster enjoys one of the finest Gothic frontages in Europe.

York's Mansion House is the only one in Britain in which the Lord Mayor and his family live during their year of office. Once, on an official tour of the city, I sat down to cucumber sandwiches with the first citizen. He told me that his gold chain, which mercifully he was not wearing at the time, dates back to 1612, and that among the other insignia and paraphernalia is an ancient half-gallon tankard at the base of whose handle is a whistle. Traditionally, when you were nearing the bottom of your tankard during a long and thirsty evening, you blew the whistle. Hence the expression 'to wet your whistle'.

I was once asked in York whether I was a Moors man or a Dales man. A pause for thought. I knew what they meant, but questions like that are a small minefield. Luckily, I was able to confess I had only seen the Dales and not the Moors, and honour was saved. It was an omission I was soon to rectify. To call the moorland country around Helmsley overlooked may strike some drivers as a very tongue-in-cheek remark, particularly on one of those eye-dazzling summer afternoons when the world and his wife are en route for Scarborough or Filey. Pickering and Thornton Dale are the sort of towns that crop up in police flashes about traffic bottlenecks ('Avoid the area if you can'). And Helmsley itself is hardly innocent of strangers, who at holiday time turn the great and spectacular market square into something akin to The Shambles on a Saturday morning.

I passed through Helmsley's great market-place at ten o'clock one Sunday morning in early May. It was deserted, except for the lady in the baker's shop laying out trays of apple turnovers and chocolate eclairs, and a boy delivering newspapers to houses on the unsunny side of the barrack-square sized expanse of tarmac. When I returned, after six hours spent on the far side of the horizon in a four-wheel-drive Japanese truck ('We'll show you the real Yorkshire,' my farmer hosts had promised), Helmsley was transformed. There were more cars in the square, where at ten o'clock you would have had room to hold a Billy Graham rally, than in any of the car parks at Ascot on Ladies' Day. Cassette recorders like pieces of vital equipment filched from space shuttles blared out reggae music, and if there had been a river people would have been paddling in it, motorcycle helmets and all. You can't blame them. Helmsley is a quite exceptional tourist centre, and it has made North Yorkshire converts from many a Sunday driver weaned on the beautiful but rather more 'obvious' and slightly self-satisfied dales.

Few people venture into 'them there hills' except to exercise a dog cooped up too long in the car, but a quicker way to experience the appeal of the moors – subtly different as they are from the more westerly dales – is either to drive from Kirkbymoorside, between Helmsley and Pickering, to Hutton-le-Hole, then to Lastingham and Appleton-le-Moors, or, if your visit is during the summer or on a spring or autumn Bank Holiday, to take the North York moors steam railway from Pickering to Goathland and Grosmont. There you can join one of British Rail's own unsung scenic routes, which connects Whitby and Middlesbrough. Much closer to 'home', however, on Helmsley's doorstep, is Rievaulx Abbey: half hidden in its wooded valley, it is an abstract, ruined beauty, all skeletal arches and fluted pillars set off by an emerald greensward.

On a second visit to Helmsley I caught the holiday mood and stayed with the traffic all the way through Kirkbymoorside and Pickering to Scarborough. One thing not a problem in Scarborough is hotels: except at the very height of the season, you can afford to be very choosy. I was there in May. The world was full of promise, and with good reason Scarborough's stallholders were counting their chickens. The streets are quiet until the first trains from Harrogate and Beverley arrive, then suddenly they are full of genteel little old ladies wrapped up against the non-existent cold (Isn't it mild for the time of year? they tell each other, several times, cocooned as they are in their Oxfam-shop coats as if en route for Siberia).

Scarborough is three places in one. There is the shopping centre, almost indistinguishable from the pleasantly predictable high street of any provincial town – *almost* because the holiday mood keeps breaking out: the main department store has a nice line in sombreros among the gents' alpaca jackets, and a sign in a sedate bookshop says 'No ice creams please'.

The second face of Scarborough is what you expect of the North Yorkshire coast: red roofs stepped down toward the harbour, parrot-green Fraserburgh-registered fishing boats in the greasy waters of the harbour. Thin hand rails set into the stone walls

Display case of spa waters, probably as undrinkable as they ever were, at
Harrogate, North Yorkshire.

Montpelier Parade, Harrogate: even if you are just popping out to buy a tin
of baked beans or a postcard, the elegance of the Edwardian and Victorian
architecture adds a fillip.

are more substantial than they look. You will hardly notice them if you walk down, but you certainly will if you walk back the same way, especially if you have been legging it up and down the seafront. For this is the third face of Scarborough – as good as you will get anywhere if what you want is rock stalls, or fresh crabs and shrink-wrap kippers ('But are they local?'); or sit down for 'fish and chips, bread and butter and tea' served by schoolgirls on holiday, with black skirts and pert bums and a tendency to mix the orders up.

Smokers' corner: seafood stall on the front at Scarborough, North Yorkshire. A token lobster sums up a problem – there are just not enough of them to go round.

I also made a small detour up the road to see Whitby where, incidentally, hotels are very much thinner on the ground. Red-roofed, seagull-shrieking Whitby never quite became a seaside resort in the Scarborough mould. People were doing very nicely thank you out of the North Sea harvest and, although times have been hard, this is a fishing community first and a holiday resort second. Whatever the weather conditions you will not find it boring. Perhaps early risers will enjoy it most: at dawn you can go down to the quayside warm in your overcoat, with the prospect of a stomach-lining breakfast in a café or hotel ahead of you, and observe the fishing boats setting off for work.

Whitby actually still has donkeys on the sands, though I thought they had a slightly hangdog look about them. Views over the town and out to sea, where there is always something going on, will more than compensate for tired feet that have to traipse up and down past huggermugger pantiled or slate-roofed fishermen's cottages. In contrast are Whitby's elegant terraces – no Georgian whimsy here, however, but solid bare stone, four-storeyed houses, some whitewashed, some unadorned. This must be one of the windiest places even on the Yorkshire coast, especially if you make it up to the abbey which is over a thousand years old, and stands on a site where there was a religous foundation three hundred years before the abbey was built. Early one March morning that contained a half-promise of spring, I brought my car to an abrupt halt in the mist swirling around gaunt Whitby Abbey. Just ten yards ahead of me was the biggest hare I have ever seen, and there was just enough sun filtering through the mist to light up the colours of its coat. It summed me up for fully thirty seconds, then turned away towards the overgrown abbey ruins.

Captain Cook, incidentally, came from Great Ayton, just inland, and his ships, the *Resolution* and the *Endeavour*, that took him on his world-beating journeys to the Antipodes, were built at Whitby. This, too, is fish-and-chip-shop country, though as I stood in a queue in the Marine Fish Bar the daughter of the man who runs the video shop told me that the fish I'd get was almost certainly imported, as the stuff Whitby catches is generally too expensive to be used locally, and it gets whisked away to Billingsgate, in London, as soon as it arrives, to end up full circle on the tables of smart restaurants in Harrogate, Leeds and York.

It was while driving between Helmsley and the Dales National Park, en route for Middleham, that I stopped at Thirsk. Between Helmsley and Thirsk, incidentally, you have to negotiate the spectacular Sutton Bank, a precipitous escarpment that virtually divides the North York Moors from the Plain of York. With gradients of up to 1 in 4, it is definitely not recommended for caravans.

Roughly, Middleham stands at the eastern gateway to the dales. It has been called the Newmarket of the North, and above this large village that *almost* qualifies as a town, strings of horses may be seen silhouetted against billowing Yorkshire skies. If you follow them, keeping a respectful distance, you can look down on Middleham nestling in its dale. On a clear day you can also take in the purple mass of the Pennines to the west, the Lake District and, across the Vale of York, the unmistakable outline of those moors. The local moors above Middleham bring back memories of sounds as distinctly as sights: the thunder of horses' hooves on the turf, the sudden silence as that noise fades away to be replaced by the distant bleat of sheep, the trill of larks. There are six racing stables in Middleham, and they have had their share of classic successes over and above

The gallops at Middleham, North Yorkshire. This could claim to be the
Newmarket of the North, in which about a third of the population are
connected in one way or another with racing.

what the law of averages would seem to offer: for example, the Derby of 1945 (the
one-eyed Dante), and three Grand National winners.

Middleham Castle, whose gaunt ruins are a continual presence in the village, is
impressive, even from the vantage point of the grassy uplands above the rooftops. It is
ruined enough to be romantic, and eerie, but not so ruinous that you pass it by without a
second glance. Richard, Duke of Gloucester, later to become Richard III, lived here
between 1462 and his coronation in 1483; before that, the castle belonged to his patron
and protector, Warwick the Kingmaker.

They say that among the Yorkshire dales the air is worth a £1 a bucket, and I
imagine the red-and-blue-anoraked hikers who straggle up the heights around Malham
and buy their ice creams from the village shop by the bridge in the village would agree.
Once described by J. B. Priestley as 'an old wild place, where you are at one with your
ancestors', the dales now comprise a national park of nearly seven hundred square
miles.

For all the cosy, snug bars in Yorkshire village pubs, the dales farmer, like many
other dales people, lives an isolated life, perhaps seeing no one between visits from the
travelling library or on market-day. I was struck recently while watching a film based on
the James Herriot stories, in which the vets' cars were seen trundling over the deserted
moors and down into the dales, that though those stories were set in the late 1930s you

would not necessarily encounter much more traffic today – unless you picked a tourist honeypot like Hawes, Kettlewell, Burnsall or Grassington, though even then you would have to go at the height of the season, or on a Bank Holiday, to experience anything like overcrowding. It is dramatic country, but it lends itself in the way that other parts of England do not to modest scaling of hills for the views, or paddling on hot afternoons in rivers that for all their fussing over stones and their weirs and little waterfalls tend to be on the reassuringly shallow side.

Richmond, very handy for the fast A1, makes a good northerly jumping-off point for the Yorkshire dales. Its name comes from the Norman, Riche Mont, and means 'strong hill'. And it was the Normans who built the great castle, seen best, incidentally, not from where you stroll down below the cobbled town square, but from the south, across the playing fields that lie below the wooded castle mound. Those cobbles come from the bed of the River Swale, and are apparently so indestructible that they have saved ratepayers a small fortune in repairs. The castle is not one of those border strongholds built to keep out the Scots, but rather, because this was after all striking a long way into alien territory, to defend the Norman invaders against the local people.

The distinctive church in the heart of the town square, which now houses the Green Howards Regimental Museum, was never actually the parish church. This stood outside the walls and was really built to serve the castle. Franciscan monks, who came here in the thirteenth century, built their own church, also beyond the walls – its tower still remains an impressive, if rather stark, medieval relic.

Richmond was never more prosperous than during the twelfth and thirteenth centuries, a focal point for trade in this part of Yorkshire, and its market was renowned for its dairy produce, its corn and salt. And its leather goods, for this was a cattle farming country.

It is the hilliness of Richmond's site (the lass of Richmond Hill was a Yorkshire girl, and knew nothing of Surrey) that really accounted for the irregularity of the streets, although more town planning went on hundreds of years ago than is generally assumed today. It doesn't matter that the old houses have hardly survived, however, because this is a Georgian town built mainly of stone. Some was local, within easy carting distance from the town; a lot of it, however, like those cobblestones in the market square, was lifted straight out of the river bed.

Brick buildings alongside stone ones, however, can be very effective indeed. One example is the King's Head Hotel: inside it has bigger-than-average rooms with high ceilings, warmly carpeted corridors with antiques and big mirrors, and one of the pleasantest dining-rooms, on the first floor overlooking the market square and the Green Howards church, that I have come across on my travels in northern England.

Richmond's theatre is a rare survival of the late Georgian era. Opened in 1788, it is exquisite. Redecorated in traditional colours, seating about 250 people, not overly spacious, with a rather narrow, deep stage, it is an architectural gem which can be visited outside the time of performances but, like the one at Bury St Edmunds in Suffolk, far best enjoyed when there is a play on.

Well to the west of here is a different kind of wild country, which seems all the wilder because of its proximity to big conurbations. Among the bleak and lonely moors above Huddersfield and Halifax, the reservoirs are the colour of pewter. The drystone walls that seem to keep the wild moors at bay run haphazardly, turning the hills above the towns into a patchwork of green, brown, khaki and olive. Isolated and abandoned mill chimneys stand out starkly like broken teeth on jagged hilltops. Heavily wooded river banks where millworkers' cottages are cheek-by-jowl can be claustrophobic for people unused to country as stark and earthy as this. The smartened-up old mill town of Hebden Bridge and the former weaving community of Heptonstall tend to cream off visitors interested in the industrial age, but Halifax has much going for it, and even if it is Bradford that has won prizes for the quality and originality of the tourist-orientated trips it now runs, confounding critics of the local authority-sponsored scheme who swore that visitors could stomach nothing more basic in Yorkshire than Herriot's dales and Scarborough's trips-round-the-bay, Halifax has succeeded in producing modern architecture that compliments and does not insult the recently cleaned-up Victorian and late-Georgian gems. The headquarters of the Halifax Building Society, all shiny black glass, is as impressive in its way as the Piece Hall of 1778, which was originally a series of galleries in which cloth buyers could inspect at close quarters a comprehensive selection of pieces of cloth brought down from the surrounding mills in other towns and villages. In the Piece Hall there are now three hundred-odd rooms in which you can buy local crafts, antiques, bric-à-brac, and there is an industrial museum here too.

It has to be admitted that for everybody who makes a special trip to Halifax, a hundred will be much more interested in Haworth. As you drive from Halifax or Bradford, even higher among the moors that surround Haworth, smoke-stacks rise from sometimes mean-looking terraces of houses on the hillside, and mist enshrouds now-redundant mills that look picturesque today but cannot have seemed so a century ago. Even the roofs are made of heavy stone flags here, as extra protection against the moorland winds. In summer it seems unreal, almost too hot if there is no wind, perhaps with the Keighley and Worth Valley Railway puffing below you (a surprisingly frequent service for a preserved steam route). It is not all that perverse to suggest that the best time to see Haworth is on one of those damp, grey, midwinter afternoons when most tourists are at home or in their warm offices. It is easier then to ignore the sight of modern buses and sleek limousines or crimplene dresses in the self-service grocers, and imagine what life was like at the Brontë parsonage a century and a half ago. In any event, avoid visiting the parsonage at busy holiday times: I have queued for half an hour to get in, and that took the edge off what can be one of the most impressive 'literary association' places in England.

Patrick Brontë, a self-made parson, brought his wife Maria and six children to live at Haworth in 1820, just a year before Maria died of cancer. Full of apprehension for her family, she had cause to worry about their health and happiness and would probably not have been much thrilled by their creativity. But creative they were, and after a whole series of disappointing love affairs and abortive plans for the future, the naive and over-protected girls took flight from dark Haworth in their imagination and began to write novels. In 1847 alone, *Jane Eyre* and *Wuthering Heights*, by Charlotte and Emily respectively, were published.

If West Yorkshire is having to work hard at its public image, what is now South Yorkshire has even further to go. But Sheffield shows what can be done. It is a phoenix from the ashes. It has transformed itself from the muckiest town in Yorkshire to one of

The Brontë Parsonage, Haworth, West Yorkshire. Its poignant, rather
suffocating atmosphere is best appreciated when there are no queues: go
'out of season' if you can.

those places that visiting delegations from other countries come to admire. Its
municipal buildings are the envy of many a place that has not had the courage of its own
convictions. I was whisked one day to lunch with the Lord Mayor, then up into the hills
to admire, of all things, a council estate, which was, well, admirable. We were then taken
to the Blue John caverns, where since Roman times they have mined semi-precious
'bleu jaune' stone, and afterwards had tea on the terrace of a mini stately home called
Oakes Park, where they had to keep reminding us that Sheffield was just two miles away,
somewhere 'over there'. In the evening we were entertained at the Cutlers Hall, built in
1832, a neo-classical monument to Sheffield's steel making prowess, and as nice a relic
of the past as was ever allowed to co-exist with chain stores and boutiques in a roomy
pedestrian-only shopping precinct. The Hall is open to the public by appointment with
the secretary: just a formality. It is worth the effort just to gaze into the illuminated
glass-fronted cabinets containing the city's finest plate, some of which dates back to the
late-eighteenth century.

South Yorkshire as a whole may be the most mundane part of the region that we rate
so highly, but even so it has the ability to surprise. If you go to the Abbeydale Industrial
Hamlet, on the edge of Sheffield, you will find that this monument to the Industrial
Revolution lies amid wooded country that was once the northernmost extreme of

Sherwood Forest. Abbeydale, which was primarily a scythe-making works until 1930, is an astonishing place. The life expectancy of an eighteenth-century grinder has since been estimated to have been twenty-nine. The commonest accident was gruesome: men grinding scythes would sit astride a stone wheel. When that broke, as it frequently did, they would be pitched on to the scythe and parted asunder from the crotch upwards.

The traumatic redrawing of the boundaries in 1974 (on April Fool's Day, as detractors have pointed out) was not entirely bad news to Sheffield, for a substantial slice of the Peak District that had previously been in Derbyshire became part of South Yorkshire – as if to give local people an extra breathing space. The village of Dore, for example, has thus brought something to the county that was historically the preserve of Derbyshire: that is, the annual custom of well dressing. It dates back to about 1350 and is believed to commemorate the Black Death. The survivors of the plague dressed the wells with elaborate garlands of flowers: biblical or historical scenes are depicted most elaborately of all. The wells receive a church blessing on the Saturday, and the decorations remain for about a week after that.

Sheffield's name has appeared on knife blades ever since Chaucer's *Canterbury Tales* were published, and probably a good while before that. (The Reeve carried a thwittel which was made in Sheffield.) It was the Labour politician and Sheffield native, Roy Hattersley, who once pointed out to me that only a place like this would let a tower where Mary Queen of Scots had been imprisoned decay, while preserving somewhere like Abbeydale Hamlet in such perfect working order that you could begin scythe-making if you needed to next Monday morning. He pointed out, too, that Sheffield has eight rivers at its disposal and something like a thousand identifiable hills within a few miles, all of which, incidentally, are accessible by the cheapest and possibly the most efficient municipal bus service in England. Hattersley moved to Leeds when he was about fifteen. That too is a city which, while not exactly lovely, shares with Sheffield a phoenix-from-the-ashes flavour. Though its outskirts are perhaps the shabbiest of any Yorkshire city, the centre has a lot of solid prosperous Victorian charm that is reminiscent of some of Northern Europe's Baltic cities. Leeds Town Hall, created unashamedly to celebrate the city's prestige during the Victorian era, and the great oval-shaped Corn Exchange are just two buildings that dwarf the walker. The railway station is tucked unobtrusively away, but the Queen's Hotel acts in its stead to provide a powerful image of the tough and prosperous railway age.

North, South or West Yorkshire suffer no identity crisis, and even Humberside is becoming rehabilitated. But Cleveland is a Cinderella county ('We're just a dustbin,' one old man told me in a pub in Guisborough) with some unlovely excrescences, but there are compensations: the village of Kirkleatham, for example, even though it is hard by a massive ICI factory. The county has its own windswept bit of coastline, and Redcar, a bright and breezy resort where golfers and racegoers blow the metropolitan cobwebs away. Where it is not untidily industrialised, it is 'invigorating'. And the best of it can afford to be very snooty indeed about those (North) Yorkshire villages that kicked up a lot of fuss in the early 1970s, when it looked as if they were going to be embraced by the new county.

Rural Cleveland is little known. People are either rushing in another direction or are put off by its no-frills reputation. Once, when I was travelling through and staying in Middlesbrough seemed unavoidable (I had visited Eaglescliffe and a couple of other villages just to the south and also sneaked a look at Captain Cook country), I remembered that this is where the River Tees flows to the sea, which gave me the excuse to strike into the heart of a countryside that I knew had compensations: I remembered photographs of uninhabited moorland dotted with the unmistakable broken-tooth remains of old lead mine workings – uninhabited, that is, except for sheep.

But first I stayed in a high-rise hotel in the centre of Middlesbrough, and was asked concernedly by the resident hall porter who helped me with my bags (a token and entirely mercenary gesture, as I travel light) if they had given me a room at the top. 'You'll get a good view,' he said. And he was right. In the fading light of a winter afternoon it was like something out of Dante's *Inferno*, great naphthalene flares, like devilish blast furnaces, illuminating the gaunt shapes of steelworks and iron foundries, chimneys of varying heights and, against what was left of the skyline on the North Sea, the shapes of tankers and freighters just a couple of miles to the east. Middlesbrough is the third largest port in Britain devoted to the export of manufactured products, and around half of those products actually stem from factories within a few miles of the town. So the county has both feet heavily implanted in the industrial camp, but there is more to see than this. The Cleveland Hills, for a start, are certainly well known to serious walkers but, significantly, there is not a single Cleveland village in the bestseller called *The Book of British Villages*. Several villages which might at one time have found themselves in the dreaded Cleveland – among them Danby, Egton and Great Ayton – escaped this fate-worse-than-death by a determined rearguard action that just happened to pay off.

Wensleydale cheese, Yorkshire pudding, James Herriot and the sheepdog trials may be the best-known Yorkshire exports, but there is at least one dyed-in-the-wool Yorkshire tradition that unites outward bound visitors who have experienced the 'real' character of the county. And yet it is largely a Cleveland preserve. There are ten-a-penny club badges and ties, but anybody who sports the black-and-silver badge showing a burning candle framed by the outline of a coffin is immediately identifiable as somebody who has 'done the Lyke Wake walk' across the North York moors and the Cleveland Hills. Inaugurated in 1955, upwards of six thousand people a year now do the walk, the only stipulation being that they must take no longer than twenty-four hours to cover its forty or so miles from Scarf Wood Manor, above Mount Grace Priory, to the most easterly point, Wyke Point at Ravenscar.

The Tees is roughly a border between the old Yorkshire boundaries, which now means in part Cleveland, and the more easily defined county of Durham. The river is not much more than a third the length of the Thames, for example, but it is full of contrasts, and even if following its charismatic course by car is but second best to going by boat, it is a worthwhile exercise. If you see nothing in Middlesbrough apart from the famous Transporter Bridge, your journey will not have been entirely in vain. Opened in 1911, the bridge swings more than a third of a million vehicles and one and a half million passengers across the river annually.

The little town of Yarm was once an inland port, and the quality of its substantial Georgian houses is an immediate indication of some kind of prosperity. It is dominated by one of the oldest railway viaducts in England, carrying the line for about half a mile. From Yarm you can follow the river upstream through Azlebury and Middleton One Row, which sounds like a street village and is. Middleton One Row is rural and attractive and belies its closeness to Darlington. En route for the other Middleton in Teesdale (not to be confused with Middleton One Row) via the A67, you arrive at Barnard Castle, which straddles the flank of an eminence on the County Durham side of the river, having grown around the twelfth century castle from which the town gets its name. This was another of Richard III's houses, and he took it upon himself to restore and strengthen the castle. Only about one visitor in three who comes to Barnard Castle, however, visits the castle itself: two out of three, so statistics say, prefer to carry on to the outskirts of the town, pretty outskirts at that, in a green and wooded, albeit suburban setting – to the Bowes Museum. This is like Versailles come to the north, an unlikely looking palace that is a treasure house of well-displayed artefacts.

Middleton benefits in a small way from tourists who have come to see the seventy-foot waterfall called High Force shuddering down from a great outcrop of whin sill. There is a small charge to see it properly, and it can be wet and uncomfortable underfoot, but it is worth every penny. More ambitious though is to visit Cauldron Snout, partly because it involves a walk of several miles from the Langdon Beck Inn, which is two and a half miles north-west of High Force on the Alston road.

Instead of going to one of Barnard Castle's coffee bars I took up a long-standing invitation and combined a visit to Bowes Museum with a few glasses of whisky in one of those mini-stately homes secreted amid the dark trees and rich brown earth of mid-Durham. The owner ran a caravan park in an adjacent field but was apologetic about it: 'It's all right – you can hardly see it from the drawing room.'

North of Barnard Castle you are en route for high, bare moors and unexpected valleys, occasionally heavily wooded. If you paddle about in certain rivers you may, as I once did, find lumps of pale-lilac, glassy amethystine washed free of impurities by the cold spring water. Spruce forests are tucked neatly away behind mossy stone walls like crowds of people inside an enclosure at the races. Sometimes, on the outskirts of a high-lying village, you pass old beech trees with trunks like stained grey silk. But you have to be careful while driving along that the outline of some attractive hill you point out to your fellow passengers is not just a grassed-over waste tip. Brown bracken-scapes, patched and brocaded like old upholstery, bask when they can in the ungenerous north country sun. Half-hidden by dark copses, the remains of old farms look grey-green and mouldy like stale loaves. The five-bar gated entrances to big houses are secretive and intriguing, like those driveways Rolls Royces turn into after you have followed them for five miles along a country road. Every tree-filled valley seems to have a stubbed-out medieval castle keep, usually next door to some rose-covered Bull Inn or Jolly Woodman with white-glossed front doors set off by polished brass. This is the England nobody knows. It is 'the-bit-in-between'. Northumberland has not yet begun. I once stayed the night in Middleton in Teesdale, which is in County Durham: it was eerie, unfamiliar, and a thousand miles from anywhere.

Gloomy Pendragon Castle, four miles south of Kirkby Stephen, Cumbria,
lays a small claim to have been the stronghold of King Arthur.

5. Long live the weeds and the wilderness yet: a northern journey

Wildest Yorkshire and the Durham moors;
Northumberland's back door, and up-and-over
the blue remembered hills

The North really *is* another country. They really *do* do things differently there. And if August Bank Holiday traffic jams suggest that England is overcrowded, a journey through the heart of the North Country may prove reassuring. I for one used to shudder at the thought of the West Riding's dark satanic mills, not knowing that smoky Hebden Bridge, for example, was only an hour's walk from the edge of bleak Oxenhope Moor, or, further north, that the grim steel town of Consett is a few minutes' drive from the exquisite Northumberland–Durham border village of Blanchland, on the sparkling River Derwent.

The windswept, peaty, craggy country that runs up and around the Pennines touches the very edges of industrial West Yorkshire. As you drive north from Hebden Bridge's nineteenth-century mills (they must be some of the best monuments to the industrial revolution in England) and breast the brow of a steep hill, to the left there falls away the untamed and treeless wilderness of Oxenhope Moor. A dozen miles beyond this lie the industrial complexes of Nelson and Burnley, though you would not know it. The best time to travel across this lunar landscape is perhaps when the weather is mixed, when scudding clouds throw shadows across the moors and unexpected sunbursts light up the hills. Oxenhope, incidentally, is the southernmost station on the Keighley and Worth Valley Railway, which runs close to the foot of the breathtakingly steep hill at Haworth, at the top of which is one of Yorkshire's biggest tourist attractions: Haworth Parsonage, family home in the nineteenth century of the Brontë sisters.

The A6033 between Hebden Bridge and Haworth runs narrowly, switchback-style, across high moors that make you think of *Wuthering Heights*, and belies the fact that in places it is only five miles from the outskirts of Halifax and Bradford. Beyond Hebden Bridge lies Keighley, which has a down-to-earth, gritty charm enhanced for me by a good handful of interesting junk and bric-à-brac shops. Skipton has long been a dormitory for commuters from the mill towns to the south: Keighley, Halifax, Sowerby Bridge. Its name originally meant 'sheep town', and it still has one of the North Country's busiest sheep markets. Its handsome, perpendicular parish church is hard by the gatehouse of the castle. (Anne Clifford was mainly responsible for the excellent state of preservation of Skipton Castle. She devoted much time and money to Skipton,

The Golden Arrow, once the pride of British Railways' Southern Region,
has a new lease of life at the Keighley and Worth Valley Railway, West
Yorkshire.

including the church. Having been born within its walls on 30 January 1590, she inherited the labyrinthine castle from her father, the Earl of Cumberland. She also inherited the castles at Appleby and Brougham, and is said to have particularly enjoyed travelling by coach between the castles by the bleakest possible route across the moors.) It occurred to me that in the right conditions, particularly at dusk on a winter's day, or under snow, this part of Yorkshire looks exactly as it would have done when Lady Anne was alive. But Skipton's surprisingly wide, tree-dotted High Street and its busy shops seem so civilised and pleasant that you tend to forget about the windswept Pennine wasteland to the north-west.

Once, just before Christmas, I drove from Skipton to Linton, or Linton-in-Craven, which won the title of 'loveliest village in the north' in a newspaper competition of 1949. It has not been spoilt since. The most impressive building, overlooking the tree-shaded village green, is the early eighteenth-century almshouse endowed by Richard Fountaine, a native of the village, who is believed to have made a fortune by superintending the burial of victims of the Great Plague in London in 1665. The Fountaine Inn is named after him. And then I drove to Grassington, down into the village square from the gloomy, rain-spattered moors, towards bright greengrocers' shops and paraffin-and-sawdust scented hardware stores. Christmas trees were already stacked up against shop fronts, ready for sale. The square has the look of a stage set, because from two corners on its north side, narrow lanes snake away uphill towards the extremities of the village, and out towards open country. Exit stage left – or right. Though the heart of Burnsall, the easternmost of these three villages, is enclosed and inward looking, there are wide and grassy river banks by the River Wharfe, making the five-arched stone bridge look all the more impressive, and the hotel at the bottom of the village street that snakes up the hill towards Grassington all the prettier.

The A63 between Skipton, Gargrave and Settle is deceptive, and cuts a comparatively fast and wide swathe through Airedale. As you leave Skipton for Gargrave and Settle, you have the Liverpool and Leeds Canal on your left. At 127 miles – the longest single inland waterway ever built in England – it was designed in the late eighteenth century to link the great port of Liverpool with the Yorkshire rivers. This is a comparatively bland part of North Yorkshire, with dark green hills only distantly to the left, and the canal a pewter-coloured ribbon on the same side close to the road. Gargrave promises more interesting things to come, with its pretty cottages by the water and a narrow lane that leads over the canal to the railway station. This is very well cared for, the sort of place that wins prizes in competitions for the best kept station. It has lots of shrubs and flowers and a well-scrubbed platform.

Probably the best-known building in the small, self-contained town of Settle is Folly House, named after the man who built it in 1679 and did not have enough money to complete the job. So the front of the house is elaborate, and the back is plain. It got him into debt: hence his 'folly'. I have seen Settle on a sparkling mid-morning in June, and during rain on a Sunday morning in February, and somehow the grimmer winter conditions suit it better, almost as if there is not room in the little market square and among the narrow back alleys for the people and the prams that emerge when the sun shines.

My journey of rediscovery to what may be the most bleakly beautiful stretches of North Yorkshire took me immediately right, outside Settle, on to the B6479 going almost due north, but it is worth the short detour along the A65 to Giggleswick. Though it sounds more like a place that processes black puddings than a beauty spot, this is one of Yorkshire's most intriguing villages. Neatly kept cottage gardens add colour to the pale limestone of the cheek-by-jowl cottages, some of which are set back behind a narrow, bubbly stream along which ducks glide, and which is crossed in the lower part of the village by a footbridge made of huge slate slabs. From the heart of the village you can see the green cupola of Giggleswick School. The school, founded in the sixteenth century, used to be famous for cock-fights, which were popular among people from the village and the surrounding area.

The B6479 from Settle to Hawes, beyond which you link up for a few miles with the A684 before joining the B6259 en route for Kirkby Stephen and Brough, crosses vast, lonely and untamed tracts of country. Beyond Langcliffe lies Horton-in-Ribblesdale, amid spectacular scenery. Fields are bordered by dry limestone walls the colour of grubby sheep bones, and the shadowy bulk of the 2,273 foot high Pen-y-Ghent broods over the land like a black-and-blue raincloud. Summer or winter, rain or sun, you will pass lots of brightly anoraked, heavily booted walkers and pot-holers. Beware: the cold may have numbed their senses, and they may step unseeingly out into the road. This is not just walking country, but embraces a famous collection of caves. Outstanding among them is the Alum Pot, with an unusually impressive entrance shaft, almost all lit by daylight, so you can easily see down it. On some days, clouds hang halfway down the shaft, resting on the thousands of cubic feet of cold air in the depths. Not all of Britain's great subterranean caves are the exclusive territory of experienced pot-holers, however, and anyone wanting to sample the caves for a day or so should contact the Whernside Moor Caving Centre, on the western edge of the Yorkshire Dales at Dent, near Sedbergh. They will advise you and hire out equipment: all you need to bring is your time and enthusiasm. At the head of the dale, you join the B6255 and turn north-eastwards en route for Hawes. But what a junction. People pull over on to the generous grass verges (well, actually, bits of moorland) to admire the scene. To the left stands the spectacular Ribblehead Viaduct, whose twenty-four stone arches carry the most impressive railway line in England across a moor which goes by the rather intimate name of Batty Moss. It is a continuous climb from Settle to just beyond here, a marvel of railway engineering. Up here, on the roof of Yorkshire, time can be measured by how fat the lambs have grown since you last passed by. In March they are appealing, but as scrawny as pipe cleaners. By May they have meaty-looking rumps, like well-fed poodles, and are already less attractive. It still rains horizontally, but less predictably, in the late spring, and there are bright, sunny days on which scudding clouds make shadows on the hills like squadrons of low flying bombers, with the sun teasing what colour there is out of the bracken and rough grass.

The bleak no man's land on either side of the road as it approaches Hawes is not to everyone's taste. It is primeval, unchanged for thousands of years, except for the railway, the road, telegraph wires and the occasional farmhouse. There are stone pens open to the skies and tumbledown barns, but they are all dwarfed by the endless brown moors. You come across Hawes quite suddenly. It is a little jewel. It could have become self-consciously bijou, but has been saved so far by being independent and workaday. I breezed blithely into the White Hart at ten minutes past two one Sunday. Of course, it was after closing time and the landlord shrugged his shoulders and pointed to the old-fashioned station clock on the wall. The beefy hikers sitting quietly in the bar, enjoying physical exhaustion coupled with a sense of achievement, grinned, embarrassed for me. One offered me his almost full glass – and really meant for me to help myself. But if the pub was to all intents and purposes closed, the shop that sells a good range of malt whiskies, for keeping out the weather, was open, and so was the little second-hand bookshop, handy for anybody who has room in their rucksack for a volume of Wordsworth or Coleridge to add a finishing touch to the scenery. You can also buy Wensleydale cheese, some of which is actually made here in Hawes: the green banks of the dale are said to provide perfect grazing.

From Hawes I drove north towards Kirkby Stephen. For several miles I crossed Mallerstang Common, the highest point of which, unmistakably on the left as one goes north, is Wild Boar Fell, easily climbable, they say, at 2,324 feet.

Like Hawes, Kirkby Stephen is too matter-of-fact to be coy, though it has enough history to keep you going for several days. The Fountain Café dates from around 1650, and the church likes to call itself the Cathedral of the Dales. Brough, to the north, is more intriguing, however. Of all the places in the north of England that have been bypassed, few can have been afforded such a new lease of life as Brough. Until a new dual carriageway took the A66 past this one-time market town, the thundering road seemed to sap the inhabitants' strength. It is as if they had no stomach for development and improvement and, as a result, the wide street, that now sees only delivery vans and cars driven by people who are either lost or local, is a rare survival. It seems hardly to have changed since the late 1940s or 1950s. The Aladdin's Cave of a general store gives a clue to its whereabouts, for among the tins of baked beans and loaves of sliced bread, there is an amazing variety of literature about fell walking, fishing, bird spotting and local monuments to visit. I paused here for a pork pie at the precise moment that the delivery van from Carlisle arrived outside the butcher's shop: not home-made, but fresh and tasty.

As I approached Alston, there were clues to suggest that the Cumbrian border was near. Perhaps the most obvious is the dark-maroon colour favoured by farmers for their barn doors and window frames. Not as pretty, perhaps, as that typical Yorkshire and Northumberland stone set off by sparkling-white trimming, but traditional and very identifiable. There is farmhouse accommodation to be had up on these windswept hills, but you cannot guarantee you will get the sort of fare that city-dwellers expect. Those romantic visions of great home-smoked hams and succulent pork served up on huge plates may have to be translated into set dinners of tomato soup made from packets, boiled chicken and crinkle-cut chips followed by tinned fruit. Ducks' eggs for breakfast or mushrooms dawn-gathered from the field outside your bedroom window will be less likely than dishes of bendable cornflakes and milk from the nearest supermarket. 'Near', of course, being relative.

Pennine landscape, near Alston, Cumbria. This is a side of Cumbria comparatively few outsiders see. Frequently shrouded in mist, with heavy rainfall, it is an acquired but unforgettable taste.

Stragglers who turn up in Alston – population 2,500 – will find one of the neatest and most unspoilt towns in the north of England. At 1,000 feet it claims to be the highest market town in the country. Several of its lanes are cobbled and breathtakingly steep. Narrow alleyways lead to unthought-of corners of the town, and there are small shops in which pre-war enamel signs and window displays more reminiscent of the austerity era of the late 1940s are not affectations, but genuine. The antique-shop minder pops into the fish-and-chip shop for cod and twenty pennyworth, wrapped in the *Newcastle Journal*, and retires to the back of the shop to eat them. The wind that whistles across the fells blows tough little old ladies up the hill towards the Post Office, and sheep farmers' landrovers jostle fairly good-humouredly for parking spaces in the steep market square. At almost every angle you can see open moorland, and in blustery weather, when the surrounding fells are forbidding, people tend to find reasons to linger in Alston's cosy, low-ceilinged, smoke-blackened pubs. At most, they might wander down to the foot of the town to the former railway station that was, until the late 1960s, the head of the line that ran along the amazing South Tyne valley from Haltwhistle. Though the original lines have been pulled up, the Tynedale Railway Preservation Society has laid a narrow gauge railway: a rather sad, defiant gesture.

I have covered the ground between Alston and Haltwhistle by bus, walking boots, diesel train and steam train, but steam train was by far the best. I remember the last time I was there. As the afternoon sun went down on a day in mid-September, the head porter-cum-handyman-cum-stationmaster slammed the doors on the last train of the day between Alston and Haltwhistle. The fading but expensively upholstered seats were occupied by schoolchildren and home-going labourers, not by the spotty youths with large knapsacks and long khaki shorts who patronise steam railways today. We left Alston and threaded our way, at never more than thirty miles an hour, through a landscape of hill farms, whose fields reached down to the shallow, stony South Tyne River. It was an amazingly pretty journey, full of sudden dioramas seen from high escarpments between banks of trees, of steep valleys and low-lying nests of houses. At that speed, you could pick out details that linger in the memory: a man sitting at a farm kitchen table, poring over a newspaper, a cowherd standing by a level-crossing with an oil lamp and a score of cattle, glimpsed dully in the twilight.

But when I last drove up to Alston the railway had long gone. I took refuge from the blustery day in the mother-and-father of all bric-à-brac junk-cum-antique shops, which stands near the top of Alston's precipitous and cobbly main street. It is the kind where you have to progress sideways between unsaleable tallboys and stuffed eagles, and if you are slim enough to try the stairs you pass people closely enough to smell not only their perfume or aftershave but also what they had for lunch.

To get to Haltwhistle, you leave the Alston to Brampton road at Lambley in favour of an unclassified road for Featherstone. The road from what used to be Featherstone railway station to Haltwhistle is narrow, little frequented, and romantic. It runs right past Featherstone Castle, now a boarding school, but a prisoner-of-war camp between 1941 and 1945. Not surprisingly, many of the German prisoners who were corralled here stayed on and settled among local people. The Tyne at this point is dark but shallow, its blackness making it seem deeper than it is. From the green footbridge that connects the lush parkland with thick and impenetrable-seeming woods, you look down into the river's shadowy waters and can easily be convinced that there are trout lurking in every pool. While I stood contemplating the scene, a raiding party of small boys was careering down the hill on their bikes from an avenue of tall trees at the top of the road, round past the castle, and coasting to a halt beside the bridge.

Haltwhistle *sounds* like a railway town, and diesel trains plying between Carlisle and Newcastle along the narrowest neck of England still keep station staff busy, if not quite as busy as when the Alston line was open. It is not a particularly pretty town, but goes about its business. Most people who see anything of it are probably killing time before getting down to the more serious business of the Roman Wall, just to the north. One of the roads that runs east of here, vaguely towards Newcastle, more or less follows the course of the Roman Wall, which in turn lies to the south of some of the bleakest and most inhospitable country in England. At Chesters, where the great Roman camp of Cilurnum used to stand, and in part still does, turn north along the B6320, as tortuous and up-hill-down-dale as the B6318 is straight and fast.

The B6320 took me for many miles alongside the North Tyne, which runs deeper and more fast-flowing than the South Tyne: when it rains up on the moors, the swollen river takes on the look of Newcastle Brown Ale, foaming, red-setter coloured. The road runs close to Chipchase Castle, a fourteenth-century fort now attractively incorporated in a Jacobean mansion, and occasionally open to the public.

I had never before been to Blanchland, which is about ten miles south of the market town of Hexham. It lies right on the Durham–Northumberland border, nestling in a fold in the wooded hills. The name of the village commemorates the White Friars, who had an abbey here and about whom a gruesome but evocative story is told. During one of the border raids of the fourteenth century, they seemed to have escaped the attentions of the Scots when the comparative remoteness of the abbey was further enhanced by thick fog. They ill-advisedly rang the abbey bell to celebrate their deliverance, and the noise of this alerted the marauding Scots, who returned over the hill and massacred the monks. It is an exceptionally pretty place now, completely unspoilt, and takes on the colour of tarnished gold from the prevailing stone. Thin smokestacks still curve upwards from the chimneys of the terraced cottages, and gardens of bright aubrietia and impossibly orange marigolds bring out the character of the gritstone. Blanchland belies its proximity to the unlovely steel-making town of Consett. Not that much steel has been produced here for several years: it is a gaunt scrapyard of a place, making days spent amid the sun-warmed heather of the hills around Blanchland seem quite sinful.

Beyond Hexham and Wooler (best reached via the A697) lie the Cheviots, which are never accorded the title mountains, perhaps because their tallest tops are pleasantly rounded and hospitably covered with grass. But The Cheviot itself rises to 2,676 feet, and its sister peaks are distinguished by giving rise to the North Tyne, the Coquet, the Till and a number of small tributaries of the Tweed. In clear weather, as on a bright early spring or autumn day, this is spectacular country. But in the depths of winter the Cheviots are as bleak and isolated as remotest Dartmoor or the wettest fens, and it is no wonder the farmsteads, pretty though their white buildings look against the hills, have such a beleaguered look about them. They can be cut off for weeks at a time when it snows. The occasional sight of a mountain hare that turns white in winter may be some small compensation for strangers who find themselves in the middle of nowhere, but a good map *and* compass is better still.

Though you get a tantalising look at the Cheviots from the A697, it's worth playing

Flodden Field, Northumberland. The scars of the Scots' defeat at the
hands of the English in 1513 have never entirely healed.

truant and veering off into the hills for a few miles. I once approached the Cheviots from the Bell at Belford, on the A1: a beautiful drive to the north-west, with sudden sweeping precipices and dramatic vistas softened at every other bend by that special Northumbrian formula of a bridge, a gatehouse, Aberdeen Angus cattle in a fenced park, tall trees colonised by rooks, moderately curious sheep.

The Cheviots straddle the Scottish border for about thirty-five miles, like packed shoals of beached whales, and newcomers should be warned that it is very easy to get lost hereabouts. Sir Walter Scott described the hills as 'huge, round-headed and clothed with a dark robe of russet'. You can stray over the border without realising it. Rushing burns know no boundaries, and putting border signs up on every minor road is uneconomic. Strangely, though, you can always tell by people's accents where England ends and Scotland begins: in this respect the boundary is as distinct as if it were built of barbed wire instead of lines on a map and a lot of history.

Even by Northumbrian standards this is undiscovered country. If you have seen it, you can laugh out loud when people tell you England is overcrowded.

Key

- – – – – County boundaries

Miles
0   10   20

0   10   20   30
Kilometres

Berwick upon Tweed

Lindisfarne
(Holy Island)

Cornhill-on-Tweed

Belford

Wooler

Chillingham

Embleton

Dunstanburgh

BORDERS

Alnwick

Cheviot Hills

Alwinton

River Coquet

Carter Bar

Rothbury

NORTHUMBERLAND

Newcastleton

Kielder Forest

Otterburn

River North Tyne

Bellingham

NORTH SEA

Chollerford

Gilsland

Housesteads

Chesters

Corbridge

Wylam

Haltwhistle

Vindolanda

South Shields

Carlisle

River Irthing

River Tyne

Hexham

Bywell

Ovingham

Newcastle upon Tyne

Lambley

Allendale

TYNE AND WEAR

SOLWAY FIRTH

River South Tyne

Blanchland

Alston

Nenthead

Caldbeck

CUMBRIA

DURHAM

Skiddaw

Penrith

Cockermouth

Keswick

Pooley Bridge

Whitehaven

CLEVELAND

Buttermere

Shap

Seatoller

Wasdale Head

Grasmere

Elterwater

Ambleside

Eskdale

Windermere

Ravenglass

Hawkshead

Bowness

Ulpha

Kendal

Oxenholme

Broughton-in-Furness

Ulverston

NORTH YORKSHIRE

N

Barrow in Furness

Morecambe
Bay

Trough of
Bowland

Slaidburn

IRISH
SEA

Clitheroe

LANCASHIRE

WEST
YORKSHIRE

Liverpool Bay

GREATER
MANCHESTER

MERSEYSIDE

Manchester

SOUTH
YORKSHIRE

Liverpool

Castleton

CHESHIRE

Buxton

DERBYSHIRE

Map 4 North-West England

86

6. The Borders:
the land that time forgot

The Tyne – North and South; the Northumbria National Park; the Kielder Forest; Alnwick; the coast; the Cheviots: Scotland-next-stop; the Roman Wall

Closer than you might think to the insouciant moors of County Durham, the serious-minded Tyne at Newcastle is not what it was. It is still an industrial river but it is cleaner, and less likely at low tide to yield a dead ship's rat or an empty bottle of Russian vodka of a brand unknown in Western Europe. Even by the standards of other North Country rivers, though, there could hardly be a greater contrast between the still black and greasy Tyne – more washing-up water than sewer perhaps – of Newcastle-proper, and the heathery National Park in which the North Tyne rises, or the moorlands of the Durham–Northumberland border where the South Tyne first makes its presence felt. Or, rather, heard – considering the way it tumbles over beds of pebbles and small weirs.

You see a lot of the River Tyne during the ride on a two-coach diesel train across the narrow neck of England between Newcastle and Carlisle, and it really *is* a 'ride', not just a duty. The small stone-built stations alone are virtually all worth a second glance, especially as it is a minor miracle that they are still there in the 1980s. Even more encouraging: if the number of people getting on and off in the course of the hour and a half that I spent en route is anything to go by, they are still much used locally. Who, I wondered, was responsible for the brave wallflowers and snapdragons at one of the unmanned halts?

East to west or west to east, this is sixty miles not of the most spectacular country in England, though it does have its moments, but of countryside packed with character and history. There is something to distract you every few miles. For example, just a few semi-rural minutes by train out of Newcastle, past lots of pigeon lofts and whippet kennels, is Wylam, a mining community where George Stephenson was born. His house is marked and is open to the public. Then there is Ovingham, whose name reveals its Saxon origins, and which has a rare surviving packhorse bridge close to the solid parish church. And, across the Tyne, amid some unappealing modern industrial developments, is the partly ruined, rook-haunted Norman castle of Prudhoe. At this point the train runs close to the Tyne, on its southern banks: the car driver will do best to stay north of the river, close enough to skim a stone over its shallow, silky grey waters, and drive along an unclassified road to Bywell. Amid parkland that feels as if it is a hundred miles from the Newcastle conurbation, though really it is only about twelve, are two separate parish churches close to Bywell Hall. The house is not open, but the atmosphere is strangely eerie and moving. There is a fragment of border castle here, too, once occupied by the Neville family. There are tall trees bordering the little-frequented lanes up to the churches, and any one of them would have a preservation order slapped on it if it stood in some suburban cul-de-sac.

Grey, stone-built Corbridge once stood on the route Agricola took when marching north into Scotland. Not big enough to be a town, and far too big to be called a village, Corbridge has resisted becoming a suburb of Hexham, which is just three or so miles away. Hexham's great abbey, which I remember vividly from the impression of feet in ancient time, and quite a few modern ones too, that have worn the steps inside the building as if they were made of wood instead of stone, is thought to have been founded by Wilfred, a seventh-century monk from Holy Island, off the Northumberland coast, who became Bishop of York. The crypt, though, is probably the only part of the original building that is still completely intact. In the little market place, part of it covered, next to the fifteenth-century Moot Hall, the Duke of Somerset was executed after the Battle of Hexham in 1464.

Quite a few tourists and others have discovered an antidote to the vicissitudes of the twentieth century along the River South Tyne. On a blustery day I clambered down past Lambley railway station on the now-defunct Alston to Haltwhistle railway towards the tumbling river, and on my way met a dentist from South Shields who had bought a local cottage to escape to at weekends. But the whole thing had misfired, and instead of just coming here on Saturdays and Sundays he had become so enamoured of the valley that he was about to give up his practice and live here permanently.

Here I have to declare an interest: Allendale, an unregarded little town about as far south from Hexham as Blanchland is, but reached by a different road, was a favourite teenage haunt of mine. When funds permitted, I would take a red single-decker bus, bright as a ladybird against the brown moors, from Hexham. Allendale seemed to me then to be the edge of the civilized world. Surrounded by untamed moors into which beef and dairy farmers make what inroads they can, it is still a self-sufficient place, physically inward-looking: the surrounding bracken and peat is kept at bay by stone houses, pubs and hotels corralled in the style of the Anglo-Scottish border.

But the border is well to the north: the only real incursions suffered by little Allendale were from local lead miners and stray cattle or sheep. One early guide-book describes the place as 'a neat little town, every other building in which is a public house for the miners', and there is a good quartet of pubs even today.

I once stayed in a small hotel overlooking the square, and my room was high up among the rafters. As the sun was setting over the inhospitable fells I sat at the dormer window and during the space of about twenty minutes watched an old, half-crippled man (a retired miner, perhaps, maybe even a descendant of the lead miners who are commemorated hereabouts by the stark silhouette of old chimneys on every horizon), going from pub to pub like a bee in a heather garden, albeit much more slowly.

Northumberland's National Park, which begins virtually on Hexham's outskirts, is not only one of the biggest in the country, but eats up a larger proportion of its host county than any other, stretching as it does in an irresistible wave from the northern flanks of the Cheviot hills all the way to the Roman Wall, parts of which stand in some places on the very banks of the jet-black North Tyne. Part of the National Park follows the line of the Scottish–Northumberland border, then veers south through the Kielder

Forest and meets the Cumbrian county boundary near Gilsland, on the old Military Road between Hexham and Carlisle. Of course, none of the National Parks are ever crowded (well, perhaps some of the car parks are on a Bank Holiday) but there is something other-wordly and untrodden about Northumberland's National Park. The Park has a curlew as its symbol. It is drawn in silhouette, which is just as well, because these birds are skilful at camouflage. (I once tried to photograph one beside the road against a drystone wall. When the prints were returned from the developers, I thought at first the bird had actually flown away and I had missed it. When I looked closely, well, it was there, but it was not a picture to be proud of.)

If the National Park has a focal point, it is probably Bellingham, although the people of Otterburn, just to the north, might not agree. The large village lies amid dark-brown moorland that seems as remote as Dartmoor or Exmoor, but is sufficiently away-from-it-all to make you appreciate the creature comforts the village can provide: groceries, a pub, a cup of tea, a garage. In other words, all those things taken for granted in built-up areas but which, even in a short space of time, when not available, assume great significance. A clue to Bellingham's former importance lies in quite a few imposing nineteenth-century buildings: a town hall with a clock tower, an impressive Roman Catholic church, an elegant stone bridge over the North Tyne. There was once a railway which stopped at Bellingham, on what must have been a surreal journey across a sea of brown moors. But the more memorable picture for me is the small cafe in the heart of the village, which always seems to be full of back-packers. Though they get closer to nature than the average mortal, devoted hikers do tend to build up an appetite, and therefore develop close relationships with meat pie and chips, accompanied by mugs of tea, followed by cream cakes.

Bellingham's parish church of St Cuthbert was founded in the twelfth century, and one of the reasons that it has a stone roof was to protect it from the firebrands of border raiders. This is North Tyne country, altogether different from the South Tyne. This branch of the river is deeper, blacker, more serious, seeming to remember days when life was not so peaceful, but continually fraught with danger from over the border, wherever the border happened to be at the time. And it is richer in fish. If you take a minor road, west of Bellingham, via Kielder Forest, you will find that the traffic peters out as you get close to the Scottish border, and you are left to your own devices. There are no villages to speak of, simply knots of modern purpose-built Forestry Commission houses: summer or winter there will be smoke from living-room log fires drifting up towards the scudding Northumbrian skies. For, as happens among the coal fields, fuel is provided free of charge for people who work in the industry.

If Otterburn has less of the flavour of the capital of the Park than Bellingham, it does have one claim to fame apart from a couple of the hotels that are few and far between up here. For it was here that, in 1388, there took place what has been called the bloodiest battle ever fought in Britain: nearly two thousand English were killed against the Scots' couple of hundred, and Hotspur, scion of the Percy family, was taken prisoner. This battle of Otterburn is also known popularly as Chevy Chase.

Rothbury, beyond Otterburn (which is really just a glorified village and a woollen mill), is another of those places like Corbridge whose pleasant, sycamore-lined green gives the place a spacious flavour. For years I went back again and again to a modest bed-and-breakfast place, where the proprietress stubbornly refused to take more than a pound for the accommodation and the sort of breakfast that has you hiding food under other bits of food, and making a lunchtime picnic out of what cannot be hidden. The terraced house overlooked the River Coquet, dark and reed-strewn, a couple of hundred feet below. It was always best on a long May or June evening, when a pearly light lingered in the sky on the far side of the town until ten-thirty or eleven in the evening and only the distant lights on the far hillside reminded you of farmsteads whose existence you did not guess at during the daytime.

For all the disadvantages of keeping a hotel even in comparatively remote country, there is one outstanding thing in its favour: it can become a focal point for what life there is for many miles around, and an oasis for lonesome travellers. So The George at Chollerford, right on the North Tyne, does well for special occasions among prosperous local farmers and picks up a nice bit of passing trade as well. It also has a following among visitors to the Wall, especially to nearby Chesters. And windswept Otterburn, where the trees have a permanent list to port or starboard depending on the prevailing wind, has two such hotels. Take care, though, not to assume that every hilltop hostelry is necessarily warm and welcoming. Pot luck is a doubtful principle up on the moors, and good planning is important unless you are completely indifferent to your surroundings.

If I had not trusted to chance, however, I would never have had such a good bed-and-breakfast as I once found at Wooler, close to the foothills of the Cheviots. I would not even have travelled as far as that farming community if I had not been too late to get a room at Belford. I had not reckoned with a coach party of Townswomens Guilders who were en route between Buckinghamshire and Holy Island. I dined among them ('Don't you have anything for vegetarians apart from egg salad?' one peevish lady asked the hapless waitress) but I had to look elsewhere for a bed.

The English–Welsh border is swathed in woodland, low-key and unassuming, but the Scottish border is flamboyant and exciting, especially when you sweep up to Carter Bar and see so many square miles of Scotland spread out before you. On a clear day on Carter Bar you can see, well, almost for ever. As I broached the heathery, wind-buffeted top and saw a large part of southern Scotland below me, the clouds parted as if stage-managed, just long enough to allow a shaft of sun to pick out the highlights. But when visibility is restricted by a Scotch mist on a Border raid, it is a sombre place – all bedraggled sheep, spray from lorry wheels: purgatory if you should have a puncture and have to get out of your car.

If Carter Bar is the part of the border to take your wide-angle lens to, and to be avoided by vertigo sufferers, Cornhill-on-Tweed is a point where you can actually wade across the shallow, rippling, trout-coloured water to Scotland. The grounds of the Tillmouth Park Hotel, a remarkable grandiose survivor of the Victorian era, run right down to the river, and they actually have a converted boathouse on the banks of the Tweed where anglers – and others – can get away from everything except for salmon.

I have already advocated those unclassified roads that strike west-north-west into the Kielder Forest from Bellingham, but they are at least leading somewhere, namely towards the border near Newcastleton; whereas the road that strikes into the hills in roughly the same direction from Thropton, near Rothbury, via Alwinton, is going nowhere in particular, except to accompany the River Coquet that rises almost on the border near the evocatively named Windy Gyle, and Hungry Law hills. Windy Gyle is over two thousand feet high. It is not exactly Little Switzerland, but more a matter of desolate sheep and curlew country, with scarcely a tree to be seen. And hardly a house either, for even the shepherds have their cottages in clefts between the moors so as to give some protection from the wind and weather. Up here, among the Cheviots, half Northumberland's rivers are born. Their birth, however, is rarely witnessed by human beings.

The A1 trunk road, well to the east, is useful but bland and does not prepare the north-bound visitor for the pleasures that lie left and right. Alnwick is one. Like many places, it owes its existence to the castle that was begun in 1095, and was sold to the Percys in 1309, when it was already an antique. J. M. Turner painted it often, but usually felt it needed a bit of romantic touching up, and tended to substitute moonlight for sunlight. Until the fifteenth century, this was virtually England's capital, because the increasingly powerful Percys kept the Scottish incursionists in check from the supreme vantage point of Alnwick Castle. The castle's interior bears no relation to its stark, if handsome, outward appearance, however. It would certainly not disgrace a Harewood House or a Chatsworth. The Percy family had an unfortunate talent for backing the wrong side, and even the most famous of them all, Harry Hotspur, was killed in a battle against Henry IV, the king he had helped to the throne. During the Wars of the Roses, the family changed sides twice, and still survived. The Percys became Dukes of Northumberland and it was the fourth Duke who went to Italy to find the craftsmen who made the interior of the castle what it is today.

Like so many other towns, Alnwick survived intact and homogeneous, unspoilt by Victorian or early twentieth-century development because there was just not the money available for 'improvement'. Even better, from the sightseer's point of view, the best of the town has been squeezed higgledy-piggledy into the space within the old walls. There is lots to see and admire, and even chain stores like Woolworths and Boots occupy premises that are mainly medieval.

There's a Black Swan and a White Swan, both of them once rival coaching inns, for this was right on the London–York–Edinburgh coaching route that reached its apogee in the early nineteenth century. But the Nag's Head is the oldest, dating back to 1598 – just one of the thirty old inns in the town.

My favourite exhibit, however, has nothing to do with medieval Alnwick. Instead, it is inside the White Swan Hotel, right in the centre of Alnwick, close to one of the surviving old town gates. When they heard that the White Star liner, the *Olympic*, sister of the *Titanic*, was being broken up at nearby Jarrow, the owners of the hotel decided to try to buy the lights and the wooden panelling from the lounge and music room of the ship, complete with carvings of musical instruments that Grinling Gibbons would not have been ashamed of. Called the Olympic Room, and used mainly as the formal restaurant, this is now a tourist attraction in its own right. Perhaps a downmarket second-best is the original Victorian cast-iron range at the Nag's Head, which, with the open fire burning, is reminiscent of cottage interiors you pay to look at in places such as the Beamish Open Air Museum in County Durham: it is nice enough there, but here it is the real thing.

If you do get as far as Alnwick it would be a shame not to take in one of the most memorable sights to be found in the North of England. If you are lucky (and success is not guaranteed) you will come back with holiday snaps almost certain to be the envy of friends and neighbours. For at Chillingham, among the foothills of the Cheviots, is a remarkable survival of a prehistoric herd of wild, white cattle, descendants of the aurochs which roamed northern Europe thousands of years ago. Though those creatures were black, except for a white strip along their back, it is believed that the Druids, by means of selective breeding and slaughter, produced a breed of pure white animals: it is certainly on record that they used white cattle for sacrificial offerings. On the Earl of Tankerville's estate for the last seven hundred years, the herd now numbers about fifty and has 365 acres to itself – except for a flock of about two hundred sheep which happily the white cattle ignore. No one, but no one, not even the custodians of the cattle and the site, ever approaches them at close quarters. There has been no direct contact with man for centuries. You will, however, need to be accompanied by one of the 'keepers' if, like a surprising total of about ten thousand people a year, you wish to see the animals even from a modest distance. On a good day you will get within, say, a hundred yards.

Chillingham lies well to the east of The Cheviot, but the further you travel towards

The Cheviot Hills dominate about two hundred square miles of northern
Northumberland and, being indifferent to political boundaries, large tracts
of Roxburghshire too.

Sheepdog trials at Chatton, near Wooler, among the Cheviot hills.

the coast of Northumberland the more the countryside flattens to deceive. The great windswept hills and craggy rocks that look so impressive against a blood-red sunset begin to take a low profile as the land reaches the sea. The flattish, exceptionally fertile littoral makes Holy Island seem all the more dramatic, with Edwin Lutyens's bizarre confection – an inwardly remodelled and reconstructed medieval castle atop the nearly conical hill that rises from the sea like a child's idea of a volcano – all the more fantastic. People confuse Lindisfarne Castle (Holy Island and Lindisfarne seem to be used interchangeably) with Bamburgh Castle: both add muscle to a coastline that for all its superb beaches is blander than many travellers expect.

Once in the village of Embleton, after a visit to the craggy dramatically silhouetted remains of another coastal stronghold, Dunstanburgh Castle, I asked my way in a village shop, but it took a passing lady rider, all jodphurs and a small face under a hard hat, towering above me on a white mare of what was surely no less than eighteen hands, to put me right. And I was invited to tea in the garden of Rose Cottage, on one of those timeless sun-dappled hot afternoons that give the lie to Northumberland's reputation for bleakness.

If every county has a colour scheme of its own, which in a sometimes subtle way it has, middle and northernmost Northumberland is dark grey and emerald green. And very effective it is. Those four square gritstone pele towers, set off nicely at the end of wide, flower-dotted grassy-verged village streets, those ancient town gates that view the progress of modern traffic with the same equanimity with which they used to put up with horses and carts and pennyfarthing bicycles, could not belong anywhere else, not even to North Yorkshire.

Probably no town in Europe, except perhaps York, provides such a spectacular walk around its original medieval walls as Berwick. It is one of the four original Royal Boroughs of Scotland, which changed hands no fewer than fourteen times before finally coming under English rule five hundred years ago. Administratively and legally it is part of England, but in other respects it has not entirely relinquished its Scottish connections: its football team, for example, Berwick Rangers, plays in the Scottish League. (An old rhyme goes, 'They talk of England and Scotland indeed: it is really Britain, Ireland and Berwick on Tweed.')

This view of Berwick upon Tweed, Northumberland, owes little to the twentieth century.

It is a prosperous-looking place of about 12,000 people and is proud of its tradition of independence. The town was mentioned specifically in Royal Proclamations and Acts of Parliament, and in 1746 it was laid down that reference to the United Kingdom should be deemed to include Berwick upon Tweed. However, in other official documents it was to be mentioned separately, which gives rise to the story that Berwick is still at war with Russia. The town was included in the declaration of war at the outbreak of the Crimean War, but omitted by name from the Peace Treaty. There are three bridges, perhaps the most impressive of which is the one that carries the London to Edinburgh trains and gives many a southerner his first look at a town that is incomparable in England. There's the Jacobean bridge, with fifteen arches, and the Royal Tweed bridge, which was opened, like Newcastle's Tyne Bridge, in 1928, in order to relieve the original bridge of the increasingly heavy A1 traffic. The railway bridge is an elegant structure of twenty-eight tall, elegant arches that was opened in 1850 by Queen Victoria to carry the main east coast railway line.

To see Berwick without taking that famous walk around the walls is like going to the Norfolk Broads without stepping even into a day boat. The first walls were built in about 1350 by Edward I of England, 'the Hammer of the Scots', and a section of them is being excavated. Then Elizabeth I built the Elizabethan Rampart, so called, to ward off Scottish and French attacks that never came. These sections were joined to the medieval walls at both ends to form riverside defences. But then, in the eighteenth century, the old walls were rebuilt as gun batteries that could command the seemingly crucial mouth of the Tweed. Beyond the housing estates on Berwick's northern side lies Scotland. To the west, you can follow the Tweed more closely than most rivers. It is a romantic river, not just because of its dramatic history but also because it looks the part.

There is no need to feel cheated if you give Northumberland a try and find yourself in the middle of a fog: those beetling crags and dun-coloured moors still look good in bad weather. For the best of Northumberland is an experience very different from the south, and bright sunny days – not as rare up here as some people say – can detract from the drama. There is often a chill in the air, and as they say up here, 'It would be lovely and warm if it wasn't so cold.'

The great metallic green hump of the Tyne Bridge, that is as much a symbol for Newcastle upon Tyne as the Liver Building is for Liverpool, was actually the model and inspiration for the Sydney Harbour Bridge. It was built in 1928, an inauspicious time for architecture. But this is just one of quite a selection of bridges over the river here (the seventh was opened by the Princess of Wales in the summer of 1983): just as famous is the High Level Bridge – built in the mid-nineteenth century and opened by Queen Victoria – by which rail travellers approach Newcastle Central Station. Happily this vouchsafes good views of several other bridges.

More and more, Newcastle is a city for pedestrians, and walking against the one-way system that cars have to endure is as much a pleasure here as in any other city, especially since there is a sophisticated new system of electric commuter trains that means people are disinclined to use their cars. The spectacular covered and pedestrianised shopping centres are the pride of Newcastle, which is not surprising, as they are probably the best of their kind in England. There is little excuse for not spending all your money here. The shops are air-conditioned in summer and heated in winter and, as the *Newcastle Chronicle* said, they are as 'modern as tomorrow'.

Despite all this the affection for the past has meant that street names in modern Newcastle hark back to history. So there is Hotspur Way, High Friars, Chevy Chase. Nor have they knocked down my favourite. This is the mid-nineteenth-century Grainger Market which, though not designed for a tenth of the millions of people who use it, throngs with jostling Geordies who are characteristically good-humoured. I always make a bee-line here for the second-hand bookshop in one discreet corner, where little old dears stock up on tenth-hand Mills & Boons, and mingle with dons from Newcastle University more interested in Hazlitt or Hakluyt.

There is a suburb of Newcastle called Wallsend, where a stubby bit of Hadrian's Wall still stands: obviously enough, the eastern extreme of England's equivalent of the Great Wall of China. But to see what is left of the best of it, you have to go west, to where the traffic travelling along this narrow neck of England starts to thin out, and moorland starts to encroach upon the farms.

It's true. Two thousand years ago England's climate was warmer than it is today, and a posting to the northernmost point of the empire was not, perhaps, as bad as most Roman soldiers expected it to be. The natives were quite friendly, and found too many advantages in living under Roman rule to make a nuisance of themselves. As always with an army of occupation, there was intermarrying with the local population, and many a demobbed squaddie could say of England: 'I came, I liked it, I stayed.'

Hadrian's Wall, Northumberland. In certain conditions, the view from the top of the wall (especially towards the north) seems not to have changed for 2,000 years. If ever ghosts walk in England, it must be along these ramparts.

You don't have to visit the Roman Wall, but it is quite hard to miss. It is easier to miss now than it was two thousand years ago, though, and is nowhere near as high, mainly due to people's canny habit of helping themselves when building a cottage, or even a castle, to the very handy stone with which Hadrian built his seventy-three mile long 'Berlin Wall'. It was built after about AD 122, which was about seventy-five years after the Romans first appeared on the south coast.

When the wall was completed, it was probably about fifteen feet high, with a wooden parapet about as high as a man on top of that. It was wide enough to take a military road of up to twenty feet across. The craggy lie of the land played right into the hands of the invaders, for steep banks virtually doubled the height of the wall, and, where it did not, great ditches were dug. Ditches were even built to the south. Every mile or so there was a milecastle (Roman miles being slightly shorter than ours) and every five miles were bigger forts that could absorb around a thousand soldiers in reasonable comfort. There were hospitals, stables, and all the paraphernalia of a thriving community.

Many a visitor from abroad has assumed, just as he walks into one of Oxford's colleges and thinks he has found 'the university', that the wall marks the border between England and Scotland. There is, of course, a substantial tract of country to be covered before you arrive at the border, and happily this gets more and more attractive mile by mile. The Roman Wall does not seem completely to have deterred the Scottish incursionaries, and the fortifications were attacked on three recorded occasions, between about AD 200 and 360. But only, it must be said, when there was nobody around to defend it.

Chesters, Vindolanda and Housesteads are the most impressive surviving Roman forts. Vindolanda is a comparatively recent excavation, much more geared to the modern demand for extensive reconstruction based on hard evidence. Chesters is more take-it-as-you-find-it, but, for my money, has ten times Vindolanda's atmosphere. You can walk among the excavated remains of the Chesters fort through gateways, along the line of barracks, visit the original headquarters, the chapel, and the commandant's house which reveals hot baths fed by hypercausts. And close to the deep, oil-black river is the regimental bath-house. Seven miles west of here, too, is the most impressive stretch of the wall proper, which follows the crest of the so-called whin sill, that tough resilient basalt which is the basis of a range of striking crags. Facing north on a good day, you can see the Pennines to the south, the hills of Cumbria to the north-west, and, due north, the whale-back moors that roll gradually upwards to the Cheviots. Excavations at Housesteads have revealed what was virtually a complete city. You can see a gateway with the marks of chariot wheels, the remains of granaries, stables, workshops, soldiers' barracks. This was, after all, a flourishing and stable community for around three hundred years.

The Wall itself is not so impressively high, but the scenery around it is more spectacular the further west you go. I am thinking of Hotbank Crags, from where you look down over wind-ruffled grey lakes, then Winshields Crag, and the 'nine nicks of Thirlwall', and then over the River Irthing, at which point the wall crosses into what is now Cumbria.

Lake Windermere, and a new generation of water bugs.

7. The Lake District and the North West: twelve million visitors can't be wrong

Keswick; Windermere; off-beat Lakeland and the coast;
Wordsworth and Grasmere; Carlisle; Kendal;
Penrith and the M6; the Trough of Bowland;
Manchester and Buxton

You can hardly see the join between Northumberland and Cumbria. It just sort of happens, especially if you follow the A97 Newcastle to Carlisle road, but it is more dramatic if you clamber over the roof of England between, say, Allenheads, Nenthead and Alston. Unfortunately there are people from the south of England who have spent twenty summer holidays in a row in the Lake District and do not know Alston from Aldershot. Of course, you can understand why they like the Lakes. A thousand people on the North Norfolk coast, for all its charms, are a crowd. Ten thousand in the same space in the hilliest part of Lakeland will be absorbed out of sight. People who are only moderately gregarious worry about what the Lake District is like in high season, but the sight of Jaeger cardigans (anoraks are different) more than a hundred yards from any main road around Windermere or Keswick is rarer than a herd of black sheep.

Despite the restless armies of people who visit Lakeland annually – they say there are over twelve million of them – the people at the Cumbria Tourist Board are not embarrassed by its popularity. They are inclined, however, to remind drivers that for the sake of parking their car, and walking a couple of hundred yards into the hills, either on well-marked-out routes, or by taking little detours down unclassified roads, they can apparently have the place to themselves. But it all depends where you go. Because of the constant traffic, in summer at least, you probably stand a better chance of losing consciousness through carbon monoxide poisoning near the top of Kirkstone Pass than of walking over the hills all day without getting rained on. The Lake District has been defined as radiating fifteen miles from Grasmere, and since 1974 it has all been confined within the 'new' county of Cumbria. Or you may prefer to take the boundary of the Lake District's National Park, established in 1949, as your yardstick. In any event it is pointless to come to Cumbria if you are going to throw up your hands and your anorak hood at the first sensation of rain on the back of your neck. There are, of course, compensations: Seatoller may be the wettest village in England but it is also one of the prettiest. Behind the village, as if on a theatrical cyclorama, is a mass of rock, lightly wooded, rising like an expertly contoured lemon meringue pie towards the sky. Between the stone – sometimes plain, sometimes whitewashed – village houses and the point where the hills start are green pastures and cottage gardens: a defiant gesture by man in the face of nature.

Just over the hills from Seatoller, about five miles if you hoof it and about twenty by car, lie Langdale and Elterwater. They are exceptionally pretty even by Lakeland standards, but have another claim to fame: they have faced up to the tourist explosion and grasped it with both hands.

To Langdale came the timesharers, building luxury chalets you can buy a piece of to enjoy, in specific weeks, for the rest of your lives. And to Elterwater came an exceptionally enterprising self-catering agency, renting out holiday cottages, as much concerned with introducing outsiders to the less frenetic way of life here as making a fast buck.

For perfectly good reasons, few self-caterers or timesharers get to meet farmers, although bed-and-breakfasting on a farm does give suburbanites a new perspective on lamb chops. Farming up here is altogether different from the prairies of Northampton-shire and the other East Midland counties. Often, farmers are a one-man band struggling against the elements, the stupidities of sheep, low market prices, and smaller government subsidies than people more used to arable farms imagine.

A local phenomenon among people who, on the whole, rarely meet the farmers, is the little knot of car drivers and passengers who, inspired by the mountains and the rippling water on the lake, alight from their vehicles and stand communing with nature. They do not generally stand for long unless it is shirt-off weather, when it is so uncomfortable inside the car that they abandon their touring plans for the rest of the day and remain by the water's edge.

If you come in the winter months you will find the roads almost deserted. But at any time between May and September there are cars, if not exactly nose-to-tail, then always in sight of each other. Ford Fiestas and little Datsuns that in school holiday time will be packed like sardines with 2.4 children and 2 adults will, in what the tourist boards call the 'shoulder season', contain just a middle-aged or elderly couple. This countryside is too pretty for some people's taste, lacking the ruggedness of the Highlands. Easier access and a milder climate than you get in the best parts of Scotland have turned the Lakes into something rather 'apart'.

For more than a decade, the tourist boards have devoted much energy into getting people on to the fringe of the region. I see their point, though I am not exclusively for out-of-the-way places. Keswick, for example, is one of my favourite towns in England. Though I have a sneaking fondness for bijou ('Bide-a-Wee') bed-and-breakfast stops, when I get to Keswick I make unashamedly for the most imposing hotel for miles around and become irascible if I cannot secure a room at the highest point of that palatial building. For this, amid the soft furnishings and with the friendly background chatter of the colour television turned down low, is *the* place from which to watch the sun set over fells that outsiders and especially East Anglians will call 'mountains'.

Even if you should arrive here after dark, all is not lost. I have supped in the hotel's sumptuous *fin de siècle* restaurant among farmers' wives on special treats and commercial travellers on generous expense accounts and then 'walked into town', that predictable and civilised pastime of the stranded traveller, to discover that Keswick does not appear to lie down and die after the shops shut: there are pubs that may remind Brummies of home, and there are also a few of the bistros that went out in Hampstead in the sixties (so this is where they came to . . .). Another reason I like Keswick is that, as far as I can tell, it has no connections whatsoever with William Wordsworth. Not that there is anything wrong with him, but it's nice occasionally to get away from his all-pervading influence.

Keswick is famous for its pencils, and even in the 1980s, when sophisticated communications and modern technology would do away with local manufacturing traditions, it still produces millions of them a year. According to local tradition, the graphite was discovered when an ash tree was blown over in a gale. The 'lead' was first used for marking sheep for identification, then for cleaning metal, then for casting cannonballs, and then, most profitably of all, for making pencils. The lead is imported now and the lead mines no longer used, but the tradition is too well established to fade away.

I once spent an hour walking by Derwentwater, Keswick's lake, after a heavy, late-spring fall of rain. The lake had swollen and the bank was awash with troubled, muddy water. The trees near the shoreline stood well inside the lake. But only a few weeks later I strolled through Keswick itself, on a warm summer night, away from that great baronial castle of a hotel that stands next to the forlorn and boarded-up railway station, down to the shores of Derwentwater. There was scarecely any moon and the blackness was nearly complete. There was, however, an oasis of light and warmth – the mobile theatre looking like a glorified dark-blue gypsy caravan.

At the risk of falling into the unseen water I walked out as far as I could on the jetty, from which, at more conventional times of the day, lake cruisers depart every half hour. I knew what lay out there: heavily wooded islands that, for people who break the rules and moor their boats, provide exquisite, silent, private picnic places; wooded shores and hillsides in which you can spot capacious country houses whose owners' greatest pleasure is that increasingly precious commodity – absolute privacy.

Derwentwater has one particular claim to distinction: in a bad winter, it is one of the first of the lakes to freeze. That might suggest it is inhospitable and exposed, but actually it is one of the most accessible lakes of all, with craggy wooded banks whose many trees are varied and softer on the eye than the conifers that dominate other parts of the Lake District. There are spectacular, not oppressive, fells surrounding the lake. The best view is probably of Skiddaw (3,054 feet) to the north. It is the fourth highest of the Lakeland fells, and Keswick lies below its protective bulk. The quickness to freeze (ice skaters love it) is a result of the comparative shallowness of the lake – up to an absolute maximum of 70 feet deep (Windermere, by comparison, is up to 220 feet deep).

A large part of Derwentwater is owned by the National Trust, as are long stretches of the banks. There are four islands, also in the care of the National Trust and accessible to visitors: boats can be hired. Small motor-boats are usually allowed on the lake, though speedboats are not. But the sailing is not particularly good, on account of the crosswinds. Close to the western bank is Brandelhow – set among 108 acres at the foot of another great landmark, the intriguingly named Cat Bells. At 1,481 feet, this is hardly in the same league as Skiddaw, but it does unfortunately have a reputation for accidents among inexperienced walkers and climbers.

Keswick is a famous place, but Windermere has a more recognisable lake. It is the biggest in England, more than ten miles long and nearly two miles across at its widest point, and Bowness-on-Windermere, which stands on the eastern side of the lake, is a focal point for thousands of visitors, especially in summer. It lies at the meeting point of several major roads, and happily it is still served by the railway from Oxenholme, on the

London to Glasgow line. This is not the place to come for cloud solitariness: that can be achieved, for example, by following the path that runs alongside part of the western side of the lake.

Windermere was used as a waterway by the Romans, who transported stones and iron ore northwards on the lake, and there were Roman settlements at Hardknott and Ravenglass. Hundreds of years later the lake was again busy with traffic, in the form of crowded steamboats. Competition between rival steamboat companies was intense, and one serenaded its customers with brass bands. The railway, which arrived in 1847, brought the holidaymakers, and it seems most of them wanted to take to the water. Fishermen can take to the lake in small boats, and they have the advantage that their sport can be most profitable at a time of the year when most tourists have gone home, for there is a good stock of perch and pike, and of carp that has been compared with salmon in taste.

I have enjoyed panoramic views of Lake Windermere from the uppermost storey of another of those wedding-cake hotels I like, and was once reminded of a film of a Chekhov short story called 'The Lady with the Little Dog'. This is set on the Black Sea coast at holiday time, and there is much promenading along the waterside with parasols and white finery. Windermere is wholeheartedly commercial, with places where you can buy miniature lighthouses made out of seashells and ashtrays in the shape of public urinals, but it is well done in its way.

The railway station is still open, and thus Windermere is the only Lake District tourist centre which can be reached by train. There is a bus service to Ambleside, also on Lake Windermere, so you can take a one-way boat trip, without needing your own car, between the two places. There is, incidentally, something incongruous about the way those blue-and-white pleasure boats have the word 'Sealink' printed on their side.

Just five miles to the west of Windermere, and somewhat overshadowed by that lake's popularity, is Coniston Water. This was previously much better known than it is now on account of the scenically superb railway that used to run to the lake from Barrow-in-Furness. The western end of the lake and Coniston village are dominated by The Old Man of Coniston, over 2,500 feet high. Three famous people are associated with the lake. One of them was John Ruskin, the Victorian essayist and critic, who lived at Brantwood, on the east side of the lake, in an eighteenth-century cottage which he bought in 1871, and which is open all year to the public. Another was Donald Campbell, who established the world water-speed record on the lake in 1959. He was killed eight years later when his boat, *Bluebird*, crashed here. A third was Arthur Ransome who wrote the best-selling children's book *Swallows and Amazons*. Ransome, who spent part of his childhood in the 1890s at a farm near Coniston village, used to say his feeling for the Lake District had been strengthened since the time his father carried him, as a small baby, to the top of The Old Man.

Between Coniston Water and Windermere is Grizedale, one of the National Forest Parks and a showpiece of the Forestry Commission, for the recreational interests of many hundreds of visitors blend in nicely with the more serious business of producing 10,000 tons of timber a year. Near Hawkshead is the Theatre in the Forest, seating 230 people, and with a twelve-month-long programme. It is very popular among walkers and local campers. Another attraction here is Treetops, a twenty-foot-high observation tower which can be booked in advance, and from where you can observe the comings and goings of foxes, hares, badgers, red deer and roe deer. Close by is a tarn which provides good viewpoints for wildfowlers. There are photo-safari hides and a nine-mile forest trail, and quite a range of goodies to take home: local people produce venison, and deerskin artefacts. There are picnic sites, camp sites, landscaped car parks. It is perhaps the best way to be introduced gently to the outdoor possibilities of the lakes without the blisters and the other discomforts of back-to-nature long-distance hiking or fell walking.

If Crummockwater, Ennerdale, Haweswater and Wastwater are comparatively little known, it is perhaps because they lie away from the main roads. Crummockwater, owned by the National Trust, is less spectacular than Buttermere, but you can get good views of it from easily scaled hills above it, and fishermen speak well of the perch, trout and pike that inhabit it. Wastwater is too austere even for the tastes of many people who prefer, say, Buttermere's wild fastness to Derwentwater's mildness. I have travelled alongside Wastwater to Wasdale Head on one of those afternoons when from inside the car the weather looks warm but which is given away by the sparkling but wind-ruffled water and the sight of people turning up their coat collars. I have also been there when the fine-weather friends had long gone and rain clouds lowered over the gorse-covered hills and rendered the hamlet of Wasdale Head alien and beleaguered. No television in the hotel here: the terrain helps to revive the ancient arts of post-prandial conversation and Scrabble. Wastwater is the deepest lake in England, touching about 270 feet. It has another distinction: its depths are so pure and clear of vegetation that it is almost sterile, and cannot, except for a particular variety of brown trout, support marine life.

I have liked more easterly Ennerdale ever since I delivered, on behalf of an estate agent friend in Whitehaven, some furniture to a deserted and echoing holiday cottage on the edge of the dark forest that dominates the lake: nearly complete isolation, but without oppressiveness. With a lick of paint, a bit of fresh wallpaper and a new cooker it could have become the sort of cottage you would want to go back to year after year, gradually getting to know the surrounding forest paths and picnic sites. At the head of Ennerdale, by the way, is what is said to be the remotest youth hostel in England.

There are several lesser lakes that rarely figure in guide books and seem to be the unofficial preserve of local people or visitors so regular they get to know their way off the beaten track. One of these is Elter Water, which gets its name from the old Norse for 'Swan Lake', and another, even though the busy A591 between Keswick and Ambleside runs past its east shore, is Thirlmere. The easily climbable and accessible peaks of Helvellyn and Dollywaggon Pike are between Thirlmere and Ullswater, and they could claim to be virtually at the centre of the Lake District.

The easternmost of the Lakes is Haweswater. It is hardly one of the most distinguished, but it does have one thing going for it. It is the most easily accessible for drivers on the M6 who do not wish to stray far from the motorway but like to feel they have seen something of the region. Haweswater is not, however, what it was, for it is a reservoir for Manchester. In 1929 the city swallowed the original much smaller lake, that was actually regarded as one of Lakeland's prettiest. It is still attractive, considering its function, and has the considerable advantage of being almost completely ignored by tourists heading for more romantic and therefore more busy lakes. Several times I have enjoyed the mood of its clear waters and cool, dark trees on a hot and transistorless afternoon.

Buttermere used to be regarded as bleak and oppressive, but it is a sign of people's more sophisticated tastes that its exceptionally deep, bleak wastes (sometimes mirror-calm, occasionally a witches' cauldron) are less awesome now. Only 250 people actually live in the village, though their numbers are swollen by guests at the two hotels.

Buttermere, Cumbria. Before the days of almost universal car ownership, Buttermere was comparatively little known. Now it is one of the most popular of the wilder lakes. It also has very good fishing.

Even though most people have never read more than a few lines of England's most prolific (and most inconsistent) romantic poet, many of them are probably searching for something tangible about him. A modest Wordsworth tour might begin centrally enough, near the Lake District National Park Centre at Brockhole, on the A591 road that links Windermere and Ambleside. The centre is on the shores of Lake Windermere itself, where among the faithfully done and low-key audio-visual displays is one devoted to Wordsworth himself, and another on the theme of Literary Lakeland. If the literary going gets too heavy, there are thirty acres of garden and parkland in which to commune with a somewhat man-made, toned-down Nature, and it is gratifying to be able to walk right to the water's edge. Wordsworth went to Hawkshead Grammar School, near to Esthwaite Water, one of the least known lakes to the west of Windermere, and least accessible, unless you take the ferry that runs at limited times across the middle of Windermere, drive via Ambleside, and then on the A593, then B5286/5285.

Wordsworth referred in his autobiographical poem, *The Prelude*, to 'Hawkshead's happy roof' and it was here that he lived for the eight years after 1778. But the real focal point for Wordsworthians is Grasmere, where you will find Dove Cottage and the Wordsworth Museum (do, on pain of frustration and misery, avoid high-days, holidays, and summer weekends here). Wordsworth lived at Dove Cottage between 1799 and 1808, and it was here that most of his best-known poetry was written. The lamer stuff, reams of it, was produced when he was older and living 'up the road' at Rydal Mount, just a mile from Dove Cottage, between 1813 and his death in 1850. He was buried in the church at Grasmere. Rydal Mount was opened to the public in 1970, the bicentenary year of the poet's birth, and embraces, among other features, a four-acre garden landscaped by Wordsworth himself.

Just north of Keswick on the A591 is the farmhouse (well signposted) where the Wordsworths lived for seven months in 1794, just a few years after the French Revolution that inspired so much of Wordsworth's early and best works.

In the hands of a private trust, Wordsworth's birthplace at Cockermouth provides a good excuse for visiting one of the most attractive off-Lakeland towns. Take the A66. Although this is a fast and functional arterial route, it does go past Bassenthwaite Lake en route for Cockermouth: this is pleasant, subtle, country, not as spectacular as you find elsewhere, and therefore much less frequented. Bassenthwaite Lake, privately owned, is the most northerly of the lakes, and one reason it is not especially well known is that public access is difficult and restricted. Wordsworth was born in 1770, in a house that was then quite new but now has the patina and ambience associated with the word 'Georgian'. Several rooms are open to the public, and contain original details. Part of Wordsworth's *Prelude* includes a description of his childhood in Cockermouth. His all-too-familiar poem *To the Daffodils* was, incidentally, inspired by a visit to Ullswater from Windermere. For the record, Wordsworth was not wandering lonely as a cloud, but had his ever-present sister Dorothy with him.

If those whom the gods love really die young, Wordsworth would have been dead and gone during the first few years of the nineteenth century. He did, however, live to eighty and, a far cry from the revolutionary and visionary who produced such memorable work, became a self-righteous reactionary and a figure of fun.

Wordsworth chose to live in Grasmere mainly because of its exquisite location. He would still appreciate the way – thanks mainly to the National Trust and the National Park Commissioners – Grasmere itself is one of the most accessible of all the lakes. And there are plenty of places Wordsworth might go to get away from it all if he found it was getting too crowded with Wordsworthians: Ennerdale, to the east, an unsung corner of the county that will yet come into its own, or Buttermere, or that extensive and astonishingly neglected area that roughly embraces what used to be Lancashire's share of Lakeland: Ulverston, Broughton, Eskdale, Millom.

Near Blea Tarn, Langdale, Cumbria. Langdale is geographically quite
central, but the absence of major roads in the vicinity emphasises its
natural feeling and remoteness.

I only found Broughton in Furness one day when I lost my way and should have been much further north. I was reminded of those towns on the outskirts of the Cotswolds, or the edge of the Yorkshire Dales, places that have not been made complacent by the attention of tourists. It is an unassuming little village, with mainly three-storeyed houses grouped around the old market square, a few shops, a couple of horse-chestnut trees in the centre. Affected by twee-ness, the cottages might be painted in pastel shades, but as it is, they are mostly of unpainted rendered stone. One village shop doubles as the mountain activity centre. But several other shops are well stocked with guides to fell walking, maps of all shapes, sizes and scales, and autobiographies by famous climbers. The village is closer to the seaside than many people realise, and there are shrimp nets, buckets and spades outside the general stores. Later, I drove from Ulpha, north of Broughton in Furness, up towards Wasdale, across bleak moorland more reminiscent of the northern part of County Durham than what you would expect of Lakeland, with stark, volcanic, dinosaur-shaped rocks across the barren wastes, and herds of that strange breed of sheep with chocolate-brown overcoats.

Skirting round the edges of the Lake District like this is not just a duty but a pleasure. From any one of the hundred points on the Lakeland fringe, including all the coastal strip, and the road that runs north of Bassenthwaite via Caldbeck towards Penrith, the bottom corner around Kendal that leads towards Ulverston and then up towards Eskdale and Ravenglass, you can enjoy both a sense of freedom and make an occasional quick, exploratory recce into the traditional heartland of Lakeland without getting bogged down with hotels and guesthouses full to the rafters.

In dramatic contrast to that country beyond the fringe is Grasmere on sports day. At such times you really could call this breathtaking scenery. Among the fells around Grasmere, to the delight of about ten thousand spectators, every August sees the Grasmere Sports. Cumberland wrestling, which used to be the mainstay of the event, has long been overtaken by fell-running, for which the participants, if not the spectators, travel from hundreds of miles away.

The most important of all the fell races (though perhaps second in spectator appeal to the hound trailing, in which forty or so specially bred foxhounds, each one a household pet, are set on an aniseed trail covering ten miles) is the Senior Guides' Race, whose name probably derives from the nineteenth-century guides employed to show visitors around the region.

The race begins from an oval arena below the summit of Grasmere's closest 'mountain', called Buttercrags, and twenty young men in the absolute peak of condition set off in full view of the crowd, some of whom will daringly have climbed half a hill in order to watch the first hundred yards of the not quite vertical approach to the 966-foot-high hill. Barring accidents, the winner, as in the Oxford and Cambridge boat race, will be known well in advance, because this is a test of fitness, and the runners' form will be well documented by the local newspapers and television. Incidentally, fell walking has rather gone out of fashion, but it used to be 'the thing'. If you were any kind of serious visitor to the Lakes you were expected to ascend a peak or two. It wasn't just Wordsworth who took to the hills: in 1805 Sir Walter Scott climbed Helvellyn (3,118 feet), and in 1802 Charles Lamb climbed Skiddaw (just over 3,000 feet).

Though it is hardly a Lakeland town, the first place most Cumbria-bound holiday makers who use the M6 motoway recognise, by name at least, will be Kendal. It lies just a few quick and easy miles off the M6. Kendal is more solid than pretty, with grey stone buildings, several hotels, and some attractive narrow lanes leading off the busy high street. There is a ruined Norman castle overlooking the town, and you can walk along the River Kent without moving more than a quarter of a mile from the town centre. In the house now used by the YWCA, Bonnie Prince Charlie slept during his retreat from Derby, which was as far south as he got on his abortive uprising of 1745. Two nights later his pursuer, the Duke of Cumberland, slept in the same bed. There is every possibility that he would have used the same sheets.

Of course, Kendal is a Lakeland gateway, but it is also a jumping-off point for the 'back way' to Carlisle, roughly parallel with the motorway. This runs via Shap, which I have liked ever since the day they completed the section of the M6 motorway that bypasses it. Literally overnight, it was transformed from a hell's kitchen of shuddering juggernauts into a backwater in which cats might chance a nap in the middle of the road. High-lying Shap, incidentally, is nearly three hundred feet above sea level, and close to where the London to Carlisle railway touches the highest point of England's rail network. About eight miles north of Shap is the Lowther Wildlife Park, in the grounds of Lowther Hall. It is not an exotic safari-park but one that specialises in indigenous or European species.

Penrith, roughly equidistant from Kendal and Carlisle, was another of the towns on the A6 that, like Shap, suffered increasingly from the effects of heavy traffic, and the M6 came as a particular relief. There are some good eighteenth-century buildings: for centuries Penrith was an important market town and commercial centre. The remains of Penrith's fourteenth-century castle are in the very centre of the town and it has the biggest bingo hall in the north of England – or so it seemed when I arrived in the High Street at about ten o'clock in the evening, precisely at the moment when it disgorged several hundred players in a matter of seconds.

Like Haweswater, which involves just a few miles' detour from the motorway, Ullswater does not mean a tortuous drive to the heart of the Lake District. Pooley Bridge, to the west of Penrith, lies at the easternmost edge of the lake. There is a good crop of tourist-orientated cafés and shops, a regular summer boat trip on the lake, and on the eastern side of the lake, at Howtown, one of Lakeland's most famous hotels, the Sharrow Bay, right on the water's edge. On a calm autumn day I have lingered over coffee and cakes by one of the hotel's picture windows, when the waters of the lake were as mirror-calm, and the hills and trees so faithfully reflected in them, that you could have taken one or two of those photographs that confuse newspaper picture-editors ('Which way up does it go?').

The M6 is a triumph of civil engineering and, south of Carlisle, between, say, Kendal and Penrith, it is far and away the most dramatic of all the motorways to travel on. Especially if you strike it when it is quiet and there are just two or three cars snaking through the hills as if on some gargantuan roller-coaster. The M6 will deposit you on the red-brick and, to be honest, unlovely outskirts of Carlisle in double-quick time, and it is not to be scorned. But it is not the best way to arrive. The prize for that must go to the train that draws in twice daily to Carlisle's nineteenth-century railway station after an energetic horizon-hugging climb up and over the backbone of England – an unforgettable trip and one of those comparatively modest journeys that everybody ought to experience at least once. The last few miles of the trip run through the Eden Valley, and the Lakes and its hills are only distantly seen through grubby carriage windows.

Though it is the administrative capital of Cumbria, Carlisle has nothing about it to suggest the wild moors and fells that make Lakeland into one of the biggest tourist draws in the country. Many drivers who have not previously followed the M6 into Cumbria are surprised how flat the surrounding country is once they are north of Shap Fell. Carlisle is a cathedral city, though the cathedral receives less attention than it deserves. It has the most impressive East Window in the country, with the exception of those at Lincoln and York and, though it is small, the interior has some fine carving. It is also notable in that it was unusually sympathetically restored in Victorian times.

The city is only about fifteen miles from the Scottish border, and much of the place's history is bound up with the strife-torn border country. The ruined castle that has associations with Mary Queen of Scots, the Civil War and the Jacobite rebellion of 1745, is open to the public. If you don't make it to the Roman Wall, try the Tullie House Museum, which contains a number of rare relics from the Wall.

Carlisle is not as romantic and impressive as its melodramatic history would suggest, but the parts of the city contained within the old walls are worth an afternoon of anybody's time. The dark-red sandstone is sombre and, for a southerner, rather alien, though it adds dignity to many ancient buildings and especially to one of Carlisle's real gems – the covered market that looks as if it would rather have been a railway station. For Carlisle is still a railway town, and the main station is as elegant and inspiring as a small and rather intimate version of York's.

The M6 motorway, they said, would make it possible to get from London to the Lake District in an afternoon. It opened up Lancashire as well, but who seemed to care about that? Lancashire is a county that maintains a low profile. Its greenery, and there is a lot more of that than most people realise, seems mainly to be the preserve of day trippers from the industrial conurbations of Liverpool, Chester, West Yorkshire and Sheffield. To call it a county of contrasts is not very original, but as you stand by some rushing stream amid the bracken of the Trough of Bowland, observed perhaps by a solitary sheep that seems very cleverly to combine aggressiveness and shyness, you may indeed relect that this is light years from the cheek-by-jowl back-to-backs and the dark satanic mills of the industrial North West. I cannot remember the Lake District ever having been cut off because it had reached saturation point, but I can remember looking at queues of traffic near the Kendal motorway exit during a family holiday, and consulting my map: I had never been to the Trough of Bowland, and I made a reasonable guess that most other people had not and would not. This corner of the North West is as secret in its way as the Blackdown Hills of Somerset. It is known mainly to local people – and hardly at all to outsiders. Not only is the heavily-wooded, heather-covered and steep terrain surprisingly overlooked, but the towns, such as Clitheroe, that lie on the edge of the so-called forest are also unknown quantities. Slaidburn is probably the best-known village and its inn, The Hark to Bounty, is famous. The name comes from a dog with a distinctive bark. Thus, hark to, or listen to, Bounty. You will hear more Scouse voices in

Trough of Bowland, Lancashire. One of the best-kept secrets among
countryside fanciers in England, it is a wild kind of no man's land that
straddles part of the Lancashire–Yorkshire border.

the bar of the Hark to Bounty than Yorkshire ones, even though Slaidburn, since the
redrawing of the county boundaries in 1974, has stood perilously close to the Yorkshire
border. Due east of Clitheroe, is Kendal Hill. An easy enough climb of about 1,830 feet
with, however, the added complication that because the distinctive hill is concave, your
path gets steeper and steeper as you approach the top. But it is worth it for the views
over the Ribble Valley towards the still smoky mill towns to the south-east, and then
west towards the Irish Sea and the Isle of Man.

The Hark to Bounty Inn, Slaidburn, is said to get its name from a
foxhound – Bounty – that belonged to a local nineteenth-century clergyman
called Wigglesworth.

It was in the bar of The Hark to Bounty that I was forcibly informed (by a
Mancunian) that Manchester's rainfall is, contrary to popular belief, slightly less than
the national average. But even so, it is probably best to see the city either on a Sunday
afternoon, when it is 'closed', and the comparatively few people who live in the city
centre are having a siesta, or when it is throbbing with life on a busy Saturday afternoon.
The worst of the traffic skirts around the city centre, and you can, as I have done, stroll
out of the quite exceptional art gallery, along to the Town Hall in Albert Square, then
sample one or two of the department stores, and for a good look at how the late twentieth
century is getting on with what remains of Victorian Manchester – which is quite a lot –
go for a stroll along the River Irwell, which still flows undiverted through the heart of
the city. There are free guided tours of the Town Hall which, like many things
Victorian, is no longer reviled but almost universally admired. There are twelve famous
murals by Ford Madox Brown, each representing a single event in Manchester's
history. The Moseley Street Art Gallery, the name commemorating the family of

Oswald Moseley, who were once lords of the manor here, was designed by Charles Barry. It is best known for its collection of pre-Raphaelite paintings, but there is much more besides.

Perhaps it is damning the city with faint praise to say that the best thing about it is the way you can quickly get away into the surrounding countryside, but Mancunians are well used to popping into their car, or up to the top deck of one of their familiar white and orange buses, to get out into the hills and moors.

Liverpool had the Lakes, but Manchester had to look closer to home for its fresh air. However, Manchester never had that tradition of free public access to the Peak District long enjoyed by Cumberland people to the Lake District. This was ironic because many more people live just a short distance from this hill country than any other of the national parks: over seventeen million live within fifty miles of the Peak District National Park's boundaries, and it is estimated that about ten million of them take advantage every year of what the Park has to offer. One of the most astonishing things, for example, about visiting Sheffield (which happens to be linked to Manchester by one of the most impressive roads in the north of England, but appears to be a closely guarded secret), is that if you are accompanied by somebody who knows their way around, you can in just a few minutes be what seems like hundreds of miles from the still comparatively grimy and industrial city. To the north of the Peak District is the industrial West Riding of Yorkshire, to the south, the industrial Midlands and Derby, to the west, industrial Cheshire, and on either side, westwards and eastwards respectively, Manchester and Sheffield.

The Peak District has no peak. One theory about the origin of the name is that it comes from the long-standing tradition of pig farming. Not that there aren't

Bakewell puddings, Bakewell, Derbyshire. Woe betide anybody who talks about Bakewell 'tarts'.

considerable heights to climb. The highest point is Kinder Scout, 2,088 feet above the neat, hardly spoilt town of Buxton, which is one of about a dozen old spa towns in Britain enjoying a revival in popularity. The Peak District underground is almost as impressive as up among the hills, for just a few miles from Buxton, at Castleton, is the Blue John Cavern, the world's only source of the semi-precious blue john stone. The biggest cavern of the several that are open to the public with an admirable minimum of formality, but just enough in the way of dank passageways and serious-looking guides admonishing unruly children to add a sense of drama, is called Mulgrave's Dining Room, after a local squire who once entertained a party of miners to dinner here. The walls of the limestone caverns reveal the origin of the rocks; marine fossils are relics of the time this was submerged under deep oceans. Probably because of the conurbations encroaching upon it, the Peak District is the most vulnerable to suffering from the hand of man; electricity pylons, that elsewhere might have been put underground, have been allowed to cross the National Park.

There is a side to Buxton that commercial travellers and package tourists do not see, unless they are more inclined to get out and about on foot than most people are, and that is the public park that borders the river flowing on one side of town. I have saved money and stayed in little one-horse hotels, and not bad they are, some of them. But I seem to return again and again to the faithful old Palace Hotel. Ask for a room with a view, which is not hard to achieve, since the hotel overlooks half the town.

It is still railway country, too, not that the trip by diesel train into Manchester is especially scenic. I have done the journey and enjoyed it, however: late at night, after alighting from the last surviving Pullman train in Britain (no great shakes anyway, and soon to become a recent memory), on to a cold and lonely platform at Stockport to wait for the connection.

I remember standing in the spacious foyer of the Grosvenor Hotel, Chester, when an American hitch-hiker arrived who had just covered the A54 between Buxton and Chester under the aegis of a BRS six-wheeler. Full marks to the imperturbable staff who treated him – done up as he was in a Vietnam veteran's anorak and muddy boots – as if he were the American Ambassador to the Court of St James. He turned out to be a Rhodes scholar en route for North Wales, and he said, 'I don't mind it rough during the day but I like somewhere cosy to go to bed at night.'

Chester was created by the Romans as a fortress – the name means simply that – and some wags have said it has remained a difficult place to get into ever since, especially since they devised the one-way traffic system. Built on an outcrop of rock looped round by the River Dee, there are only two bridges. The city was in the forefront of those banishing cars from ravaging the city centre and creating a ring road which, it must be admitted, has caused some intending visitors to miss the place altogether – the first time round (round being the operative word) at least. It is the archetypal black-and-white city, but not tediously or too self-consciously so: there is many a Georgian doorway set off by classic symmetry and enhanced by pastel colours that perhaps surprisingly bring out the best of the ancient brickwork. In 1975, Chester was chosen as one of four British cities to represent European Architectural Heritage Year, which was the impetus for a restoration scheme in several Georgian houses and a Tudor building where Charles I is thought to have stayed after the battle of Rowton Moor.

Winterscape in Buxton, Derbyshire. In the foreground, St Anne's Crescent; in the
background, the Palace Hotel

The countryside immediately surrounding Chester is bland, and the coastal road
that takes you and the Rhodes scholar towards Caernarfon only partially inspiring.
Better is the sylvan approach to Shropshire and the no man's land of the Welsh border
thereabouts, which is the kind of countryside where people stand at crossroads with
their route maps out, scratching their heads.

8. The Welsh borders and the 'heart of England': letting the world go by

*The Long Mynd; Ludlow; Shrewsbury; Malvern;
Worcester; Hereford; Weobley; Hay-on-Wye;
Shakespeare Country and the Vale of Evesham;
Warwickshire; Stratford-upon-Avon and the
gateway to the Cotswolds*

The 170-mile-long border between England and Wales has been compared with the line of a half-finished jigsaw puzzle. Here Wales infiltrates for no apparent rhyme or reason into England, there England gets its own back. The Welsh Marches are a half-forgotten stretch of Britain that keeps its secrets, and reveals its charms only grudgingly: it is well worth a detour.

The name Marches derives from the medieval Marcher lords, aggressive and ambitious even by the standards of the times. March itself comes from Mark, or dividing line, and the Marcher Lords ruled, with semi-official sanction, the uneasy land between the occupied territory of Wales proper and the comparatively settled, fertile farmland of middle-England. Most historians settle on Offa's Dyke as some kind of national boundary. Built between 756 and 796, the great earthwork once stretched the entire length of the border, and by the tenth or eleventh century, people came to accept it as the border-proper.

Several impressive stretches of Offa's Dyke still remain around Knighton, right on the border, and in 1971 some kind of security for this great international monument was established when the Offa's Dyke footpath was opened. This runs from Prestatyn, in the north, to Sedbury Cliffs in the south. During the Middle Ages the Marches became neglected, partly because people who did have farms here even when hostilities died down preferred to opt either for Wales or England rather than live in a no man's land, albeit a softly contoured and fertile one.

In the right weather, if you half close your eyes, you can ignore the progress of eight or ten centuries. Little has changed, except the shape of this wood or that field, or the amount of luxuriant undergrowth in a valley through which a rarely visited river goes tumbling down. Where practicable, explore the countryside on foot. Drive, say, towards Church Stretton in Shropshire, and devote half a day to exploring the Stiperstones ridge, north of the village, or the Long Mynd, also accessible from Church Stretton, from where there are spectacular views. It is almost as if these outcrops of steep wooded hills are there as an introduction to the massive hills of mid and north Wales.

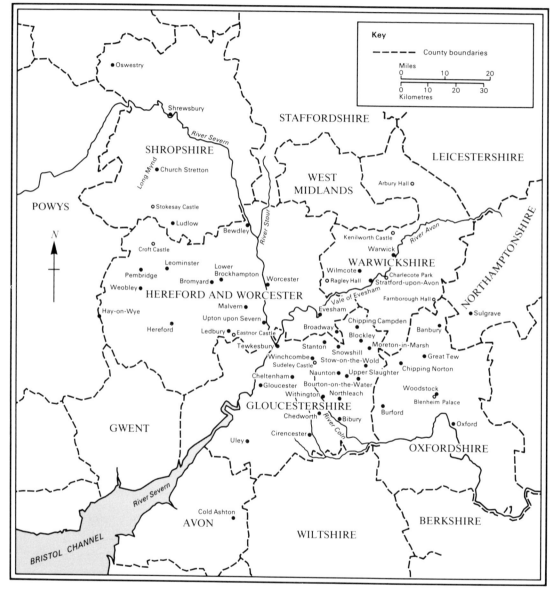

Map 5 The Welsh Borders

The whaleback mass of what is part of the Long Mynd (it means long mound), and a scattering of woodland among the cornfields, are clues to the location of this scene. It is in fact near Church Stretton, Shropshire.

The Long Mynd (the word simply means 'mound') is safely in the care of the National Trust. Reminiscent of a beached whale, stranded inside a great loop of the River Severn, it is not as high as it seems, no more than 1,690 feet above sea level at its highest point, and therefore easily climbed or rather clambered up. Because the Mynd, which embraces four and a half thousand acres of open moorland, makes such a recognisable hump, it is as if the surrounding countryside has been smoothed out and made fertile, and this great rocky outcrop somehow forgotten by the landscapers.

A few of the distinctive buildings that are a cross between houses and castles give a clue to the character of the region. Stokesay Castle, for example, is a fortified manor house. Its builders wanted to put the past behind them, but didn't quite have the courage of their convictions, and made a few concessions to defence, just to be on the safe side. Croft Castle, another National Trust property, near Leominster, is also a stately-home-cum-castle whose luxurious interior belies its more defensive outside.

Never is it more true that England's appearance changes chameleon-like minute by minute than in Shropshire, Herefordshire and Worcestershire or, as new parlance refers to the latter, Salop and Hereford-and-Worcester. It is as if all the elements that make up the characteristic English scene have been thrown together at the last minute before Wales arrives, as if there were extra hills and valleys, copses and rocky ridges to get rid of before they were impounded at the border. There is something, too, about the market towns of the border country, including Shrewsbury and Ludlow. Although Ludlow has a castle, neither it nor Shrewsbury have cathedrals, which tend so often to overshadow the place they are in. (A classic example of this elsewhere is Ely, in Cambridgeshire, which is a delightful town seen for its own sake by a tiny minority of visitors.)

A. E. Housman was buried in Ludlow but actually came from Worcestershire, which means he was not really a Shropshire lad. In any event it was absence that made his heart grow fonder. For Housman, who died in 1936, forty years after 'A Shropshire Lad' was published, spent most of his life a hundred miles away as a Cambridge don. Housman's links with Ludlow add a little in the way of literary associations to this handsome place. John Milton's *Comus* was first performed here on 29 September 1634, though it is unlikely to see any more performances, say, at the Ludlow Festival for, to put it mildly, though the music is pleasant it lacks, well, dramatic power. But I did once watch an open-air performance of *A Midsummer Night's Dream*. There is nothing amateurish about the plays at the annual Ludlow Festival; instead they are professional shows at which, however, it is advisable to bring your own cushions and blankets, so as not to allow bodily discomforts to distract you from the play itself. If your own backside is numb from inactivity there is an uncomfortable irony in watching the cavortings of Bottom the Weaver.

Shropshire is England's biggest inland county, and has retained an air of secrecy, perhaps fostered by the proximity of a stretch of Welsh border that is only, it seems, infrequently crossed: people do tend to go specifically to North Wales or South Wales, via much busier crossing points, and the whaleback hills which are relics of great geological upheavals many millions of years ago, and which characterise the best of Shropshire, do not encourage much stumbling across the county by accident. It is well worth at least half a day to climb one of the hills, in order to enjoy views which would compare favourably with those afforded to a glider pilot.

From the summit of the Long Mynd, incidentally much recommended for moderately energetic walkers, are very good views of the Stiperstones: pronounce it as in 'viper's bones'. They are a mass of severe rocky outcrops in which the wind howls eerily and thus recaptures something of the magic of this part of the country. This border wears its troubled history more lightly than, say, the country which straddles northern England and southern Scotland. Just to take one example: Oswestry, north-west of Shrewsbury, was twice set alight by the English and the Welsh armies in a space of less than twenty years during the thirteenth century.

Shrewsbury itself has been knocked about a bit by more modern vandals – read planners – but it remains a place that, if you stand where the skyline is broken by church spires and towers, with the English bridge across the Severn in the foreground, you might just be able to sell lock, stock and barrel to some gullible American millionaire. In short, it is a gem. It was once quite a fashionable place, a focal point for high society both from North Wales and Shropshire, and it is just possible (say on one of those tranquil summer evenings when all the people and the traffic have gone home) to see the town's half-timbered Tudor buildings as they would have looked two or three hundred years ago. It is place-name country again: Dogpole, Grope Lane, Shoplatch and Wyle Cop have appeared in local records for hundreds of years.

The public school, founded by Edward VI in 1552, is famous. Among its old boys were Sir Philip Sidney, and the 'enfants terribles' who started *Private Eye* magazine in the 1960s.

The Severn that flows under both the so-called English bridge and the Welsh bridge, not to mention eight other bridges that have cropped up in the last few hundred years, is, like Offa's Dyke, in places almost a natural boundary between England and Wales. The English bridge and the Welsh bridge are, incidentally, known thus because of their geographical situation. You traditionally used the former if you were en route, say, for London, and the latter if heading for, say, Welshpool.

At Bridgnorth, you don't see the river so well from the water's edge as at Shrewsbury, and you will do better to climb to Castle Walk, a footpath from where there are extensive views of the town. From here, you can watch the serpentine river snaking its way round the town. Bewdley, which gets its name from Beaulieu, has kept its elegant Georgian houses, overlooking the water, and Stourport, all red-brick, industrial archeology and canal boats, is at the junction of the Severn and the Stour.

Worcester, Gloucester and Malvern lie on the Severn. Malvern is a cliff-hanger. Though it is not actually on the Severn, you do look down over the Severn Vale from any one of a hundred places. When the Ironbridge Gorge was in full industrial swing and the waters of the Severn as it flowed through it were black and nasty, Malvern water was being bottled at the then iniquitous price of one shilling a time, roughly the equivalent today of a magnum of champagne. It was so pure, they said, that early Victorian doctors described it as 'water with nothing in it'. When you travel by British Rail you are provided with Malvern Water in the restaurant cars and, most notably, on their sleepers. Many a lonely vigil that I have suffered through the wilds of Cumbria or Northumberland in a British Rail sleeper has been accompanied by the bottle's familiar rattle.

As it straggles along the whale-backed Malvern hills, Malvern looks like something out of Scotland's Trossachs or, as you get closer to it, the shores of Lake Lugano. Unlike most towns which look elegant and impressive from the distance but bring you down to earth with a bump when you arrive, Malvern is as good when you reach it as it is from afar. One of the main reasons it seems so unspoilt is that there is just no room for ugly development. From any high point in the town, and the terrain means there are many, you enjoy a roofscape par exellence.

The people who live in the tall four- and five-storeyed Regency, Victorian and Edwardian houses, all pinnacles, fretted woodwork and steep-pitched roofs, are probably very fit, because walking around Malvern tends to make demands on the calf muscles and the lungs. Even as you stroll along the backstreets following the contours of the lower slopes of the hill, you will be vouchsafed spectacular views across the plains of the River Severn. But it would be interesting to know just how many Malvern people have ever reached the Worcestershire Beacon – 1,395 feet above sea level, from where they say (don't they always?) that you can see seven counties. On my very first visit to

Great Malvern and Malvern Priory, Worcestershire. On a clear day from
this remarkable, high-lying survivor from Edwardian and earlier days, you
can see half of England.

Malvern, despite the effect on my breathing in just seeing the town itself, I summoned
up the energy to climb to the Beacon. Lest anyone pour scorn on the modest height of
the Malvern Hills, though they loom above mainly flat country and therefore seem
much higher than they are, they should be reminded that the rock is older than that of
the Cuillins of Skye, or Snowdonia, and thus deserves veneration.

This is Edward Elgar country. He was born in 1857, just three miles from
Worcester, and in 1878 he played second fiddle at the Three Choirs Festival, which is
held every third year at Worcester. Elgar came to live in Malvern in 1891, after a
disastrous attempt to break into the London scene. His talent had not been recognised
there, and he had no great ambitions left, until the Enigma Variations, which he
composed when he was over forty, received its first performance in London in June
1899. He composed his Dream of Gerontius while living in a house at Malvern Wells,
below Malvern itself, where the steep town begins to flatten out towards the plain. He
subsequently lived in Hereford, went back to London, but returned to this part of
Worcestershire after his wife's death in 1920.

Perhaps the greatest boost to Elgar's renewed popular appeal in the 1970s and '80s
came from Ken Russell, the highly idiosyncratic film-maker. He shot memorable
scenes, for a BBC TV film about the composer, among the Malvern Hills, all scudding
shadows and panoramic views, accompanied by the uplifting – in this case literally
– music of Elgar's Serenade for Strings.

They say that afternoon tea has declined. I do not mean the office worker's pallid plastic cupful of unboiled liquid half infused with a tea bag, but sitting down in front of teacakes that are impossible to pick up without getting your fingers sticky with melted butter, gooseberry jam in crystal glass bowls and fairy cakes that arrive laughably too numerous until you end up paying the waitress with some embarrassment because, unaccountably, they have all gone. If this has disappeared, nobody has told them in Malvern. I walked up two steep flights of stairs, rather reminiscent of the more seedy type of privately owned betting shop, turned left at the aspidistra and entered a rather genteel orgy: the air was heady with the aroma of strong teas – 'real' tea that is, not tea bags. Good teashops and good bookshops often go hand-in-hand. The order in which to enjoy these two notably inexpensive treats is as follows: take the bookshop first, walk to the teashop and when you are there carefully unwrap your purchases to gloat over what almost inevitably will seem like bargains. The bookshop I have in mind is hard by the abbey gardens. It is the kind where you do not see the owner but hear him, just feet away from you behind a maze of shelves, filling his pipe, stirring his tea (tea again!), chatting in low tones with another customer – but, if you eavesdrop, rarely about books. Equally rarely, if he is on his own, does he read. On a cold day, the room will be heated by a portable gas heater, and a too-warm soporific fug will steal over it.

From high up the abbey tower you look over half of Worcestershire. Not that I climbed it, because my room in an ivy-covered hotel close by afforded a view just as good. A double bonus was that between the hours of 7 am and 11 pm – or certainly the ones during which I was around – the sound of the abbey's bells chimed the hour, the half hour and the quarter, with a good few trills and carillons thrown in.

East-facing Malvern is always highlighted by early morning sun. Milk bottles are wet from the dairy and their contents, even though the day is warm, still drinkable. A ginger cat is sufficiently invigorated by the incipient warmth of the day to go walkabout, but it is not yet hot enough for it to lie mindlessly in the sun.

The few minutes' drive from Malvern to Worcester, or vice versa, are duller than you might expect – all between-the-wars housing and uninspired shopfronts. Well, nearly all. And Worcester itself was saved in the nick of time: another couple of years, a few more insensitive planning decisions, and it would have been past redemption. As it is, it has been heavily criticized by some for its apparent failure to keep through-traffic away from the city centre. A pedestrian precinct that runs right through the centre of the city from near the cathedral close has, however, undone a lot of the damage wrought by bad planning. It allows one, for example, time to gaze at the elegant Queen Anne Guildhall which stands right on the High Street. And despite the rush of traffic between the cathedral and the smart Trusthouse Forte hotel opposite it, the cathedral precincts are quiet and peaceful.

The cathedral was heavily restored by the Victorians, but the view of its west front from the cricket ground across the river is a chocolate-box favourite. Quite close to the cathedral is another world-famous Worcester institution: the Royal Worcester Porcelain works, in which visitors can join a guided tour and browse among the showrooms, including a big 'seconds' department.

For a while I wandered round the cathedral and then sat beside the fast-flowing Severn. Re-invigorated, I joined a guided tour of the porcelain works and the Dyson Perrins Museum (yes, Perrins did help to invent Worcester sauce and yes, it is still made here). Worcester seems to have missed out on the extra space it deserves. It is a cramped city, but one advantage of this for the visitor is that everything worthwhile is cheek-by-jowl. You do not have to go far to get from riverside to cathedral, from Royal Porcelain works to pedestrian precinct. There is a racecourse, and a semi-professional theatre where I once saw a rollicking performance of *The Canterbury Tales*, by Neville Coghill out of Geoffrey Chaucer. In the porcelain works you discover that bone china really is made of bone and that these long-established English porcelain factories were experimenting and risking huge amounts of capital at precisely the same time as the big European factories in Meissen and Sèvres. For my money the most memorable exhibit of all was the Blind Earl pattern of embossed wild roses on a pale background: the Earl of Coventry had been blinded in a hunting accident and wanted a braille-like pattern he could feel and enjoy. If you can see as well as touch this is doubly impressive.

I first saw Upton upon Severn a few hours after the severest storms in living memory

The Talbot Head pub, Upton upon Severn, Worcestershire. The town pays a price for being so close to the river, for it is prone to flooding in this low-lying corner of green England.

had finally subsided. Fields that in their summer finery are like bowling greens were half water, half mud, and the willows growing along the river banks looked like drowned rats. The little town is, if not dangerously, then certainly uncomfortably close to the river. It has, however, many compensations. Among its many advantages, Upton enjoys the sight of the Malvern Hills rising to the west. Not too dauntingly, but just enough to give perspective at the end of one or two of the town's half-dozen streets, most of them made up of outstandingly neat and pretty black-and-white half-timbered cottages and pubs. There is a sprinkling of antique shops, an ironmongers, a couple of junk shops, an off-licence, a red-brick Midland Bank on the corner opposite the Talbot Hotel (which has some superb stained-glass windows), and several enticing little lanes snaking away off the High Street. Every other person seems to be walking around with a fishing rod or a Chinese meal from the curiously named Wing Yuk takeaway.

Tewkesbury's abbey, which people often take to be a cathedral, was built of stone from near Guiting, in the Cotswolds. It is the second abbey to have been built on the site, replacing one in which a West Saxon king called Brictric was buried in the year 800. The 'new' church was consecrated in 1120. It is handsome enough from the outside and, being just far enough away from the bustling main street of Tewkesbury, exudes an air of peace and tranquility. But it is when you are inside that you appreciate it most, especially for something which always feels good to me: the characteristic Norman circular pillars about six feet in diameter and over thirty feet high, reminiscent of the nave of Gloucester cathedral. 'Feels' good? Yes, literally: you are tempted to embrace them, or at least surreptitiously feel the texture of the stone. The fan vaulting which crowns these lofty pillars is said, incidentally, to have been originally inspired by a forest roof, and the feeling of being in a forest glade is enhanced by the 'light at the end of a tunnel' mood the pillars create, that is underlined by spectacular stained glass at both the west end of the nave and, more elaborately still, the many-windowed sanctuary. After Henry VIII's dissolution of the monasteries, he was offered and accepted the sum of £453 for the buildings, and therefore Tewkesbury kept for posterity one of the least-known and best churches in the heart of England. You can climb the steps of the tower, more than two hundred of them, for an educational bird's eye view of the layout of Tewkesbury and its surrounding hills.

Herefordshire is – or was – the England of people's expectations. Life does move at a different pace, though you might not think so if you find yourself on a fruit farm at the height of the season, or waiting to be served in a roadside vegetable mart. Herefordshire is one of those counties that is going nowhere very fast. It likes to think of itself as the centre of England, but will settle for being the heart of England. The county town, or city in this case, is Hereford which is, unlike some, conveniently in the middle of the old county, thus making a handy central point for that breed of visitor intent on fanning out madly in all directions. As with several neighbouring counties, Herefordshire seems to have amassed a private collection of intriguing village names. Even if they are not, you feel they should be worth a detour. Amongst them are Stretton Sugwas, Ocle Pychard, Hope-under-Dinmore.

Hereford cathedral is one of a group of great churches known as the Old Foundation because their origins were rooted in the pre-monastic age. Some visitors with a specialist eye come to visit the library, in which part of a collection of priceless books is secured by metal chains. There are very few of these chain libraries remaining: another, which I have seen and admired, is in Maldon, in Essex. If you cannot make it to the Three Choirs Festival, held here every third year – on the other two occasions taking place at Gloucester and Worcester – a good substitute might be the afternoon short evensong service: it is famous for its subtle, unself-conscious beauty.

One advantage of the frustration that assails people who try to see Hereford from their car is that they simply have to park and walk – especially on market day, when they might actually see farmers' wives selling home-made produce, including butter at the Butter Market that has stood here for hundreds of years. The Cattle Market is a different proposition from the once-a-week affair of most so-called market towns, and is very big business indeed. It operates most days in the middle of the week: this really is the place to get your Hereford cows or even one of those bulls that fetch thousands of pounds after sweeping the board at the Smithfield Show. The only sign of life in the market place one Sunday afternoon, however, apart from the flashing lights beside the zebra crossing, was the thin red-and-black line of Salvation Army men and girls arriving with their tubas and tambourines for the open-air evening service of hymns, mainly modern.

The biggest milk-producing farm in Europe is in this county, but a comparatively high proportion of the farms of Herefordshire are small, virtually one-man bands, and these help to give that intimate, nice, old-fashioned patchwork look to the landscape that is the despair of economic planners in Brussels high-rise offices. One low-key quality about the county is the handful of little-known stately homes. Among my favourites are Eastnor Castle, near Ledbury, Lower Brockhampton at Bromyard, and Berrington Hall, Leominster. Much of the best of the county hides its light under a bushel, so whereas Yorkshire makes no small song and dance (with some reason) about its fabulous railway museum in York itself, Hereford has quite an impressive railway museum where they do, actually, on high days and holidays, get up steam.

If you have time to see only one of the outlying villages, make that Weobley, whose name is spelt Wibelai in the Domesday Book. Charles I spent the night here after his defeat at the Battle of Naseby. Another claim to fame is that, around 1800, there were said to have been fifty practising witches. Weobley is as black-and-white as a handful of liquorice allsorts. The island in the middle of the wide main street, where any common- or garden-village would have a village green, is actually a rose garden, originally the market square. Although the half-timbered houses – a bit of a bay window here, an elaborate doorway there – are mainly just two storeys, there is a rare enclosed and comfortable feeling about the place.

Nor is it as twee as you might expect. It has not yet become a tourist honeypot. The Red Lion Hotel dates back to the fourteenth century, and the parish church of St Peter and St Paul had its finishing touches added at about the same time, although some of it is Norman. There's a statue here to Colonel Birch, one of Oliver Cromwell's officers who had the temerity to take him on and question some of his decisions. He is said to have been imprisoned twenty-one times for his trouble.

If I would single Weobley out as a special case for treatment as a village, Ledbury wins by a short head from Bromyard and Pembridge as the town to see. John Masefield was born here in 1878, and described the town as 'pleasant to the sight, fair and half-timbered houses black and white'. It is a metropolitan version of Weobley, and its handsome wide main street, which you half expect to echo with the clatter of coach and horses, and its narrow 'back-doubles', would do for a film set. The best of these is Church Lane, where three- and four-hundred-year-old black-and-white half-timbered houses frame a view of the 203-feet-high parish church spire. I especially like Ledbury because it is not pretty-pretty, because you can park your car and potter around the

No colour bar in Ship Street, Oxford.

The Roman Bath, Bath, Avon. Sympathetically reconstructed and
containing many original details, it was the most luxurious of its kind in the
Roman Empire.

Cheddar Gorge. Among the caves here, in which prehistoric tribes lived, evidence of cannibalism has been found.

Glastonbury Tor, Somerset, is claimed to be the place where Joseph of
Arimathea buried the chalice used in the Last Supper. The simple church
he built here is said to have received the first Christian converts in Britain.
The building at the top of the hill is a fourteenth-century church tower.

Nunney Castle, Somerset, was built in 1373. Outwardly it is a fort, but inside it used to have many of the essentials of a country home.

No sails in the sunset: the Helford River, Cornwall, from near Mawnan.

Cranborne Chase is a chalk downland that, no respecter of county boundaries, sprawls across part of Dorset, Wiltshire and Hampshire. For centuries it was preserved as a royal hunting ground and was protected from development.

Berwick St John, Wiltshire, and local beer.

shops on a Saturday afternoon in as matter of fact a way as if this were Guildford or Dagenham, while drinking in the atmosphere of one of England's most ancient towns.

Parts of Herefordshire are actually very exposed to wind and weather, but in a sheltered valley, the sight of the Malvern Hills on one side and Wales's Black Mountains on the other make it seem enclosed and secure. Sometimes you can catch a cone of sunlight on top of one of those rounded hills looking like a monk's tonsure. And those black-and-white timber cottages that you can't take all that seriously have a fairy-tale look about them.

Just a few minutes' drive south-west of Weobley is Hay-on-Wye. The Welsh Border actually runs through the town. The geography, however, is incidental. To call this a bookish town is to put it mildly. There are not just more bookshops here than in any other town in the country, but *ten* times more. Not only is this a border town, but it is the meeting point of three counties. About twenty miles from Hereford itself, Hay-on-Wye is very pin-pointable on anybody's map. You might just come to see the Elizabethan Hay Castle, built into the ruins of its Norman precursor, but the bet is that even though the man behind it all never advertises Hay as nirvana for browsers and antiquarians alike, they would come in their thousands anyway.

The only thing that tends not to be a bargain, not just here but in any bookshop, are old volumes about the immediate surrounding area. You are more likely to pick up bargains about the Welsh borders on the outskirts of Birmingham or Newcastle than any of the places you can see from the Long Mynd or Symond's Yat, a massive green and wooded escarpment overlooking the River Wye.

I suspect that only a handful of those people who visit Upton upon Severn carry straight on through the western end of the village and out towards the Vale of Evesham. But if it were not for the proximity of the so-chic Cotswolds to the south and east, this low-lying, unspectacular rural hideaway would probably be a tourist magnet in its own right. I remember a day spent meandering through the Vale of Evesham for, among other things, the names of its villages. There was Cow Honeybourne, Upton Snodbury, White Ladies Aston, Flyford Flavell, Norton-juxta-Kempsey. There was Wyre Piddle, Wyre Lock, Bretforton, Cleeve Prior and Wickhamford. And there are the towns of Pershore and Tewkesbury, which are prettier than they sound. I noticed incidentally how some local people added an extra gloss and an extra syllable to Evesham itself: it becomes Eva-sham.

It is said that the monks of Evesham Abbey were responsible for the early fame of the Vale of Evesham as a fruit-growing area. When the Domesday book was compiled, there were no fewer than thirty-eight vineyards. Labourers were ten a penny then, but nowadays this is 'pick your own' country (road signs say PYO), where Victoria plums are known to guide-book writers as Pershore eggs: the best of them really are egg-shaped and approximately the size of Grade 1's. Apples and other soft fruit are available, especially in the autumn, at below high-street prices. Even asparagus will usually be a few pennies cheaper from roadside shops than in metropolitan green-grocers, especially early in the season.

If you are there in the autumn and get off the main roads in order to admire the lush orchards close to, you might get close enough to the real thing to smell the creosote painted on to dismembered boughs. Apples can be so plentiful that if only they could be stored a bit longer you would want to fill your car with them for just a few pennies a pound. My own long-standing weakness is for plums, so my autumn journeys through Worcestershire are interrupted by the search for the perfect Victoria. There is nothing twee about these fruit stores, none of the slight embarrassment you get as you tinkle a bell outside somebody's porch or ponder over a box of rhubarb by some rustic wicker gate. It is matter of fact stuff: a man in a grey flannel suit gets out of his new Rover and buys a stone of Worcester Pearmains and a pannet of Victorias, a transit vanload of Boy Scouts swarms over jars of local honey and pears, pressing the flesh and jostling damsons in distress.

Whereas most of Worcestershire is still highly rural, the best of Warwickshire has long been on the tourist beat, and takes itself fairly seriously. Warwick itself is what expatriates might still expect a county town to look like. It also has the advantage (from the point of view of tour guides stuck for something to say) of being as close as makes no difference to the centre of England. It has a castle that offers everything that coach operators and historians could ever want, and a good handful of half-timbered medieval buildings besides. There is a racecourse where viewing from a somewhat antiquated grandstand is exceptionally good, a clutch of antique shops, several elegant Georgian buildings and easy access not just to Stratford-upon-Avon but to the much underrated town of Leamington Spa, faded but still elegant. Warwick Castle is one of the finest inhabited castles in Europe, all turrets and battlements, round towers and square towers, dungeons and places where you can pour boiling oil on to troubled coach drivers. The castle was begun by William the Conqueror in 1068 as part of a string of fortresses planned during a long march north to remind the local population that resistance was to no avail.

Rural Warwickshire has more than its fair share of stately homes and castles. There are the Marquess of Hertford's family home at Ragley Hall; Packwood House, with its ancient sculptured yews; Arbury Hall, a Gothic mansion set in an estate on which George Eliot, the novelist, was born; and Kenilworth Castle, which at one time was a much more impressive structure than Warwick Castle. One writer has said of Kenilworth 'the face of history is scarred now, but its bone structure is as sound as ever'. At least it is on a main road: I came across Farnborough Hall, which is not, quite by chance one day when I was actually looking for a municipally owned Country Park. The Hall is set in sleepy parkland and, while not in the major league of stately homes, is safely in the hands of the National Trust, and contains exquisite tapestries, porcelain and paintings.

In 1932, when Stratford-upon-Avon's 'new' Shakespeare Memorial Theatre was completed, replacing the original which was burnt down in 1926, it was immediately nicknamed The Jam Factory. It enjoys a twelve-month season, and its average audience is 95% of capacity, easy enough to credit as you stroll along the banks of the Avon in May half an hour before the performance begins, but doubly impressive when you turn up on a freezing January night and find that instead of being able to breeze in without a ticket, you have to stand ignominiously in the queue for 'returns'. Incidentally, remembering the 'upon' in the town's name may be deemed locally to be more important than having read Shakespeare, or even agreeing that all the plays were written by just one man. The story goes that a Stratford postman, on seeing letters marked 'Stratford on Avon', returned these to the sender with the scribbled message 'place unknown'. Whether they pick up such nuances or not, however, Americans can, with some justification, regard the Shakespeare Theatre as partly their own. When the grandson of the Warwickshire brewer, the Falstaffian Charles Flower, who built the first theatre, attempted to raise money for the replacement, he found little cash forthcoming from subscribers in England. Two million pounds, however, was raised in America. The theatre foyer is much smaller than many people expect of such an institution. The 1930s art deco is nice, and so is the way you are suddenly slap bang in the auditorium as the foyer door opens. There is very little of that familiar peering and wondering and watching your step as you descend towards your row. The auditorium is surprisingly intimate and warm, and the red seats are plush and comfortable. Just along the river a little way from the theatre is another building which had people hot under the collar, though in this case it was before it was actually completed, for this 250-room hotel, as sleek and luxurious as any metropolitan building, is very much in the low-rise idiom, and does not intrude.

There always used to be much fanciful elaboration of the Shakespearean myth ('How well we can imagine the young Shakespeare leaning over a bridge and watching his reflection in the waters of the Avon' – a difficult feat today when you have to keep an

Half close your eyes, and this amazing survivor of medieval Stratford owes absolutely nothing to the twentieth century. The Victorians favoured wooden cladding on old buildings, which helped preserve the original fabric.

eye out either for juggernauts or Japanese tourists wanting directions to Marks & Spencer). But I rather like the idea that Shakespeare was caught poaching deer in Charlecote Park, a few miles away from Stratford. It adds spice to a visit there, although it is a delight anyway. There are wide, bee-humming, flowery borders sheltered by high red-brick walls, terraces and gardens leading down to the River Avon that only just flows past and looks like smoked glass.

The Shakespeare Properties, as they are known in and around Stratford, are, I suppose, essential viewing. And the guides are excellent – probably as good as you will get anywhere. But I thought the family home of Mary Arden, Shakespeare's

Holy Trinity Church, Stratford-upon-Avon, Warwickshire. In any other town this beautifully proportioned church would be a tourist attraction in its own right. Here it is frequently overlooked, though it *does* contain Shakespeare's tomb.

mother – far enough from Stratford to be in the heart of the countryside – was the best of all. Perhaps because I was virtually alone there on a cold autumn day that probably had most visitors sitting round log fires in the lounges of their hotels. Being solitary here had a special piquancy, because when Mary Arden ran what was then a farm all the farmhands would have slept together in the house. Shakespeare would have brought Anne Hathaway here before their marriage to spend heavily chaperoned evenings together in the snug parlour. Older anyway than William, she was well past the usual age for getting married and was probably resigned to spinsterhood.

It was a Stratford-upon-Avon coach operator who quite recently came up with one of those 'why didn't I think of it myself' ideas. Having watched waves of tourists mooching aimlessly about the town after doing their duty by Shakespeare, peering into shop windows long after closing time and comparing the prices of the electrical goods unfavourably with home, he thought it would be a good idea to offer them evening tours of the Cotswolds. He is still counting his money.

Sleepy hollow at Naunton, Gloucestershire. Up on windy ridge the wind
blows colder than you think, and being tucked away is the name of the
game.

9. The Cotswolds, Oxford, and the limestone link: sermons in stone

Owlpen, Great Tew, and pretty things in-between;
Bibury; Burford; Bourton-on-the-Water and Broadway;
our all-time favourite and some shrinking violets;
Oxford as a Cotswold town

Choose one of those Cotswold villages that nestles in a valley and has largely been overlooked by the twentieth century. Pick a mid-week morning, when there are no sightseers around. Leave your car and clamber up the protective hillside and, instead of seeing the village at close quarters, look down on it. This is the way to imagine life as it was hundreds of years ago, especially if you can walk where there are no massive electricity pylons or yellow lines that snake two by two through the heart of a village, sometimes on both sides of a lane that is no more than about ten feet across, so that from certain angles the lines seem almost to touch. But more important than the yellow lines: who planted those three-hundred-year-old oak trees on the horizon? Who drew up plans for that manor house surrounded by flower-dotted meadows where sheep have grazed for about four hundred years? What would the beer once brewed in the Fox and Goose have tasted like, and how would it compare with the stuff that now comes from Devizes every Tuesday afternoon?

The only thing to be held against the Cotswolds is that there are no road signs which simply say 'Full Up' for use on Bank Holidays on all the main and side roads that lead into the region. I am an advocate of using public holidays for staying at home and catching up with the interior decorating. Never is that more applicable than here: cottages, churches, and even barns, may be irresistibly honey-coloured and twice as old as time, but they should be enjoyed if possible on quiet weekday mornings when everybody else is at work.

The Cotswold boundaries embrace much of Gloucestershire and Oxfordshire, but touch Avon, Worcestershire, and border on Wiltshire. To the north, parts of Northamptonshire have a Cotswoldish look about them, and since the oolitic limestone knows no administrative boundaries, if you do happen to be here at the same time as the world and his wife, you could do worse than the Cotswold fringe, say around Banbury, in Oxfordshire, and Sulgrave, in Northamptonshire. The Cotswolds defy administrative lines of demarcation but are distinctive and independent-minded, happy about tourists but also intent with getting on with the serious business of the day, which in many cases is a mixture of arable and sheep farming. The Cotswold hills are generally just a few hundred feet high, though they may seem more, even when they are just bumps on the horizon. The highest point, at 1,134 feet, is Cleeve Hill, just a few miles north-east of Cheltenham. In a way, it is downhill from then on, though not scenically.

The Cotswolds were not always regarded as especially pretty, though William Cobbett once referred to the criss-cross, drystone wall demarcation of fields as uglier than anything he had seen before. In spite of that view it is the way that limestone buildings, generally unadulterated by brick or timber, seem to spring from the landscape that appeals to town dwellers used to a heterogeneous mass of all kinds of buildings of different shapes, sizes and styles. Hardly any Cotswold villages were planned. They just happened. But it is the stone and especially the way the stone allows lichens to grow on it that appeals.

Owlpen, Gloucestershire. On the very western edge of the Cotswolds, this hamlet of golden-stone cottages, bobbing around a fine mansion like tugs around a great liner, is secret and self-contained.

People talk about Cotswold stone, but it is basically no different from the limestone you find elsewhere, as far apart even as Dorset and Yorkshire. It is not very durable, though that can be charming in itself: the crumbly, old-cheese look gets people reaching for their cameras. The secret is that the ease with which Cotswold stone is worked has made it possible for the most humble buildings to be made of basically the same material as the grandest 'wool' churches built by medieval tradesmen and farmers, who made so much profit out of the sheep – which were even more visible hundreds of years ago than today – that they wanted to secure as comfortable a place in heaven for themselves as they had on earth. So barns, pigsties, bus shelters and scout huts look homogeneous and good, and they too seem to belong to the scene rather than superimposed on it. The grander buildings came first, of course, but as the great prosperity of the region began to affect everybody down to the humblest farmworker, all that accessible and good quality stone became part of common use. Though it varies from silvery grey to the dark, almost orange ironstone of the Northamptonshire border, the best Cotswold stone has a luminous quality which seems to retain the sun, as if it has mopped up its warmth during the last days of summer, and stored it to sustain local people and visitors alike through the winter months.

The Cotswolds are extensive enough to embrace all sorts of geographical variations. It is not just the colour of the stone that varies, but the type of farming, the soil and the lie of the land, and, not least of all, the extent to which the place is geared up to and used to tourists. Only a handful of the people, for example, who make it to Bourton-on-the-Water, a village that has become commercialised, ever see the furthermost extremes, such as Uley in the south-west, near Cirencester (which is not, incidentally, really known any more as 'Sisester'). Uley is the heart of *Cider with Rosie* country, what Laurie Lee referred to as 'a mystery land of difficult hills and deeply wooded valleys'. At the nearby hamlet of Owlpen is a superb manor house surrounded by its own hamlet of cottages, a mill, a seventeenth-century court house next to the parish church, where the lords of the manor of Owlpen held their Court Leet, a kind of petty sessions. This is a classic hideaway, archetypal honeymoon country, mellow and golden against the protective greenery of the surrounding hills on a late summer afternoon, or comfortable, warm and secure inside one of the cottages on a winter evening.

There is no traffic to speak of on the back lanes which lead from the nearby village of Uley to Owlpen, and no aeroplanes. The Tudor house that slumbers among tall trees next to that pretty and ancient church is like an ocean-going liner around which lesser craft cluster. Owlpen is much more hilly and, being half cloaked with protective trees, more secret than, say, Bibury, apart from the fact that Bibury is usually swarming with camera-toting tourists.

Bibury's one-time weavers' cottages, called Arlington Row, that form a backdrop to a grassy meadow, and have the River Coln sparkling past, are enhanced by a church famous for its elaborately carved headstones. Although it may never be coupled with the great churches of Chipping Campden, Cirencester and Northleach, it is a good enough example of how much money there was available four or five hundred years ago after the ordinary business of living had been dealt with. And there is Arlington Mill, a museum of local crafts as well as a carefully preserved monument to the business of corn milling and cloth manufacture. The River Coln that powered the mill is, incidentally, a Thames tributary.

Bibury, Gloucestershire, is well on the tourist beat. Play truant if you can and see it when everybody else is back at work – mid-week in winter is a good time.

A rare exception to the unplanned character of most Cotswold villages is Great Tew, which is not to be missed if you are travelling north or north-west of Oxford, or wanting, say, an extra diversion during a visit to Blenheim Palace. There is a reason it looks the way it does, why its yellow- or brown-stone cottages, thatched roofs (several of them badly in need of replacement) and gardens are all so much of a piece. The heavily wooded village was reshaped, prettied up and its boundaries redrawn by the estate manager of landowner General Stratton. It was either that or move it wholesale to a new site that would not offend the squire's eyes. The physical decline of the village, which was a matter of scandal in the early 1970s (the cottagers not being masters of their own destiny), has been halted, but it is interesting to see the place – not just for its own sake but as an example of how villages can go into decline unless they are treated with kid gloves. Great Tew is a slice of English history preserved in aspic, and it is easy to see how quickly the weeds and the wilderness, the foxes, rabbits, and badgers, would colonise such a place as this.

Years of acquaintance with the Cotswolds have made me able, not exactly to find my way around the area blindfold – though they do say it is possible with your eyes shut to tell all sorts of things about where a stone wall or the side of a house has been quarried, and by whom, and when – but certainly to manage without a road map. There was, however, one nagging detail that I was never quite able to fathom. I suspected that the mushroom-shaped stones now used for decoration outside many Cotswold village houses – I noticed several around Blockley, and a few near Bibury – were originally functional and not decorative, but I could not work out how. I heard the answer in a village pub – the best source of local knowledge. Called staddlestones, apparently they were used by farmers as cornerstones for haystacks, to allow ventilation and to keep rats away.

Incidentally, if nothing else tempts people meandering around the Cotswolds up into the hills where the wind blows cold, and reminds them that these are exposed and often icy hills, it should be the Cotswold Farm Park at Bemborough, above the village of Guiting Power. Joe Henson, son of Leslie Henson the music hall star, took over Bemborough Farm in 1962 and, on land owned by Corpus Christi College, Oxford, helped create a 'rare breeds' park that is now part of the Rare Breeds Survival Trust. The Cotswold Farm Park, as it is called, attracts more than 100,000 visitors every year. The sheep, horses, goats, poultry and cattle, seen distantly from the road that passes the Park's entrance, were once common sights in the Cotswolds, and elsewhere in England.

A generalisation: Cotswold village names are blunt and prosaic: Snowshill, Stanton, Cold Aston, Northleach, Chedworth, Chipping Norton – a short sharp shock for people weaned in the mellifluous Vale of Evesham or rural Dorset. But you could stick a pin in a Cotswold map and find that virtually any village is worth a roll of camera film.

If you visit Blenheim Palace, it makes an appropriate detour if you also visit both the Barringtons, Great and Little. Although well away from the essential tourists' Cotswolds, they are built of the same stone as the great Palace, created for the Duke of Marlborough in recognition of his defeat of the French armies at the beginning of the eighteenth century. Also off the tourist beat (except when people are looking for bizarre, even eerie, Snowshill Manor), the village of Snowshill, near Broadway, contains many exceptional architectural details, gables of different sizes, that nice combination of a drystone wall set into a grassy bank, good small stone tiles, all set off nicely against the wooded, sheep-dotted green hill behind. Stanton, a little to the west, is even more of a rarity. Close to the wooded lip of the Cotswold escarpment, surrounded by some of the lushest greenery in England, Stanton's mellow stonework feels more like a natural crop of rock than something created by man. The principal house in the village was built by Elizabeth I's chamberlain. This cosy corner of the Cotswolds, incidentally, is very well endowed with public footpaths, including the Cotswold Way, a hundred-mile route that follows the limestone escarpment. This is the England that makes expatriates wistful and full of nostalgia. It should be bottled and shipped to the Australian outback and the South African veldt.

'Broddy', as Broadway is known locally, has been shaped and its way of life altered by the main road that slices right through it. It is tempting to imagine what Broadway would have been like if it had been hidden away over the top of some looming hill, protected by screens of deciduous trees, and accessible only by a narrow lane undiscovered by jumbo Euro-lorries.

Assuming you do not travel by juggernaut, the Cotswolds lend themselves to a circular itinerary that can be picked up at any point and left just as easily. Most drivers will begin their exploration at one of the towns on the Cotswold fringe, and this trip happens to start at Oxford, taking one along the fast and functional A40 dual carriageway to Burford. It would be a pity not to stop here, even if just for a drink in one of the pubs on either side of the exquisite wide main street that runs downhill at right angles to the A40. These pubs were coaching houses at a time when Burford was an important stopping point just two days' coach ride from London. It was very prosperous as a wool-producing community in the fifteenth and sixteenth centuries. Now tourists flock here in their thousands: the town enjoys a different kind of prosperity, and has never looked back.

A little off-beat, to the west of Burford, are the Barringtons, Great and Little. Little is better: an unusual village whose cottages, mainly terraced, are ranged around a great, largely overgrown patch of rough ground that was originally a limestone quarry. So you could say lots of Cotswold villages were virtually born here. Partly on account of the wild flowers that thrive on limestone, in summer the centre of the village is alive with butterflies and birds.

Next make your way from Little Barrington, back towards the A40, and take that road for a few miles as if towards Cheltenham, turn off at the sign for Compton Abdale and Withington. You plunge at once into a sea of greenery, wooded and fertile, down a sharp incline beyond which flatter (that is, comparatively flatter) country opens out in front of you. Withington is not quite on the tourist beat. It is surprisingly large and straggling, with several fine-looking houses close to the road. The ancient-looking Mill Inn, incidentally, is not ancient at all but was built in the 1960s from old Cotswold stone, some of which had previously been Northleach prison before it became a museum. From Withington it is worth a detour to Chedworth Roman Villa, whose mosaic floor is famous, and which was discovered by chance early this century by a farmer's dog that had gone after a ferret. The tranquil setting of Chedworth, protected by banks of trees and what is now lush rolling farmland with plentiful supplies of fresh water, is a reminder that life for the Romans, especially well on into their occupation, was not necessarily harsh and uncomfortable – and Chedworth villa must have been a desirable residence by any modern standards.

Return to the A40, but instead of continuing for Cheltenham, take the unclassified road north of Andoversford for Winchcombe via Brockhampton and Charlton Abbots. On the outskirts of this underrated little Cotswold town, not as bijou as, say, Broadway (that 'painted lady of the Cotswolds'), stands Sudeley Castle, open most of the summer months to the public. Once the home of Catherine Parr, Henry VIII's last queen, it was substantially remodelled in the mid-nineteenth century, but has lost none of its romance. Between Winchcombe and Broadway, you pass (just a couple of miles off the road) Hailes Abbey, where there is also a small limestone quarry, and, in the tiny church, some exceptional Saxon wall paintings. Also just off the main road, the village of Stanton, a rare gem even by Cotswolds standards, is on the way to nowhere. It has managed to preserve a village street that in almost every single respect, except perhaps for a Rolls-Royce or a tandem leaning up against the walls of the pub, has scarcely changed in three hundred years. North of here lie Broadway and Chipping Campden. They can't be ignored, but ignore them if you can on Bank Holiday afternoons. Not that Broadway is the least bit embarrassed about its pulling power for tourists. Indeed, it is quite hard to imagine real people living in Broadway at all; most of the shopkeepers are unofficial purveyors of hard tourist information and the receptionist at the Lygon Arms is probably inured now to people popping in just for a peep at this famous hotel, with no intention of having a meal, let alone staying.

Take the road through Broadway, which is, in fairness, a fine example of a linear development of many periods, but all of a piece and hardly spoilt. Up Fish Hill, you pass the golf course on your left, and hope for clear weather: the views over the Vale of Evesham can be quite remarkable.

From Broadway, follow signs for Chipping Campden. There has been a market here since 1180, and the prefix probably derives from the Saxon word for market. The covered market-place here has probably figured in more calendar photographs than anywhere else in the Cotswolds. It was built by Baptist Hicks a few years after Shakespeare's death. The parish church, one of the three or four of the best in the Cotswolds, which is saying something, was built by the grandfather of one of Shakespeare's most important patrons. Called William Greville, he made a fortune ten times over during the height of the wool industry and was known as 'the flower of the wool merchants of all England'. Chipping Campden has several good small hotels, pubs, little restaurants, and I always suspect most of the people taking photographs of the market-place or pottering about on the well-worn stones (talk about those feet in ancient times) have just emerged from one of the local hostelries or tea rooms. From Chipping Campden follow signs for Blockley.

At Blockley, Victorian workmen's cottages are juxtaposed higgledy-piggledy with much earlier dwellings. The village straggles, going nowhere in particular, and mainly two-storeyed cottages overhang the narrow village street in a way reminiscent of York's tightly knit Shambles, albeit with very much of the rural flavour. The brook that flows with some force through Blockley, by the way, was the reason several water-powered mills prospered here in the eighteenth and nineteenth centuries. From Blockley, follow signs for Batsford where, in spring or autumn, the Batsford Arboretum is open to the public. It contains about a thousand trees, including a 'handkerchief tree' (of which there are thought to be just three or four in the country), and a direct descendant of the mulberry tree believed to have grown in Shakespeare's garden in Stratford-upon-Avon (there is another with the same pedigree in John Milton's garden in Buckinghamshire). Batsford, which dates mainly from Victorian times, provides a different angle on Cotswold life and is a respite from the medieval and Elizabethan villages that are dotted around this landscape like pepper out of a pot. Moreton-in-Marsh, just a few miles east of Blockley, suffers a little from being on the A429 Warwick to Chippenham road, and

Chipping Campden, Gloucestershire, gets more than its quota of tourists, but is a community in its own right. It lies close to the northern edge of the Cotswolds that, some will say, is less 'pretty-pretty' than the south or the centre of the region.

there is a railway station too, a rare occurrence in the Cotswolds, yet its very wide main street, its several hotels, and its (not particularly cheap) antique shops, which at least deserve a browse, make it worth a stop.

From Moreton-in-Marsh, go due south to Stow-on-the-Wold, and then Bourton-on-the-Water. They are contrasting, though both well and truly on the classic Cotswold tourist itinerary. Stow-on-the-Wold would probably carry on much as it is whether or not people came to admire it. Whichever direction you approach it from it is attractive, which is not something to be said even of most tourist towns. There are real shops, not just boutiques catering for visitors, for this is a genuine market town. It is 1,000 feet above sea level. 'Stow on the Wold where the wind blows cold' they say about it, though it must be pointed out that people say that Bisley, near Stroud, is windier still. (It used to be known as 'Bisley, God Help Us'.) There are several hotels and pubs with accommodation, and if you have time on your hands, Stow would make a good central point from which to explore the Cotswolds. In the seventeenth century, the great market-place was used by local farmers to buy and sell sheep: the square is said to have been able to accommodate up to 20,000 of them. The last battle of the Civil War, incidentally, was fought here in 1646. The Royalists lost, and 1,500 of them were incarcerated in the parish church.

En route for Bourton-on-the-Water, you follow signs for The Slaughters, just a couple of hundred yards and about a mile off the main road respectively. Lower Slaughter is one of those sleepy Cotswold villages beside a babbling brook where

'Which way up does it go?' Winter scene at Broughton Castle, Oxfordshire.

weekend painters are apt to sit and grimace at the curious faces of the tourists. There is a manor-house kind of hotel, terraced stone cottages, and nothing as crude as a village shop. Upper Slaughter is slightly more real, but seen by fewer people. I have walked from Lower Slaughter in a fit of righteousness when it seemed indecent to take my car up all the narrow lanes and to disturb the rural peace, in which the only memorable noise came from a distant wood pigeon, and on a summer afternoon it is an ideal way to get close to the Cotswold scenery without straining yourself too hard. Not that there is much to Upper Slaughter, apart from another hotel, a few gingerbread cottages, and a manor house set in twenty tranquil green acres.

To get to Bourton-on-the-Water, return to the main road and drive for just a few minutes due south. Bourton is not quite the Disneyland of the Cotswolds, but is decidedly the place to take fractious children who may wonder what there is that's so special about all those predictable stone and thatch villages. There is a model village, in stone, at the New Inn (which is, of course, nothing like new). And yes, there is a model of the model, and a model of the model of the model. There's a motor museum, a bird garden, knick-knack shops and low bridges over the River Windrush, where people are at liberty to paddle, and green banks where they can have their picnics. There are ducks to feed, model trains to admire, several restaurants, picture galleries to buy souvenirs in, and generally to have a good time as long as you do not imagine this is what the Cotswolds is really all about.

From Bourton, make your way across country towards Chipping Norton, geographically only just a Cotswold town, but handsome all the same. From here, via the B4026 through green, flattish parkland dotted with pheasants, to Charlbury, which is just within London commuter distance, and then, perhaps, Woodstock and the Duke of Marlborough's Blenheim Palace and then Oxford. On a journey like this the detours are best, and those are often taken at random or by stabbing at the map with a thumb.

I have always thought of Oxford as belonging to the Cotswolds rather than the Home Counties. It is a spectacular eastern gateway to rural Oxfordshire and Gloucestershire. Unfortunately, though, it is somewhat weighed down by clichés. Those dreaming spires were never very dreamy except during a summer heat haze or when you had had too many glasses of cheap sherry with the Dean. Or both. Open-topped sports cars in The High were generally something of a liability (apart from the fact that it was illegal for undergraduates to own them) and garden parties were, in retrospect, all too frequently rained on. For most visitors Oxford is inevitably more a matter of wondering where to park or, for the really enterprising, a matter of which end of the boat you are supposed to punt from.

The city may be nearly as famous for its cars as its scholarship, but see it without the traffic if you can. For me it is a Sunday morning city: tramps (they seem to come out of the stonework) accost you outside Christ Church or All Souls, but always very politely, quite plummily spoken. Who are they? Redundant dons? Research students fallen on hard times? One of them engaged me in a comparatively erudite conversation to the background of pealing Sunday morning bells, though it quite spoilt the effect when, having touched me for 20p, he failed to recognise me twenty minutes later and asked me again ('You know, I don't usually do this sort of thing').

It is also not at all bad after dark. Then, the twentieth century fades into insignificance. Converted gas lamps that at first and second sight are the real thing cast unearthly shadows along little-frequented passageways between college buildings: a favourite is the one that cuts at right angles from The High past the high wall of All Souls and the Bodleian towards Hertford College and The Broad. I once joined a two-hour walking tour of the city, among complete strangers. But it turned out, because everybody got on well, to be a three-hour walking tour, and dusk had fallen by the time we had finished. Our guide knew what he was doing, because we hardly saw a single car during the whole late afternoon and early evening. Our romantic illusions were not shattered.

Dining Hall, Magdalen College, Oxford. Pronounce it 'Maudlin', and note that Cambridge's Magdalene College has a slight difference in spelling.

The city has looked back unashamedly at all stages of its creation towards its medieval origins, particularly when the Victorians got going (not just with new colleges and old college extensions but even when they were building substantial red-brick villas on the city outskirts to house the families of university lecturers and administrators). The city is not ashamed of its red brick the way some places are, perhaps because it has so much confidence in its Cotswold stone. Most colleges, being built of limestone, are the colour of honey mixed with honeysuckle. And when it rains they take on the colour of old mustard.

The reason, of course, most people respond so rapidly to the cheek-by-jowl buildings is that the best of them have hardly changed for two or three hundred years. The Oxford that Dr Johnson knew when he was up at Pembroke College in the 1720s still exists, though you may need to suspend your disbelief a little if you happen to hit the city centre during a Friday rush hour: in which case keep to the back lanes. Not that Johnson was at all nostalgic about the place. He was so poor as a student – at one point his toes actually showed through his best pair of shoes – that he lived on a prison diet in the confines of his own room and remained in college even during the holidays, when everyone else had gone home, simply because he could not afford the stagecoach fare back home to Staffordshire. In December 1729 he gave up the ghost and left, never to complete his formal studies.

The best English cities enclose you comfortably and are good to look at at the same time – of course Oxford qualifies. The railway station is nothing for language school students to write home about, and it can do nothing to uplift the spirits of newly arrived undergraduates, hatless and hapless, some of them seeing Oxford for only the second time. Nor does the one-way system endear motorists to the place. It is all less of a piece than Cambridge but, at both town and gown level, more broadminded and more prosperous. You suspect that students and lecturers spend the occasional weekend in some leafy Cotswold hamlet at a house party. It is also more down to earth for, even when the motor trade is up against it, skilled car assembly workers at Cowley earn as much as most dons.

Some of the shops, despite the chic new paperback emporia and the Chelsea-style boutiques are not just old but venerable with it – like Blackwell's, Oxbridge's most famous bookshop, in Broad Street: if you could distil it it would surely taste like vintage port. Nearby, incidentally, Archbishop Cranmer was burnt at the stake in 1556, spice being added to the spectacle by the fact that he had recanted in vain, reputedly begging for mercy the whole hideous night through before being dragged to his unimaginable death.

At Blackwell's I bought a paperback copy of Jan Morris's *Oxford*, but inadvertently left it, still wrapped in its paper bag, in a greasy-spoon café in the city's famous covered market. When I went back, trudging irritably through shoppers and sightseers, it had disappeared without trace. I knew that if it had been snapped up in such unpromising circumstances it had to be good, and I bought another one. Despite this unhappy experience I am as likely to spend an hour in the covered market as to potter through Merton's sleepy quad or Magdalen's manicured gardens. For your nostrils are assailed by a not very delicate but nevertheless heady concoction of aromas: sawdust, fresh meat, seeds and cereals, potatoes from the greengrocer's stall, fish, peat from the flower stand and steam from the urn in the tea bar which seems to be full from opening till closing time. Butchers boys' delivery bikes are propped up against Victorian shop fronts and barrows with herring boxes stand, incongruously, next to a bright-red pillar box. The surprisingly elegant iron girders that support the roof are reminiscent of a small railway station – like London's Marylebone.

One thing that can take the edge off a visit to Oxford, however, is that the city is surprisingly short of really good hotels. Perhaps canny tourists or tour operators have discovered the trick: that is, hole up somewhere in the Cotswolds and just come into Oxford for the obligatory rubbernecking.

If the Stratford man who takes Americans around the Cotswolds wants to expand his horizons he might do well to introduce a limestone tour. Of all the building stone that gives England its postcard appeal, limestone is the prettiest. It makes for honey-coloured cottages, police stations that look much too bijou and 'cute' to be taken seriously, villages that are all-of-a-piece. Limestone and thatch make an unbeatable combination, and when I once came across a Northamptonshire baker's shop housed in a thatched cottage, I knew I had found its apotheosis: the dark, bird-nesting thatch was complemented by trays of home-made ginger cake and chocolate fancies, the pale and mid-yellow limestone by treacle tarts and lemon curd.

The limestone belt cuts diagonally across England, roughly from the Dorset coast up to where the fishermen of Staithes, North Yorkshire, put up a very good pretence of ignoring the twentieth century and carry on as they have for hundreds of years.

People talk fondly of Cotswold Stone, but there is really no such thing. It is basically the same stuff as you find in Yorkshire and Somerset and, if it is slightly less durable, especially true of Northamptonshire, this merely enhances its eye appeal. Here it tends to go all crumbly, and comparatively quickly – say in 150 years – gives a building that half-as-old-as-time appearance that is so attractive and goes so well with dark woodlands and bubbling streams snaking through man-made culverts, set off perhaps by little bridges that would not disgrace a Japanese garden.

Parts of Leicestershire are not only remarkable for the quality of the stone villages, but that part of it that used to be Rutland actually had two famous limestone quarries from which much that was admirable and photographic emanated. Here, in England's most famous fox hunting country, the picture postcard view of a hunt meet on some frosty autumn morning is not complete without a rambling old stone manor house that seems to spring from the countryside in which its stands rather than being imposed upon it. The only reason that Rutland, Leicestershire and Northamptonshire never became quite so prosperous and famous as wool-producing regions is simply that there was not the same dependable water supply. We take for granted those tumbling Cotswold rivers, criss-crossed by model village bridges that look more decorative than functional, but without the water there would be few of the great 'wool churches' that add so much to the Cotswold skyline, and fewer still of the great country houses and gardens for which the place is famous. Sheep were farmed, but the wool fulling in mills that needed a good water supply had to be done elsewhere.

Northamptonshire ironstone is every bit as varied as Cotswold limestone, which ranges from the golden yellow of Bath to the translucent, light-reflecting off-white of the southern Cotswolds, and is so dark in places that it even has a mauve or bluish tinge within its orange-brown. Not to be missed are those unsung glories of the East Midlands: Oundle, Stamford, Fotheringhay, Rockingham, Cottesmore, as well as the more regarded Rutland twins, Oakham and Uppingham. Collyweston is no picture book, but it is worth seeing, for it is the place where Collyweston tiles come from. There has been a quarry here for several hundred years, producing blocks of what is called fissile limestone, which when deliberately exposed to the elements split into surprisingly thin sections.

I stumbled across Hallaton, in Leicestershire, on a bright winter morning after staying overnight in Market Harborough. The contrast between the fine and subtle red brick of busy Market Harborough, once full of stagecoaches and now full of heavy lorries, and Hallaton's village houses grouped around its green, left me with a lasting impression of this remarkable village. The unusual conical 'market cross' that is itself solid and substantial and contains lots of skilful work, speaks volumes about the ready availability of good workable stone in the neighbourhood. Among the villages worth visiting are Ketton, where stone has been quarried for over four hundred years, and which contributed to the building of several Cambridge colleges, and Barnack, which produced a rougher limestone known as ragstone. It was quarried by the Romans and much used in medieval times in, for example, the cathedrals at Peterborough and Ely, but Barnack's stone was exhausted by the end of the eighteenth century. Not surprisingly, the village did well by the proximity of such good material, and is very handsome. Some Ketton stone has a pink look, though on ageing this weathers to a paler, greyer appearance. The stone here is generally tougher than Cotswold stone and lasts longer, even if it lacks that more malleable texture of Cotswold stone. Then there is Lyddington, an interesting village in its own right, with the Bede House now a museum. This used to belong to the Bishops of Lincoln until the seventeenth century, when it was converted into a hospital by Lord Burghley, who was now doing very well for himself at Burghley House on the outskirts of Stamford.

Lincolnshire is underrated in almost every respect, and may just as well be underrated for the quality, in places, of its limestone. But anybody who has driven from Grantham, where there is a remarkable tall spired parish church of limestone, and an ancient inn, the Angel and Royal, which is more Cotswold than Midlands in the way its exterior is pockmarked by old age, will quickly be convinced that even if you had to forsake Leicestershire, Northamptonshire, Oxfordshire, Gloucestershire and points south-west, there would be lots of evidence of the limestone tradition. Take Fulbeck, for example, which the unsuspecting driver comes across quite by surprise. It is a gem, and would do as a backdrop for a film portrait of some fox-hunting eighteenth-century country squire. The pub, the Hare and Hounds, draws people from Lincoln for a glass of local beer and a bowl of home-made soup during their lunch hour, and the big house, Fulbeck Hall, which dates from 1733 is, appropriately, reached from the road (though unfortunately it is not open to the public) by an avenue of lime trees. Better still, and much closer to Grantham, is Belton. Belton House, the family seat of the Brownlows, was offered for sale intact for somewhere in excess of six million pounds during the early 1980s and finally sold in 1983 to the National Trust. A grade I listed building, it is said to be the finest Restoration house surviving in England, yet it sits quite modestly behind the parish church in the estate village. Much of Belton was built during the mid-nineteenth century, and it has all the best characteristics of a limestone village –

good carving, nicely planned houses, a feeling that this is a living community, even though there is not a hair out of place. The whole thing is much enhanced by great trees, and even more by the fact that the main road lies a couple of hundred yards away: you have to take a small detour to get into Belton.

Just off the A607 Grantham to Lincoln road lies Ancaster, also set lower than the main road and, though almost all its rooftops are clearly visible from it, technically reached by a detour. Ancaster stone, quarried nearby since the time of the Romans, was used for several Lincolnshire churches, which is quite an accolade. Cream rather than yellow in colour, the stone is very closely textured and, while moderately workable, lasts eons. Fulbeck church and hall were made of Ancaster stone. From Fulbeck, high on the limestone ridge, there are good views of large stretches of this western side of the county.

Like one of those rivers in North Staffordshire that disappears into rock, and re-emerges some distance later as if nothing untoward had happened, the limestone belt is dormant on its north-easterly journey until the North York Moors rise up, though the Howardian hills and some stretches of the unregarded East Riding provide enough of a diversion to slow us down. Like the Cotswolds, the Yorkshire Moors used to be populated primarily with sheep, and communities were generally small: there are few substantial towns between, say, Thirsk and Bridlington (Malton is an exception). It is worth noting that Castle Howard, virtually a town in itself on account of the number of people employed and the space occupied by the house, is actually of sandstone and not limestone, though limestone was readily available.

There are good limestone houses on each side of the wide street at Coxwold, pleasantly set back from the road itself by steep green banks. The village has changed scarcely at all since the time the row of almshouses just downhill from the Fauconberg Arms were completed in 1662. Just a mile and a half from Coxwold, on the Ampleforth road, are the ruins of Byland Abbey, itself built of good oolite limestone. A good example in Rye Dale of sandstone as opposed to limestone carving is to be found in Rievaulx Abbey, well hidden (though Henry VIII found it and virtually destroyed it) in a green and wooded dip among the surrounding hills.

The Dales have charm enough, but I enjoy introducing people who think they know a bit about Yorkshire to the villages among the North York moors, particularly those to the north of the generally busy A170 road between Helmsley and Scarborough: that is, Hutton-le-Hole and Lastingham. Lastingham's church was re-endowed in 1078 on the site of a much older one. Many mainly detached stone cottages complement the handsome church, whose first version is thought to have been destroyed by the Vikings: the original foundation was created by St Ced in 654, and the new church has a crypt built over his burial place. The pub, over 250 years old, is a good example of a village inn built entirely of limestone. Hutton-le-Hole is much more of a tourist draw. It is one to avoid, however, during Bank Holidays.

Late summer on two-tone-brown Fylingdales moor: people go hang-gliding, and potter around the bizarre and sprawling village of Goathland. The limestone belt has a final fling before petering out close to Robin Hood's Bay. Goathland is architecturally very mixed, though it does contain some stone houses, and does not have just one village green, but several. The greens are like stray patches of heathland between the houses, sheep graze close to the little gardens fronting pantiled and worked stone houses, where 'roses round the door' and ivy up the side are set off prettily by white-painted windows. The fact that I was rash enough to buy a packet of toffees from the Post Office in the village and thus lost a filling that caused me much pain en route for Whitby, did not detract from my fondness for Goathland, a village unlike any I have come across in Yorkshire or anywhere else.

If you do ride on the Pickering to Grosmont railway, make Goathland the place where – for no extra charge – you break your journey, and walk up the lane from the station in the valley to enjoy a remarkable place. Happily, the unassuming late nineteenth-century parish church of St Mary is at the far end of the village, which makes sufficient justification for a walk right through it. As you approach the coast, and especially when you arrive, most cottages are of pale limestone under bright-red pantiles, washed in stormy weather by salt spray. The cliffs here are vulnerable to coastal erosion, and are said to recede by several inches a year.

Of course, there is more to England's backbone than limestone, so anyone with time on their hands should not neglect Cornwall's granite or West Yorkshire's gritstone or the slate of Cornwall and of Cumbria, with its subtle green tinge. Pennine stone, too, is another story, running from the Potteries of Staffordshire up to Northumberland: plenty of limestone, but less subtle in colour and harder, less easy to work and, although sharing that more conventional limestone look of being part of the scenery, not quite so attractive as the oolitic. The limestone you find in Derbyshire, near Buxton, for example, in ugly, massive quarries, around which great excavators trundle like mutant caterpillars, does not produce stone for building, but is excavated for chemical additives and the ingredients of animal foods or for making roads. The millstone grit of West Yorkshire, with all its connotations of grimy industry, causes some people to shudder. Personally, however, I like it. The colour of the stone, though not made any lighter by the effect of detritus from the factory chimneys, is natural.

Stone is often surprisingly localised: an odd village here, a church there, a country mansion among the trees, may be the only visible example of what an individual quarry has produced. The fact that West Yorkshire and County Durham will have been inclined to paint the natural stone is an indication of the low regard in which it is often held. Not so in Blanchland, on the border of Durham and Northumberland, which is built of brown gritstone, a planned village with stone tiles that, if it could be transplanted to the Cotswolds, would be one of the four or five most famous villages there.

The belt of limestone that cuts diagonally across England north-eastwards of the Cotswolds really has its beginnings on the Dorset coast, close to Durdle Door, that spectacular and unreal sculpture that looks as it if has been wrought by the hand of some eccentric but has actually been carved out of the rock by the sea and the weather. This southerly limestone is pale and silvery, a million miles from Staithes or Northumberland, but its parentage is the same.

10. The West Country:
Camelot and sandcastles

Cornwall, North and South, and Devon, North and South;
Cheddar Gorge, the Blackdown Hills and the Wiltshire
heartland; Bath and Bristol, and a winter journey

Devon really is full of local colour. Not just on account of its limestone cottages, or its rich dialect, or the old codgers with dewdrops at the end of their noses who sit in the inglenooks of cosy whitewash-and-thatch pubs, but literally, by virtue of its exceptionally rich red earth – redder here even than in Cumbria's Eden Valley – and the deep, almost Irish greenness of its pastures. Cottage gardens show up like the pictures on seed packets against those whitewashed houses, and if you pass a newly thatched roof, its colour will be flaxen, much brighter than the more resilient Norfolk reed. Add to all this a few of Devon's secret, swift flowing rivers reflecting a summer sky, and you know why such a lot of it appears on Beautiful Britain calendars.

Much of the county keeps itself to itself. There are large expanses of Exmoor and Dartmoor that are about as heavily frequented as Greenland, and both the north and south of the county are memorable for tightly packed coombes, and rivers that you know are tumbling somewhere below you but remain out of sight until you have meandered through the bracken to pin-point them exactly. It is partly this lie of the land that gives so many Devon villages their characteristic straggling quality. There are, of course, exceptions to the rule, but many villages are built attractively along the course of some stream, sometimes snaking away as if intending to disappear only over the horizon, but usually stopping short below a bank of trees or some steep wooded escarpment.

The county has the rare advantage of two distinct coasts, which are as different as chalk cliffs and cheese. North Devon is not simply a slightly more off-beat version of the better-known side of the county, but a different proposition altogether. The resorts are comparatively private and self-contained, and appeal to people not averse to a bit of rock climbing or to making an effort to get a good view from this or that headland. Several of them are more inaccessible than the southerly resorts, and this makes them seem more for the initiated than for the run-of-the-mill tourist.

It is at the north coast that the rivers which rise on Exmoor eventually reach the sea: the Lyn, the Barle, the Bray, all of which take it easy among the valleys before they gather momentum. And they really do gather momentum: the junction of rivers, for example, at Watersmeet and Lynmouth, is quite dramatic.

One reason people like Exmoor so much is that the villages make more inroads into the twenty-mile-wide wilderness than happens with Dartmoor. Simonsbath is small enough, but Exford is surprisingly substantial, with its village green, two or three hotels, a garage and quite a lot of activity winter and summer.

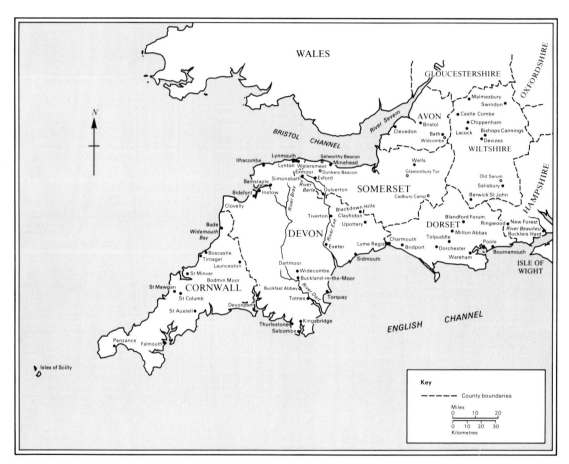

Map 6 West Country

Cornwall dislikes as much as Devon the way the two counties are so often lumped together as one. Cornwall-and-Devon: they go together like peaches and cream or, as Cornishmen or Devonians might say, peaches and gravy. Of course, each county considers itself superior to the other. Cornwall is, on the whole, leaner and tougher. It is more exposed, more windswept, despite the famous seaside resorts and the suntans, than its more easterly neighbour. Some of its place names have a surprisingly foreign sound – surprising until you remember that within living memory people in obscure pockets of the county spoke their own Cornish language, and even the saints' names attached to the parish churches have an alien ring: St Minver, St Mawgan, St Columb, St Austell. There is a Welshness about the old language, as well as about the conservatism of the people here. They share Celtic roots, and, Wales aside, they would probably have more in common with a fisherman from Brittany than a Durham coal miner.

Taken with the south, North Cornwall is 'separate but equal'. It has at least one beetling castle, and sea-wracked stone harbours, as well as yellow sands and surf, but it is certainly different, more exposed, more of 'an experience'. The south of the county makes much of its sub-tropical plants, its waving palms, its sheltered bays, and they do a brisker trade in suntan lotion in Falmouth and Penzance than in Boscastle or Tintagel. In Devon the sea is an adjunct to the land – decorative or functional, depending on whether you hail from Torbay or Devonport, depending on whether you make your living as a Clovelly fisherman or play the role of a tourist. In Cornwall the relationship is much closer and more fraught: nowhere in the county are you more than fifteen miles from the sea as the crow flies. But in both counties those taciturn men who turn out the lifeboats have a good chance of ending up dashed against the rocks below those high cliffs that are so pleasant to stroll along to watch the sunset.

Cornwall is as far west as you can go in England, apart from the Isles of Scilly, which are just twenty minutes from Penzance by helicopter. That is perhaps the best way to travel to the islands, though the three-hour crossing via the *Scillonian*, also out of Penzance, has a charm of its own if the water is not too choppy, for the ship is virtually flat-bottomed, on account of the harbour bar at Hugh Town, St Mary's principal and only town. But in any event you should never expect the sea to be millpond smooth, for this is an exceptionally exposed corner of Britain's coastline.

I have been to Cornwall the smart way, which is by plane from Heathrow to Newquay, and the laborious way, which is by train. Nothing makes the peninsula seem more remote than the latter's curious mixture of the slick and the pedantic: breakneck speeds as far as Exeter, followed by a sluggish meander all the way to Penzance, stopping at every lamp-post and tree, slowing down for the driver to admire the view, giving way to lugubrious cattle. Or so it seems from several coaches back from the front. For once, car is best unless you are in a hurry, even if you have an aversion to knife-through-butter motorways. That way you can strike at the West Country's heart, into Wiltshire's deep, heavily wooded and secret enclaves, up and over Dorset's surprising hills and unexpected views, while at the same time making good and comfortable progress.

I once played truant towards the end of an interminable week-long conference in Southampton and took off into the sun for a follow-your-nose jaunt into the West

West meets west: Isambard Kingdom Brunel's railway bridge over the
River Tamar, which divides Cornwall from Devon.

Country. Driving south-west on the M27, I found the New Forest well signposted, but
with approaches guarded as jealously as the Prime Minister's official country residence
at Chequers. The Forest has, after all, remained virtually unchanged since William the
Conqueror went after deer here, and people obviously intend it to stay that way. On a
cool late-autumn day on which it threatened to rain but never did, the cloud formations
ahead of me as I climbed slightly, with forest on each side, were reminiscent of some
fantastic Himalayan snow-scene. The cleverly backlit clouds were as exciting and
impressive as in any television commercial for naturally sparkling Swiss spring water.
Hereabouts the forest is much thicker and seems more impenetrable than most people
ever imagine. Just as they say of Stonehenge, 'Isn't it small?', they tend to say of the
New Forest, 'Isn't it big?'

When William Rufus was killed by an arrow during a stag hunt in 1100, the New
Forest was so strictly guarded as a royal preserve that a man could be imprisoned or
even mutilated for as much as disturbing, let alone poaching, the royal deer. Even in

these more easy-going times, you can still be fined for feeding any of the two thousand or so forest ponies that are one of the main reasons people make a bee-line here whenever the weather starts to turn for the better. The Forest is notably alive with foxes, and badgers are quite common. Less agreeable are the adders that are a scourge of picnickers and hikers during dry, hot summers. They (that is, adders *and* picnickers) are said to favour the sandy heathland because this retains its warmth once it has been exposed to the sun. The Forest covers about 140 square miles, and although, inevitably, farmland has encroached on its borders, those square miles might be able to remain self-contained and unassailed in the future. William the Conqueror dispossessed around 150 families when appropriating the Forest for his own preserve, but, of course, if he had not cornered it off so effectively it would not have remained as intact as it does today.

The New Forest, however, is almost as much about small country towns going about their business as leafy glades where ponies graze. If you see Brockenhurst and Lyndhurst, you will have had the best of it, and if you are really taken with the ponies you can actually buy one at Lyndhurst's annual pony sale. Lyndhurst means 'wood of lime trees', though lime trees are comparatively rare now. Horse-chestnut, hazel, birch, holly, hawthorn, oak and pine (the latter superimposed on the Forest and not to everyone's taste), are predominant, but another distinctive feature of Lyndhurst is a six-hundred-year-old oak tree with a girth of over twenty feet. It may not compare with Nottinghamshire's Major Oak but, being less well documented, is often a nice surprise for visitors. One of Lyndhurst's buildings is the Verderer's Court. The Verderers number six, each of whom must own the freehold of no less than seventy-five acres in the Forest. They are primarily custodians, responsible for caring for ponies and preventing the ravage of the Forest by outsiders.

The New Forest does not run quite all the way to the Solent, that stretch of water that separates the mainland in this corner of Hampshire from the Isle of Wight, but Buckler's Hard, a one-time boat building centre on the lower reaches of the River Beaulieu (very well placed, as Henry VIII and others discovered, for regular injections of oak from the Forest) is a genuine maritime contact for forest dwellers and visitors. The boatyard once employed 4,000 men, and forty of the ships that took on Napoleon under Nelson were built here. Craft that sail out of Buckler's Hard now are on a more modest scale, for this is a major yachting centre.

I was once a bingo caller on a holiday-cum-caravan-camp in the depths of the New Forest. When life in a cramped and archaic gas-lit caravan became too claustrophobic for comfort I would get a green double-decker bus from Ringwood and trundle into Bournemouth. The town was always invigorating, by no means as stuffy as some people say. It has more grand hotels than Scarborough has guesthouses, and is reminiscent in some ways of Miami in the thirties and forties: spacious, wealthy, with palm trees and occasional flashes of art deco on buildings. It's a cosmopolitan place, with a big Jewish community, kosher butchers that are (of course) open on Sundays and closed on Saturdays. If the hotels closed down (there is quite a constellation of AA stars), I suspect the pine forest would eventually take over. One street seems to be exclusively devoted to Indian and Chinese restaurants, but everywhere that is not a *slightly* sophisticated version of the traditional pleasures of the seaside seems to be given over to luxury apartments, their approach drives graced by sleek Rolls Royces and Mercedes.

It is probably the most moneyed seaside resort in England and, at its best, it is architecturally not bad at all. Bournemouth never quite belonged to Hampshire, even before the county boundary changes put it into Dorset, and it is still something of a city-state.

As I drove from Bournemouth due west into Dorset I was much impressed by the sight of old, dark thatch with so much moss on it that it was green: the effect is green and black – like Aberdeen Angus cattle against a hillside. Low hills are crowned with mixed woods, and green fields are so lush and emerald that you think of Ireland. There seems to be nearly as much colour in the winter months as in the summer, and the sun, being noticeably low in the sky at two in the afternoon, gives a different angle on the colour and the shape of buildings.

Wet or dry, Dorset is full of puddles: Affpuddle, Turners Puddle, Tolpuddle and Briantspuddle, among others. Famous Tolpuddle is disappointingly red-brick and plain, but its spine-chilling story is as fresh as ever. And there are piddles as well as puddles: Piddletrenthide, Piddlehinton, Piddle-this, Piddle-that. To see them all from Poole, as I once did, drive north-westwards on an unclassified road marked Puddletown, just off the A352, less than two miles west of Wareham. This road rises to one of the highest points in this part of Dorset, which is Gallows Hill, 283 feet above sea level.

Turners Puddle is a two-men-and-a-dog sort of place. Down a lonely pitted lane bordered by meadows, with a sad and neglected little church, it is almost, but not quite, a deserted village. Affpuddle church, St Lawrence's, gets more than its share of American visitors, however, because it contains the tomb of Edward Laurence: 'Near this place lyeth the body of Edward Laurence – gent: Who departed this life October the 2nd, 1751, aged 67'. Laurence was a relative of George Washington's mother, and it was believed to be her family's coat of arms that inspired the design of the American flag. Tolpuddle is one of England's most famous places. Under a huge sycamore tree is the Martyrs Memorial, which tells the story of the Tolpuddle Martyrs. In 1833 a Methodist lay-preacher and labourer called George Loveless organised a secret Friendly Society of Agricultural Labourers, composed just of himself and five others. Their aim was to raise their wages of nine shillings a week, which was barely subsistence level. The reaction of their employers was quick and simple: namely, to cut their wages to eight shillings a week. When they appealed to local magistrates, their pay was cut yet again, to seven shillings, and they were told that if there was any more trouble it would be reduced still further. In desperation, they met under the sycamore tree to try and agree how best to get off the horns of their dilemma, but events were taken out of their hands. They were arrested, given a 'trial', and sentenced to seven years transportation-in-chains to the Australian Penal Colonies. Their case caught the public imagination, but almost too late, and it was only after two years of hard labour that they were pardoned. Four years later they returned to England. It is said that one of the exiles would never have known of his pardon if he had not seen it mentioned in an old newspaper found when he was still in exile in New South Wales.

In the very depths of inland Dorset, just a few miles to the west of Piddletrenthide, is Cerne Abbas and, a little bit further to the east, Milton Abbas and the market town of Blandford Forum. It is all reminiscent of that 'heart of England' country, mostly embraced by Warwickshire, Herefordshire and Worcestershire. Wareham, just west of

Tolpuddle, Dorset, is just one of several Piddles and Puddles in this soft
and historic county. It is pretty enough, but most closely associated in
many visitors' minds with the Tolpuddle Martyrs of 1834.

Poole, enjoys the happy combination of Saxon origins (it is still partly surrounded by ninth-century earth ramparts) and an eighteenth-century elegance, arising from a fire that destroyed much of the old town, causing it to be substantially rebuilt, all in the same period. (It is nearly always a successful formula: Sir Christopher Wren was so quick off the mark after the Great Fire of London in 1666 in seeing Charles II with his plans for rebuilding the ravaged city that some historians have even wondered whether he started it.)

The A35 between Dorchester and Bridport is one of those roads that, because they are high, offer wide-ranging, bird's eye views of the landscape. The sea is over to the left, beyond a craggy moonscape of green hillocks and black crags. As I drove west, I noticed many pubs that offer a traditional roast Sunday lunch, often at very reasonable prices indeed. Presumably they arrive at these prices on the assumption that people will drink lots of their wine and beer. A sign outside one pub in Charmouth promised 'interesting bar food'. A good sales gimmick: it gets you wondering just what they mean by 'interesting'.

I drove into Lyme Regis with the sun sparkling on a calm sea, so bright that it hurt my eyes. It was Jane Austen's favourite resort and is the home of John Fowles, the contemporary best-selling novelist. There are lots of hotels of the one and two AA star variety. At first you think there is no room for the spacious, high-ceilinged Bournemouth seafront sort of place, but there is at least one three-star hotel, nicely situated among trees on one of the hills above the pastel-coloured town.

In Sidmouth, over the Devon border, the seafront is dominated by sandstone cliffs and small hotels with fretted wooden balconies, quite a number of them blue-and-white, with lots of ironwork and yellow AA signs. As you glance into the dining-rooms, there are no sauce-bottles on the tables, so you know that these are a cut above ordinary guesthouses. Instead, there are restrained alabaster table lamps with neatly coifed napkins of linen, silverware, potted plants in the dimly lit lounges. Several hotels do not have stars, but are 'Approved': all part of the pecking order. There was quite a little enclave of fishermen at the eastern end of the promenade, where you can buy crabs and other shellfish, and, not least, turn your car round, for the seafront road is too narrow to allow that in comfort. It occurred to me there was a surprising amount of activity for off-season, mainly provided by suede-coated senior citizens with labradors in matching colours.

There was quite a breeze getting up as I drove through the wooded, inward-looking, generally unspectacular 'middle bit' of Cornwall, and in Launceston it began to hail. Fond as I am of English weather and all its vicissitudes this was a bit too much, and I wavered in my resolve. Suddenly the prospect of sitting down in front of the television in a four-star hotel and watching the racing, began to appeal. It was the realisation that I was just an hour's journey from a stretch of the Cornish coast that I had not visited since I was a child that gave me the incentive to press on: nostalgia time again. I remembered how as a child I had learnt 'By Tre, Pol, Pen, you will know these Cornishmen.' I certainly travelled past a whole forest of Tre's: Tremaine, Treburtle, Treneglas, Trelash, Trevivian, and more.

Tintagel is well geared up to tourists. There's a King Arthur car and coach park, and one hotel has a separate entrance to its 'Excali-Bar'. There are pottery shops, 'cottage crafts', a betting shop to peep into in case they have chalked up the odds on King Arthur

Looe, Cornwall. No quiet backwater this, but one of the county's busiest resorts. During the winter months, however, it takes on a different character.

ever having *really* been to Tintagel, take-away pancakes and waffles. A stiff walk from the village is a green headland where cows graze, looking as if they might fall into the sea. There are some nice looking three-storeyed houses overlooking the sea and the weather, but their windows rattle when there are westerlies. Along the road that links Tintagel with the National Trust owned village of Boscastle, bungalows tend to be called 'Four Winds', or 'Westering'.

Boscastle harbour is a glorified crack in the north Cornish cliffs. If it didn't exist, it might be necessary to invent it, otherwise fishing boats would have nowhere to escape from the cruel sea. It has escaped the worst of the commercialism and has just two or three rather welcoming, busy, well-stocked general stores-cum-souvenir shops. It was almost exactly a quarter-century before that I had come here as a child. Now, on an increasingly windswept day I was still unprepared for the witches' cauldron that greeted me as I drove northwards from Tintagel. The sea that beat its head in fury against the harbour wall was the colour of ginger beer, and as fishing smacks tossed and rode helter-skelter at anchor in the harbour I wondered just how long they would fare in the open sea. I hugged the shelter of some fishermen's cottages by the harbour edge and watched a thin red line of hikers toiling up the footpath winding from the harbour up towards the headland along the edge of the protective cliff. Just a few days later the same

St Ives, Cornwall, and a cat ignoring a camera.

wind plucked a teenager off the same path and flung him into the foaming water, where he was dashed against the rocks.

I remembered a childhood fortnight of which Sir John Betjeman would have approved, at Widemouth Bay, north Cornwall's surfers' paradise. With just two or three outcrops of rock to add interest to the eye, this is the Cornwall of the tourist brochures, and the wide skies and far-reaching green sea is as good as anything in East Anglia.

Bude, the first sizeable Cornish resort, is very Cornish in flavour, although it is so close to the Devon border. Both it and Widemouth Bay are outstanding resorts, where Atlantic breakers provide the nearest equivalent in England to Bondi Beach. On revisiting Bude I realised I had forgotten how much *space* it occupies: terraces of three-storeyed Edwardian villas beyond greens like displaced patches of moorland, a cinema standing alone like a hotel in a Hollywood cowboy film, a blustery promenade, separate beaches.

I had never been to Clovelly. If there are as many cats in Mousehole as there are here, there are probably no mice. On a steep walk to the bottom of the almost perfect village, literally hacked out of the precipitous cliffs, I saw no fewer than eight cats: black, tabby, ginger and off-white. A curious thing about Clovelly is that the whitewashed houses tumbling on top of each other all the way down to the harbour seem to be trying to make sense of the crazy angles they have to live with: many of them have fenced-in balconies and terraces that are on exactly the same horizontal line as their neighbours' rooftops. Hanging baskets of flowers make a dash of colour against the white in summer, though when it rains these drip down your neck as you struggle uphill towards the car park and find yourself wishing the famous donkeys were available all year round to transport you to the hilltop. Even during that unseasonal journey I didn't entirely miss the tourists. There was a coach party from Bideford milling around the car park at the top of the hill, but some of the little old ladies among them never did see the village proper ('If I go down them steps, my dear, I'll certainly never get back up again').

I remember Bideford for its distinctive layout: a broad river – the Torridge – low hills that are sufficiently well defined to give perspective, and houses that rarely rise to more than three storeys, or two storeys and a gable. There is not much colour among them. A bit of pastel here and there, but mainly white or black-and-white. If I had stayed longer I could have watched an amateur performance of 'South Pacific' at the Queen's Hall, Barnstaple, colourfully and aggressively advertised between Bideford and Barnstaple – a satisfactory alternative from time to time, I have found, to looking at the four walls of a hotel room. The village of Instow promises a seafront, although really all you have here is the wide river. Barnstaple is similar in layout to Bideford, though it is much more industrialised, and somewhat larger.

It is an increasingly intriguing journey, over hill and over dale, to Lynmouth and Lynton. They are rather like what Great Malvern would have been like if it had been evacuated to the seaside – wooded, hilly, craggy, with turn-of-the-century houses, and small shops that sell knitting wool or electrical goods that cannot compete with hypermarket prices. The villages haven't become too brash and commercialised, perhaps because the beaches are mainly mud and rock. There are signs on the clifftops that say 'To the lighthouse', and you can get Virginia Woolf's books along with Jack Higgins's in one or two well-stocked bookshops. And in spite of the predominant mud and rocks, you can buy buckets and spades. Much recommended is the toll road through the Porlock Estate off the Lynmouth to Minehead road, which also saves negotiating a gradient of 1 in 4. It consists of a series of hairpin bends through forest that is not too thick to allow generous views of the headlands and of the sea lapping into the spacious bay. Minehead is another north coast resort where holidaymakers from Exmoor go to get sea breezes in the middle of a sunny spell, when the interior of the brown and secret moor gets too hot to handle.

Of England's seven national parks, Exmoor is the smallest, but in terms of the appeal that has people saying 'Why haven't we been here before?', it consistently scores highest. It is light-under-a-bushel country, and what claims to be the capital of Exmoor, Simonsbath, consists of nothing much more than a country-house hotel and a meadow beside the River Barle, where I stopped early in the morning to watch sleek mahogany-coloured horses (no moorland ponies these) grazing in a picture-postcard scene. If I had wanted a *real* village, or somewhere to buy petrol and post a parcel, I would have had to go to Exford which, like so many village-sized communities, takes on greater importance than its size warrants because it is a focal point within a rural area.

Between Simonsbath and Dulverton, I passed a stag hunt: the last, I was told, of the season. Deer hunting is as important around here as fox hunting is in the rural Midlands. Deer are the largest mammals in Britain, and the National Park gets its insignia from the deer's antlers. The population of these descendants of the prehistoric red deer hovers around the five hundred mark. They are, incidentally, more likely to be seen in spring than in high summer or autumn, because the planting of new grass on open moorland tends to flush them out from their secret, scrubby hideaways among Exmoor's deep and riveted coombes. As on Dartmoor, Exmoor's other famous creatures, the ponies, are technically owned by farmers but to all intents and purposes run wild. When rounded up and broken in, they make pets and mounts for children.

People say Exmoor is a poor man's version of Dartmoor, but the terrain is dramatically different, and a further distinction is that the moor virtually has its own coast. The clefts and coombes that break up the moor are generally thickly wooded. Comparatively shady and cool in warm weather, they give Exmoor a distinctive look, and soften the effect. Although there are tracts in the heart of the 260 square miles of moor that are very bleak and seemingly impenetrable, the impression Exmoor gives overall is of a softer, more pastoral place into whose wildest stretches carefully nurtured farmland manages to penetrate. The terrain is mainly of sandstone on which are superimposed heather moors. Prehistoric man is said to have neglected Exmoor because the woods that cloak the coombes, and render the rivers that criss-cross the moor obscure, were too difficult to clear. Leaving Exmoor, I drove through Dulverton. In almost any other part of England, this small town would have the reputation of one worth spending half a day in, but, because of the nearness of Exmoor, people tend to hurry through. Even hurrying through, though, you will find enough evidence that this is in the heart of hunting and farming country. Landrovers give way to black-hatted riders, yellow-and-black posters inside the greengrocers' windows announce Young Farmers' meetings and gymkhanas.

The highest points of the moor from which to get orientated are Dunkery Beacon and Selworthy Beacon. From both of these you can take in virtually the whole of Exmoor and that dramatic coast. The land does not peter out, as it does in so many other places in the West Country, but ends with a flourish, with headlands and precipitous roads that have people parking cautiously because they are unable to combine looking around with concentrating on the difficult and narrow roads.

To put it simply – the AA will not approve – there are two ways into the West Country. The low road goes into the deep south of the peninsula, the high road stays on an axis from London, and arrives – via the M4 motorway if you must, and via a series of tucked-away alternative routes if you can, in the new county of Avon.

The banks of Badgworthy Water, Exmoor, Devon, are surely the ultimate
in romantic picnic country.

First impressions are a very hard act to beat. The first time I saw Bath I was picked up
from the station and whisked by car to the Pump Room for coffee and then, because my
host had an inexplicable passion for it, a glass of kümmel, followed by a second, and a
third. Somewhat light-headedly, I spent the next two hours on a walking tour of the city
so uncompromisingly energetic that I was more often at a trot than a stride. The only
real respite I had was because there was a queue, or rather a small mêlée, at the entrance
to the Museum of Costume. It gave me a chance to get my breath back.

Never go back, they say, but I suspect that is only if you have been especially happy somewhere. The next time I saw Bath I had driven from Dartmoor, and I was en route for Tetbury, in Gloucestershire. The city was still in Somerset, then, and you did not have to make the same mental adjustment that a county boundary seems to demand (each county has so many connotations, is so fixed in tribal memory: Somerset is cider, Glastonbury Tor, Wells Cathedral, whitewashed cottages. Avon makes sense as a name, but is still a culture shock). It was half-past-six in the evening. The offices and shops had closed and the empty streets seemed exhausted by the heat. Traffic was muted, and I longed to take a trip round the Georgian streets, up and over the parks and through avenues of trees in one of those horse-drawn open landaus that seem so incongruous in Rome and New York but would actually suit Bath very well.

In the early 1980s Bath's citizens decided, after much soul-searching and juggling with funds, that it would become a real spa again. Many millions of pounds will have been spent by the end of the decade. The Romans, who developed the natural spring waters and a whole mini-civilisation around them, would have approved. It was in the eighteenth century that Bath was rediscovered as a spa and that is when the best of the city dates from. The original Pump Room was rebuilt in 1795, but the extent of the Romans' development of Bath was not realised until the ruins were excavated nearly a century later. If you come to admire the city's inspired honey-coloured façades, as most people rightly do, and bask in the glory of a confident and ambitious architectural grandeur, you could do worse than take out an overdraft and stay a night or two in the exquisite Royal Crescent, which has been called 'the finest street in England', for one of the houses has been turned into a last-word-in-luxury hotel. This crescent, in which thirty houses are cheek-by-jowl in a semi-elliptical terrace with fine views over the city, was created by John Wood the Younger.

Bath and Bristol together used to be British Rail's most popular combined day return trip from London. In the middle of the seventeenth century, Samuel Pepys visited Bristol and declared that it was 'in every respect, another London'. His journey, by the way, would have taken him about three days by stagecoach. Springs had not yet been invented and he would have been bruised black-and-blue by the trip. The real prowess of Bristol as a seafaring town began in the 1490s, when John Cabot planted the English flag in what he prosaically called 'the New Found Land'. He had discovered 'America', which has yet to decide whether it owes its name to Amerigo Vespucci, or to John Cabot's chief benefactor, Richard Amerycke. Naturally Bristol capitalised on the to-ing and fro-ing of ships (between 1654 and 1675, about 10,000 Britons passed through Bristol on their way to settle in the New World), and a network of trade routes was quickly built up when this country acquired a taste for spices, tobacco, sugar, wine and spirits. Sixteenth-century England exported mainly wool to Mediterranean countries, including Spain and Portugal, and the ships came back not empty but full of port, sherry, olive oil and soap. Slaves were never bought and sold in Bristol itself, though it is true that more than fifty Bristol ships were involved in the transport of slaves from the Gold Coast of Africa to the southern states of America.

High above Avon Gorge, spanned by the Clifton Suspension Bridge, is England's most famous suburb. Clifton could stand up with the likes of Bath, Harrogate, Cheltenham and others. As it is, it is now just an appendage to a bustling city, and correspondingly matter-of-fact. Clifton combines the atmosphere of a university town, which in effect it is, with the architectural distinction of one of the great spas, which it never was. It has something of a Greenwich Village atmosphere about it, with a bit of north Oxford and some of Edinburgh's fierce independence of spirit.

Bristol is surprisingly modest about its charms. There is the smart Theatre Royal, whose interior, like that of Richmond's Georgian theatre and the one at Bury St Edmunds in Suffolk, has remained unchanged since the mid-eighteenth century. There's the SS *Great Britain* moored in dry dock, Britain's first ocean-going iron ship, created by Isambard Kingdom Brunel. There's the elegant shell of the mid-nineteenth century railway station, whose future use is somewhat in doubt, but which is unlikely to be destroyed. There's the elegance of Clifton itself and its famous suspension bridge. There's the first Wesleyan Chapel to be built in England. And not least there is the clutch of Berni Inns which, for all the unpretentiousness of the steak and chips on which their reputation is founded, have some outstanding premises, including the famous Llandoger Trow. This is believed to have been the model for Robert Louis Stevenson's Spyglass Inn in *Treasure Island*, in which the reader first meets Long John Silver.

The *Great Britain* was, at 3,000 tons, the biggest ship ever built. She was launched here in 1843 and crossed the Atlantic in fifteen days, easily a record for the time. She made the voyage to Australia no fewer than thirty-two times and became a troop ship for the Indian Army and the Crimea. Finally, in 1884 she ran aground on the Falkland Islands until, in 1970, she was refloated and towed back to her home port. Like the Clifton Suspension Bridge, the Temple Meads railway station is a legacy of Brunel. It would be nice to record that Brunel, who has left an impression on Bristol, was a local man, but he actually came from Portsmouth.

Towards the end of the 1970s, with minimum fuss, the city introduced to the largely uninterested public and the only vaguely interested trade, a wine fair that has since become a staple of the English calendar. For about ten days every July, Bristol re-affirms its position as capital of the wine trade. The fair has, after all, a good pedigree: it is unusual in being open to the public as well as the trade, and most wines can be tasted by the glass for a modest sum, added to which your entrance ticket contains several vouchers which include 'free' wine tasting. Even better, most of the wines can be bought by the bottle as well as the case. There are full bodied wines from Chile, crisp whites and easy-on-the-palate reds from California, wines from new producers such as Barbados and Japan. In one year, about thirty wine-growing countries were represented here, and over 80,000 people turned up.

The stretch of the M5 motorway that links Bristol to Exeter, and thus back to what people inevitably call 'the real West Country', may not have quite the scenic grandeur of the M6 in Cumbria or the undulating and wooded charm of the M3 in Surrey and Hampshire (a motorway for all seasons, but autumn is best). It does, however, link some very interesting places indeed. I have much enjoyed sneaky little detours to Clevedon and Weston-super-Mare, to the extreme southwestern corner of the Cotswolds around Uley and Owlpen, to Cheddar, to Tiverton and its museum (by far one of my favourite small museums in England), and the Wellington Monument and the Blackdown Hills. I have even – this must be heretical – admired and enjoyed several of the motorway restaurants. Vilified as they are, if you stop for a late breakfast chosen from a bright and newly replenished display in a freshly hoovered and scrubbed interior, or for a midnight snack in a nearby deserted neon-lit space-age service area in the middle of nowhere, you may discover a peculiar charm that reminds me of the slightly other-worldly paintings of Edward Hopper, especially his lonely country garages and his eerie late-nite city diners.

Clevedon Court, which can be seen from the motorway, is sometimes confused with Cliveden, on the banks of the Thames in Buckinghamshire, once the home of Lord Astor and rendezvous of the 'Cliveden set'. Clevedon Court is less grand, but more ancient: it is a rare example of a fourteenth-century manor house. Among the rooms that are open to the public during the summer months is the so-called Justice Room, for the Lord of the Manor was also Justice of the Peace and responsible for trying petty offences. Architecturally so well preserved and so characteristic of its time, the building is better than any textbook.

The Wellington Monument stands almost exactly on the Somerset–Devon border. There are superb views even from the base of the great obelisk, so you can imagine how much more impressive these are if you climb its 235 steps. On clear days you can see – well, if not forever – certainly the Black Mountains of Wales. In *very* good conditions, you can see Snowdonia. That this is possible is due not only to the impressive height of that strange obelisk built in commemoration of the Duke of Wellington, whose family home is nearby, but primarily to the Blackdown Hills on which it is built. The Monument, 170 feet high, is National Trust property, and its stairs are climbable during official opening hours.

Part of the Blackdowns, whose name will have many Westcountrymen scratching their heads ('it rings a bell, but . . .'), straddles the border between Somerset and Devon. It is not mountainous country, just secretive and hilly, where narrow lanes that never see much traffic unless it is lost, meander between hills down into coombes, up over bits of abandoned moorland, and woe betide anybody who tries to find a hamlet or a natural feature without a good map. On two occasions in my attempt to explore the Blackdowns, I made completely false starts, found myself going nowhere in particular, and gave up. The villages of the Blackdowns ring no bell at all for people who do not have roots in the area, easy though they may be on the ear: Upottery, Clayhidon, Widcombe (not to be confused with the Widecombe of Dartmoor), Staple Fitzpaine, Castle Neroche. The country is heavily wooded, and the Forestry Commission owns much of it. In a hedge in Clayhidon is a plaque to a murderer, an unusual distinction. It records how one William Blackmore was murdered on that very spot in Rosemary Lane in 1853 and how his murderer, George Sparkes, was hanged in Exeter in front of a crowd of 12,000. A public hanging was always an excuse for a day off, roughly the equivalent of today's Bank Holidays. But these Roman circuses were banned in 1868, and the nearest equivalent sport came to be keeping vigil outside the walls of a prison.

I like the last few miles of the M5 as it approaches Exeter, with just a hint of green hills not too far away, and newish service areas where they have learnt the lessons of planning mistakes elsewhere. Though many an English city claims to have seen thousands of years of unbroken occupation, some are fanciful. Not so in the case of Exeter. It was a place of some importance before the Romans appeared, not least because of the abundance of salmon which used to swim in the River Exe. The city probably benefited from its westerly location, being allowed to get on with its own business without undue disturbance by invaders, except, that is, of the more domestic kind: one of the first branches of Marks and Spencer was opened here in 1912. Access from the southernmost point of the M5 even into the heart of Exeter is quick and pleasant. Interchange 30 takes you via a fast feed road to the city centre, and from the very end of the motorway there is a fast link road to the city's southwestern edge, and thence without difficulty into the shopping centre. (Though the heart of the city has severe traffic restrictions, car parks are adequate and well signed.) There are some very old pubs in the city and several outstanding museums: perhaps most notable of all is the Maritime Museum, which occupies part of a canal basin, where over a hundred craft of historic interest are moored. Of course, there is a cathedral, which happens to have an exquisite vaulted ceiling and exterior stone carvings that get people from Rouen coming in pilgrimages, so that seeing it is a pleasure and not just a duty.

It was during a stay in Exeter that, inspired by a series of humorous advertisements, and jaded with hotels, I decided to try out that special independence much vaunted by a photographer friend. I hired a camper caravan and, with warnings in my ears from dubious friends who associated me exclusively with four-star comfort, I set off down the narrow lanes of mid-Devon. Not only was the vehicle, which was nearly seven feet wide, and nearly eighteen feet long, quite happy to handle those twisting West Country lanes, but it even negotiated that notorious Porlock Hill near Lynmouth. After staying in the caravan park on the edge of Ilfracombe, I made my way via Barnstaple and Bideford towards Bodmin Moor, and then, on my way back to Exeter, over Dartmoor in autumn sunshine. Such a vehicle gives one the advantage of being a couple of feet higher than ordinary car drivers, and does wonders for those panoramic views.

As with forests (so often nothing of the sort) the word 'moor' is misleading. Dartmoor is much more memorable for its scrubby hills leading up to granite outcrops called tors. Hay Tor on the eastern edge of the 'moor', is one of the best points from where to get an overall impression of this eerie landscape, and Hound Tor, another, gets its name from its resemblance from a distance to a pack of hounds. There's Devil's Tor, Laughter Tor, Vixen Tor, Yes Tor, which, at over 2,000 feet, is the highest of the lot. Diamond-shaped Dartmoor is about twenty-seven miles from north to south, and the same east to west, and within it rise several of the most famous rivers in the county, including the Dart and the Teign. Not many people read Charles Kingsley, author of *The Water Babies*, any more, but they might appreciate the literary associations of Holne, where he was born in 1890, and which is in the heart of the moor. I once had bed-and-breakfast with Mrs McFadyen, though the sign on her window said 'No Vacancies'. 'I am not really open for the season yet,' she explained, as she sunned herself among her ostentatiously tall daffodils, 'but I don't suppose it matters for just one night.' Alas, she had nylon sheets and noisy plumbing, but she also had a copy of *The Water Babies* along with her Agatha Christies and the odd Dick Francis. Oh, and she also served crispy bacon for breakfast. There's also Buckfast Abbey, Buckland-in-the-Moor – again misleading as it is surrounded by woods – and Widecombe, which is worth going to not just because it is famous for Widecombe Fair, but because, if you come from Exeter, you enjoy the most impressive approach of all, when the road rises gradually from Bovey Tracey and passes close to Hay Tor. Buckland-in-the-Moor, incidentally, is all but on the course of the River Dart, and its thatched cottages below tall trees and in the hollow of the moor, have made it a bit touristy.

You will never appreciate anything of Dartmoor if you do not leave your car and walk at least until the car park is out of sight. It has to be admitted, though, that if your main intention is to see Dartmoor ponies first, and the prison second, you can actually do that without opening even the car window. The ponies, one of half a dozen breeds of wild ponies in England, often come to you unbidden, and working parties of prisoners still loom out of the mist in their blue overalls like a scene from the film *Papillon*.

I also took a trip to the famous South Hams and en route I happened to stumble into a furniture auction in the market town of Kingsbridge. This bustling little place was a nine-day-wonder in the mid-1970s because of a ruse by the landlord of one of Kingsbridge's oldest pubs to beat the Inland Revenue. Quite simply, he revived the age-old system of barter: if you were a farmer and brought a sheep into the public bar, it could be used in payment or part-payment of, say, a solicitor's bill or a new back boiler for your house. The whole thing worked like a dream for several months, but then the taxman put his foot down.

It was too hot and stuffy for Kingsbridge, and I made my way further south still, to linger among the boutiques and jaunty yachting caps of Salcombe, where I had an argument with a Hooray Henry in a sports car who nipped into my parking space. I stayed in Thurlestone, where there is a pub whose supporting beams are said to have come from a wrecked hospital ship from the Spanish Armada. Not many coach parties make it here: for them the narrow high-hedged lanes typical of Devon are virtually impassable with comfort. Thurlestone gets its name from a curious rock in the bay that has been 'thirled' or pierced from the constant wearing down of the waves. It is mentioned in the Domesday Book as Torlestan. There is a big hotel, white and imposing, a local landmark, and one of the best hotels in the south-west. Along the coast at Slapton Sands (not so much sandy as composed of very small pebbles which are fairly comfortable to the feet), the D-Day landings of 6 June 1944 were practised.

It was after a night in that unlikely wedding-cake hotel that I took time off to see Totnes. Its High Street is one of the best I know, and even if old ladies with shopping bags are panting a bit by the time they reach the end, they probably appreciate why this is one of the handsomest towns in the country. Several of the houses in the High Street are Tudor, though you might not know it from the more recent façades; most buildings date from between the sixteenth and eighteenth centuries. Some of the best of them stand above covered walkways or arcades, which are known in Totnes as the piazzas. More important is the fact that the stone pillars supporting the overhanging shops and offices not only keep the rain off but look good too. At one time stalls used to be set up under the overhanging buildings, but these took so much trade away from the proper shops that they were banned.

I had first seen Wiltshire after being press-ganged into joining a coach tour from central London that took in Guildford, Winchester and Salisbury cathedrals, and the best thing about the trip, apart from the light and unpretentious beauty of Guildford's cool and abstract interior, was probably the insight it gave into rural Wiltshire. One of the villages we passed was Berwick St John. It has always stayed in my mind, and seemed for a long time to be the archetypal ordinary country village: not another Castle Combe, with its double yellow lines and its Rolls-Royces, and not a Malmesbury, which gets

Dartmouth, Devon. Hugger-mugger houses are positioned to see what the
rest of the world is up to, and windows are designed to catch all the light
that's going.

more than its share of tourists. But in an unspectacular way, as happens so often, my brief glimpse of the place gave me the incentive to go back.

Autumn sunlight in Charlton, Wiltshire.

It was almost exactly a year later, on a hot weekday afternoon in June that, perilously near to closing time, I stopped for a pint of Badger beer at the Talbot Inn, amid the mustard-coloured stone and thatch of Berwick St John. There was just one table outside the pub, and in the course of half an hour, as I sat there and drank in the village scene and a further glass of beer, nothing passed on the road through the village except a Post Office van and two people on a tandem. I said hello, but the pained concentration on their faces clearly militated against a reply.

It was the landlord who told me why Wiltshire people are traditionally known as moonrakers. The story goes that two yokels from the village of Bishops Cannings were discovered raking the surface of a village pond on a moonlit night. When people asked what they were up to, they said they were trying to retrieve that 'great yeller cheese' in the middle of the water. This was, simply, a reflection of the full moon. They were probably up to no good, and were attempting to retrieve stolen goods hidden in watertight barrels at the bottom of the deep pond. Bishops Cannings is one of those villages that have seen busier times. Its population used to be much bigger, as its expensively built, substantial, perfect Early English spired church indicates. John Aubrey, whose *Brief Lives* has tended to mask his painstaking chronicles of Wiltshire life, described how village people could beat anybody in the country at 'music, football, and the ring', by which he was referring to bell ringing in St Mary's church. A nice local touch: in the early 1700s the vicar of the church left a legacy for the bells to be rung at eight o'clock every winter night, in order to guide travellers who might be lost on the downs above the village.

For all the hustle and bustle of Salisbury, which is well on the tourist beat, and the moderately heavy industry of Swindon, Devizes and Chippenham, I think of Wiltshire, more than most counties, as a place of villages that reveal themselves only grudgingly to the visitor, hidden as they so often are, tucked safely away from the winds that howl across the downs. Not that Castle Combe hides *its* light under a bushel. It is content to be a picture-postcard village, high up in the league-table of 'places of interest to the visitor'. It has never quite recovered from being the real-life set for the film *Doctor Dolittle*, made in the mid-1960s, a film, curiously, which seems to have sunk without trace and is rarely seen. The village was transformed into a make-believe seaport with jetties and boats, and local people were not inclined to welcome the invasion with open arms.

Castle Combe, Wiltshire, is one of the better known villages in a county
that for the most part plays its cards close to its chest.

Just a few miles to the west is Devizes, which makes a good focal point from which to see Wiltshire: it is almost in the very centre of the county. It has hotels and restaurants, and an exceptional market square, almost in the same league as Salisbury's.

I had a Wiltshire pork pie in a Devizes pub, and enjoyed it, but I preferred Lacock partly for the fact that you have to park your car in the car park on the outskirts of the village: irritating for some people but usually a sign that you are in for a treat. Lacock is not quite such a classic as Castle Combe, and, anyway, its wider streets and little side turnings and alleyways, not quite labyrinthine, but accommodating all the same, can absorb far more people on a Sunday afternoon. Not all of them who bring cameras realise that Lacock Abbey is one of the most important places in the world in the history of photography. This was the home of Henry Fox Talbot, a photographic pioneer and founder of the photographic firm still in existence. The first photograph negative ever produced is in the museum here – it dates back to 1835.

Fox Talbot beavered away quietly and transformed the way we look at everyday things. What they did at Salisbury several hundred years before, however, was more spectacular. They abandoned the first town and tried again down on the plain. One unlikely tale is that in the year 1219 at Old Sarum, which the Romans called Sorbiodunum, the monks here found themselves locked out of their abbey by Roman soldiers, and decided to settle down the hill. A legend is that Bishop Poore, who led this exodus, had an arrow shot into the air: like the Mormons, they would settle where the arrow landed, and Salisbury cathedral was built on the very spot. Although it is just a ruin, it is worth going to Old Sarum, not just for the atmosphere and, incidentally, the open-air plays performed there on summer evenings, but for the view of Salisbury down below, especially that exquisite cathedral spire that John Constable could not get enough of.

'New' Salisbury does not go short of tourists, and Saturday afternoons in high summer could give the opposite effect from what is required. The cathedral too, for all the tranquility of its exceptional precinct, where there are Georgian houses almost as well-worth looking at as the cathedral itself, is likely, even at the best of times, to have two or three conducted parties disrupting what should be an atmosphere you can cut with a knife. If this happens to you, go at teatime, before the cathedral doors are closed, when all self-respecting charabanc parties will have left for the day or gone back to their hotels for the table d'hôte meal promised in the brochure.

Not that there is anything wrong with coach parties. I have conducted several here myself. And I took the same forty Americans from an East Anglian Air Force base who once accompanied me around the baking back streets of Salisbury (and, gratefully, into the cool and shadowy cathedral) to Stonehenge, Avebury and Marlborough. Here is an interesting point: if Marlborough, an outstanding example of largely mid-eighteenth-century town planning, had been forced to remain exactly as it once was, it would now lack that delightful leavening of Victorian, Edwardian and early-twentieth-century domestic detail that makes it worth a long detour.

We waited until the cool of the evening before we climbed back on to the bus for the tedious journey through London. Happily, they had discovered there is more to England than Breckland and Ipswich, and, perhaps across a hazy field, or in a back alley of an ancient town, spotted a ghost of neolithic or medieval times: go this way, via Wiltshire, towards the West Country and you will be vouchsafed just a hint of how strange and other-worldly things can be beneath their late-twentieth-century veneer, even a hundred or so miles from London.

The classic view of Salisbury Cathedral, Wiltshire, across the water-meadows. The spire was completed in the fourteenth century and, at 404 feet, is the tallest in England.

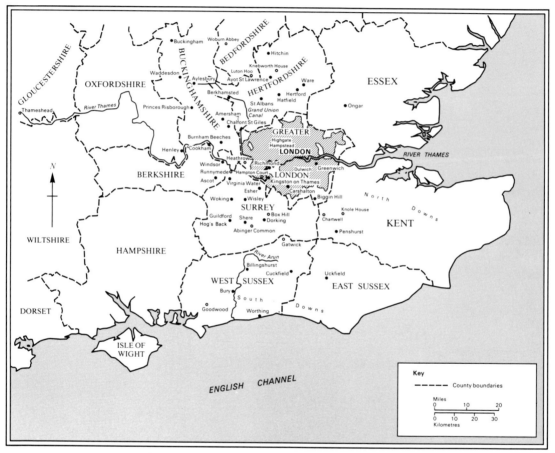

Map 7 South-East England

11. London ('just passing through') and the South East: commuters and country lanes

Sussex almost by the sea; Virginia Water
and rural Surrey; Kent despite the motorways;
Hertfordshire and Buckinghamshire

I was on my way back from Perth, Australia. It may have been the effect on the brain of twenty-one hours in the air – rosy-fingered dawn on the tarmac at Bombay, otherwise just whisky-drugged limbo and a losing battle with badly designed headsets – but London at ten o'clock on a Saturday morning was spectacular. I could almost have believed the pilot was a part-time London Tourist Board guide who was wanting to show off the city, awash as it was in hazy autumn sunlight, to his two hundred or so passengers. If so he must have been gratified by the response, because normally straight-laced passengers began to risk the wrath of the stewardesses and undo their seatbelts, banking steeply to get a better view.

I had never followed the course of the Thames from the air. 'There's London Bridge,' people exclaimed as we passed a few hundred feet over Tower Bridge, which from this big bird's eye view dwarfs the White Tower – the oldest readily identifiable building in London – and renders the city church of All Hallows by the Tower pathetically small. A naval history buff from Hobart spotted the HMS *Belfast*, and one bon viveur was even quick enough to make out the Savoy hotel on the northern bank of the river. The Palace of Westminster, as it is rightly called but rarely referred to, stands out like a fortress painstakingly assembled by a precocious ten-year-old, the pinnacle of Big Ben more noticeable for its squeaky-clean clock face than its Victorian Gothic frippery, and somewhat put to shame by the disproportionately massive Victoria Tower that lords it over Britain's upper chamber at the westerly end of the Palace. When there is any reflection at all from London's much maligned skies you can see the Thames slithering eastwards, more serpentine than most maps suggest. You also notice how flat the eastern approaches to the capital are, and begin to understand why they built a spectacular Thames Flood Barrier. Another thing you notice is the profligate amount of city greenery, not just in the very heart of London but on its outskirts: on Hackney Marshes, apparently, there is enough space to accommodate about a hundred full sized football pitches side by side.

There is of course not an inch to spare in the heart of the city, which makes the grass that grows in London's parks as precious as jade. Yet I once met a man who lives in rural Suffolk who told me that he goes to London, where he has a small mews cottage just off Eaton Square, to get away from it all. 'In a small town,' he said, 'everybody knows what you're up to, but in London you are your own man. It can be lonely, but that is usually because if you are on your own you tend to see a lot of other people having a good time.'

Even those Londoners who do not have a country retreat and are averse to the idea of living in suburbia have their favourite hideaway that defies the city's sardine tin reputation. For somebody I know it is the inner courtyard of the Wallace Collection in Manchester Square, for somebody else it is the slightly faded Belgravia restaurant that has disappeared from the good food guides but hasn't actually changed much. For others it is a stroll around the back streets of Mayfair on a Sunday afternoon's window shopping spree, or Bloomsbury at dusk in autumn, when for once the attic rooms and obscure academic libraries of the University begin to take on something of the ambience of one of England's ancient universities instead of being swamped by traffic and office workers. Or it might be the Inns of Court, which are, like the best of Highgate or Hampstead, bordered by elegant iron railings, wide walkways and handsome Georgian houses of a kind that the old London County Council tried to emulate when building blocks of flats in the 1930s and then the 1950s, but didn't quite succeed. It is all reminiscent of a more leisurely and in some ways more elegant age. Visitors are not

No 1 Court, Old Bailey London. Even though there is no longer a black cap for judges to reach for, much of the drama attached to this room has survived.

discouraged from pottering around the courtyards, just as if they had stumbled across some transplanted Oxbridge College, but have to apply to the Porter's Lodge for admission to the individual halls and chapels. Apart from a chapel, each Inn has a library and dining-hall where successful legal students are 'called' with due ceremony. In Gray's Inn, incidentally, the first performance of Shakespeare's *Comedy of Errors* was given in 1594, and Charles Dickens was one of the students at the Middle Temple, though he was seduced away from the law by the idea of journalism and writing.

In contrast to those hallowed precincts, I once spent a month of nights as a security guard on the Barbican site, on what is now one of the most prestigious residential apartment complexes in the City. My contribution to the security of the place was negligible, and the only time I had to exercise my extremely limited authority was when there was a knife fight in the small hours of the morning between two Irish labourers working on the foundations. The police took twenty-five minutes to arrive, by which time the erstwhile combatants were sharing a bottle of Guinness. It was an eerie place to be, with or without workmen: great tarpaulins flapping in the wind like something out of a scene in *Mutiny on the Bounty*, rats scurrying underfoot if you veered from the walkways created over a sea of mud. The Barbican is now a vast complex of about two thousand flats, a girls' school, a fine theatre, arts and conference centre. Its high-rise luxury flats are a landmark, and if they give a space-age look to this part of the City, it should be remembered what a mess this was for about twenty years after the London blitz during which most of it, it seems, was destroyed – apart from, by some trick of fate, a handful of Wren's thirty-two city churches.

The City on a Sunday morning or in the middle of the night does more for the history buff than climbing to the top of the Monument, which used to provide panoramic views of the City but has long been overshadowed by skyscrapers. The Monument used to be *the* place for schoolchildren to go: it made a pleasant double-bill coupled with a visit to the Tower of London, which is within easy walking distance to the east. The Monument is 202 feet high, which corresponds exactly with the distance from the base of the Monument at which the Great Fire of London is said to have started. Running to the top used also to be a challenge for keep-fit fanatics before joggers began to appear on the City streets.

Off nearby Cheapside lie Bread Street, Pie Corner, Poultry Lane and Pudding Lane and Milk Street: the open-air seventeenth-century equivalent of a twentieth-century hypermarket. Cheapside is probably the oldest street of any size in London. The name first appears in 1067, roughly at the time when the Tower of London, or the White Tower at least, was being built by William the Conqueror. The origin of such familiar names as these is easy to guess at. Haymarket actually did hold a hay market three times a week for about three hundred years. During Elizabeth I's reign, washer-women had been allowed to dry their clothes on the grass, but in the early eighteenth century the road was paved, paid for from money raised by taxes on every load of hay and every load of straw.

Regent Street, which is separated from the Haymarket by Piccadilly Circus, gets its name from the corpulent but handsome Prince Regent, eldest son of George III, who was to become George IV. It was originally planned as a royal road leading from the Prince Regent's house, Carlton House, to Regent's Park, though it was never completed. It was the same architect, John Nash, incidentally, who created Marble

Pincus Rose, garment dealer, Brixton Market, London.

Dim sum (lunchtime snacks – read 'feast') at the Chuen Cheng Ku
restaurant, near Piccadilly Circus, London.

Arch, which stands at the bottom of Edgware Road, on an island circumscribed by pounding traffic at one end of Oxford Street. It was intended as the gateway to Buckingham Palace, but proved too narrow to take certain types of horse-drawn carriages, and so it was moved to its present site.

Pall Mall, where it is so hard to get a taxi between two-thirty and four o'clock on weekday afternoons, because that is when the clubs disgorge their members after lunch, was named after a French ball game, *paille maille* (similar to *boules*), played here during the seventeenth century. Piccadilly, once the heart of fashionable London rather than what it is now, which is a glorified traffic roundabout, got its name from the *pickadiles*, or ruffs, fashionable during the seventeenth century. Holborn commemorates a dried-up river, which created a hollow, or hole, for itself, a dip in the lie of the land that is now crossed by a viaduct. Parallel with Holborn runs Fleet Street. Its name derives from a river, too, but it has not, contrary to popular misconceptions, dried up. A tributary of the Thames, it flows underground, no longer a sewer, and it can in fact be seen by intrepid visitors who venture under the cellar of the celebrated pub Ye Olde Cheshire Cheese in Wine Office Court, just off Fleet Street. Wine Office Court? That comes simply from the collection of wine taxes that were paid here. Wine Office Court, incidentally, leads through to Gough Square, where one of my favourite London museums is Samuel Johnson's former house. Lacking the intimacy of Johnson's House at Lichfield, Staffordshire, it is still elegant and much recommended, incidentally, as a cool retreat on a hot London afternoon. Johnson is thought to have used Ye Olde Cheshire Cheese as his local.

Dr Johnson's House, Gough Square, London. It is intriguingly similar inside to Johnson's birthplace and one-time home at Lichfield, Staffordshire. Its utter peace and quiet belies its closeness to Fleet Street.

More people see something of the City than they used to because the London Museum is there. It is harder to get lost in this museum than most because its exhibits are planned not just in chronological sequence, but in one continuous gallery. The gallery does have twists and turns and different storeys but, in their determination to make sense of London's many-sided history, the organisers of this outstanding place have tried very hard to prevent people going round and round in circles. The still new (it was opened in 1977) Museum, which is within walking distance of St Paul's Cathedral, was an amalgam of the Guildhall Museum and the old London Museum that used to be housed in Kensington Palace. One of the reasons that the Museum has won so many accolades is that you can spend an afternoon here without needing to know the difference between the Stuarts or the Tudors, or whether Henry VIII was on the throne before or after Elizabeth I. Inevitably, there are the favourites. The diorama of the Great Fire of London of 1666, which was always a great attraction at the Kensington Palace Museum, tends to have queues during the school holidays or, during term time, complete classloads of children waiting to thrill to the voice of Sir Michael Hordern reading extracts from Samuel Pepys' diary: Pepys was an eye witness at the Fire.

Then there is the Lord Mayor's coach, several tons of gilt and lacquer, built about 1757, with its elaborate painted panels, its red-and-gilt wheels. Once a year it is not confined to barracks like Cinderella, but is rolled out of specially constructed doors for the Lord Mayor's Show in November. The new Lord Mayor climbs into its opulent seats and, pulled by six brewers' drayhorses, travels from the Guildhall to the Law Courts to swear his oath, and then back. There is more of Samuel Pepys: his chessboard, his specs, a pocket watch, a walking stick. There's a real prison cell from Newgate which was last occupied in the 1890s, on whose walls there are genuine inscriptions by prisoners, now long forgotten, who were incarcerated there.

Most Americans seem to treat New York City as an entirely different animal from the rest of the eastern United States. Many Englishmen do the same with London, at least if economic necessity means they have to work there, as they have done for a century or more in fact: witness those sepia photographs of commuters pouring out of Holborn offices in the 1880s en route for outer suburbia. A hundred years later this nightly exodus from the city and The City transforms London, though you would hardly notice any difference among those enclaves of good living like Mayfair and Belgravia, but it does wonders for the back streets around the Mansion House and St Paul's, and summons up long-departed spirits from the dank and eerie precincts of the Tower, which are worth seeing at dead of night because that is about the only time they are deserted.

If I had to choose my favourite London pubs the short list would probably centre around those close to or right on the Thames, especially that part of it that Sir Christopher Wren would have strolled along while he was living on the south bank of the river as St Paul's Cathedral was being completed.

The George, just off Southwark High Street, is a rare survivor from the days of the galleried inns, whose galleries were not, however, just an architectural conceit – like the imitation green shutters you see superimposed on the outside of new executive houses – but simply an early equivalent of the passages that linked upstairs rooms: there was no other way around. The Anchor is hard by the south bank, though you have to clamber up a specially constructed viewing platform to see the river from any sort of perspective.

The Museum of London is – literally – an incomparable introduction to the city. This stone figure of a Roman legionary dates from about the first century AD, and was discovered in what is now Camomile Street.

The last time I was there the restaurant and bars had absorbed three coachloads of Italian tourists, who had upset their English guide greatly by leaving their visits to the lavatory until the moment before they were due to depart for the second half of a London tour. Things were not going his way at all, for in all the confusion and his intense desire to get back on schedule he had physically pulled from their seats – hard won in the mêlée – two English customers who had nothing to do with the tour.

Of course the Anchor has been tarted up, but it is surprising how easy it is to hark back to the days of Hogarth and of Dickens. And there is the Samuel Pepys, a more cavernous and less crowded adaptation of a Thameside warehouse. It looks from north to south across the river, and from its terrace you may just catch the whiff of stale seaweed and drowned rat. It is not, therefore, uncomfortably twee.

This part of the city is a favourite among those small-scale entrepreneurs who organise walking tours of London. I once joined one, finding myself among as motley a collection of people as you will find this side of Chaucer's *Canterbury Tales*. I felt about as comfortable as if I had slipped alone in my shabbiest mac into a film-show off Piccadilly of *Swedish Love Games* and found myself sitting next to the vicar. But in fact the tour was not half bad. It was called Mysterious London and was one of several that were advertised in the *New Statesman*. It cost £2 a head, which included the price of a drink in the first of the two pubs we went to, but no refund if you could not stay the course.

We were in the charge of a retired headmaster, and there was an unexpected pleasure in letting ourselves be shepherded and marshalled as we snaked untidily from the crypt of a fourteenth-century church to a low-ceilinged pub of much more recent date – around 1650. It was better than letting the train take the strain, and just like being back at school, for our guide was no slouch at keeping order. ('Keep up at the back there. If you don't want to listen to what I have to say, then please leave.') He was, however, quite entertaining and informative, and everybody did stay the whole two hours. In the last pub of the evening I bought him a drink, partly because he said he did not accept tips ('Thank you very much, I'll have a barley wine') and it seemed small enough compensation for an evening that could have netted him only £20 after expenses, and partly because I wanted to ask him if he had ever had nobody turn up. 'When nobody turns up it's easy,' he said, 'because then you just go home. It's when one or two turn up that you can be in trouble. You have to go through with it. Once I had three people, one of whom was extremely fat, and would not go at more than two miles an hour, and one of the other two kept wanting to go to the lavatory. Well, as you know, that's easier said than done in the middle of London. In the end I gave up and we all went to Ye Olde Cheshire Cheese for a few drinks.'

Walking as a means of getting around has its supporters, but for my money it has to be a taxi or the top of a bus. It was my aunt from Windsor who told me that certain London taxi drivers were qualified guides and would I please arrange one to take her and her friend from Winnipeg on a tour of the sights. I argued in vain that these arrangements were entirely informal, and that any taxi driver would take you the long way round so you could see a bit of the city. 'That's not it at all,' she protested. 'The taxis have silvery tops and the drivers organise a whole day tour for you, or less if you want it. And I have heard tell', she went on, 'that it's traditional that you take them to lunch.' Of course, she turned out to be quite right, and she got her tour. I found a taxi guide by asking a driver who took me from Euston to Waterloo (which is in itself not a bad way to see a bit of London life), and by all accounts my aunt and her friend got their money's worth. The nicest thing on such a jaunt is that if you are taking the driver to lunch there is absolutely no problem about getting a cab after you leave the restaurant. I am well disposed anyway to London taxi drivers, and impressed by their knowledge. I have only twice knowingly offended one. Once was when I opened the door while he was still coasting to a halt, and the other was when I began to give him directions to a street which I thought was obscure but which he knew intimately.

It is the jostling crowds that put me off big cities, the feeling that you cannot look up at some detail – a statue, a clock – without the risk that somebody will cannon into you. The fact that you will *both* apologise is neither here nor there. But when you are in a coach or on top of a bus you are immune, cocooned from the real world, unless a small child gets on at Marble Arch and dollops ice cream in your lap. And if you take a London Transport Round London sightseeing tour, even though there is no guide, but just a map, you will learn more about London in a couple of hours than most natives do in lifetime. The next best thing is to take a bus during the rush hour through the very centre of the city – just as long as you are not in a hurry. The painfully slow progress that can give you indigestion if you are late for an important appointment turns out to be an advantage in itself.

In London I prefer to be a fly on the wall or a night bird, but most people are able to participate in the everyday cut and thrust of the city without it getting them down. A problem is that two thousand years or more of civilisation, layer upon layer, generation after generation, makes it very hard to get to grips with the place the way one can with some bit of West Yorkshire moor or Devon fishing community. London was the very opposite of a planned city. Its location was pure fluke: it happened to be possible (just) for the Romans to bridge the Thames at the very point where a straight line between Newhaven and York and from Dover to Chester, crossed. Being an easily negotiable river, London's prowess as a trading centre was assured.

You cannot begin to appreciate London without spending some time near or preferably on the Thames. At the very least, take a journey downstream from Westminster Pier or Tower Pier to Greenwich. Preceded by, say, a couple of hours in the Strangers' Gallery in the House of Commons during Prime Minister's question time (possibly the best free show in London), or avoiding the crowds in the Tower or on HMS *Belfast*, it could be more fruitful than a whole day spent traipsing around Oxford Street or half a dozen museums. Of course, a lot depends on your guide, but the salutary experience most of them have had of American tourists who are far more knowledgeable about English history than most Englishmen tends to put them on their toes.

If it were not for the Thames, I suspect, people would know London better than they do. It has kept South Londoners from getting to know North Londoners; it has meant the inhabitants of Hornsey know Suffolk better than they know Sydenham, that people from Catford consider Islington very foreign. If I were charged with giving outsiders some sense of what London is like I would not give priority to St Paul's or Westminster Abbey, Trafalgar Square or Horseguards Parade. All that can come later. I would get people criss-crossing the city: a number 36 bus from Kilburn to

Camberwell, a number 30 from Islington to Kensington. More ambitiously, a tube ride from Amersham to Ongar, the far extremes of west and east, to that point where the countryside meets the suburbs, can make Londoners who rub shoulders in their offices with people who think nothing of commuting from Norfolk and Dorset, feel as if those towns are just down the road.

Suburbia and commuter country are rarely enjoyed for their own sake. The southerly suburbs of Dulwich, Beckenham and Bromley are more salubrious than what you will find north of the Thames – with the exception of Hampstead and Highgate – partly because of their proximity to Surrey and Kent. Those packed Metropolitan Line tube trains en route for Amersham are not a patch for style on First Class carriages bound for Woking, Carshalton and Esher. And you would hardly believe that inconsequential railway halts like Burgess Hill and Hever take about the same length of time to get to from the sweat and smoke of rush hour London as it takes directors in their City dining rooms to consume their main course. There is a whole world outside the city about half an hour by train or, especially if you live to the west, just a few minutes more by motorway.

To call London a collection of villages has become something of a cliché. But the outsider who has perhaps once taken a day trip to Madame Tussauds from Blackpool (yes, it can be done) may find that an afternoon pottering about, say, Dulwich Village or Highgate and then taking a bus ride to picnic in one of the royal parks may, in the space of a few hours, might change his misconceptions about the concrete jungle. Though it is only twelve minutes by train from Victoria Station, and then a five minute walk, Dulwich Village, not to be confused with the more workaday East Dulwich, could actually be some rigidly preserved village in, say, stockbroker belt Surrey or on the edge of the New Forest. Unlikely though it seems, it lies in the metropolitan borough of Southwark. It would not come as too much of a surprise to see post-chaises scurrying through the main street of the village, past houses set back from the road beyond wide grassy verges, much enhanced by white fence posts and chain fences, that must have been universally admired and envied when they were first built in the middle of the eighteenth century. Opposite what was once known as the College of God's Gift, founded in 1613 and opened for business in 1690, stands the Dulwich Picture Gallery, which would be exceptional by any standards even if it did not enjoy such a delightful location. Opened in 1814, its collection of Old Masters is outstanding. Both pictures and gallery have suffered quite a few vicissitudes: apart from a severe bombing raid in 1944, the gallery is notorious for having been robbed every few years – or so it seems. At least one painting seems to regularly turn up in some suburban garage or in the back of the taxi of some bemused driver from Ilford. Dulwich College proper stands in all its late-Victorian grandiosity half a mile away. The only time most of the thousand-plus pupils get to see the original school is on Founder's Day, on which they commemorate Edward Alleyn, an Elizabethan actor-manager who made good – especially when he was appointed to a lucrative sinecure by James I.

Hampstead is probably the nearest north London equivalent to stockbroker-Dulwich, though the differences are quite marked. For one thing it stands on a hill over four hundred feet above sea level, thus affording its residents good views of the Post Office Tower. 'Good' in terms of clarity rather than aesthetic appeal, perhaps. John Constable found in Highgate and Hampstead a quality of light to be compared with his

Dulwich Village, London. You could happily believe you are in some corner of Salisbury or Cheltenham, but central London is only twelve minutes by train from West Dulwich station.

own rural Suffolk, but even he is just one more famous name associated with the tree-dotted heath, the ponds that seem to ice up at even modest December frosts, the Montmartresque steep steps, the restaurants and the boutiques. Dr Johnson, Bonnie Prince Charlie, Guy Fawkes and George Orwell lived here, and Henry Moore and Barbara Hepworth shared a house while they were struggling to make a name for themselves. Not that this cuts any ice with the people who turn the bars of internationally known pubs, like Jack Straw's Castle and The Flask, into madhouses, nor the thousands of Londoners who swarm over Hampstead Heath for the August Bank Holiday Monday fair.

People who would settle in Dulwich or Hampstead but who need the calming influence of the River Thames, often settle for Richmond. You can get there by Underground (though most of the journey is actually in the open), bus or conventional train, but *the* way to go, if time allows, is by boat from Westminster. On a sunny day, people stroll along the river and enjoy something approaching a seaside atmosphere. There are ice creams, deckchairs, pubs with flowery gardens, people taking it easy. This is one of those places, like Hampton Court and Kew, that are not so much London suburbs as country towns in their own right. Grassy stretches of the river bank invite people to bathe: the river is clean even at Tower Bridge now, and is cleaner-than-clean at Richmond. Thus refreshed, you may feel energetic enough to climb to the highest parts of this elegant but liveable-in town in order to test whether you really can see six counties from the top of Richmond Hill. (The lass of Richmond Hill, though, much to the disappointment of many visitors, belonged to Richmond in Yorkshire.)

Hampton Court Palace, Surrey. By far the best way to get there is by river boat from central London. Many of England's kings and queens did just that.

Richmond's handsome five-arched bridge over the Thames is a good example of eighteenth-century architecture, but this was no new town even then. The Richmond Theatre, the original 'Theatre on the Green', dates from 1765, though the present one – a good deal more comfortable, incidentally – just got in while it could be called Victorian: it was completed in 1899. In Henry VIII's time, the green was part of the grounds of the old palace. It had been built by Henry VII in about 1500, but it is Henry VIII people remember when they go to buy the 'maids of honour' cakes produced here as closely as possible to the way in which they were made four hundred plus years ago.

A few curves of the Thames beyond Richmond, along banks where farmers are more predominant than commuters, you come to Cookham. It is pretty enough for its own sake, but it also happens to have within its boundaries one of southern England's best art galleries, just the beat of a swan's wing from the Thames. This is the Stanley Spencer Gallery, founded after the artist's death in 1959 as Cookham's own testimonial to the local boy made very good indeed. Spencer was born in a tall semi-detached house near the gallery in 1891, and lived in Cookham for almost fifty years. Shy and gauche, it is said that when he was studying at the Slade School of Art, between 1910 and 1914, he always ran for the earliest possible train back to Cookham after his day's work. The village, which despite the modern traffic in the High Street retains much of the tranquility that Spencer loved, was one of the main influences in his life. The other two were religion, particularly his reading of the Bible, and his personal experiences during the First World War, and the most striking thing about Spencer's paintings is the way he interpreted Biblical events as happening in the everyday Cookham scene. But not all his paintings have a religious theme: one of the most famous is 'Swan Upping at Cookham'. Swan upping, an event regularly seen and much loved by tourists, when young swans are marked by their owners, takes place in July each year.

Cookham is still surprisingly unknown; Henley is a different proposition. If you came here at any time other than July, you would have no idea that for several days of the year the stretch of river hard by the red-brick and whitewashed houses overlooking the wooded green knoll by a bend in the Thames is the setting for the Henley Royal Regatta. Elevated in some people's minds to the same level as Royal Ascot and Goodwood in the social calendar, it is not as exclusive as some people would like to think. You stand more chance of getting into the Stewards' Enclosure here than Ascot's Royal Enclosure, though you do have to be proposed and seconded by a member. Henley Regatta takes place over just a mile and 550 yards of river, and upwards of 50,000 people come for the July event. The Regatta authorities own 120 acres of riverside and, as long as you obey certain rules, some written, most unwritten, you will not be uncomfortable. If offered a drink, ask for Pimms. If wondering what to wear, any bright blazer will do, as long as you wear a collar and tie too, and you will not remove your blazer until edicts are issued from the Stewards' Enclosure. Women are expected to be 'bright and formal'. A colleague who failed to gain entrance to the enclosures insisted that nothing was lost. 'Most people say the best view is to be had from the riverbank anyway,' he said, 'and that is free.'

The source of most rivers turns out to be a trickle of nothing very special somewhere among a mass of peat bogs, or, if you are really lucky, a spring in the middle of a cow pasture, where cow pats are less of a hazard than the sodden grass underfoot. The source of the Thames is a little more impressive, but only because somebody has had the sense of drama to construct a statue around the spring at Thameshead in Gloucestershire, where the river first appears, but even then, most of the time, it is dry: only after heavy rainfall among the Cotswolds will there be anything worth seeing. I have to admit this is taken on hearsay. A friend drove, walked and stumbled to Neptune's Statue, as it is known locally, and wished he had just stayed in the pub instead. 'There was more to look at when we had a burst pipe last January,' he said.

I was once put upon and made to help manoeuvre a cabin cruiser from Kingston upon Thames, going upstream: not exactly in the path of Jerome K. Jerome, but certainly through the heart of what you would never imagine to be one of the most densely populated stretches of southern England – densely populated, too, with ghosts of the past. Saxon kings used to be crowned at Kingston, long before there were any coronations at Westminster Abbey; Hampton Court was where Henry VIII honeymooned – not once but several times – and it was a favourite, too, of Charles II, who used to ride here all the way from his London palace at Whitehall in time for lunch overlooking the river. That Charles used to make such a journey on horseback would

Follow that. A Royal Ascot winner is led into the unsaddling enclosure.

have seemed unusual, because then, and for a couple of hundred years before, the river was a thoroughfare in itself. You could pop out at certain fixed points along the water and hire a chauffeured rowing boat as readily as you can call a taxi today.

King John signed Magna Carta at Runnymede. Windsor Castle, which King John did not use, is a few miles upstream. The oldest inhabited royal castle in the western world, it has had its cut-out cornflake box look only since the early 1800s, when it was extended and remodelled by George III. No fewer than eighteen kings and queens had lived here by the mid-fifteenth century. It is said to be the present Queen's favourite London home, and is full of family memories. She and other members of the Royal Family came here to escape the London blitz.

A short detour from Windsor offers a chance to see stockbroker belt Surrey in all its contentedness. The drive from Windsor-proper to Virginia Water happens to run through Windsor Great Park, thereby producing a double bonus. The name of this suburb par excellence derives from the lake two miles long, amid woods at the southern end of the park. The park was laid out by the first Duke of Cumberland as a way of recuperating after his crushing defeat of Bonnie Prince Charlie at the battle of Culloden. Occupational therapy indeed! He decided where the lake should go, planted the first cedars, oaks and beeches, and in so doing, left a legacy for the population of north-west Surrey that, though much mocked, is a model of urban life in a country setting. Even the shops stand in a row as neat and tidy as in toytown.

Best of all for people who would know the Home Counties are probably Green Line buses. Being comfortable to sit in and let the world go by, they will appeal to the armchair traveller: the countryside without muddy feet, the big city without being pushed and shoved. One minor advantage of coach or bus travel is that you can with impunity peep over garden walls into people's living-rooms, through supermarket windows and the cabs of lorries, enjoying impertinent views of people's private lives. These familiar and reassuring buses, whose drivers regard themselves as something of an elite, are green and white: just green enough when you spot them in the middle of the metropolis to suggest those rural backwaters that lie so surprisingly close to London. Green Line buses do not only ferry people to outlying parts of the capital and its on-the-doorstep forests and farms, but have introduced many who are daunted by the business of joining organised coach tours or getting to the appropriate rail terminal to make excursions by train, to the pleasures of the rural Home Counties. A hundred leafy enclaves in the stockbroker belt are no longer just names on the map.

Green Line buses strike right at the heart of cities and towns, and there are no parking problems. Nor are there treks from railway stations or tour-coach parks. There is room on the luggage racks for that outsize lampshade you might buy in the spectacular open-air market at Hitchin, in Hertfordshire (take Route 732). And that exotic plant you might pick up in the shop at the Royal Horticultural Society's fabulous gardens at Wisley, in Surrey, will remain as firmly rooted in its compost as Green Line buses are in the affections of Londoners. A perhaps unexpected market has been carved out of the London suburbs among business travellers who, rather than make a couple of changes on the Underground (despite the tremendous advantages of the Piccadilly Line extension to Heathrow) prefer to go to the airport by Green Line, to Gatwick as well as

There is more to Windsor, Berkshire, than the castle and Windsor Great
Park. The town has a number of surprising corners and modest back streets
that provide relief from the mass of tourists.

Heathrow. You can also get to Biggin Hill and the famous wartime aerodrome, where the annual International Air Fair is held, and to Hendon, a few miles north-west of London, known for its RAF Museum. Green Line also have an extremely useful link between Gatwick and Heathrow: they gave it the rather tongue-in-cheek number 747.

Among country houses, there are Green Line connections to Chartwell, Winston Churchill's much-loved home, but a lovely house in its own right; Hatfield House; Woburn Abbey and the Wild Animal Kingdom; Knole House (you could have tea in stockbroker-Tudor Sevenoaks afterwards); Hampton Court; Knebworth House; Luton Hoo – an almost perfect eighteenth-century house designed by one of Scotland's best exports, Robert Adam. Among beauty spots that can be reached direct from central London are Surrey's Box Hill, which Keats was so fond of, and Runnymede. Among historic country towns are Aylesbury, Hertford (surprisingly unspoilt for a county town), Hitchin, the cathedral city of St Albans, Dorking and Guildford.

It was an enforced stay in Guildford, and time to kill that took me, on the advice of a long out-of-print guidebook I found in a second-hand bookshop smelling of old attics, to a green enclave that seemed a hundred miles from anywhere, and not – as it actually was – well inside commuter country. I explored the eerie Silent Pool, just off the busy Guildford to Dorking road, near Shere, and Abinger Common, just a short excursion from the more famous Abinger Hammer, and near to Sutton Place, which used to be Paul Getty's country home. You do not even need a Green Line bus, or a more parochial and darker-green London Country bus: a run-of-the-mill red one gets you here – though it will usually be a single-decker.

Surrey is also about sandy commons and banks of pine trees, beech forests and spectacular views from the top of hills. The more accessible these are, the more they are inclined to be visited at weekends. The trick is to get just outside the commuter belt, though those commuters are inexhaustible in their search for the best of both worlds, which is what commuting is all about. There is always a good chance of finding somebody's BMW parked outside a rural station that looks at first sight as if it could be two hundred miles from the city but is, you discover by judicious perusal of the Southern Region timetable, actually only about an hour's train-ride.

Box Hill is one of those famous viewpoints. Though only six hundred feet high, it is as much a landmark for rural Surrey as, say, Kilnsey Crag is for North Yorkshire. It gets its name from the box trees that grow here. And the Hog's Back is to Guildford what Box Hill is to Dorking. You can stick a pin in almost any corner of Surrey where the North Downs run and a find a viewpoint and, from Gibbet Hill, the second-highest point of Surrey at 895 feet, probably the best views of all. To the north, almost directly below, is the hollow of the Devil's Punchbowl. To the south, the ground falls steeply away into the wooded valley where, somewhere below, Haslemere is lurking. Much as Sussex people will set the South Downs against the North Downs, it is not just the nearness to London and the opportunity for millions of people to get away from it all that gives the latter a special quality. They are more wooded, less exposed to the wind, more sudden and more steep, and less rolling, which means they are more difficult to get to at first sight, but once you have dealt with gradients of one in four or five, the work is done. The highest point of all, incidentally, is Leith Hill, which at over 960 feet is also the highest point in the whole of south-east England.

Northern and mid Kent have made a virtue out of a necessity. They do not deny the

The old blacksmith's shop, Abinger Hammer, Surrey.

London link, but capitalise on it. A London Transport bus stops directly outside a four-hundred-year-old red-brick pub, a village street has boutiques and butchers' shops almost as chic as Hampstead's, a Women's Institute has a lot of members who think nothing of taking a day return on Southern Region's grubby electric trains to go shopping in Oxford Street and Knightsbridge and to have tea at Fortnum and Mason. Oasthouses are no longer in danger of being razed to the ground, but are converted into talking-point residences with picture windows. ('A special feature is the circular sunken bath.') Pick-your-own fruit farms are cheek-by-jowl with half-timbered mock-Tudor roadhouses. Much of the county is tucked away in nooks and crannies left by the most aggressive pick-a-stick arrangement of motorways and trunk roads in the south of England. On a mid-autumn morning I drove from Victoria, via Bromley, to Otford, and then to Sevenoaks. In Otford, farm labourers rub shoulders in the snug of the low-ceilinged local – rarely any jukeboxes or space invaders – with accountants and stockbrokers and headmasters, and are not patronised by them. Half the contents of a wickerwork and knick-knack shop spill out on to the pavement to catch the last rays of the year's sun. Round the willow-shaded sun-dappled green, complete with pond, elegant red-brick Georgian houses put up with the vicissitudes of the twentieth century, and less than half a mile away a new dual-carriageway sweeps arrogantly over the motorway.

Sheep graze unconcernedly: do they have any preference for quiet country lanes or are they actually indifferent to their surroundings as long as the grazing is good enough? But in making for Sevenoaks that bit of road flatters to deceive, and you are quickly back on to a winding lane into the town centre. Sevenoaks for me means toasted teacakes and a steamy crowded teashop bursting at the seams with tired shoppers, middle-aged waitresses and the occasional schoolgirl on a Saturday job. There is usually a queue ('Quick Elsie, there's a table over there'), and you might find they serve 'real tea', not tea bags.

Once, after tea in Sevenoaks, I spent a late afternoon walking around Knole Park and Knole House itself and, after two hours of meandering, it was a pleasure to sit back on a Green Line bus and return to London. The closer it is to the rush hour the more pleasurable it is, and even mundane Streatham and Brixton become objects of curiosity as you gaze at them from your elevated position at the back of the bus. By car and by bus this part of Kent is all about leaving frantically busy roads and turning off into rural backwaters. Sudden views too can be spectacular, even if those views embrace a stretch of motorway in the distance.

Virginia Woolf has left probably the best impression of Knole House slumbering in its great park close to Sevenoaks. In her novel *Orlando*, she writes of the house, 'There it lay in the early sunshine of spring. It looked like a town rather than a house . . . courts and buildings, grey, red-plum colour, lay orderly and symmetrical; the courts were some of them oblong, some of them square; in this was a fountain, in that a statue . . . spaces of greenest grass lay in between and clumps of cedar trees and beds of bright flowers . . . This vast, yet ordered building, which could house a thousand men and perhaps 2000 horses, was built, Orlando thought, by workmen whose names were unknown.'

It is handy to be able to pin convenient labels on corners of the country that have memorable characteristics. Kent is always tagged 'The Garden of England', but I think the Vale of Evesham makes a better garden of England than Kent, although fruit farms, hop fields and apple orchards are common to both. I think of it more as it was once, perhaps three or four hundred years ago, cloaked (almost suffocated might be a better description) by great waves of deciduous woodland, when there were more charcoal burners than hop pickers. The best of it is a county of steep lanes and heavily wooded escarpments, of bracken-filled, sudden little valleys and fierce winds that sweep up from lower lying land as you walk through beechwoods or lean over a stile, say, to admire an arrangement of red-brick and pantiled cottages clustered together to manage a quorum and call themselves a village.

Chilham, Kent. Winter is the time Chilham's famous medieval banquets at the Castle come into their own, drawing coach parties (often in period costume) from London and beyond.

For many Londoners Kent is probably all about leafy lanes and Sunday afternoon cricket matches. Or deckchairs at Margate, or waiting around at Dover to catch a ferry. But winters can be severe: Kent gets more snow than all the Home Counties combined, for example. The more you examine the county the more it resists too easy a categorisation. What for example have the Medway towns got to do with those apple orchards, and what have the coalfields of the county got to do with the White Cliffs of Dover?

Losing your way in rural Kent, if you are not in a hurry, could be the best thing to happen to you. On the outskirts of Penshurst once, in trying to make a short cut, I

The doorway into the Chapel of St Benedict at Canterbury Cathedral,
Kent. On 29 December 1170 Thomas Becket entered here while being
pursued by the knights of Henry II who were to murder him.

stumbled across a cream-washed and timbered house that, reliably dated about 1270, turned out to be older than Penshurst Place itself. Over a glass of local cider I commiserated with the owner of the house: he had just finished excavating a lake and poured into it a million gallons of water that had, to his consternation, simply drained away. It transpired that in medieval times, this had been marshy land that needed draining. The original fourteenth- or fifteenth-century drains still operated all too well. I say commiserated, but the fact that he was living in such surroundings clearly militated against excessive sympathy. Again I was reminded of the proximity of London, because he said, 'Most days I commute. It's easy. I just go to Tunbridge Wells station and it's an hour to Charing Cross.' Tunbridge Wells seems hardly to belong to Kent, and though it makes no pretence of ever being a spa again, it still has more in common with Cheltenham, Harrogate, Droitwich, or Buxton, than with any other Kentish town.

If you drive towards Uckfield on the Brighton road, Sussex is just down one hill and over the brow of the next. The difference in terrain as you cross the border is as marked as the difference in accent in the space of three hundred yards on either side of, say, the English and Scottish border. You expect more shades of grey, more of an indistinct blur between the two counties, but distinctions are surprisingly marked. Perhaps this is the way England survives in its compartmentalised, individualistic way, like a small town preserving what is left of the past and resisting incursions from developers. Trees and hedges are, however, a common factor. Everyday roadside copses, or those avenues of overlapping interweaving oaks and ashes that Sussex people take for granted, are noted casually only when the sun is high and filters through the canopy of a wood. The small country towns of east and west Sussex do not seem to have the same everyday problems experienced by the real world. You can't quite take them seriously: all those half-timbered cottages next door to intricate redbrick, with low ceilings and small doors, more geared, it seems, to Walt Disney gnomes than real people with mortgages. Even place names cannot be taken all that seriously. One crossroads near Billingshurst offered me Partridge Green to the right, or Nuthurst to the left. There's Uckfield and Cuckfield, Muddles Green, and Small Dole. Going west towards Billingshurst and then south, you could almost imagine that the sea is close, for the countryside is becoming more open, farms are flatter and the South Downs are still to be negotiated. One advantage for cottage dwellers in Sussex and other hilly counties is that you have a good chance of finding a place to live that is tucked protectively under the brow of some hill. En route for Worthing from Billingshurst I made a detour to the inconsequential village of Bury, which consists of little more than a few cottages and a typical Sussex church leading to what used to be a ferry over the River Arun but has long since been closed: all the better for people living in the cottages who now have virtually no traffic passing their studded oak doors.

I stayed overnight in Lewes, which was described by William Cobbett when he visited it in 1822 as 'a model of solidity and neatness'. There is a handful of churches, but more antique shops and bookshops. It is a nice architectural mixture set off by cobbled streets, lots of greenery and a hilly position that is not too hard on the muscles but nevertheless allows prospective angles and viewpoints not generally vouchsafed to the visitor to towns amid completely flat country. The best view of all is from the battlements of the Norman Castle, which used to be a much more imposing place even

Lewes, East Sussex, succeeds where many smaller communities have failed:
it is a text-book example of sensible conservation, a rare mix of different
architectural styles.

than it is today, until about 1620, when most of it was broken up and sold to local people
at sixpence a load, for them to use as they wished. The bowling green was once a
jousting ground but those knights of old are remembered nowhere near as vividly as
Guy Fawkes, for every 5 November Lewes is the venue for the most famous bonfire
night celebrations in the south of England: Lewes had a long Protestant tradition, and
was violently anti-Catholic during the first few years of the seventeenth century, when
Guy Fawkes's plot to blow up the Houses of Parliament and restore a Catholic
monarchy was discovered. On the big day, five thousand flaming torches are paraded
through the centre of Lewes.

The following day I retreated behind the Sunday papers in a small congenial, smoky
pub in Bosham (which is pronounced 'Bozzum'), at the head of one of Chichester

harbour's many subsidiary creeks. (Along with Bellingham in Northumberland, and Wymondham in Norfolk – 'Bellinjam' and 'Windum' respectively – it catches nearly everybody out. But beware Wymondham in Leicestershire.)

The Romans' Fishbourne Palace has been excavated nearby, and the Danes were subsequent invaders. King Canute, who was king between 1016 and 1035, also had a palace here, and a girl believed to be his eight-year-old daughter was buried in the church. The story of Canute standing at the edge of the English Channel needs amplification: what he was doing was proving to his courtiers, who were flattering him and cajoling him to ridiculous lengths, that he was, after all, only human.

It is one thing to admire the white cliffs of Dover from an incoming cross-channel ferry, but altogether a superior matter to walk over them from inland west Sussex along the South Downs Way, an eighty-mile route that is, unlike some of England's long distance walks, easy to appreciate in short doses. Hardy, dyed-in-the-heather walkers regard the South Downs Way as very easy meat indeed, but do not be discouraged by this, especially since some of England's prettiest villages, including Steyning and Alfriston, are just a stumble down the hillside from the route and, car free, this could turn out to be the best way to visit them. You are within a short detour to Devil's Dyke and Ditchling Beacon, and also close to the great Iron Age fort called Chanctonbury Ring, north of Worthing, probably the most famous landmark of all on the route. The walk takes you over the Seven Sisters, which are, incidentally, much more impressive white cliffs than Beachy Head, and ultimately to the promenade at genteel Eastbourne. People are sometimes surprised to hear that the South Downs, which extend tortuously from Hampshire's eastern border – they are first evident near Winchester – are never more than a thousand feet high. But it is only as you approach Beachy Head, near Eastbourne, walking over the great chalk masses on which the Downs lie like a thin and crumpled carpet, that you really see much evidence of the white chalk.

It was a drive I made to East Anglia from Eastbourne that proved to my surprise that it is just an hour from rural Sussex, via the M25 and the M11, to the best of Hertfordshire: heavily wooded, arable, hilly enough to annoy cyclists and to create sometimes spectacular views, albeit occasionally of the outer edges of the metropolis itself. Much of the best of the county is easily accessible by road, up the A10 towards but stopping well short of Cambridge, or even the unlovely but satisfyingly fast A1, with its sporadic stretches of motorway. My own preference is for the eastern side of the county, but since it is not much more than thirty-five miles from west to east, and since the exception proves the rule, and there are indeed some exceptional corners in the far west, that is a spurious distinction.

It is therefore the easiest of the Home Counties to find if, like the Automobile Association, you take Marble Arch as your starting point for most journeys by car. You head for Barnet, almost part of London yet surprisingly rural (on a misty autumn evening you half expect a highwayman to spring at you from a bush), and follow your nose. It should lead you via the whiff of woodsmoke or fertile earth, or mushrooms ready for picking, or locally brewed beer, up through Potters Bar towards the Green Belt, to the ancient and unspoilt county town of Hertford – which seems somehow to have escaped the ravages of chainstores and supermarkets, and to have specialised in antique shops instead – to Ware, whose Great Bed now reposes in the Victoria and Albert Museum: the Great Bed used not to be unique, but simply a particularly substantial example of the sort of bed found in many a coaching inn on the outskirts of big cities. Unless you were a very important person indeed, not only did you not expect to find a room to yourself but you probably had to share a bed as well. The Great Bed of Ware, and many others like it, could accommodate eight or ten people together, generally too exhausted by their travels to indulge in any monkey business.

Hertfordshire is a densely populated county, as any journey on one of the crowded commuter trains that ply to and from King's Cross, Finsbury Park, St Pancras or Moorgate indicates. But in any one of a hundred villages you could believe you were a day's journey from London. Farmers are as prosperous as the city financiers who are disgorged from Eastern Region's new electric trains at St Albans and Welwyn Garden City. Once, in December, I stood on Letchworth railway station with two farmers who were on their way to the Smithfield Show, for all the world in their brogues and their tweeds like easy-going, slow thinking Herefordshire yeomen. Their weather-beaten look and their inexpertly knotted ties belied the fact that they had, respectively, just parked an XJ12 and a new Range Rover.

Many a dowager and deb who never thought they would be seen dead north of Hampstead may find themselves in and around Berkhamsted en route for one of the country's most famous health farms, which manages very cleverly to be both sybaritic and ascetic at the same time. Some debs can be seen cycling along West Hertfordshire's leafy lanes on summer Sunday afternoons, but in Berkhamsted itself they quickly learn to avoid the High Street on account of its traffic fumes, and to prefer the tow-path of the Grand Union Canal that runs through the town, parallel with the busiest railway line in Britain – London to the Midlands, out of Euston. If you have the energy you can thus walk or cycle all the way to Hemel Hempstead and, if you are lucky, find a good excuse to lean and watch canal boaters negotiating a lock, rising up to meet the higher water level, sometimes looking rather embarrassed, as if part of some elaborate National Theatre stage set. People often get into a tangle. One man in particular was quickly losing his cool in 70 degrees of heat in front of dozens of spectators as he failed to understand the intricacies of the lock. His wife was no help: 'I said all the time we should have had a holiday cottage,' she shrilled.

I once asked a lock-keeper on the Grand Union Canal near Berkhamsted on one of those warm shirt-sleeve Sunday afternoons whether he got bored. 'I used to work in a factory,' he beamed, as he surveyed all he was master of, 'so you can imagine what it feels like to work here.' I followed his gaze along rows of bright geraniums and along the shadows of tall poplars, past Constable-esque pastures and copses, past unmodernised cottages with vegetable gardens, back to where a Sunday school party of ducklings was crossing the canal, and understood what he meant.

Old Hemel Hempstead is an antidote to the bland modern part of town, and should be taken at least once a quarter. It is excellently preserved – two fine and labyrinthine pubs, the King's Arms and the White Hart – and on one side of the High Street are pretty municipal gardens with gnarled trees (and gnarled gardeners) that have miraculously survived the ravages of property developers. I once took a coach party of Women's Institute ladies for an evening in one of Hemel Hempstead's haunted pubs, but unfortunately the landlord's enthusiasm for a quick profit had militated against the good feed we had all anticipated. In the end we all had to fill up on fish and chips down the road, but very nice they were too.

Like Berkhamsted, St Albans has too much traffic to contend with, but it does have enough redeeming features to make it worth finding a place to park – even apart from the abbey. Rural Hertfordshire is surprisingly easy to get lost in. I once took a mini-bus load of Canadian tourists, who were fans of George Bernard Shaw, along the Devonshire-narrow lanes to Shaw's longtime home at Ayot St Lawrence. A mini-bus had to suffice: a full-scale coach could hardly have negotiated the tortuous back doubles. When it is opening time at the Brocket Arms and when the almost adjacent tea shop and tea garden are in business, the sleepy village street of Ayot becomes quite animated.

Ayot St Lawrence would probably have never been discovered had it not been for the fact that Shaw lived here from 1906, when he was fifty, until his death after falling from a tree in the garden at the age of ninety-four. They say he settled here because on a country walk he noticed a tombstone in the churchyard which read 'Mary Anne South. Born 1825. Died 1895. Her time was short.' If seventy was to be regarded as 'short', this was the place for GBS. Part of Shaw's house is open to the public, but what appealed to me most was the revolving kiosk in the garden that was his summer workroom. By means of one of those mechanical contrivances which intrigued Shaw but seemed to plague him, you could and can move the hut round as the day progresses in order to make the most of the available sunlight.

If Shaw's house were for sale, and not in the hands of the National Trust, it would fetch as much as some Border castle or Knightsbridge penthouse – not because of the literary connections (they might add a couple of thousand pounds, at the most) but because of the proximity of London: no more, via Welwyn Garden City railway station, than an hour and a quarter away. Such are the best corners of the Home Counties. For people who *think* they like living in the country, they can be so near but so far.

Perhaps because it is something of a buffer-zone between workaday Essex and Buckinghamshire, Hertfordshire has always been overshadowed by more rural Bucks. For one thing, you can get there by Underground. Amersham on a soporific Sunday afternoon, as you pass the time of day with the London Transport guard, may seem the most unlikely stop on the whole of the Underground network – though far from being a sybaritic experience, it is at least very convenient and therefore smart. Much of the best of the county is well on the tourist beat. There is Marlow (riverside walks, half-timbered coaching inns), Old Amersham (Georgian architecture, more pubs, a historic market place), Chalfont St Giles (John Milton's cottage, stockbroker-Tudor, even more pubs) and Waddesdon Manor, built by the Rothschilds as a rural retreat at the end of the nineteenth century.

The lanes of Buckinghamshire make a pretty back way into Oxford, if you have time on your hands and eschew the M40 motorway. Go via the Chalfonts (Chalfont Park, Chalfont St Peter, Chalfont St Giles) via Amersham, Little Missenden, Great Missenden and Princes Risborough. And if there is time make secondary detours to Burnham Beeches, which is a more genteel and parochial Epping Forest, and to Brackley, whose wide and handsome street has not changed fundamentally since stagecoaches used to stop here in the eighteenth century, to revive the inner man and the inner horse on the journey between Banbury and London.

Buckingham itself is not, many people are surprised to hear, the county town –

although it was until a great fire, in 1725, destroyed most of the place. After that the administration of the county's affairs was taken over by Aylesbury. Thus much of Buckingham immediately post-dates the first quarter of the eighteenth century and is therefore a pleasure in itself.

There is nothing about Buckinghamshire that will frighten the horses or upset old ladies, unless it is poor old Slough, which has never recovered from the things Sir John Betjeman once said about it. I am, however, grateful for Slough. I have relatives in Windsor and live in Hertfordshire: there is a very convenient shopping centre directly between the two, in the heart of Slough, and on several occasions I have refuelled on Mars bars, TV dinners and cans of Fanta.

Milton's Cottage, Chalfont St Giles, Buckinghamshire. John Milton came to live here in 1664 to escape the Great Plague of London, and it was here that he wrote *Paradise Lost* (for which he earned the sum of £5).

II

Map 8 The Coast

Coastal England:
down to the sea again,
and again, and again

Round the ragged rocks, and the best beaches in Europe;
ozone, mudflats and the smell of wet dog;
the resorts in spring, summer, autumn and winter;
rock shops and rock pools

We do like to be beside the seaside. But we take our pleasures seriously. Ice-creams are rarely refused at Bexhill simply because a chill wind is bowling senior citizens along the prom like spinning tops, and a final dip before going home for tea is not to be turned down simply because everybody else left half an hour ago and the sea is already pounding against the promenade. (Actually *bathing* in England in cold weather can bring you close to death. Immersion for five minutes in water of 40°F. will cause a stiffness in the limbs, and death will follow between half an hour and two hours later: the temperature of the seas around England is at or near 40°F. for seven months of the year.)

Apart from swimming or promenading in winter, at all times of the year people do things which would make their toes curl with embarrassment at home. Where else but in an English seaside resort, for example, would you find people walking into shops devoted exclusively to the sale of rock which is contorted into such bizarre shapes that the walking sticks and false teeth seem quite bland and unimaginative?

Many towns that are distinguished in their own right have the further advantage of the seaside either at their door or just round the corner. A short car or train ride from the centre of Newcastle or Liverpool to the sea will rejuvenate the jaded city dweller. Half the considerable charm of Hull derives from its workaday docks, largely unseen though they might be, and the proximity of one of the most impressive rivers in the north. And not even people who have discovered the subtle pleasures of seafaring towns like Grimsby and Fleetwood necessarily know that there are open days in the docks and on the trawlers, or that visitors are allowed at the early morning fish markets from which – even when times are hard – such places get half their living.

Grimsby may not immediately appeal, but you might just be tempted, if you have time on your hands while travelling north by train, between say, London and York, to pick up a train at Doncaster that will take you to Scunthorpe, Grimsby and Cleethorpes. Being totally disregarded, such places often turn out to have much to recommend them. Workaday Grimsby has quite a history. Norwegian ships were trading here in the eleventh and twelfth centuries, and the docks that were built mainly in the second half of the nineteenth century turned this into the most versatile fishing port in the world, bringing in haddock and cod from the seas off Greenland, as well as shrimps from eerie

Tetney Haven, just over the Lincolnshire border. The fish market is an entertaining place. Go any later than about six-fifteen or six-thirty in the morning, and you will have missed the best of it. All that will remain is a pungent smell of fish, and lots of ice and innards on the greasy floor.

Apart from fish markets there is enough going on in most seaside resorts to make the traditional day trip and the stroll along the pier look like very small beer indeed. You can visit lighthouses, take a ferry just for the fun of it and not because you are going anywhere, explore naval dockyards, go for harbour cruises. In some cases you can combine the last two, as at Portsmouth. Nearly every seaside resort has boat trips of some kind available, from Seahouses and its trips to the Farne Islands to bob around among the seals, to the famous Mersey Estuary cruises of the SS *Royal Iris*, on which you can eat and drink at the same time as absorbing some scouse ambience.

There are traditional maritime ceremonies, among them the blessing of the sea at Hastings, in which a lifeboat is used as a pulpit, and Brightlingsea's formal opening of the oyster season, in which the mayor goes out in a boat for the ceremony. There is the Blessing of the Salmon Nets at Norham, near Berwick upon Tweed, and, at Berwick itself, the Tweedmouth Feast and Crowning of the Salmon Queen, a week-long carnival. There are Roman coastal forts and castles whose situation alone has thrust them on to the apron-stage of history: Hastings, Dover, Dunstanburgh, Tintagel and Orford are just a few that spring to mind. There are the town walls of Berwick upon Tweed, highly recommended for a summer evening stroll, even if putting the finishing touches to your suntan is more appealing than the history. You can go diving for sunken treasure, or at least maritime bygones, especially in the Isles of Scilly.

You can even join a barge taking part in one of several races arranged annually off the Essex and Suffolk coast. Some barges used to sleep up to sixty merchant seamen but most have been luxuriously refitted with just a handful of double cabins, and while sailing with the owners (not necessarily in a race) you have all your meals provided. Incidentally, the distinctive brown or rust colour of the barge sails used to be derived from a hand-mixed composition of linseed oil, fish oil and red ochre, which kept the sails in working order despite the ravages of sea spray. Today a commercial preparation is used.

Piers are physically and financially even more vulnerable than railways, being devoted purely to enjoyment. In 1978 alone, two piers were destroyed or so badly damaged that their future was in doubt. They tend to catch fire, and more than once they have been cut in half by passing ships. A walk along the pier, of which fifty still survive around the coast of Britain, is like going to sea without all the hassle. For most people brought up in England it is a nostalgia trip, past knots of anglers more gregarious on piers than on river banks or the shore; past toffee-apple and candy-floss kiosks, what-the-butler-saw machines (there is, at the time of writing, still a special minor thrill in discovering antique machines that should only take old pennies but have been adapted to modern coinage); past mahogany-coloured old women devoted to sea and sun and who 'wouldn't go abroad if you paid me'.

The air really does feel better on the pier, the sea on a good day sparkles more and is bluer. It is a place to meet people, to waste time, to see the town from a distant enough vantage point to add extra enchantment. There are piers open to the public, some of them in winter as well as summer, at Weston-super-Mare, Paignton, Weymouth (whose pier is believed to be the oldest surviving one in Britain), Ryde, on the Isle of Wight, which has a railway, and, also on the Isle of Wight, Sandown and Shanklin, and Totland Bay. Perhaps the most famous pier of them all is Brighton's Palace Pier and, still standing but with a doubtful future, the town's West Pier. (In the 1890s a Professor Reddish charmed visitors by repeatedly riding off the end of West Pier on his bicycle.)

The pier at Worthing has a pavillion and minature railway and, against all the odds, Southend in Essex, which has the longest pier in Europe, may still be able to retain its railway. Elsewhere in Essex there is a pier at Clacton and at Walton on the Naze, and, in neighbouring Suffolk, at Felixstowe and Southwold (but only the stubby shore end), and Lowestoft. Further up the coast there's Great Yarmouth, Skegness (half the length of the original of 1881), Cleethorpes, in Humberside, and the short pier at Redcar, in Cleveland.

Ferries go one better than piers, and provide a breath of air, often for only a few pence, that adds considerably to the enjoyment of the seaside. Even though the unforgettable steamer that once plied between Hull and New Holland has sadly gone for good, you can still, for example, go to Walberswick from Southwold in Suffolk by passenger-only ferry: perhaps the best way of all to visit Walberswick. Similarly, there are passenger ferries from Felixstoweferry to Bawdsey, and between Harwich and Felixstowe. You can go from South Shields to Tynemouth, from Kings Weir to Dartmouth, from Falmouth to St Mawes across the River Helford, over Weymouth harbour. You can – except at high season, when bookings are essential – take a casual trip from Portsmouth and other places on the mainland to the Isle of Wight: more ambitious perhaps, but well within the scope of half a day's jaunt. Incidentally, probably the best way to approach Liverpool is via the ferry from the Wirral peninsula, the way the locals travel to and fro, using the ferry like a bus. It is a tricky and potentially hazardous crossing, even though it is done in only ten minutes, for the Mersey is the fastest-flowing river in the country, and the tide rises about thirty feet. Rumours have it that the Mersey ferry will one day be closed, and that people will have to use the existing alternative tunnel. Inevitably, the ferry has to be heavily subsidised by a local authority which hardly has a lot of cash to spare.

The coastline of Britain is said to be better protected by lighthouses and lightships than any other in the world. Most lighthouses can be visited except on Sundays or during the mornings, and visitors must leave an hour before sunset. Since most of the best of them (from the visitor's point of view) have been built on headlands or promontories, lighthouses are ready-made tourist attractions. They look good, almost as if they are part of the landscape, and are full of interest. Lighthouses open to the public include those at Whitby in North Yorkshire, Seahouses in Northumberland, Cromer in Norfolk, Flamborough Head near Bridlington in Humberside, Portland Bill in Dorset, St Catherine's near Ventnor, Trevose near Padstow, Pendean near St Ives, The Lizard near Helston, St Bees and Whitehaven in Cumbria, and Lundy, off that unlikely island in the Bristol Channel.

Some spectacular beaches are well charted but little visited: I have had virtually the whole of Bamburgh's marvellous flat beach to myself on a sunny August Bank Holiday Monday, and shared the dunes and the empty damp sands of Theddlethorpe, in Lincolnshire – just a few miles north of teeming Mablethorpe – with sporadic low-flying aircraft from the RAF hugging the shoreline. I have walked across Morecambe Bay, being careful to join a conducted party lest that notorious track of half-land half-sea claims me as one of its many victims. I have swum off Jacob's Ladder, near Felixstowe, and off the shingly beaches bordering the mouth of the River Deben on a hot day that has seen police turning traffic away from the town-proper because it has reached saturation point.

I have enjoyed family picnics among the Sahara-like sand dunes at Littlehampton and been away-from-it-all even when the secret hollow in every dune has had its occupants, and I have chatted with contestants in a sea angling competition at Hopton, Norfolk, amid shifting banks of shingle whose constant grating combined with the ebb and flow of the North Sea to produce the kind of unearthly music that Benjamin Britten was able to recapture.

I have stood on the cliffs at Dunwich, in Suffolk, and listened, perhaps half-seriously, to the sound of the sea as it calms down after a storm, for the ringing of long-submerged church bells: a persistent local legend. Dunwich was an important medieval port, and what was once the town (except for the church on top of the hill, whose original graveyard has half-tumbled over the cliff) now lies under water.

If I could live anywhere in England I chose, it would probably be at Southwold, Walberswick, or Dunwich, with the great, heaving grey North Sea for company. You could really believe you are on the edge of the world here, and if the wind sometimes makes you bend double to make any progress along the cliff top or the shore, it helps to render this side of the country safe from too many prying eyes.

Actually, summer holiday beaches can be sad places. Not when people pour on to the sand full of hope, when the sea sparkles enough to hurt your eyes and the aroma of suntan lotion is nostalgic and heady, when you have no sooner settled down in your deckchair than you want to walk along the promenade to buy an ice-cream or investigate the stock of paperbacks at the seasonal kiosk. Rather, at the end of the day, when people start to drift off the sands and a cool breeze reminds you you are not wearing a shirt, and you have got a slight case of sunburn; when litter is picked up by the wind and eddies irritatingly round your feet, and it is an effort to walk back to the promenade, laden down as you are with a deckchair that needs to be returned lest you lose your deposit, and thermos flasks and children's woollies that they would probably have refused to wear even if it had snowed. The concrete was warm and sensual to your feet when you strolled along it at lunchtime but now it turns out to be cold and gritty. As the sun goes down over the terraced Edwardian houses on the far side of the golf course you remember it is a long way to walk back to your hotel or to the only car park you managed to find a place in. It is as melancholy as the end of a decade or a lifetime.

Most seaside resorts have a particular beauty out of season. The more they depend on holidaymakers for their existence, the more vulnerable they seem to be on a blustery Monday morning in November or February. The first time I saw the seafront at Skegness was early on a midsummer evening, at about the time families with toddlers were calling it a day and the men on the dodgems were switching on the fairy lights for the night. The second time was on a misty January afternoon when I was the only person in a cavernous Woolworths.

One of the reasons for the great diversity of English beaches is the geological structure of the country. Inland, it needs a trained geologist to know what is going on. At the seaside, you only need a cliff cut away like a slice of layer cake to give you some idea of how – literally – the land is structured. So you have chalk ('young' rock, only up to 225 million years old) on the South Coast – which is those famous White Cliffs of Dover, for example, and the even more impressive Seven Sisters – and in Cornwall you have granite that can be as old as 600 million years.

Just as varied, and just as noticeable, are the tides. In the Bristol Channel the tidal range may be as much as forty feet (hence the unforgettable sight of glistening mud banks, like cliffs of wet elephants, below Clifton Suspension Bridge), and at Southampton or Portsmouth just a matter of inches.

During the war this island people put their buckets and spades away. Invasion was a constant threat, and even such unlikely landing places as North Devon and what was then Cumberland were mined and obstructed. The Ministry of Defence still controls about 150 miles of coastline, and large stretches of the Dorset, Cornish and Cumbria coast are virtually out of bounds.

Including the Ministry of Defence property, you would need to travel 7,000 miles or so to 'do' Britain by its coastline. And by road, it would be further still. If to the tortuous and ravaged coastline you add the temptations of rivers and estuaries, you would need half a lifetime. I was once sidetracked into a journey up the River Dart in Devon, a memorable experience on a hot summer afternoon, and was burnt almost to a frazzle under a sapphire sky. Better still, I have escaped from the maelstrom that is the heart of the Lake District in high summer, and by way of the Eskdale to Ravenglass railway, travelled through a fairy landscape to a blissfully cool coastline that is one of England's best-kept secrets. On the far side of the country, almost across its narrowest neck, lies an equally wild but comparatively well-charted stretch of coastline around Bamburgh and Dunstanburgh, several miles to the south of which, almost among the suburbs of Newcastle, are the bright and brash resorts of Whitley Bay, North Shields and South Shields.

Perhaps the nicest thing of all about getting away from things and travelling on the edge of England, is the way traditional resorts alternate conveniently with fishing villages that have never seen a bingo parlour, and genteel eventide watering places that would never allow space invaders to darken their doors. Seldom, it seems, are local authorities and conservationists as vigilant as in seaside resorts, perhaps because when they get a whiff of ozone people tend to cast their inhibitions aside. Even seaside architecture has traditionally reflected a sense of liberty, being on the whole generously proportioned, especially compared with the big cities and suburbs. It was railway engineers, however, and not architects who really changed the whole face of seaside resorts, and although you could have taken a pleasure boat from London to Margate as early as 1815, you would have had the place to yourself and a few handfuls of well-heeled Londoners. But by 1835, there were 100,000 people a year (and that mostly concentrated in a few weeks) coming to the town.

Brighton and Southend used to argue about which of them was really 'London-by-the-Sea'. For generations, ever since open-topped tourers and charabancs bowled along the London-to-Southend arterial road, new in the 1930s, Southend's easy access had more than compensated for the predominance of its mudflats over the sands.

There is more to the Essex seaside than Southend, of course. Among my favourites is Clacton, on whose pier I once won a prize at bingo on – of all days – New Year's Day; there is Frinton, with its peace and quiet and its gently shelving sand; there is Walton-on-the-Naze, whose cliffs and dunes lead to a marshy estuary.

In spite of the cold North Sea and the constant coastal erosion, Suffolk and Norfolk generally have better beaches and more sand, but several Suffolk resorts have succeeded in spite of the predominance of shingle rather than sand – among them Felixstowe, Aldeburgh and Southwold.

Sometimes the beaches even seem incidental. You could visit Orford, for example, and enjoy it, and never realise the village is just a flint's throw from the North Sea. Unless, that is, you climb up into Orford Castle and survey the raw marshes that stretch down to the water. It is a toss-up, in the absence of detailed market research, what takes people to Orford: the castle or the food. For not only is there a pub with an exceptional restaurant, as well as a pub with a reasonable restaurant, but there is a famous seafood emporium. If Orford is like a film set (low-ceilinged cottages, a chandler's shop, groceries that despite the number of visitors seem geared just to the needs of local people) then the Butley-Orford Oysterage is a ready-made scene stealer. The little restaurant, with the atmosphere of a well-scrubbed farmhouse kitchen, is famous for its smoked salmon, its oyster soup, its eel stew, and just round the corner, down a little side street, is the 'takeaway' part of the business that enables strangers to bring back home a little bit of the Suffolk scene – mainly smoked fish (mackerel, salmon, trout, cods' roe, eels, whiting, herring, crabs, losters, oysters). Almost everything is locally caught.

The closest the North Sea ever gets to resemble the Aegean is an occasional bottle-green colour. Out of its depths come the huge cod that you see for sale in little wooden booths on the shingle beach at Dunwich. But beware the fishmonger who may just be dressed up in his oldest blue jersey masquerading as a sea-salt, like the greengrocer on the bypass selling 'fresh farm produce' who has never been nearer to a farm than Nine Elms vegetable market.

On a Sunday morning in Southwold, a few minutes' drive north of Dunwich, I found a pub that suited my mood perfectly. Instead of fifty large tipplers rubbing shoulders and buttocks in a space actually intended for twelve, the bar was half full of people sitting quietly behind the Sunday papers. Even the barman was leafing through the *Observer* colour magazine with one hand and dispensing gin and tonics with the other. Conversation, if it existed at all, was muted. Outside, more energetic people than me strode across a greensward that would not have disgraced a West Suffolk village bypassed by the twentieth century. Two men and a dog, bowed against the wind blowing off the North Sea, strode purposefully towards the seafront.

The coast of North Norfolk is more famous than Suffolk as a holiday destination. Cromer, for example, has been a popular resort since Edwardian days and has enough traditional amusements to keep it that way. Near-neighbour Sheringham is more down-market and has massive complexes of holiday caravans, but it too has its following among coast-fanciers, and it also happens to be the eastern terminus of the breezy North Norfolk Steam Railway, which, miraculously, you can reach by ordinary British Rail trains.

Beyond Sheringham, the further west you go, the more impressive the sands become. I was much taken with Holkham beach, and remember looking back inland from the water's edge at the grassed-over dunes and banks of pine trees in two-tone green, nicely set off by the deserted sands. Close to where I stood, a lone shelduck glided inland to the very edge of the water, coming to a halt in that swampy mess that marked the ebbing tide. Later that same day, at dusk on the road between Holkham and Hunstanton, I found I had lingered so much among the flinty, red-pantiled villages dotting this part of the coast that I was behind schedule, and night fell before I reached my destination. Under a milky moon, mist was rising above fields of bruise-coloured cabbages.

I have, incidentally, a fondness for Wells-next-the-Sea, an unlikely combination of the sea-going east coast – all grubby coasters with the skipper's washing strung up on deck to dry – and of resorts like Great Yarmouth, with their rock shops, amusement arcades and greasy-spoon cafés.

Between the traditional resort of Hunstanton and the Lincolnshire coast near Wainfleet, there is silence and solitude, but little for the family with buckets and spades. Much of the marsh that makes it so hard to find the sea hereabouts is in the process of reclamation, and nearly half of the two hundred square miles of the Wash dries out at low tide, making a tempting but occasionally dangerous place to go walking. Some parts of the coast are growing at the expense of others. The coast between Bridlington in Humberside, for example, and Spurn Head in Yorkshire, is composed of shifting sands, and what used to be a coastguard station at Gibraltar Point, home of a fine nature reserve easily accessible to visitors, is now all of a mile inland.

Gibraltar Point is an exceptionally exciting place to be in the autumn, to see the waders, gulls and wildfowl, and the colourful berry-feeders. A major contribution to conservation here is the protection of shore birds in the summer, which allows the ringed plover, for example, to feed on the exposed foreshores of the reserve. But the rarest of the shore birds is the Little Tern: once in danger of extinction at Gibraltar Point, this beautiful little bird now thrives, thanks to a twenty-four-hour guard by wardens and volunteers during the breeding season.

Skegness, just north of Gibraltar Point, is bright, brash and breezy. North of here, caravans tend to dominate the coast, along which flat sands are mostly backed by dunes. Mablethorpe is a smaller, slightly more low-key version of Skegness, and it has its own loyal followers: the hinterland is especially pleasant. North of Mablethorpe, you are in flat, wide-skied country again, with few facilities for family holidays. It is a region of wide beaches, nature reserves and, occasionally, intrusion from low-flying military aircraft, for this is RAF country too.

Cleethorpes is South Humberside's main resort. There are dunes and a mixture of sand and mudflats. It became a holiday resort partly because of its low cliffs, on an otherwise flat coastline, from which you can get a good view of the sea and shipping in the Humber. It was the railway company that first stopped the erosion of the cliffs by building a promenade, and then it took over the pier, which had been built by a private company in 1873. Bridlington, in 'North' Humberside, has cliffs, and mostly smooth sand, with some shingle. It is another of the traditional resorts and, like Skegness, has a very strong following among the towns of the Midlands: flat Leicestershire and Nottinghamshire accents can be heard in the fish and chip shops and the pubs.

There could hardly be a starker contrast between Bridlington and the great high chalk cliffs of Flamborough Head, beyond which the rocky limestone coast has suffered none of the erosion of the softer sandstone further south. Approach roads become steeper, and walking is harder: this is an infinitely more dramatic stretch of England's coast than you will find further south.

Filey is an underrated place with good sands. It has pretensions but is not pretentious. On anything like a bright day its white-painted hotels (a sprinkling of AA signs) make a pretty backdrop behind the well-stocked gardens that fall steeply away towards the sea. It is a kiss-me-quick, toffee-apple and candy-floss sort of place but it is not a Scarborough. It is much more discreet than that, though there is sauce on the tables in cafés and guest-houses, and there are saucy postcards at the newsagents' and in the souvenir shops.

Scarborough is one of the great seaside places, with cliffs, rockpools, spacious sands, a roomy promenade with rock-shops and children's amusements. Whitby is as much a fishing community as a seaside resort, but each benefits from the other. The harbour dominates the town, but there is a small sandy beach on the east as well as the main beach on the west (for a challenging walk with a spectacular view of this coast, visit the abbey up on the clifftop). Redcar, like Filey, is comparatively little-known among southerners, but has fine, three-mile-long sands. I once discovered from talking to some local Filey people that Yorkshire families traditionally moved from south to north up the coast, depending on their relative prosperity. So you begin with somewhere like Withernsea, then move perhaps a year or two later, as funds improve, to Bridlington, then, say, to Robin Hood's Bay or Whitby, but perhaps doubling back to the most prestigious of them all – Scarborough – where the Grand Hotel, opened in 1867, was heralded as the most modern in Europe: in addition to one bedroom for every day of the year, it had speaking-tubes for servants, and palatial public rooms.

The seascape between Redcar and Whitley Bay, has few easily accessible sandy beaches, except for Tynemouth itself, which has dunes and gently shelving sands dotted with rocks and rockpools (interesting for children who like to mess around after the tide has receded). Whitley Bay is Newcastle-by-Sea, a traditional resort with long stretches of sand. Like Tynemouth, and South and North Shields, it is an unsung seaside town that Tynesiders are content to keep to themselves. Whitley Bay's side-kick incidentally is Cullercoats. The two places have the same sort of relationship as Hastings and St Leonards, or Brighton and Hove, and if you live in Cullercoats you never admit to being from Whitley Bay.

Tynemouth is not quite the Frinton of the North East but it is greenswarded and genteel, and Tynemouth Priory has just that element of history that might justify a detour. The stretch of coastline that runs roughly from Amble to Berwick upon Tweed, a border town that has the big toe of one foot in Scotland but belongs in most respects to England, is officially an area of outstanding natural beauty. It has benefited from very little industrial pressure, and has too small a population to have any real effect. A visit here is much enhanced by easy access to offshore islands, including Holy Island, a near-island that is reached by a causeway only accessible at low tide. Going to Holy Island, or Lindisfarne as it is also known, has something of the appeal of walking along a pier. There are boat trips here from the busy little resort of Seahouses (which has managed to embrace space-invader machines and fish and chip shops without too much detriment to its windswept, aromatic maritime atmosphere), and to the Farne Islands, where you are virtually guaranteed sightings of seals and rare bird life.

On Holy Island, incidentally, there is a mead distillery that harks back many hundreds of years to the liqueur distilled by monks. It hardly compares with Chartreuse, but is at least a good local tradition nicely preserved, and is widely available in pubs and off-licences. Bamburgh and Dunstanburgh are well on the tourist beat, but most people have never hear of Boulmer (pronounced 'Boomer'). Of course, it has its following among local people who bring their Sunday papers and stare at the heaving North Sea from the comfort of their cars. Boulmer's beach is more down to earth than Bamburgh's: white, but scarred with long strands of dried seaweed, with upturned fishing boats, lobster pots, and seagulls screaming overhead.

You can see the Farne Islands from Bamburgh, and you can certainly see Bamburgh from the Farne Islands, for that great looming castle on its grass-covered cliff is, like Holy Island itself, one of the North East coast's greatest landmarks.

North of Berwick upon Tweed, which is like a Tower-of-London-on-Sea, even down to the green and the cannons people sit on to eat their sandwiches, the coast changes as if under some Scottish decree, and instead of the low-lying, easy-going pastoral nature of Northumberland's coast, one's impression is of a stark, rugged place: a different world.

The coastal explorer who turns off at Berwick with the aim of picking up the sea again in Cumbria, and who does not know the narrow neck of England, is in for a treat. He will travel back in time through England's most troubled history, and at the same time, through outstanding countryside.

Then if he drives from, say, Carlisle (a good focal point for communications) to the workaday and shingly harbour of Silloth (there are, however, dunes and gently shelving sands too), he will be near the northernmost point of a coast that goes unremarked by the hundreds of thousands of holidaymakers who take the Lake District as the be-all and end-all of their Cumbrian foray.

The Solway Firth is a muddy tidal estuary, not quite land, not quite sea. It is wildfowl country, not bucket-and-spade country. South of the estuary, the Cumbrian coast does not score many points out of ten for its sands or amusements, though it can look very good from the point of view of somebody who has found the Lake District, for all its beauty, rather claustrophobic. Industrial waste has been dumped on some beaches and although recreational zones are in the process of creation, there are some years to go. South of the industrial towns of Maryport, Workington and Whitehaven, however, there are wide flat sandy beaches. One of my favourite resorts near here is Seascale, which with its pastel-coloured terraced cottages facing the sea, and one or two rather bleak-looking hotels, is slightly reminiscent of Ireland.

Ravenglass is an exceptional seaside by any standards. People do manage to do some sunbathing on the beach, and it is worth bringing buckets and spades (bring them on the Ravenglass–Eskdale railway if you are based at the centre of the Lakes), as at low tide there are wide expanses of rather muddy sand. A good excuse for visiting Ravenglass is Muncaster castle, within range of an afternoon stroll from the village – the most famous artefact contained within the castle, though it is rarely on view, is the six-hundred-year-old glass, enamel and gold goblet called 'The Luck of the Muncasters'. Legend says that if this were to be broken, the fortunes of the family will be pitched out of the window, (and perhaps end up somewhere among the rhododendrons). At Ravenglass, the sea makes a three-pronged attack on the shoreline along the estuaries of the Esk, the Ert and the Mite. The poet Norman Nicholson, who is not a Lakeland poet in the sense of exclusively writing about Lakeland scenery, but is probably thought of as a Lakeland man, was actually born on the coast at Millom. He has described it as 'not spectacular, except perhaps for St Bees, where behind the dunes, you have about a mile and a half of flattish land, then suddenly fells rising up very bare, like a bowler hat. It is very unspoilt, and because it faces west, this part of the country has a warm coastline. You can sit on the beach in the evening with the sun in your face, with the light still strong, when, inland, dusk has already arrived.'

Probably the best way to get an impression of the Cumbrian coast is to take the coastal railway line from Barrow to Carlisle. Since the middle of the nineteenth century the coast of Lancashire has been the holiday choice for the industrial north-west, an alternative to the Forest of Bowland or the Peak District. Railway lines were laid quickly: this was a private enterprise business, and there was money to be made not just at the seaside, but in the fares. The character of individual resorts quickly became established. Blackpool was noisy and brash, while adjacent Southport, though its character today is rather mixed, was genteel: no rude young men bringing telescopes to the sea to spy on girls' bathing machines, as happened, to much consternation, in many resorts. Which reminds me that one of the things that history books, dealing with the growth of the traditional Victorian seaside resorts, often miss is that the beach was one of the few places where you could (and young women literally did) let your hair down within a rigidly structured Victorian society.

Many new resorts sprang up: Morecambe, Southport, New Brighton, Lytham St Anne's, and it wasn't long before people's lives were not complete without two weeks in a boarding-house, regardless of the reputation of the landladies.

Mother of them all, Blackpool, is not only England's most celebrated seaside resort, but the tower is a European landmark in its own right. No other resort has one. It is a superb publicity gimmick that was erected in 1894, and which, as somebody else has pointed out, is really a pier stood on its end. Of course, the other Lancashire resorts suffer from the inevitable conclusion by outsiders that they are just as bright and breezy as Blackpool. But even within the suburbs of Liverpool is a mass of flat sands that are reminiscent of Lincolnshire. Here is a different world from Blackpool or New Brighton, even from genteel Lytham St Anne's or Southport, which is a bit brash and a bit genteel at the same time.

If you follow the shores of the Bristol Channel towards the south-west, you will be rewarded with at least one unsung little place. In a way, it is an introduction to Weston-super-Mare. Clevedon is old fashioned, and benefits greatly from the way the coast here is broken up into bays and coves topped by surprisingly steep green hills. The M5 motorway runs only a handful of miles away, but I travelled on it for years before ever guessing at the existence of such a resort as this.

Weston-super-Mare, because of its great bay and its view of South Wales on the horizon, doesn't have so much a seaside as a lakeside flavour about it. Even at high tide, when those famous sands are exposed (unlike Morecambe Bay's sands, completely safe) you never really have the feeling that you are on the edge of an ocean. It is, of course, the sands that have kept Weston so popular, during a period in which England's seaside resorts have taken such a hammering from the Mediterranean and more exotic destinations. There are donkeys on the sands, but no donkeys among the canny tradesmen: Weston used to get well over two million holidaymakers every summer, and you might think numbers are similar today when you are shopping in the 'real' town that lies behind the smart stuccoed façades on the houses and hotels, mainly three-storeyed, that face the Bristol Channel and, on the far horizon, the coast of Wales.

J. M. Turner, the first of the Impressionists, painted several of his sunsets here ('Mr Turner, I have never seen such a sunset' . . . 'Then, madam, you haven't lived'). The good old days of the steamers that used to take people on trips up and down the coast to Minehead, Lynmouth, Ilfracombe and Clovelly are long gone.

From Weston the coast runs more or less due south to Burnham-on-Sea, before making a turning, almost at right angles, to the west towards Watchet and Minehead. Minehead is a snug place, all tall trees and pristine guest-houses, that lies under the lee of the great promontory called North Hill. Though much used as a jumping-off point for people more intent on discovering Exmoor, it has a lot going for it. The wide main street that leads inevitably to the seafront makes me think of Skegness with a bit of Cornish Riviera about it. Its main street is straight and prosperous, with just a bit more greenery and a slightly more tranquil flavour than any of those east coast resorts.

At the beginning of the nineteenth century, Lynmouth and Lynton were just off-the-beaten-track fishing villages, but Lynmouth, especially, became fashionable, not because of its beach, which is mainly rocky and shingly, but because of the beetling coastline, the pine trees and the bracing air. Shelley, the Romantic poet, visited Lynmouth – still off-beat, with its little harbour and guest-houses and small hotels where people return year after year – in 1812, and lived here with his schoolgirl bride. Lynmouth is not quite as invulnerable and cosy as it seems for, in 1952, thirty-two people were killed by floods here.

This is altogether an exceptional coastline: Ilfracombe is by far the best known and biggest resort, and is North Devon's largest. There are no fewer than eleven beaches, two of them actually reached by tunnels through the rock. The old harbour is, rather surprisingly, the centre of town, where holiday yachtsmen pass the time of day with local fishermen. Not quite so famous, but with superb beaches, fringed by low hills and heavily wooded, Woolacombe is good for surfing and safe bathing. It is rock pool country and children love it.

Between Lynmouth and Bude, the broad sweep of what is curiously known as 'Barnstaple or Bideford Bay' (Barnstaple is rather a long way inland, though still functions as a port) incorporates the best coastal view in England. Great, rocky headlands provide exceptional views of the sea and the surrounding country.

Barnstaple and Bideford are not too far inland to make them well within a half-day's visit for people who are holidaying on the coast but, inevitably, they take second place to Clovelly, which is inclined to take its hundreds of thousands of visitors for granted. Clovelly was one of the last West Country tourist honeypots I saw. It had eluded me for years. Of course, it knows full well it is pretty. It even used to be that people could only hang out washing on an appointed day. There are no garish signs, and cars may not – and probably could not – descend to the tiny harbour. They call this main thoroughfare down to the harbour the High Street, though a place less like the high street of any town or village would be hard to come by. The village was built with great daring on an almost perpendicular slope, and they got away with it. And it owes its existence to the

Lynmouth, Devon, could almost be called Exmoor-by-the-Sea, for here the
mysterious brown and rolling hills and combes of Dartmoor's more
northerly sister meet the Bristol Channel. Architecturally, there is a
Victorian legacy that people like or loathe.

herring fishing, which though it is no longer the case, was said to be the best in North
Devon. You can see the isle of Lundy out to sea and, if you continue to Ilfracombe, or
possibly, in due course, Bideford, you can travel out to that most unlikely of islands: you
might expect to find it among the Channel Islands but to come across it in the Bristol
Channel is quite disorientating.

People who live on Lundy have an address as distinctive as the one enjoyed by the
Duke of Wellington (when he lived at Apsley House, now at London's Hyde Park
Corner, his address was No. 1, London). If you live on Lundy your address is Lundy,
Bristol Channel, via Ilfracombe. The island is twenty-four miles from Ilfracombe, and
from there the crossing takes about an hour and a half, though the nearest mainland
encounter is Hartland Point, eleven miles from the island.

Steamers have been bringing visitors to this 400-foot-high fifty-two-million-year-
old slab of granite since the late nineteenth century. The island is owned by the National
Trust, and has a resident summer population of about forty. There is one hotel, which
was built in about 1830, and this is the first island building you see as you approach. I

Lundy. Nobody can say they really know the West Country until they have
had at least a day trip to this unlikely outpost.

was glad, during a stay of just two days, to find that I was to sit at a communal table
rather than be shunted off, Terrence Rattigan style, to a separate table, to talk only to
the waiter – because when you travel alone, there is nothing more daunting than a place
where local knowledge is essential. The islanders are allowed to travel free to the
mainland (they call it 'going ashore'), but surprisingly few bother, as they have here
most of the advantages that, say, the isolated and tightly knit community of St Kilda, off
the coast of the Outer Hebrides, had until they were 'evacuated' in the 1930s, with none
of the horrific disadvantages of such bleak loneliness. Not surprisingly, the grassy cliffs
of Lundy are reminiscent of the north coast of Devon. Your arrival on the *Polar Bear*
could hardly be more dramatic, for the landing point via a little butty from the steamer
is at the foot of a massive headland. Your luggage is transported by Landrover, but you
are expected to make your own way to the top on foot.

All over the world, people who never have any intention of visiting Lundy, are familiar either with the huge number of bird species which have been recorded here (over 420), most famous of which is the puffin, or with the Lundy stamps that used to be issued, but are no longer, and now have great value. Both coins and stamps were issued in two denominations only: one puffin and half a puffin. The name Lundy, incidentally, comes from the Old Norse. Lund means puffin and the suffix 'y' denotes an island (as with Orkney), so it is tautological to refer to Lundy Island but 'Puffin Island' *is* right. In 1958, Lundy received its first and so far only visit from the Royal Family, when the Queen Mother came, and the document on the wall of the island's only pub proudly commemorates this event.

South of Clovelly, you cross into Cornwall near the villages of Welcombe and Meddon, and if you are sensible you allow time to see Bude, which is a strange, windswept, easy-going throwback to the Edwardian era. Tintagel and Boscastle have resigned themselves to being swamped by tourists. As ever, see them if you can out of season, though Boscastle has, to give it credit, escaped the worst of the commercialisation that has ravaged Tintagel. Much of the village is National Trust property.

The Cornish Coastal Footpath, especially upon its northernmost section between, say, Tintagel and Bude, has been designed partly to appeal to people who have only modest athletic ambitions. The main point about it is that you can take a slice here, a slice there, and if you have co-operative fellow travellers, sink back into the comfort of your car without any blisters. The great trick, if you can manage it, is to use two cars and to plot roughly what you think you will be able to walk, and then to leave each of the cars at either end of your route.

At Newquay, south of the blustery, tough but touristy little villages of Boscastle and Tintagel, you will find a different Cornwall. This is more in line with Torquay and Torbay, or any number of traditional seaside resorts. There are several good beaches (which is why these places developed in the first place) and a few substantial hotels.

Land's End marks the dividing point between the two Cornwalls: that of the west, and that of the south. This may not be quite the most westerly point of the British mainland (that privilege, which catches most people by surprise, belongs to Ardnamurchan, in West Scotland), but Land's End certainly takes the English trophy. It is unashamedly commercial, though new ownership in the 1980s may do much to maintain the atmosphere it deserves, even if people who want to drive their cars almost to the water's edge have to pay a price to stand and watch the Atlantic breakers hurling themselves on the black rocks. Land's End is probably an essential port of call for anybody holidaying within the peninsula anywhere between Penzance and St Ives, but it is the Lizard that is the southernmost point of mainland Britain, though it attracts comparatively few people.

It is not xenophobia that accounts for severe restrictions on new building on the Isles of Scilly, especially of hotels. It is that these islands, twenty-eight miles south-west of Land's End, don't have the water supply or other essential services to support more than a limited number of people. The permanent population is about 2,000, and about 1,700 people live on St Mary's. So there is conservation without the hassle. So important is the need to book your accommodation in advance that you may be asked

Boscastle, Cornwall. Largely in the hands of the National Trust, this is as much a fishing community as a tourist attraction.

when buying tickets for the three-hour sea passage whether you have somewhere to stay. If you say no, you won't be refused the tickets, but you might get an old-fashioned look and a warning that, at the height of the season, unless you are just a day-tripper, you may be turned away and have to return to the mainland.

Scores of visitors literally book their next holiday on Scilly even before they go home. They are either cautious or they have learnt the hard way, for there are only half a dozen hotels on St Mary's and two on the idyllic, privately leased island of Tresco. The limited accommodation, however, is not a weakness but a strength, for these tranquil, flower-covered islands are never crowded, and it is not all that rare to have a sheltered sandy cove on a little-frequented part of St Martin's or Tresco or Bryher all to yourself on a hot August Bank Holiday.

Even the setting of Hugh Town bay, adjacent to the island's capital, is impressive in itself: a harbour with anchored boats and yachts bobbing, the low outline of St Martin's and Tresco in the near distance, a salty, seaweedy smell in the air that will be all the stronger if the tide is out, and the sparkling blue sea beyond the high jetty wall. If you are on the quay at about ten o'clock in the morning you will probably be taken aback by the fact that it seems all the holidaymakers you thought had come to St Mary's are piling into open motor boats in a desperate effort to leave the island. The demeanour of the boatfuls of happy people may reassure you. They are in fact departing for morning or all-day trips to some of the other islands in the archipelago. The newcomers are

The jetty, Tresco, Isles of Scilly. This is where you arrive and, if you can ever bring yourself to do so, leave Tresco. These have been called 'The Fortunate Isles', and Tresco is probably the luckiest of them all.

probably going to St Agnes (the locals call it 'Agnes'), or to St Martin's – well known for its superb white beaches – to Bryher or Tresco; the more adventurous will be going to the now uninhabited islands of Samson or Teän, which are rare-bird sanctuaries, or to the rocky Eastern Isles or even – conditions permitting – to the impressive, Atlantic-buffeted Western Isles and the Bishop Rock Lighthouse. The trip out to the Bishop is probably the most spectacular of all. By all means go to Tresco for twenty-four tranquil hours, or go to St Agnes for a stroll on the most exposed and apparently most loved island among local people, but if your stomach can cope with the heaving seas, go to the Bishop Rock Lighthouse when they are delivering mail and supplies by helicopter, or even changing over the lighthouse crew. Twice a day, right through the long holiday season, come low or high water, the boats leave for the so-called 'off islands'. Should the sun disappear behind the clouds for more than a couple of hours you will see chalked on a blackboard on the quay in some bold seaman's hand a notice: 'Weather on St Mary's will be dull and wet. On the off islands hot and lovely.'

As the island's flower-growing traditions would suggest, even the winter climate is mild. Snow or frost is very rare, almost unheard of, and Mediterranean resorts come off badly in a mean-temperature comparison. Hotel prices are lower in the early spring, and if you can have a beach to yourself in August, at times you can virtually have a whole island to yourself in January, February and early March. There's one other great bonus in a winter visit: that is the drama of the sea that surrounds you. It's an aspect of life here that almost all visitors miss, and it is altogether unforgettable. The sight of smallholders picking daffodils as these start to bud, against the backdrop of foaming breakers on the beaches below, is surely unique in the world. It's open to argument which is the more impressive – the sight of an angry sea in a winter storm or the appearance of the islands at an exceptionally low tide. At such a low tide hundreds of rocks that are usually submerged become islets and ridges, lying like sleeping marine animals in a calm green-blue pool. Even in good, still conditions, they remind one of what another writer has said of the islands: 'They are like torn strips of granite, floating on the surface of a sea full of terror and grandeur.' If the surface of that sea were to be lowered by only twelve feet, some of the islands would no longer be islands. There are actually stories of people who have *walked* from St Mary's to Tresco at an exceptionally low spring tide.

Of the 140 islands that make up the Scilly archipelago, five are inhabited, though if you include the two families on Gugh, which is linked to St Agnes by a sand-bar (an impressive sight, that, to watch the tide come in and cover the bar), then there are six. At one time the island of Samson was inhabited, too, though now it is the haunt of a strange breed of black rabbits, of gulls, ground ivy and a variety of exquisite wild flowers that puts even the other islands into the shade – and that is saying something. Visitors can land on Samson, though if they miss their five o'clock boat back to St Mary's – an unlikely event – they must be resigned to a lonely night in the open. People land on Teän (pronounced Tee-an), too, when conditions permit. There is evidence that there was a prehistoric settlement here, and that it was occupied as late as the eighteenth century, when people made a poor living from making 'kelp', which basically meant burning seaweed to make a substance that was exported and then used, among other things, to make iodine and dye.

Until the arrival of a plutocratic zealot called Augustus Smith, in the 1830s, kelp-making was the main source of livelihood on the Isles of Scilly. Smuggling – often from ships anchored off the north coast of Tresco and out of sight of coastguards on St Mary's – was a bonus. Smith soon appointed himself governor of the islands, with the tacit approval of the Duchy of Cornwall, under whose jurisdiction they were. It was Smith who was almost certainly responsible for saving the islands from de-population. Though detested by many, he geared the population up to organising themselves and their agriculture. He 'banned' smuggling (well, tried) and under the Smith dynasty shipbuilding flourished and the tradition began of spring flower growing that until recently was Scilly's main industry. The origins of this now flourishing trade are obscure – some say narcissus bulbs were presented to some islanders by an Italian sailor in the early part of the nineteenth century, but it is probably only a romantic theory. Tourism has now overtaken flower growing as the number one money spinner, but the two go hand-in-hand in importance to the islands' economy.

Descendants of Augustus Smith, who were to all intents and purposes 'lords of the manor', alternately called themselves Smith-Dorrien and Dorrien-Smith, and although they handed back all the inhabited islands except for Tresco to the Duchy of Cornwall in 1927 for economic reasons, their association with and influence over the islands are still felt. Beautiful Tresco is even now their domain. The family still occupies the substantial house built next to the ruined abbey by Augustus Smith. The house is not open to the public but the world-famous sub-tropical abbey gardens and the Valhalla Museum, composed of astonishingly colourful and even gruesome figure-heads from ships wrecked on the Isles of Scilly, are open every day except Sundays.

On a warm day on Tresco you can stroll along some shady tree-lined lane and forget that you are on a small island of seven hundred acres. You could be in some peaceful rural part of Dorset or the much larger Isle of Wight, far away from any town, let alone city. On a summer day the sweet scent of pines, the sight of foxgloves beside the road have a heady, unreal effect. The sea is turquoise, the sand is almost white, the place is totally silent except for the excited cries of a few city children unused to the sensation of hot sand on bare feet.

Penzance is a grey and lively though not particularly pretty town, which in my experience sells the best Cornish pasties in everyday baker's shops and supermarkets. The Cornish way, which mass-producers ought to emulate, is to use lots of diced potatoes, real meat, turnip and lots of pepper. Humphrey Davy, incidentally, the inventor of the Miner's Lamp, was born not in some grimy North Country pit-head village but in Penzance in 1778.

When I think of summer in Cornwall it is less of those yellow-ochre expanses of sand with jagged rocks and deep, intriguing rock pools, than of translucent crème de menthe water lapping against whitewashed granite jetties. Further out to sea there are breakers to be seen – nothing too dramatic on a fairly calm day, but inoffensive-looking frothy rollers that make a break between sea and sky so you know where the horizon is, and the white, pastel or primary colours of yacht sails. In the cove are fishing boats having a weekend off: lots of red and green among their colours.

The Cornish Riviera has become as distant from south-east England, it seems, and nearly as expensive to get to as the South of France. But its day may yet come again. It extends roughly from Land's End in the west to Looe and Polperro to the east, and embraces a coastline of around one hundred miles. If, that is, you allow for the tortuous shoreline that meanders around, say, the Lizard, which bulges out into the Atlantic Ocean and is marked dramatically by one of the most famous lighthouses around England's coast. There are cliffs and beaches, fishing villages and substantial resorts. The trick, as in so many parts of England, especially where it is well-trodden, is to acknowledge the existence of the well-known resorts, but then to strike inland for a satisfying bit of contrast. Falmouth is a classic case, and happily the business of getting inland and seeing a slice of the county that other visitors miss is made doubly enjoyable by the opportunity to sail up the Fal by cruiser to Truro.

The River Tamar all but separates Cornwall from the rest of England, and there is no reason to suppose Cornish people would have any objections if the severance was complete. It is the independent flavour of Cornwall, and not just the quality of its beaches and rock pools that draws people to what is, after all, a comparatively long way for their holidays.

Between Mevagissey and Whitesand Bay there are more holiday beaches than anywhere else on England's south coast, with sheltered beaches that are rarely uncomfortably windy, and cliffs that, being lower than the north coast, are not daunting for grandmothers and small children. Fowey, Polperro, St Austell, Mevagissey and Looe are the chief attractions for holidaying families.

Between Plymouth and Dartmouth, in Devon, the South Hams, whose chief on-the-map town is Salcombe, jut out into the sea like a cow's udder – an unromantic description, perhaps, for one of coastal Devon's most attractive locations. Plymouth, despite its interesting history, has been ravaged by 'progress', and has little in the way of a beach to offer. Better to make for Thurlestone or Salcombe. Thurlestone is a very tucked-away little place, and the adjacent Hope Cove is a real live small community of fishermen who are slightly surprised to see visitors, but always welcoming. The sailors who come to Salcombe may disdain pottering around on the sands, but still the beaches are good, and there are places to buy buckets and spades along the narrow little main street of this maritime place.

Torbay sounds like a local government or a public relations man's concoction, as if the three resorts contained within it – Brixham, Paignton and Torquay – would rather do their own thing. The merger began in 1968, and mutual interest made opposition very short-lived indeed. The idea was that this should become England's Côte d'Azur, and in a good summer, when as in Cannes or Nice, you cannot park within half a mile of the seafront unless you are very lucky indeed, there seems to be something in that claim.

Nearly all the seaside between Dawlish and Swanage has been developed; only Chesil Beach, for very good reasons, has remained inviolate. The sound that this primeval stretch of coast makes when the tide is running at night has been compared with that of an old man wheezing and snoring. It soughs and shifts with the waves, but for all its sound and fury reveals nothing of its secrets. Like Spurn Head, in Humberside, it forms and reforms and reshapes itself. It is ten miles of steeply banked shingle, whose most amazing characteristic is that the size of the stones increases evenly from one end to the other, so that the pebbles are as big as cricket balls at Portland Bill, and down to the size of peanuts nearer Abbotsbury. They say that fishermen always know, even by dead of night, what point of the beach they land on, depending on the size of pebbles they find.

Even before the railways came – normally the salvation of a seaside community wondering how it was going to survive into the second half of the nineteenth century – several places were flourishing as spas. It is just that they never quite achieved the fame of places like Cheltenham and Bath. The cliffs are as varied as the coast itself. Budleigh Salterton, where the beach is backed by sandstone cliffs, is dramatically unlike Beer Head, which is primarily chalk. The Dorset coast was unknown territory for me until I accompanied a born-and-bred Dorset man to Bridport and Portland Bill while en route for, eventually, a Channel Islands ferry from Weymouth. We did see Lyme Regis, but were sidetracked to a place called Seatown, via Chideock, down a gap in the many miles of high sea cliffs that dominate the coast at the western end of Lyme Bay. Seatown is a tiny place, probably not seen by more than one visitor in a thousand who settles for Lyme Regis. All red-sandstone cliffs and dark-green foliage, it will at least be happened upon by hikers on the South West Coastal Footpath, and a good number of them, according to the landlord, find their way into the Anchor pub, near where the pebbly shore slopes steeply into the sea.

Durdle Door, Dorset. Never did the chalk downs meet the sea quite so dramatically as this. The bite out of the chalk promontory has been eaten away by the sea over millions of years.

Late afternoon on Hope Cove beach, near Thurlestone, Devon.

Low tide on Holy Island.

Worthing, West Sussex. Seaside architecture among the south-east resorts
is literally in a class of its own.

St Katharine's Dock, near Tower Bridge, probably represents the most
imaginative transformation of workaday London into a tourist attraction.
(*British Tourist Authority*)

The Guildhall, Guildford, Surrey, dates from 1683. It is still used for
formal council ceremonies, including mayor making.

New thatch at Singleton, West Sussex. Made of straw, this roof will last about thirty years, compared with the lifespan of a Norfolk reed roof of about seventy-five or eighty years.

Sandringham House, Norfolk, is a rare example of a royal home open to
the public. Much frequented by the Royal family, it was here that
George V and George VI died.

The ruins of Rievaulx Abbey, near Helmsley, North Yorkshire. The
Abbey's heyday was probably around 1150, when there were 150 monks
and about 500 lay brothers but by Henry VIII's dissolution only a couple
of dozen remained.

Bridport has its own seaside resort, called West Bay. The town was once famous for producing ships' cables and rope: hemp and flax were grown here locally, and the art of ropemaking helped Bridport people to survive economic ups and downs. 'To be stabbed with a Bridport dagger' was a colloquial expression during the eighteenth century for people who were hanged. Fishing nets, sailcloth, ropes and twine are still one of the basic products of the town, which consists mainly of one long, straight main street, wide enough to do justice to little architectural flourishes. From Westbay, it is about twenty miles to Portland Bill via the B3157, from which you get quite spectacular views of the coast. At one point, when you are up to six hundred feet above sea level, you can actually take in a stretch of about seventy miles in a vast arc from Portland Bill through Burton Bradstock all the way to the distinctive white cliffs of Beer Head, in Devon, and beyond there to sandstone Sidmouth and thence to Torbay.

Beyond Weymouth is Lulworth Cove and Durdle Door. Lulworth Cove has inevitably become a South Coast beauty spot. Almost encircled by cliffs up to four hundred feet high, it is on the way to being a landlocked sea. Take care, by the way, not to make too many ambitious plans about embracing the whole of the coastline here, for much of it is in the hands of the Ministry of Defence, and is used for army exercises and firing ranges.

Weymouth was once two separate towns, Old Weymouth and Melcombe. The cliffscapes that elsewhere along this coast overshadow the beaches (depending on where the sun is) peter out into almost nothing at Weymouth. This makes the place accessible to massed ranks of caravans. Never quite recovering from his ignominious defeat in the American colonies, George III came here in 1789 while his son, the Prince Regent, was turning Brighton into Belgravia-by-the-Sea, and he became the first reigning monarch to try out a bathing machine. It is a comparatively well-protected resort, though whether or not it became a holiday place never had much bearing on its importance as a port. It was used by the Romans, and Melcombe is thought to have been the port by which the rats carrying the Black Death arrived in Britain in 1348. Weymouth is now the main terminal for ferries to the Channel Islands.

Poole Harbour has a coastline almost as long as the whole of the Isle of Wight's – that is, fifty-two miles at high water compared with the Isle of Wight's fifty-seven miles. There is no doubt though about which of the two has the better seaside. Sailors may be content with water in any shape or form, muddy or not, whereas for family holidays, the Isle of Wight beats most of the Hampshire coast hands down. Poole Harbour is virtually a landlocked estuary, exceeded only in its marvellous natural resources by Sydney Harbour. Even better, it is surrounded by a hospitable mixture of pinewoods, soft hills and heathland. Poole is not just a port and yachting centre, but a seaside resort too. Yet it is quite an industrial town in its own right, mainly making bricks and tiles and building boats. The ravines, or chines, in the cliffs that penetrate inland are probably the most distinctive natural feature along Poole's coastline. To walk up Branksome Chine, for example, will take you inland for over a mile, under the overhanging branches of pine trees, and, during the spring, rhododendrons enhance a spectacular natural setting. Poole Harbour has double tides, which means that in the course of twenty-four hours there are approximately fourteen hours of high water.

Neighbouring Bournemouth is a survivor among seaside resorts. It seems to have been unaffected by the economic ups and downs that have local councillors in other places wringing their hands. It is smart, cosmopolitan, always busy, consistently popular.

The trouble with Southampton is that, unless you are about to embark on a transatlantic cruise in the QE2, you are going to feel like a poor relation. It is so firmly entrenched in the popular imagination as the principal port of entry for visitors to Britain between the 1930s and 1950s that it makes Heathrow and Gatwick look very prosaic indeed. The city might have become the capital of England simply because of its easier access, and it actually did develop as a port to save the long drawn out and uncertain business of travelling round the coast and up the Thames to London Docks. It had a small following as a fashionable watering place but that never really caught on – there were too many rough and uncouth sailors. The modern layout of the docks dates roughly from the 1830s, and though passenger ships are few and far between and there are no big ones apart from the aforesaid QE2, freighters, and particularly oil tankers, have more than made up for the shortfall. Southampton belies its closeness to Beaulieu and Bucklers Hard, near the southernmost extremes of the New Forest. Being a port is almost incidental.

Portsmouth is less functional than Southampton, more worth seeing in its own right. Perhaps the best way of all to get to grips with this intriguing place, flanked by natural harbours, and more nostalgic for most Navy men than the late-lamented rum ration, is to take a pleasure boat from Southsea's shingle beach on a harbour cruise.

North-west of the railway line stands the great naval base which, despite swingeing military cutbacks, has the single most impressive and moving relic of Britain's maritime past. This is Nelson's flagship at Trafalgar, HMS *Victory*, a wooden warship of 3,500 tons that has been meticulously preserved and is open most days of the year to the public. It will get even more attention in years to come, for the Royal Navy Museum in the nearby dockyard is being extended to cover the whole history of British sea-power. Among the ships to see is Henry VIII's *Mary Rose*, whose salvage from a muddy place of several hundred years' rest at Spithead, the famous anchorage between Hampshire and the Isle of Wight, was completed in 1983.

Portsmouth Point and Old Portsmouth, the original city, graced by Georgian houses, are just a ten-minute walk from the centre of Portsmouth. Old Portsmouth used to be a fortified city, and you can walk along ramparts that have become breezy, sea-tangy promenades. Better yet: walk a little further to the south and east and you reach Southsea proper, a seaside resort in its own right.

They call Queen Victoria's island home, Osborne House, 'wet weather Osborne', because when it rains people congregate there, abandoning the beaches and the amusement arcades. Yet the Isle of Wight's royal connections go back a lot longer than the Victorian era: Edward I took a liking to the place in 1293 (perhaps the first recorded example of a royal holiday), during a respite from grinding the faces of the Scots into the heather, and ever since then the Governor, which is now little more than a courtesy title roughly equivalent to that of Lord Lieutenant of a county, has been appointed by the sovereign.

There is a memorial to Victoria in the market square in Newport, county town of the island, and one of the few places of any size not actually on the coast. Well might people

Godshill, Isle of Wight. The island's seaside resorts are a match for any on the south coast of the mainland, and the countryside of the interior is soft and generally unspoilt. This scene has appeared on many a jigsaw puzzle!

have inscribed a memorial to Victoria in 1903, two years after her death. For she was responsible, as she was in so many places in Britain, for concentrating the minds of future holidaymakers on the delights of the island, and would be worth her weight in crown jewels to any tourist organisation. But Victoria was merely the catalyst. For the Isle of Wight has everything going for it for unhurried, not over-expensive, traditional family holidays. Its location ensures a comparatively mild climate and an exceptionally long season. The diamond-shaped island is no more than about twenty-three miles long, and only about twelve miles from north to south, which will satisfy people who like to visit a place and feel that they need to come to grips with it by seeing every corner. The terrain is varied, from marshland that is the domain of waterfowl, to chalky downs and those wide, smooth expanses of sandy shore that are chiefly responsible, along with the generally mild weather, for bringing people from all over the country on holiday. As yet, the island has only a comparatively small following among overseas visitors. West Wight is more rural and less frequented than the easterly side of the island, where Ventnor, Shanklin, Sandown and Ryde provide a 1980s link with the breezy, unashamedly self-indulgent atmosphere of the Edwardian era, especially Shanklin pier, which is privately owned. Here electric organ music wafts seaward from a far-from-haunted ballroom (lots of old ladies with cotton frocks and fat knees, drinking Double Diamond), and if you are not careful you trip over seagulls pottering about on the boards waiting for a bit of somebody's bacon sandwich. I remember taking the August evening air on the pier, and then walking up the chine towards my hotel, alongside people in white summery shirts or strapless dresses. The fairy lights were winking on the pier behind me, and the evening was Riviera-warm: the Isle of Wight at its best.

There are no really big towns, though the population of the island does rise to well over 100,000, even outside the summer – surprising, perhaps, for the average visitor who is not actually here on an August Bank Holiday. The Isle of Wight does, incidentally, have its own Member of Parliament, who generally follows his constituents' unenthusiastic views about a long-mooted bridge to connect the island with the mainland. But this stands no more real chance of success than the idea of building a tunnel. For the Isle of Wight is just far enough to make a journey in either direction not too much of a daunting undertaking.

Since every square mile of the island is well picked over by tourists, this is not the place to get-away-from-it-all easily, unless you come in the winter months. And then you should be warned that only about one in five of the island's many hotels and guest-houses are open. In summer, though, the island is geared up superbly well to the needs of high-season visitors. I have never, for example, seen so many tea shops and tea gardens. Even on the less visited west coast, you will find that Brighstone and Mottistone, essentially quiet villages, have their coach parties all through the season. Well recommended for people wanting to see as much of the island as possible is to take a trip on the upper deck of one of the island's green buses. If an ordinary coach vouchsafes much better views over hedges and stone walls than a car, imagine the effect of being ten feet higher on the upper deck of an double-decker. The fact that it can be almost bumpy enough to make you seasick does not detract from the experience.

Beyond Portsmouth is London-by-the-Sea. Around three million people live within a couple of hours' drive of the resorts between Selsey Bill and Beachy Head; that is, Bognor, Littlehampton, Worthing, Hove and Brighton, and subtler, more low-key places like Shoreham, Rottingdean and, one of the most undeservingly unsung of the lot, Seaford. Fortunately, the nature of the coastline means that tens of thousands of people can be absorbed without detriment and if the sands do get too crowded or the sun gets too hot (or the lack of it makes it too cold) the South Downs are never far away. Among them it is possible to put other day-trippers out of sight and out of mind just by strolling a couple of hundred yards from the nearest car park.

Bognor would probably not be in the least offended to be called a small version of Brighton. Like hotels that don't allow dogs and get good business from dog-haters, it will always attract people who are put off by the more brash and sophisticated places.

Littlehampton was a childhood favourite of mine because of the dunes which add extra fuel to childish imagination, and the limpid green sea, not too far away to make it inconvenient to return for egg sandwiches and Tizer. A hundred years ago Littlehampton was a port serving Arundel, and it still has a number of cargo ships and coasters mixing in among the yachts and dinghies. The mouth of the Arun here is one of the most dangerous places to attempt to swim on the whole of the south coast.

Until the middle of the eighteenth century Brighton was a simple fishing village, known as Brighthelmstone. Daniel Defoe referred to it in 1722 as 'old and built on the very edge of the sea'. He would have been astonished to discover what happened to it during the following half century. In 1783 George III's son, the Prince Regent, patronised the town, and it has never looked back. Nothing you can throw at it – its one time nickname Sin City, or the raffish image it acquired after the publication of Graham Greene's *Brighton Rock*, the terrible reputation its racecourse had in the 1930s – has apparently diminished its prowess. It has become a city of elegance. Architects come to admire its Georgian terraced cream-and-white stuccoed houses. Antique and bric-à-brac hunters come from many miles to potter about the Lanes, virtually all of which are devoted to antiques, and, if they are canny enough, among the narrow streets – unkempt though they look – close to the railway station. Even in the 1980s with all the other possibilities for getting out to enjoy yourself, Brighton received around seven million day-trippers and more than half a million people spend the whole of their summer holidays here. All this in spite of the fact that there is little sand but rather steeply shelving shingle.

Between Brighton and Beachy Head, Seaford happens to possess the last in the line of seventy-four Martello Towers which were erected at the beginning of the Napoleonic Wars to keep a watch on the coast between Seaford and Folkestone. The beach at Seaford is almost entirely of shingle but it is a sheltered place that is quite content to take just a tenth of the visitors Brighton gets, while retaining a sleepy, rather suburban, atmosphere.

Eastbourne and Bexhill have an unfortunate geriatric public image, but this is partly because they have resisted (not always that successfully) incursions by certain manifestations of the late-twentieth century – specifically hamburger emporia: Eastbourne lost to the great McDonalds in 1981 and you can walk on the promenade with your big Macs, even when no rain is threatened.

Beachy Head, which is altogether more famous, dominates the resort of Eastbourne. At 530-odd feet above the sea, and therefore the highest headland – though not the highest cliff – on the south coast, it is topped by springy downland turf and of course the summit has its share of evidence of human interest; there is a café, a police station and a stone inscription: 'Mightier than the thunder of many waters, mightier than the waves of the sea, the Lord on high is mighty'. The Beachy Head Lighthouse built in 1902 is dwarfed by this great promontory, even though it is over 150 feet high itself.

Hastings is less genteel, more earthy. Of all the south coast seaside resorts this is the one that has changed least in the last twenty-five years, except that behind their Victorian bay windows and their high-ceilinged flats or in their hotel rooms, people are sitting more comfortably than they used to do. It is surprisingly white, positively gleaming in the sun, and there is quite a lot going on in the town. You hear remarkably little about it, and it does not sell itself.

West Pier, Brighton, East Sussex. A seaside resort without a pier is, well, not quite the ticket. Brighton used to have three. It now has two – the West and the Palace, but only the Palace is open at present.

Folkestone and Dover are inevitably functional places but there are seasidey characteristics in both, and anyway, with the proximity of Dymchurch, Hove, St Mary's Bay, which is sandy, and Sandwich's dunes, there is enough to build a sandcastle with. Both Folkestone and Dover, as well as Walmer and Deal, are interesting enough as old communities in their own right. Folkestone especially is to my mind an underrated place. A little bit rough-and-ready, perhaps, but that is a common enough characteristic of a working port that has to be realistic and look after its maritime interests more than its tourists, but I have had some of the freshest cod and chips outside coastal Suffolk or Yorkshire, and have particularly enjoyed the flavour of the town at six or seven o'clock on a summer weekday evening when the traffic has miraculously faded away from the centre and there are no ferries due in for a while.

Folkestone seems much smaller than Dover, in terms of the numbers of ferry passengers it handles and even in terms of the numbers of holidaymakers who come here for its own sake. Folkestone would make a good base from which to explore towns and villages inland including, for example, Lympne and Canterbury. There is Winchelsea, and Romney Marsh, one of the last wildernesses: I once took a train from Ashford to Rye, and that was my first sight of the marsh. It has turned out to be a great favourite, no less so because of the way that people raise their eyebrows when you suggest it as an underrated corner of the country that could turn out to be a tonic for people daunted by Brighton's teeming millions.

The coastline between, say, Pegwell Bay and the Thames Estuary has been much maligned. Despite the muddiness of much of the shore, there is a desolate, gull-haunted beauty, similar – not surprisingly, for it is just up the coast – to parts of south-east Essex. At Herne Bay and Margate you can build sandcastles and get sticky with candy-floss along with the best of them. Broadstairs is more genteel than either, and has six beaches. Charles Dickens wrote *David Copperfield* and *Barnaby Rudge* while living here, and an annual Dickens Festival has done no harm to the town's public image.

This cursory look at England's coast ends not with a bang but a whimper, at Sheerness, on the Isle of Sheppey. Yet this grey wasteland, disfigured by electricity pylons and factories, has a whiff of ozone and, if you half close your eyes, or at dusk (always an advantage in a 'iffy' place) there is a subtle beauty – even if in the touching shanty towns of holiday chalets in which Londoners try to get back to nature at weekends.

III

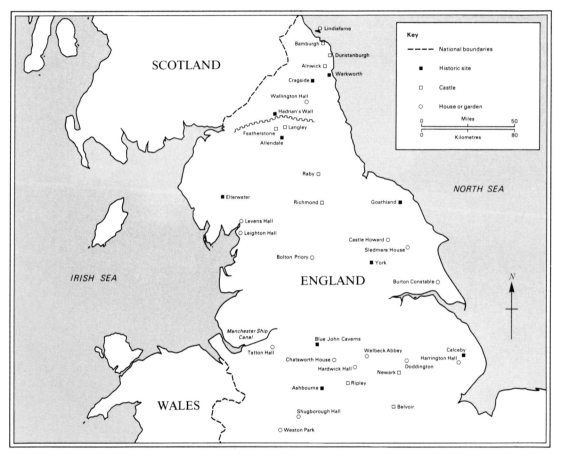

Map 9 Castles, houses, gardens (North)

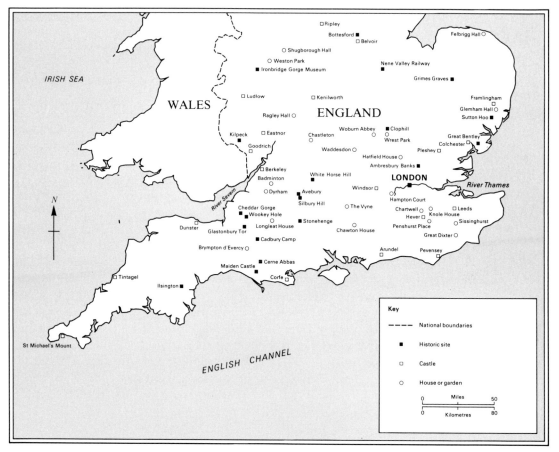

IRISH SEA

WALES

ENGLAND

□ Ripley
Bottesford ■
□ Belvoir
Felbrigg Hall ○

○ Shugborough Hall

○ Weston Park
■ Ironbridge Gorge Museum

Nene Valley Railway ■

Grimes Graves ■

□ Ludlow
□ Kenilworth

Ragley Hall ○

Framlingham
Glemham Hall □
Sutton Hoo ■

Kilpeck □ Eastnor
Chastleton
Woburn Abbey ○
Clophill ■
Wrest Park

Great Bentley
Colchester ○

Goodrich ■
Waddesdon ○
Pleshey ■

Hatfield House ○
Ambresbury Banks ■

□ Berkeley
Badminton
White Horse Hill ■
LONDON
River Thames

○ Dyrham
Avebury
Windsor ○
Hampton Court

Silbury Hill
Chartwell ○
□ Leeds

Cheddar Gorge
○ The Vyne
Hever □
Knole House
○ Sissinghurst

Wookey Hole ■
Stonehenge
Penshurst Place □

Dunster □
Longleat House ■
Chawton House ○
Great Dixter ○

Glastonbury Tor

■ Cadbury Camp

Brympton d'Evercy ○
Arundel
Pevensey

Maiden Castle ■
○ Cerne Abbas

□ Tintagel
Corfe □

Ilsington ■

St Michael's Mount □

ENGLISH CHANNEL

Key

— — — National boundaries

■ Historic site

□ Castle

○ House or garden

Miles		50
0		
0	Kilometres	80

Map 10 Castles, houses, gardens (South)

1. The making of England

Small boys would have loved it. It was better than Disneyland. Around two hundred million years ago, most of England was covered by a kind of brackish lagoon, dominated by dinosaurs. Most of the country's familiar rust-coloured sandstone dates from this period, and these rocks contain an exceptional number of monster fossils. Between twenty and fifty million years later, most of Europe was covered by a sea of coral, dotted with islands, in which swam huge numbers of reptiles.

Gradually, massive geological changes took place. In a warm climate, plant and animal life flourished, and mammals developed apace. But then came the Ice Age. Great glaciers transformed the country in their drive southwards, and most of Britain and northern Europe were covered by ice thousands of feet thick. Four times this happened, but then the climate became warmer and the ice melted. At this time, Britain was still part of the mainland of Europe, which is why European plant species tend to be widespread here. Then, during the penultimate Ice Age, man first appeared: the earliest human fossil found in what is now England dates from about a hundred and fifty thousand years ago.

There is some evidence of human occupation in Europe of 40,000 years ago, but England was not colonised by men crossing the swampy North Sea until around 8000 BC. They came during much warmer weather than is normal today, when summers were long and hot, and trees and other vegetation were rapidly cloaking the hills. They were peaceful people, mainly farmers, and quickly made their impression on the landscape. Forests were felled, hills cleared of trees for timber to build shelters and to make enclosures for domestic animals. Between the Bronze and Iron Ages, life here was comparatively prosperous. Farms were efficient in their limited way, and, incidentally, much of the heathland we take for granted, dates from that time: the trees have never been allowed to reappear.

The first Celtic invaders, around 500 BC, caused the peaceable Bronze Age men to seek safety among the hills of the north, and Wales, but it was the Celts who brought an understanding of the use of iron. And then, about 450 years later, the Romans appeared. It is said they were surprised to find pockets of genuine civilisation and that stories they had heard about the barbarous wasteland were often inaccurate. For most people, the Roman occupation was more stable and safe than that of the British 'kings'.

Between the disappearance of the Romans and the arrival of William the Conqueror, both Saxons and Danes proved to be great cultivators, laying down a feudal system that anticipated the Norman invasion. Although primitive to contemporary eyes, at least it had the advantage of being fairly efficient. (It was the Angles, from north Germany in the fifth century, who gave England, or Angle-land, its name.)

When the Normans arrived, about a third of England was covered by forest.

The Corbridge Lion is the most famous exhibit in the museum of the
Roman Camp at Corstopitum, Corbridge, Northumberland. The carving
was unearthed in about 1906.

Penalties for poaching the royal deer, for example, may have been Draconian, but
people enjoyed some privileges. Among other things, the old Roman roads were
protected rights of way, though not many people had reason to travel any great distance.
They were, for example, allowed to graze cattle and sheep on common land, and let their
pigs root around for nuts and acorns. They could fish for free, and cut peat for fuel: it is
believed, for example, that the Norfolk Broads began at this time to take on the shape we
know today, being created by people digging for peat.

A Georgian country park dominated by a neo-classical mansion is simple enough to
come to terms with, and planned villages – attractive as they often are – contain fewer

A model of the Roman Fishbourne Palace, which stood near Bosham, West Sussex, and which has been substantially excavated.

secrets than, say, a green but pock-marked field in the middle of nowhere. Calceby, in Lincolnshire, comes to mind. It still contains the traces of a long-lost medieval village whose church, which used to be on the outskirts, is intact even now.

Seven or eight hundred years ago the population of such seemingly untamed wildernesses as Dartmoor or the North York Moors was quite high: there is evidence at, say, Ilsington on Dartmoor, of continuous occupation prior to the Romans. The process of rapidly increasing population was reversed, however, during the time of the Black Death of the mid-fourteenth century. The plague lasted for over one hundred years and, in many cases, wiped out the population of several villages at a time. Many romantically deserted communities, evidence of which is often best seen from the air, date their mysterious, mis-shapen, overgrown mounds and ditches that seem to go nowhere, from this time.

In many instances, people simply got it wrong and found that the surrounding farmland was not adequate for their needs, and even though the foundations of a town had been laid, people tended to wander away, and leave the place to its own devices. But sometimes more dramatic reasons than this were responsible for a village or town disappearing: the plague, as already mentioned, or the water supply drying up – one reason why comparatively few villages on the chalk uplands of the Lincolnshire Wolds and the South Downs have survived. Water simply drained away, and people had to go elsewhere. There are perhaps three thousand lost or deserted villages in England, most of them having disappeared off the map between about 1450 and 1550, when the population of towns increased dramatically, and large stretches of countryside became depopulated.

The countryside began to take on its patchwork-quilt look, with many small fields and free-range woodlands, all criss-crossed by high-hedged narrow winding lanes, simply because the first farmers really to leave an impression on the countryside were peasants, each looking after their own small patch of land. The hedges added protection from the wind and rain, encouraged crops to grow, and kept cattle and sheep where people could keep an eye on them. Those lanes themselves seem to sink so deep into the land, and meander so much, because some of them were originally drainage ditches dug yard by yard by hand, and had to avoid natural obstacles that were difficult to remove, like big trees or deep ponds: a far cry from the Romans, who had almost limitless and well-organised labour at their disposal. So it was not the rolling English drunkard who made the English road, for some local roads were simply created by generations of cattle rolling haphazardly home. Long-distance cattle tracks gradually turned into roads as the population of the country became much more peripatetic.

All the other distractions obscure a simple fact: in some parts of the country there are more villages than others. In much of the West Country and upland Yorkshire, for example, people did not need the economic structure of a village to support them, but could, almost literally, settle down where they felt like it, and where there was, say, a source of fresh water, shelter under the lee of a hill, trees to supply fuel and building materials, good pasture for cattle, and soil that was full of potential.

The classic English village, slumbering beside the clump of great chestnut trees on its green, or straggling along a quiet country lane, seems such a permanent fixture that natives of the place who return after only fifteen or twenty years may feel outraged to discover how much it has changed. And the feeling that unless a place is wrapped in cotton wool, it might actually disappear, is responsible for the rarified atmosphere of many of the ten thousand or so villages in Britain. But you do not need to be a historian to guess at how vulnerable the village is. Look at that church on high ground, for example, well away from the main body of the village. The church is obviously fifteenth or sixteenth century, the majority of the village houses are Georgian or Regency. This might have been a village stricken by the plague, or it might have been uprooted and rebuilt in order to make room for some grand country estate. One of the gratifying things about such planned villages – I am thinking of the ones at Badminton, close to the home of the Duke of Beaufort, or Ripley, next to Ripley Castle, near Harrogate, or Waddesdon, a street village that runs past the gates of the Rothschild home in Buckinghamshire – is that it is easy to get to grips with how they evolved. Elsewhere, it can be a hit-or-miss business: things are not always what they seem.

Lavenham, in Suffolk, for instance, does not exist as such a perfect example of a medieval 'wool' town because its inhabitants were particularly conservation-minded, but because the community was unable to compete at the dawn of the industrial revolution with cheaper wool-processing machinery and the cheap labour provided by bigger conurbations. So it went to the wall economically but its buildings remained intact. (In certain pockets of Britain, notably the Cotswolds and Suffolk, local laws ensured dead bodies were buried in woollen shrouds, so as to give the trade a boost.)

Church Lane, Ledbury, Herefordshire, where there has been sympathetic conservation. It is child's play for the casual visitor to see how the English townscape was created, generation by generation, layer upon layer.

Until the end of the eighteenth century, the process of creating wool to be woven was extremely long and laborious. Firstly fleeces were cleaned, then spun into yarn, then washed, and the fibres were aligned by dragging the matted wool through cards. Then the wool was spun, usually by spinning wheels worked by the feet. This was often a job for life for single women, hence they became known as spinsters. Then, after spinning, the wool was woven into cloth on a hand loom. The cleaning and compacting of cloth for the loom was known as 'fulling' and Bibury is one place, happily very photogenic, that has its original fulling mill intact; it is open to the public. As methods of production became more sophisticated, and the industry expanded, it was necessary to improve communications, which was the main reason why canals were dug and rivers improved.

Pubs, coupled with the parish church, will tell you more about a village than most of the inhabitants' reminiscences put together. Every tenth pub in the heart of rural Britain will claim it is six or seven hundred years old, but until about a century ago almost all beer was brewed at home, and *real* sixteenth- and seventeenth-century pubs are extremely rare. The situation is not helped by the pleasure a lot of Victorian and twentieth-century developers and historians took in inscribing dates on to the front of buildings: beware the possibly early-Victorian stuccoed pub that announces a date of origin of 1650.

Even today, seemingly remote villages well away from motorways and railways are evolving. So a pub closes down after being owned for decades by a brewery and reopens after two fallow years as a free house, whose survival will depend on the landlord attracting a new clientele from a wide catchment area. There may be fairy lights, a new car park, probably a restaurant, and the hardworking owner will go as close to the letter of the planning laws as he dares. A redundant church has become a holiday cottage or an antique saleroom. A railway station is a coal merchant's yard and office. And of the more workaday houses, one in three may be owned by city dwellers living seventy or more miles away (frequently they will be the most lovingly cared-for houses in the whole neighbourhood). And the new executive estate houses that are only *just* in the village look more cottagey than the four-hundred-year-old houses in the village centre. There will be pretty, factory-made Regency bow windows inserted into neo-Georgian frontages. There might be white railings and wicket gates that would do justice to cottages Anne Hathaway would have known, and there will be double garage doors with a classical Greek motif.

Even today there are valuable buildings in danger of being razed to the ground. It has always been so. Often, village houses fell down after what today would seem a surprisingly short time. This was partly because of one law that allowed a cottage to be tenanted by anybody who could produce a key. No repairs were ever done, and eventually a house would become uninhabitable. When it came to surviving, location was all-important, and a Fenland village constructed out of not very good quality brick and inferior thatch, and ravaged by marshy, badly drained ground, would not last a quarter as long as a village constructed of good local timber. For wood is a much more durable material than most people realise, easily lasting, if properly treated, for hundreds of years.

Political upheavals often did a lot for the quality of building in a community. For example, the dissolution of the monasteries during Henry VIII's reign was a disaster for the building trade. Or so it seemed: many master masons who lost their livelihood soon found employment in building houses (around many of which small villages developed) for the new aristocracy who found favour with the king. Village houses now generally complement 'the big house', but hundreds of years ago they would have been much less substantial. Yet, grouped as they were around the green, and surrounded by plots on which vegetables could be grown and the odd cow or sheep grazed, they literally set a pattern that has survived. As the status of the master mason declined, and he and his kind no longer travelled extensively throughout Europe, he aped fashion less and evolved an English style of architecture which, on the whole, sits more happily in the landscape.

The decline of this particular trade also gave a boost to what had been known in Roman times, but had since declined, and that was the making of good-quality brick. For my money this is a much underrated building material which, perhaps on some moated Elizabethan house with the late afternoon sun on it, can be outstandingly beautiful. The masons' work might be relegated to a fire-place in the dining-hall, or decorative work on a window or a garden arch, but was none the worse for all that. The substantial village houses you admire as you walk along a quiet street may have been divided and sub-divided into smaller units than was ever intended, and then, in the hands of somebody with money to spare and a sense of the past, have been returned to their original function as a single house. The traditional timber frame of the exterior is something the Victorians would never have known and, even if they did, it would probably have been stained black and not the pleasant, biscuity-coloured, rustically pock-marked timber we see today. Pock-marked, incidentally, because of the Victorian custom of nailing plasterboard on to the timber: unadorned framework was not admired for its own sake, as it is today.

Even inside the cottage, things are not necessarily what they seem. The 'traditional' low ceiling might be masking a network of beams – perhaps even numbered ones revealing that they were originally ships' timbers – and a brick wall at the side of a cottage, perhaps pleasantly overgrown with ivy or roses, might actually encase an original structure of wattle and daub. One of the commonest mistakes made in the twentieth century is the assumption that preceding centuries were peopled by simple, uncultivated and brutish people. In fact many medieval village houses, if you throw in central heating and hi-fis and double glazing, would be the envy of most people today. In the 1600s, for example, the country was quite prosperous, and village houses were of several rooms, many well planned and well constructed. It was later, during the Industrial Revolution, as divisions between rich and poor became more marked, that village houses became downgraded, were subdivided, and their more able-bodied occupants, or those with several mouths to feed, moved to the developing cities and towns. The village green survives in a wide variety of forms, and so, less frequently, does the village pond. Sometimes the green is big enough to absorb cricket matches in one go, and has even learned to live with being dissected by major roads. Sometimes, with less equanimity, it has seen the encroachment of modern houses on to its fringe, and in one or two very rare instances, allowed itself to become completely covered over by a new housing estate.

Though I have admired the green at Great Bentley in Essex, said to be the biggest in Britain, and the greensward at Long Melford that sets the Perpendicular church off superbly, and the hillocky, much dissected, village green at Elterwater in Cumbria, upon which, in season, people picnic as on the beach among the dunes, I am especially fond of the green-dominated, sprawling, surprising village of Goathland, among the North Yorkshire moors. The greens here are more like heathland than conventional village greens; sheep graze close to carefully fenced cottage gardens, there is marram grass among the thistles and burdock, though the greens are more carefully tended than they seem at first glance. A happy blend of greenery and urbanity. Sometimes the village green, as in the famous example of Elsdon in Northumberland, was potentially kept for coralling cattle during border raids. Village ponds were not just decorative, as they often are today, with duck and geese, but often the only source of fresh water or fresh fish. The source of fish also applied in many cases to moats around houses: in certain parts of Suffolk, until many of them were overgrown, there were moats around hundreds of houses of a substantial size. The village green was sometimes used for common grazing, and a pond therefore provided water for cattle and sheep.

The commonest shape for the village green is triangular. It is not hard to ascertain why, for this was the natural shape created by the junction of two roads that both came from, say, the north or from the south, and however functional some greens may seem, they have all benefited from a complicated legal position. Though technically somebody owns the village green, it is often not clear who, and even if it is used for common grazing, there is little danger of any individual 'developing' the green. Where there is a pond, it was often thought in earlier times to have been holy (hence the tradition of well dressing in Derbyshire), and this too helped to preserve it and the green from encroachment.

The pub that overlooks the village green is as much a part of the community as the church. But if you are particular about its authentic antiquity, a good rule of thumb is to find an inn that has obviously – even if bypassed in modern times – served its purpose on a trunk road, preferably an old coaching route. If it has a low-ceilinged and cottagey look about it too, it is probably an establishment in which an ale-wife was permitted to brew her own beer and sell it on the premises – usually without any formality such as a bar. The oldest pubs around often had such a history. Many people resent the standardisation of beer that has come with the acquisition of such places by large breweries, but even in the seventeenth and eighteenth centuries, an ale-taster, wearing leather breeches, would be required to sit on a bench in a puddle of beer to test whether the brew had been too liberally sugared. If at the end of the required time his trousers stuck to the bench, the landlord, or more often landlady, was in trouble.

The name of the village pub is changed only on very rare occasions – a handful that had been called The Feathers, for example, after the insignia of the Prince of Wales, became The Princess of Wales following Prince Charles's marriage in 1981. The name and the sign swinging outside are usually as old as the pub itself. Decorative though they are, pub signs originally had quite a simple purpose, which was to indicate to people who could not read (until the eighteenth century this was the great majority of the population), that strong drink was to be had, along with a better chance of food and lodging than it is customary to find today in ordinary pubs.

The names of the pubs are a source of infinite delight, and there is even something in the theory that a place gains in atmosphere if it is appropriately named, so you will find many a Fox and Hounds in hunting country, and many a neatly executed sign outside a Wheatsheaf in arable farming land, or even an occasional Three Conies where local farmers once despaired over the rabbit population. But it would be interesting to know just how many people on a Saturday night in a country pub called, say, the Cat and Fiddle know that this comes from a corruption of the name of a French nobleman, Caton le Fidèle, or that the Bull and Mouth derives from Henry VIII's capture of the Port of Boulogne, or that the Goat and Compasses comes from the phrase 'God encompasseth us'. Sometimes the names of village pubs defy all comprehension, or at least certainty of origin: one of these is The Case is Altered, which usually has more theories attached to it than regular customers.

The best villages, with or without greens, are those where local materials for building, rather than imported ones, are used. Considering the outside influences to which they are vulnerable, these villages have remained identifiable and thus appealing. Take the high lying, air-cooled villages of the Pennines. Seldom do individual buildings in villages such as those around Huddersfield or Hebden Bridge or Haworth, reveal in one stroke the history of their surroundings and the preoccupations of their inhabitants. For hundreds of years this was a sheep-rearing area and the typical, long, two-storeyed house next to a farm or in a village street had rows of windows, sometimes eight, nine or ten in a row, divided by sandstone mullions. These allowed as much light as was practical to enter upper rooms, thus enabling weavers producing woollen cloth to work at their livelihood as long as the daylight lasted. Then came steam power in the valleys, producing soot and grime that over the decades transformed the brick and stone to the familiar black associated with the industrial north. Roofs were usually made of stone slabs, which were easily split into layers as thick or thin as was required and were readily found among the moors. So easily honed are these, that roofs are not steeply pitched, as even at 30 degrees they were proved to be watertight.

If you move over the border into Lancashire, you will find the same type of house, but with bright-white or cream pointing between the stones, which gives them a disconcerting boldness until you get used to them. If you travel just a few miles to the north-east into the Yorkshire Dales, however, the change is dramatic, since the main building stone is paler, even blue or lilac in certain lights, and individual houses and even complete villages somehow mirror the prevailing impression of the rugged, rocky outcrops among sheep-dotted moors and steep crags looking down over rushing shallow rivers.

The total effect of authentic village architectural detail is much greater than the sum of its parts. Doors, chimneys, ornamental stonework, timber cladding, the pitch of a roof, the effect of rain on Westmorland slate, a thatcher's 'signature' – which might be a pheasant or a fox or a Cheshire cat made out of thatch – these are just a few of the little cameos that render the best English villages so memorable.

Most architectural details are taken for granted, but they all have a story to tell. Doors, for example, were the only outside feature of most houses for many hundreds of years, as well as being the only source of light (hence the familiar phrase 'don't darken my door again'). And it is often forgotten that letter-boxes are a comparatively recent invention, which is why they can look out of place on, say, Georgian houses.

Windows are even more crucial visually, and more varied historically: the Romans, it is said, were perfectly capable of making the kind of plate-glass windows used in most modern shop fronts, though in practice the techniques they developed were not used until after they abandoned these shores. But windows began to appear very early in the

Middle Ages, mainly in churches and great houses. In more modest houses, they used to be treated as part of the furniture and would be taken out by the owner when he moved. As windows became more universally used, economics dictated that small panes became fashionable. These were much cheaper to produce than large ones, though highly decorative small-paned windows are now treated as a rarity. They are most commonly seen in Shropshire and Cheshire, set off to best effect in a traditional half-timbered black-and-white house. The origin of the word 'window' is 'wind hole', indicating that they simply began as holes in the structure to allow smoke or unpleasant smells to escape.

Chimneys had a similar beginning, and the word itself derives from the French word for 'fireplace': they were simply holes in the roof. They really began to have some significance in the building of a house only after the introduction of coal as a fuel for heating, for while the smoke from wood was not too unpleasant, smoke from coal was intolerable. They served a double function in that they were also built-in smoke houses, particularly for bacon, and the reason so many of them are so large is that they had to be big enough for a small boy to get in to clean them. Food was often preserved by smoking, for these were the days before refrigeration (though some grand dwellings had underground ice houses), and winter diets were poor.

It is the most harmonious villages of all which seem most pleasing to the eye, even though in theory a village in which houses of different materials come together is more varied and interesting. The main materials for building come down to four. Put most simply, these are: wood, stone (including flint), mud and brick.

Most timber houses were built of willow, elm, chestnut and hornbeam. Oak was usually reserved for important buildings or pieces of buildings, and it is generally oak that has survived. The familiar timber-frame houses developed as wood became scarcer, and these have survived more generally than pure wooden houses, having developed a very harmonious style of their own. Many of them were so well built that it has become quite feasible for them to be raised up and moved to different locations. The increasing rarity of timber for building provides the best clues to the age of a frame house. Usually, the more timber in it, the older it is. The shortage of timber, too, is responsible for that very distinctive style of infilling between wooden struts, known as wattle and daub, which is a common sight when builders are at work renovating an ancient East Anglian house. Mud was used to fill panels between the wooden struts, and staves fitted into holes drilled into the main framework were used as strengthening. Hazel branches were then woven between these like basketwork.

Carved wooden buildings reached their peak during the fifteenth century, mainly because this was a bad time for church architects and artisans. Weatherboarding, the method of using slats of wood vertically or horizontally on the exterior of a house, was simply protective but it is a very attractive and underrated building method.

One of the first things a visitor to the Roman Wall learns is that even five hundred years ago it was much higher than it is today. The simple reason is that local people used to help themselves to the original stone for their own farmhouses and cottages. It was only in the early nineteenth century that a stop was put to this. Three thousand years before the Romans appeared, quite a few stone houses were built of 'field stone', simply picked up from the ground. But the strongest traditions of building in stone developed where trees were virtually non-existent, hence those dramatic northern moorscapes with harmonious houses and farms built of the prevailing grit and limestone. Until the late seventeenth century, stone was cheaper than brick, and using bricks was something of a luxury, so modest village houses might be of stone, and a manor house on the outskirts might be of brick.

Building stone appeals in the same way as the product of local breweries, or malt whiskies, for the stone varies tremendously even from one quarry to another. The easy and attractive way in which one type of stone, perhaps paler, perhaps darker, perhaps more variegated, blends into another, enhances a journey through those regions of the country where stone is the prevailing building material. In some places, things are even more heterogeneous, and you might find, even in one building, sandstone, flint, chalkstone, brickwork, clay pantiles, and, say, in a nineteenth- or even early-twentieth-century extension, a slate roof to boot. This particularly applies in ports where varied materials were passing through and occasionally available. Chalk is attractive, easily quarried and easy to carve, but does not weather well, a reason why it tends to be combined with brick or limestone. Sandstone, too, a characteristic feature of parts of east Cumbria, is soft and is frequently seen combined with brick or even gritstone.

Despite the eternal look of some stone houses, mud is much older, and more common than is realised. Even though inherently a weak material for building, mud houses (still frequently seen in Somerset and Devon) have survived if they have been well protected from the weather. Called cob in Devon, this is made from loamy earth mixed with straw or reed, chalk if it is available, or gravel, sand and small stones, mixed together like a Christmas pudding. Mud buildings were frequently much more common around the Solway Firth, in East Anglia, and the southern Midlands.

Building mud houses was a highly localised activity, the sort of thing which might have appealed to people who now go in for ambitious do-it-yourself schemes. Topped with thatch of West Country straw – which has a shorter life than Norfolk reed – these attractive houses have been described as looking like 'well-fed pigs', mainly because of their rounded and uneven corners.

Brick is more subtle and varied than it is usually given credit for. Bricks have been used only since the fifteenth century for ordinary houses, and brought strength, fire resistance, and ease of handling that had not hitherto been available. Dependent for colour and size on the method of firing, the number of additives and the minerals present in the ground, bricks are bright red in an iron-rich area such as Lancashire, while in Staffordshire they even go blue at high temperatures. The Romans made bricks, but for hundreds of years they were luxury items. Perhaps the greatest proponent of brick building was Sir Christopher Wren, in the second half of the seventeenth century, though even he was criticised decades later for choosing brightly-coloured brick: the Georgians preferred things more low key – yellow, brown, rust and grey.

The worst thing that has been said about the tourist boards is that they are turning England into a museum piece. And there is a limit to the number of villages that can be embalmed: they have to adapt to survive, and there are enough lost or deserted villages as it is. A village in the depths of the countryside is probably safer than one on the edge of a growing town, but even those can take comfort in the fact that there is a back-to-the-village movement: small is beautiful again, and while modern shopping precincts and housing estates are built to resemble traditional village squares and village streets, then there is lots of hope for the real thing.

On the whole, though, villages have changed much less than the countryside itself, though not always in the way one might think. The much maligned prairies that modern farming methods tend to create where the lie of the land makes it feasible, and which in some cases have only been avoided by a strong tradition of fox hunting, are not actually a twentieth-century phenomenon. In the seventeenth century large, open fields, especially in the Midlands, were the norm. It was only when it was gradually discovered that fields of just a few acres, carefully walled or hedged in, were economic for cattle and crop production, that the face of the landscape began to change again.

The enclosure of former common grazing lands and woodland during the eighteenth century deprived many rural communities of security and grazing for cattle, but bringing peasants under the control of all-powerful landowners did provide alternative employment. Then the massive onslaught of the new industrial age ravaged the countryside at a time when planning laws were non-existent, and the fields and woods of England were suddenly very vulnerable. Paradoxically, farmland became all the more important to provide food for the increasing metropolitan population. Gradually the face of England was being transformed. Formerly abandoned or unused land was suddenly vital, woodlands had to be conserved, and organised road and rail and canal communications were essential to bring food into towns and to allow goods to be transported, particularly to ports.

Industrialisation had begun to change the look of the countryside about three hundred years ago, even though as far back as the Romans, who had sought mainly gold and lead, England's mineral wealth had begun to be exploited. Hundreds of years before the Romans, primitive man had taken advantage of his surroundings. The earliest mines in England were probably those dug at Grimes Graves, near Thetford, Norfolk, in the heart of flinty Breckland. Hundreds of pits were sunk, and tunnels dug from the bottom of those pits as miners hacked out the flint they were to use as axeheads, arrowheads and knives. Breckland is such a strange place, all pinewoods and sandy heather, that it is worth visiting for its own sake, but I was rather disappointed to find that the mines the tourist sees at Grimes Graves were not the intriguing and labyrinthine network of secret passages I had believed, but just moderately deep pits.

Real industrialisation began in the Elizabethan age. There was mining for tin, lead and copper, there was charcoal burning for smelting, and already the foundations for the iron and steel industries were being made. There had been some far-sighted afforestation (for the navy on which the security of England depended was made up of wooden ships). In parts of the country, however, even timber for smelting began to run short, and this is why sea coal began to be used as an alternative – an unpleasant, unpopular, and noxious substance, which is still mined, and gives the north-east coast of England between Middlesbrough and Sunderland a strange look. Except as curiosities, the lead mines have largely disappeared now, but it was they, rather than the Blue John mines that were important to the economy of the Midlands. (One of the few mines that still exist, and is accessible to the public on special occasions with permission, is the Magpie Mine. On open days you can descend with a conducted tour

Grimes Graves, near Thetford, Norfolk. Though people who expect a
labyrinth of passages may be disappointed, they can descend into chambers
where flints were hacked by prehistoric man.

the remarkable, cold, dank frightening depths to which people sank. Our guide dropped
a fairly heavy stone into one of the shafts, and we counted fully eight seconds before it
finally reached the bottom.)

People who appear in their many thousands at one of the Ironbridge Gorge
Museum's five separate and distinctive sites (one of the best bargains anywhere is the
combined ticket, allowing access over a long period or in a short time, to all the sites) are
following a longer tradition than they probably realise: sightseers from all over Europe
came here, all agog, in the 1760s. But it was fifty-eight years after Abraham Darby's
death in 1717 before the symbolic construction of the world's first iron bridge across the
Severn near Coalbrookdale was authorised. It required an Act of Parliament and was an
ambitious and even daring project. The construction was in the hands of Abraham
Darby III, who proposed to span the River Severn with a single arch in the first bridge
ever to be built of cast-iron. Not only did it work, but it was a minor wonder of the
man-made world, and can be enjoyed and marvelled at today exactly as it was over two
hundred years ago.

Richard Arkwright was another revolutionary whose entrepreneurial skills not only

Ironbridge, Shropshire. The practical value of this, the world's first iron bridge, was less than its prestige value. It was cast in 1778 at Abraham Darby III's foundry at nearby Coalbrookdale, which is now home of several Ironbridge Gorge museums open to the public.

affected the lives of millions but who literally shaped the landscape. What happened was this: the first cotton cloth was imported from India, but it was soon realised that if raw cotton could be sent here, there was the capacity to produce finished cloth. Thus began the links with the southern states of what was much later to become the USA. Richard Arkwright created a machine that would spin cotton fibre into yarn, and at Cromford, in Derbyshire, on the banks of the River Derwent, he found the premises that would allow such a machine full rein. When Arkwright's patents ran out, entrepreneurs stepped in, and the familiar mill chimneys came to dominate the horizon all over what is now the industrial north.

Steam engines, which transformed the industrial scene, actually began down the mines, and steam pumping engines were created to remove dangerous and uncomfortable water in the shafts. As industry prospered there was further demand for an even better transport system. Canals got better and better, and just as important was the improvement of roads and bridges, and here the emergence of John MacAdam and Thomas Telford gave yet another boost to the industrial advance. In the same league was Isambard Kingdom Brunel, who enabled railways to negotiate daunting terrain. There had been railways long before steam engines appeared to work them: colliery trains pulled by horses had existed nearly a hundred years before the Stockton and

Canal Bridge at Norton Green, near Burslem, Staffordshire.

Darlington railway. Interestingly, even today, steam engines are in full commercial use at collieries, because of the ready availability of coal – it would be pointless running them on electricity.

Colliery engines will probably outlive the Bluebell Railway and the trains that chug to and fro along the Nene Valley. But elsewhere the scars of the Industrial Revolution are healing – slag heaps are being grassed over, theme parks and yachting marinas are covering up old gravel workings, low-ceilinged pubs where navvies ate their lunches are being prettied up. Who knows what the Manchester Ship Canal will be used for in three generations from now?

It is those stretches of England where the hand of man is not always in evidence that are increasingly popular among holidaymakers. About 90 per cent of England is now farmed, which means that there is very little wild country left but, just as an abandoned suburban garden will turn to something resembling a jungle in about ten years, it is not hard to imagine just how quickly the neat and nurtured countryside could return to nature.

One of the reasons that England is so beloved of overseas travellers, especially those from huge continents, is the astonishing variation within short distances of the nature of the landscape. This is mainly due to variation in soil and the kind of crops that grow best in any particular area. In the West Country, for example, you might have many acres of cider apple orchards around a trio of villages, and then, just a couple of miles further on, typically lush green romantic pastureland divided into comparatively small fields with lots of shelter for dairy cattle and then, beyond that, outcrops of rough moorland, leading over some headland to a sandy beach fringed in turn by rich arable farms. The soil can change even in the space of one farmer's field, and the same variation is even found in domestic gardens – which makes a rail journey all the more enjoyable (all those revealing back yards). So in the industrial North East, where people have tended to grow vegetables out of necessity, you have a tradition of gardens producing leeks, onions, cabbages, often enhanced for the eye by walls of sweet-peas (which take up little room), or tall sunflowers, hollyhocks, irises and the like. It has been estimated that half an acre is the minimum amount of ground necessary for a small family to make themselves self-sufficient, but allotments or small suburban gardens need only be a fraction of that size to provide extra vegetables or meat from chickens, ducks, and even a pig.

Perhaps it means we have come full circle. 'An acre of ground and a cow' is still many a city gent's ideal, and there is a regular exodus of jaded ad-men in the direction of the hills and a smallholding. Those peaceable neolithic farmers would have understood full well. But it's nice to pop into town sometimes, and if 'town' is graced by a Georgian terrace here, an Elizabethan courthouse there, a bit of Le Corbusier or Lutyens infilling, so much the better.

2. An England built to last: castles, houses, gardens

You cannot go far – certainly no further than a day's march – without stumbling across the rubble of some ruined castle, or the ramparts of something in a better state of preservation. England has castles the way New York has skyscrapers, and there is a small fortune waiting for the entrepreneur who, Department of the Environment permitting, takes a historic castle in good order and recreates the interior as it was the day after William the Conqueror built it. Most people find it hard to imagine what things were like in the not-so-good-old-days, but life surely had its comforts, even when King Arthur was ensconced in Camelot.

As you scale the battlements of Framlingham Castle, in Suffolk, which dominates the substantial and attractive village, you wonder if people could actually have lived in it. But its seemingly impregnable curtain wall – fun to walk around the top of – used to contain vaulted chambers dating from around 1200, proper glass windows (even the Romans were adept at making plate glass), fireplaces and chimneys. Walls would have had draught-excluding tapestries, floors covered with straw or loose matting – revolting, perhaps, if left unchanged for long, but perfectly acceptable when freshly laid. The sixteenth-century writer Erasmus put it succinctly when he described one particular room that had been neglected: 'An ancient collection of beer, grease, fragments, bones, spittle, excrement of dogs and cats and everything that is nasty.' As castles became more domesticated and less geared up to war, medieval architects would indulge themselves. It was believed, for example, that whitewash preserved stone, and the combination of gold-painted pinnacles and brightly painted doors and window frames were the architectural equivalent of illuminated manuscripts. Add to this the lavishly painted interiors in which murals depicting noble and Biblical scenes predominated, and you have a world at odds with the impression most of these places convey today.

The serious building of castles began many hundreds of years before such embellishments appeared. William the Conqueror used them as a way of establishing stable government – and very successful he was too – under a hierarchy of regional overlords. But even under the Normans, contrary to popular belief, most castles were made of wood. By AD 1100, out of eighty-five castles commissioned by William, only six or seven were of stone. These included the White Tower (which is the oldest part of the Tower of London), Richmond Castle in Yorkshire (the oldest of them all), Pevensey in Sussex and Colchester in Essex. Most were either of the motte type, based on a truncated conical earth mound surrounded by a ditch and topped with a timber palisade, or the motte-and-bailey type, which was simply a motte with an outer court enclosed by walls.

Far more Norman castles would be around today if they had been capable of conversion into domestic dwellings, but generally they were not, and most were sold for the value of their materials. The first castles were usually built on the top of natural hills, and although none of the original wooden structures remain today a sharp-eyed helicopter pilot would be able to pick out tell-tale markings of ramparts and ditches. And sometimes the hills themselves are so distinctive that you think 'if there wasn't a castle up there sometime, then there jolly well should have been'. One of the best examples is Cadbury Camp, which was such a strong natural fortification that it was reoccupied and rebuilt several times, long after its original function had been forgotten.

But there is no castle country to match Northumberland. It positively bristles with them. Some are intimate and parochial, like the pele towers that stand next to country vicarages and kept clergymen comparatively safe from irreverent incursionists from over the border; some, like Alnwick, are lavish stately homes masquerading under the guise of rude and warlike forts; some, like Bamburgh, Dunstanburgh, Warkworth and Lindisfarne, are castles in the traditional mould, and others, like Langley (where they have 'medieval' banquets for the delectation of coach parties from the Newcastle suburbs) and Featherstone (now a boys' school and once a prisoner-of-war camp), have been dragged kicking and screaming into the twentieth century. Langley stands on a great rocky mound, partly hidden by trees, just south of Haydon Bridge, which straddles the River Tyne close to the middle of the narrowest neck of England. The castle was once part of the great barony of Tynedale, and until you enter the building, you have no idea of its new-found contemporary function. An interesting architectural point: the foundations do not go below ground but are built right on the base of the rocks. The castle walls, incidentally, are six feet thick: strong enough to withstand even the ravages of all those women's clubs from Blaydon and Ponteland having a night out.

Bamburgh Castle is much vaunted by the guide books, and it is easily the most impressive man-made landmark on England's north-east coast, brooding as it does over the most spectacular beaches in the north. Grassy dunes separate the castle walls from the beach – cold and windswept, even eerie, when fair-weather visitors have gone home. What is not generally known about Bamburgh Castle is that it contains a number of luxury apartments. The view of the North Sea these enjoy is exceptional, but the great, angular red-sandstone castle, especially when viewed at close quarters, is not itself exactly beautiful. It gives the impression of being totally impregnable, having been built on a great rocky outcrop that lies near the easternmost extreme of the so-called Whin Sill, the ridge of volcanic rock that rises from the Pennines to the Farne Islands. But it has been much extended and altered, particularly during the late-Victorian period.

One of the most striking things about Alnwick Castle is the life-sized figures that are placed strategically along the battlements and on top of the turrets. The figures, which look smaller than they are because the walls of the castle are so high, were originally used to confuse enemy scouts, who would not have dared to come close enough to be disillusioned. Ancestral home of the Dukes of Northumberland, and as impressive inside as some of the country's finest stately homes, this could have been the inspiration of all the toy castles ever sold to the parents of small boys. The castle was left to rot in the sixteenth and seventeenth centuries, but from all vantage points it still looks as a castle should. By the same token, from its battlements and its state rooms, the views of the surrounding country, with the sea only five miles away, are outstanding. Dunstanburgh

Castle's location is almost too good to be true. Poised on an exposed grassy promontory of basalt rock beside the unruly North Sea, it has the added advantage for the historically-minded visitor, who finds that cars and coaches detract from a place, of being accessible only via a footpath that runs close to the shore. It is as romantic a ruin as you will find in England, and that is saying something, but it is an especially lucky sightseer who ever gets to see its stark black silhouette from the seaward side. The headland on which Dunstanburgh stands was probably once the site of a Romano-British settlement. The castle itself was begun in 1316 by the Earl of Lancaster, who probably wanted to turn it into a fortified port. It was enlarged and modernised in 1380 by John of Gaunt, who was Lord Lieutenant of the Scottish Marches, but it was already a ruin by 1538, and outwardly has changed hardly at all since then. If you go to Dunstanburgh, you feel you *have* to enjoy it, because getting there is quite an undertaking. There is a shorter approach, but for most people it involves a walk of a good mile along the green path by the North Sea from the village of Craster, where you may reward yourself for your exertions with a couple of home-cured kippers. The smokery here still keeps up a tradition going back hundreds of years, unadulterated by any idea of fast food.

I have visited and admired almost enough English castles to compile a gazetteer, with just a couple of irritating gaps to fill: Queenborough Castle, in Kent, has gone for ever, and Jedburgh, a favourite, is unfortunately just over the Scottish border (had the reivers always had their way, of course, it may not have been so). There was Arundel in Sussex, reminiscent, partly because of its round tower on a central conical mound, of Windsor Castle. Like Windsor, the castle was heavily restored in the early nineteenth century. The tenth Duke of Norfolk, whose family seat this is, spent over half a million pounds creating a Gothic fantasy, most of which was dismantled by the fifteenth Duke in the final years of the nineteenth century. He tried to recreate the original state of the castle, but it was really too far gone.

There was Corfe Castle in Dorset, whose impressive ruins are all the more impressive for being silhouetted on a steep hill above the village of Corfe. It has the look of a wedding cake enthusiastically attacked during a reception and left for dead. And Dunster Castle, in neighbouring Somerset, which, under one Colonel Wyndham, held out against Parliamentary troops for 160 days until April 1646. Though it has stood on its hillside for almost a thousand years, it has the look of a lush stately home rising elegantly among mixed woodlands and gardens.

Eastnor Castle, in Herefordshire, has appealed to me since the day I saw it, just glimpsed through the trees after a visit to nearby Ledbury, when I did not have time to stop. It too is much enhanced by gardens, but its ivy-covered turrets and battlemented towers, for all their medieval appearance, date back no longer than 1812. So instead of being the apotheosis of the medieval castle, it is actually a fake, but beautiful to look at and charming inside, with some spectacular early-Victorian rooms. There was Framlingham, in Suffolk, and Goodridge Castle, in Herefordshire, yet another that was knocked about a bit by Cromwell. It was finally cowed into submission by Cromwell's troops with the help of a cannon called Roaring Meg, which now stands on Hereford's Castle Green. On its wooded hill above the River Wye, it was a border defence against the Welsh.

Hever Castle, in Kent, was sold on the open market in 1983, and the new owners

Scotney Old Castle, near Lamberhurst, Kent. The half-ruined tower is
over six hundred years old, its appeal much enhanced by the moat and the
great trees that surround it.

were concerned when the number of visitors dropped dramatically: many people
thought that the castle was no longer open to the public. Hever's previous owner, Lord
Astor, struggled to preserve the castle intact, but his dissatisfaction with the effect of
tourists on the grounds and the castle fabric got the better of him. Once the home of
Anne Boleyn, Henry VIII's second wife, Hever had been reduced in social status to a
farmhouse in the first few years of the twentieth century before being bought by the
Astor family. The Long Gallery here is an exceptional survivor, and the gardens are a
rare example of early-twentieth-century work. There is an exquisite tree-fringed lake
overlooked by a stone piazza. In the same county, though there is no public admission, it
is worth seeing Ightham Mote from the outside. A fourteenth-century domestic castle
near Tonbridge in Kent, its moat was really meant as a defence against wandering
robbers, rather than enemy soldiers. The Mote of the name is one of those misleading
words. It has nothing to do with the moat but derives from the same route as meet,
indicating a place where the local Council convened.

Battered old Kenilworth, in Warwickshire, seems to play second fiddle to Warwick

Castle (but there's many a good tune . . .). It was once the home of Robert Dudley, Earl of Leicester, Elizabeth I's favourite, but now little remains except a romantic empty shell. When he lived here, Leicester is said to have spent £100,000 converting the castle into a palace suitable for a queen. Ludlow Castle, to the north-west, can be seen for many miles around, and was the most important strategically of all the Welsh Marcher fortifications. The interior is open to the elements, but provides a spectacular setting for plays performed here during the Ludlow Festival. Maiden Castle, in Dorset, is said to be haunted by the ghosts of Britons who resisted the Romans. Straddling a hill over a half a mile long, it is thought to have incorporated a Stone Age settlement around 2000 BC and later became a great earth barrow, or funeral monument. It was abandoned until 300 BC, when Iron Age men arrived and, taking advantage of the site, created a town that covered the whole of the hill. They made ramparts and put up some resistance to the Roman invaders in AD 43, though without success. In the 1930s a burial ground containing the remains of the defenders of the town was uncovered.

Newark Castle, in Nottinghamshire, withstood three civil war sieges, but after the surrender of Charles I, Cromwell's troops rubbed salt into the wound by making the townspeople dismantle the castle themselves – but most of the river wall and a gatehouse survived. Fraught even though it is with traffic, and suffering the indignity of an admittedly rather handy public lavatory hard by, it nevertheless adds a certain grandeur to the town.

Pleshey Castle, in Essex, is one of the greatest secrets in the country. The whole of Pleshey village lies within the two-mile-circumference enclosure of pre-Norman earth works, and although the castle has unfortunately long since completely disappeared, the moat – still containing water – is spanned by a remarkable fifteenth-century bridge that still remains. When you reach the top of the mound you are at one of the highest points in Essex and it is well worth a detour.

Raby Castle, I can confirm, is one good reason among several for visiting County Durham. Legend says that it is built on a site once owned by King Canute. It is a classic, looking as good on the skyline, set back from the passing road behind rolling parkland, as any castle fancier could wish: it was considerably altered and 'improved' in the eighteenth and nineteenth centuries but without detriment to the original fabric and the atmosphere it still conveys. Clifford's Tower, for example, which is at the north-west corner of the castle, has walls ten feet thick and is the largest of several towers. It is scarred with arrow slits. The kitchen has that great high ceiling common in medieval times: it was hoped that most cooking smells would be somehow wafted away.

It is St Michael's Mount, off the south Cornish coast, however, that must surely have the most impressive situation of any English castle, especially at high tide, when the causeway by which the island is accesssible from the mainland is covered by the sea. It is thought that this was once part of Lyonesse, an ancient legendary kingdom that stretched from Land's End to the Isles of Scilly, most of which is thought to be now under the sea, and it achieved a moment of fame as the last pocket of resistance by the Lancastrians during the Wars of the Roses. The Earl of Oxford stood out against the Yorkists, but a six-month siege reduced his troops to the edge of starvation.

In the same county, Tintagel Castle's ruins stand on a windswept headland very different from urbane and gentle Penzance. Almost separated from the mainland through the effects of the weather and the waves over thousands of years, some people

Leeds Castle, Kent. Come here when the crowds have gone, and the
twentieth century seems a very long way away. It is not surprising so many
kings and queens felt at home.

say it was King Arthur's Camelot, and, happily, enough that is tangible has survived to
get the imagination working.

I have enjoyed a picnic lunch at Uffington Castle at the very top of White Horse Hill,
Oxfordshire. On a fine day, when visibility is good and the wind is just ruffling the long
grass and larks are trilling above, this is a romantic spot. And I have had afternoon tea in
one of the border country's pele towers. These were simply clergymen's houses built
during warlike times as mini-castles.

But after all the sound and fury, signifying much, the most indelible memory I have
is of Leeds Castle, in Kent. I saw it at about three o'clock on a January afternoon, when
the world was closing in around the great park in which the moated six-hundred-year-
old castle stands. The twentieth century could have been a figment of anybody's

imagination. It had been snowing during the previous night and all that day, but now it had nearly stopped: just a few odd flakes. The park was covered with a foot and a half of new snow and without this I would have seen nothing. With it, however, came a pale and ghostly light that showed up the shapes of the dark trees bordering the park. As I made sluggish and almost silent progress towards the castle itself, and rounded a bend in the winding approach road, that light showed the outline of a fairy-tale building that in Hollywood you would dismiss as too good to be true. Just two or three windows were illuminated and, though I didn't know it until I had crossed the deep slate-coloured frozen moat and gone inside through the portcullis, those lights came from ecclesiastical-sized candles and the glow of several log fires that only lacked Irish wolfhounds lounging in front of them to complete the picture. That evening was the closest I have come to going back in time.

Everyone enjoys such places differently. I am constantly drawn to the windows of a great house to admire the view from milady's bedroom, or to look down on the people milling about among the fountains, or to observe some three-hundred-year-old oak from squirrel height. I especially like to hang back behind the last visitors of the day. I remember Belvoir, in Leicestershire: the last-but-one visitor's footsteps echoed ahead of me on polished marble floors, and already the shadows in little-frequented corners of yet another Gothic fantasy of the 1830s seemed to merge with those stealing silently over staircases and landings. It was only because I was hassled by the custodian that I did not linger until it was completely dark. Belvoir is really just a glorified country house. Intricate and intriguing, with a good sprinkling of battlements, castellations, terraces, great stone stairways, corridors ennobled by suits of armour, priceless silver, solid-gold punchbowls, stern oil portraits, the building is like a cross between something out of the *Wizard of Oz* and Windsor Castle. It also happens to contain one of the outstanding private collections of paintings in Europe, with works by Hogarth, Joshua Reynolds, Van Dyke, Rubens and Holbein, among others.

Like museums and art galleries, great houses do not reveal themselves all in one go. It is the details that remain in the mind: like Winston Churchill's marmalade cat – now dead but replaced by an almost identical mog – inscrutably contemplating the stream of visitors at Chartwell, in Kent. Like the child collecting tadpoles from the rhododendron-bordered lake at Cragside in Northumberland or, beside another lake, at Dyrham Park, near Bath, with the fish snapping at flies at dusk. Like the authentic broughams and open landaus in the carriage museum at Doddington Park.

One historian has remarked on the lack of ambition of a recent Duke of Rutland at Belvoir. But the Duke thought anywhere else in the world was a poor substitute for his place in the country, and as you stand on the terrace you cannot blame him. And it was Churchill who said of his favourite home, possessed as it is of a fabulous panoramic view of the Weald of Kent, that 'a day away from Chartwell is a day wasted'. It might be because he was so patently fond of Chartwell, which he bought for £9,000 in the 1920s, that it remains more a home than a great house. That of course is the big secret: Waddesdon Manor, in Buckinghamshire, for all its exquisite furniture and pretty figurines, is a glorified museum.

Houses like Waddesdon were showpieces, designed as much for displays of power as

Chartwell, Kent. This was Winston Churchill's country home for over forty years, but by any standards it is a civilised, welcoming and peaceful house, with spectacular views of the Weald of Kent.

well as the ordinary business of living. Sometimes country house owners merely went through the motions of living in the country and spent as little time as possible there. Until communications improved, it was a long, tedious, and uncomfortable business simply getting from London to, say, the Shires, and it was only at the beginning of the nineteenth century that habits began to change and people were able to contemplate a dual existence in town and country.

Visitors find the elusive lived-in flavour all-important, and the wider and more windswept the countryside a house stands in, the more welcoming and luxurious its interior. One such is Wallington Hall, in Northumberland, a great, creamy-grey mansion, best approached from the south, over a fine stone eighteenth-century bridge from which the house appears on a slight hill. It is almost, but not quite, masked by tall trees. The view from the house is of barren but not depressing moorland country, into which some farms have infiltrated, and the impression the house makes on the arriving visitor cannot have changed much since about 1750.

The grounds of Wallington Hall, which was built by successful manufacturers from Newcastle, are exceptional – especially the formal gardens and the water gardens – and it is likely that when the gardens were being laid out, a teenager from nearby Kirkharle would have passed by and observed what was going on. Lancelot Brown, later to become 'Capability Brown', was to leave an indelible impression on the English landscape as a gardener and a setter of landscaping trends. Wallington was described in the eighteenth century as 'huge and handsome, which appears from dispensation of the apartments, to be very convenient'. In 1777, it was taken over by the Trevelyan family, who have lived there ever since, although in 1941 Wallington was presented to the National Trust, along with 13,000 acres, so great was the financial burden of running it.

The garden and lakes are laid out on three sides of the house, and the walled garden has been the preserve of rare flowers for over a century: there are fuchsias, for example, that date back to 1908. In the wooded garden, you could be a hundred miles from wild Northumberland, so effective has been the transformation of a corner of moorland enclave to a classically inspired water garden, bordered with great trees. If you catch it when most visitors have drifted away – perhaps even during those stolen moments when the clock tells you you *should* have left – it is silent except for wildfowl on the lake or when, after a shower, rainwater drips from the trees.

There is a much more formal garden at another favourite house of mine, which is Penshurst Place, in Kent. It too was always more than just a house, and it was one of Henry VIII's favourite homes. He was so enamoured of it, cynics say, that he contrived to have its owner, the third Duke of Buckingham, tried for treason and beheaded, simply in order to acquire the property for himself. When the house passed to the ill-fated Edward, Henry's only male heir, he in turn passed it to his friend and protector, Sir William Sidney. Penshurst was already well over two hundred years old then, having developed around an early-fourteenth-century manor house, whose Great Hall, with a square chestnut roof, is one of the finest medieval survivals of its kind in Europe. Even so, it remains a family home: the present owner is Lord de Lisle, VC, who inherited Penshurst forty years ago. The house has been open for centuries, and attracted floods of visitors to the house and the grounds. I thought that, apart from the Great Hall, the most memorable part of the house was the Long Gallery, created after 1599 and finished in 1607, and quite mundanely designed simply as a place where

Lord de L'Isle and gardener, Penshurst Place, Kent.

people could get exercise in bad weather or walk up and down as they chatted. You could certainly go jogging in it. The room contains several fine portraits, including one of Elizabeth I, part of the 'Gloriana' series that was initiated in order to enhance her national prestige, and one of Philip Sidney, for whom Elizabeth I had a soft spot.

On the other side of the narrow neck of the country from Wallington Hall, the southern hills of Lakeland form a backdrop to Leighton Hall. The original house was medieval, and it had a chequered existence until the happy decision, around 1879, to remodel virtually the whole building. This is one of the best memorials to rustic Victorian taste, full of romantic details and mock-Tudor embellishments. There is a lot of late-eighteenth-century Gillow furniture, for the house was bought in 1822 by Richard Gillow, grandson of the founder of the Lancashire furniture makers, Gillow and Co, later to become half of Waring and Gillow. (Best of all the pieces is probably the Victorian four-poster bed.) When I first drove down the lane to the hall, I assumed from the house's appearance that it was white-stuccoed, but in fact the colour of the stone is natural. It is a curious, unusually pale local limestone which picks up even the weakest sunlight and reflects it in an almost eerie way. A falconer was entertaining the early-season visitors on the lawn, though his falcon seemed disinterested.

Other great houses have been in the path of what is loosely called progress. 'Hardwick Hall, more glass than wall', they used to say of the great, gaunt house that now looms high above the M1 motorway near junction 29 in Derbyshire, but today it is much admired. It is a spectacular memorial to the irrepressibly ambitious Bess of Hardwick – a gold-digger of circa 1542 who would have put the most opportunistic Ziegfeld girls to shame, and who crowned her remarkable career with this remarkable place. She even had her initials, of very immodest size, inscribed into the top of the great square towers on the west front of the house. Bess of Hardwick married four times, the last time to the Earl of Shrewsbury, and grew richer and more powerful with each marriage. She became a widow for the fourth time at the age of seventy in 1590, and it was just a year later that she began the creation of her great monument. It took six years to complete, and, untypically for Tudor England, is uncompromisingly symmetrical. There really is more glass than stone in the walls. There are no fewer than fifty windows, several of them huge. In the care of the National Trust, Hardwick Hall has been kept very much as it would have been in Bess's day, especially the tapestries.

The Gallery, Hardwick Hall, Derbyshire. Even as great houses go, this is
larger-than-life, and the formidable personality of Bess of Hardwick
dominates its curiously intimate rooms.

A far cry from the great houses that have the support of the National Trust or substantial endowments, are those historic piles that have been rescued in the nick of time by individuals, their energy fuelled by a desire to keep a piece of history alive. One of these is Brympton D'Evercy, occupied by Charles and Judy Clive, who bought this leaky one-hundred-roomed house in Somerset in the early 1970s and have fought a slowly winning battle against rainwater and numbing cold ever since. I met 'Mr Clive', as he is known locally, and he told me, 'Every time it rains, I have to go round and make sure none of it is coming in. We were once about to sit down to an evening meal, and I had to get up on the roof in my dinner jacket and replace a slate. When we have visitors, we warn them to wear fur boots and thick underwear, and every bed has an electric blanket – otherwise no one would stay. Space, of course, is no problem: the dog and the cat have separate bedrooms, and we have occasionally had indoor cycling.' There are other compensations too: in one recent summer they made five hundred gallons of cider on a press that stands in the priest house. Brympton D'Evercy has one thing in common with Hardwick: it has a great tapestry. But this, 23 feet by 10 feet, is actually modern, the work of a team of more than thirty relatives and friends who, during one complete winter, helped to make its forty-four panels. Building on the house began in 1678, and in 1731 it was bought by one Francis Fane, who left it to his younger brother who later became the eighth Earl of Westmorland. Through family connections, the house was inherited by the Clives. There is a lovely back garden, and even on a Bank Holiday it absorbs scores of people without fuss.

People living in a semi might not think so, but Brympton D'Evercy is quite a modest country house. Others are almost city states. Vita Sackville-West, who saw her family home, Knole House in Kent, as more like a large village than a country mansion, was not really far off the mark. Although some great houses were built all-of-a-piece, more often than not they just grew and grew. Some of them extend from the fourteenth or fifteenth century to the present day, or at least to the work of the late-Victorians: I am thinking especially of Sledmere House, the early-twentieth-century reconstruction of a much older building that has faithfully recaptured the warm domestic atmosphere that must have prevailed in this richly endowed mansion in a part of Yorkshire – Humberside to be strictly correct – that few people see.

Among the great houses that were more like fourteenth-century Italian courts – independent, prosperous and prestigious – are Castle Howard in Yorkshire, Chatsworth in Derbyshire, and Woburn in Bedfordshire. Castle Howard dominates the surrounding countryside, and the fact that it redoubled its worldwide fame because of the success of the television dramatisation of Evelyn Waugh's *Brideshead Revisited* – partly inspired by Castle Howard, which was only thinly disguised in the book – has left it largely unmoved. The house is remarkable for dozens of reasons. Not only is it architecturally superb but it is unusual for having originated as the inspired jottings of a man who had no training as an architect. For John Vanbrugh was actually a successful playwright. Castle Howard's vast echoing chambers – it is much more of a palace than other buildings that go by the more grandiose name – and its hundreds of acres of gardens, set off by temples and fountains, can absorb many thousands of visitors without detriment. On a warm summer afternoon, I walked to the Temple of the Four Winds and where I sat down with a book: there were more people in the souvenir shop than in the grounds.

Chatsworth, the 'jewel of the north', as it has been called, is almost on the same scale. Though its grounds are not as extensive as Castle Howard's, nor its treasures as staggering as Harewood's, it is still palatial. The first Duke of Devonshire, who inherited Chatsworth in 1684 and found a 'decaying and weak' building that Bess of Hardwick had built, was essentially a city-dweller. After leaving London for political

The Chatsworth Violin, Chatsworth House, a spectacular example of
trompe l'oeil, originally created by Vandervaart in about 1723 for
Devonshire House, London.

reasons, he brought a taste of high society to the country, and Chatsworth was long associated, particularly in the late-nineteenth century, during the time of the sixth Duke, with glittering house parties. It was the sixth Duke who built the private theatre – a great rarity even among such houses – that still exists. The first Duke had been a passionate gambler and though he was immensely wealthy when he began the renovation and extension of Chatsworth, he was embarrassingly short of money at the end. His problems were aggravated by his inability to imagine the finished product from architects' plans, and a lot of new work was destroyed when second and third attempts were made to get things 'right'. The Duke also argued with his architects, and it is said that, following one such quarrel, in which Christopher Wren was called to adjudicate, the Duke himself may have had a hand in some of the designs. I happened to visit Chatsworth one Derby Day, in the company of a party of Irish travel agents, and our peregrinations among the dark panelled rooms and up and down heavy oak staircases were interrupted shortly before 3 pm by the need to return to our executive coach to watch the race on television. Not one of us had the winner, as it was a three-legged outsider, but the first Duke would probably have approved all the same.

Though it stands in a man-made landscape, Chatsworth's surroundings are wild and windswept. Its atmosphere is restrained. It would not be seen dead in the company of exotic animals, performing or otherwise, and carousels. It is not a Woburn. That is a place I liked for one reason in particular, which is that it is able to perform a dual role: circus and museum. For behind the fun-fair and the antiques emporia and the safari park, there remains one of the most exquisite country houses in Britain, with an interior as richly decorated and endowed with furniture and paintings as any in the country. The safari park, however, was just an elaborate extension of what had already existed for nearly a century – an interest in wildlife preservation by the Russell family that began with the introduction of Père David deer in the 1870s from their threatened habitat in China. There are now several hundred.

I have been to Woburn several times, but best of all was the day of the Game Fair. There was pheasant plucking against the clock and a demonstration of fly casting in the lake, sheep trials, exhibitions of historic firearms and mounted butterflies, clay pigeon shooting (for beginners, too), *real* pigeons in aspic at the buffet, real ale, ox roasting. And that was only before lunch.

Some of the great landowners may have been no better than feudal overlords, but they did the countryside no harm. Fine houses like Wallington Hall and Sledmere lie on the edge of comparatively wild and little-populated country. But as communications became easier, a great landowner who skulked in London and did not take part in rural

Burghley House, near Stamford, Lincolnshire. Home of the annual horse trials, it perhaps comes into its own when the visitors have gone and the ghosts of winters past steal up.

activities and look after the welfare of his tenants began to be very much looked down upon. There was much to-ing and fro-ing, even among people born and bred in the country, between country and city. As carriages became more comfortable and stylish, people not only travelled between London and their country homes, but would travel within their county or even beyond, going to race meetings, and spending weeks at a time in one of the spas that were becoming fashionable during the eighteenth century. Fashion and social interests began to dictate the shape and size of houses in which expense was no object. Rooms were larger, being designed for balls and parties, and a series of interconnecting rooms, a very common phenomenon to be noticed by today's visitors to great houses, allowed for an easy flow of people through from one chamber to another. Then, as the eighteenth century progressed, people began to travel and collect more *objets d'art*, and more space was needed to house these. Artefacts became more important than families, libraries were enlarged. Whole wings were even added to some houses, particularly where sculpture had been collected on trips to Mediterranean countries. People were less in awe of books, though libraries were by no means used exclusively for them – games, maps, scientific toys were commonplace. What country house library would be complete without a globe, or a sextant or an astrolabe? I came across a superb example of what a library could become at Felbrigg House, Norfolk: an oak-panelled rhapsody in buff, brown, oak and leather in which to while away a whole winter of rainy afternoons.

Although it is probably the eighteenth-century houses that excite most interest today, it was really during the nineteenth century that people seemed most to appreciate the delicate balance of comfortable living and ready access to what they thought of as 'the countryside', but what was really a compromise between a garden and a wilder world outside. If you visit certain houses, among them Burton Constable in Humberside, and Doddington House in Gloucestershire, you may stumble across a rabbit warren of corridors and separate rooms, inevitably more dank and unappealing than the main parts of the house. As houses changed, and ideas about country house life became more fixed, servants were allowed to be neither seen nor heard, except when absolutely essential.

All too many houses have gone down – literally. Unintentional neglect has done for some of them, while others, protected by preservation orders but millstones nevertheless, have sometimes deliberately been set on fire. A senior member of that exclusive club of people who have literally saved great houses from becoming rubble is the Marquess of Hertford. In the early 1950s you might have picked up the national papers and seen photographs of the Marquess scrubbing the seventy-foot-long Great Hall of his ancestral home with, as it was reported, 'not a thrall or a serf in sight'. Times were hard, and the future of Ragley Hall lay in the balance. It was of course a marvellous publicity gimmick, and ever since those dark days, people have driven to this corner of 'the heart of England' to visit the house. In terms of the number of visitors it gets, it is one of the ten most popular houses in England. That Great Hall, incidentally, would double quite nicely as a garage for double-decker buses. Apart from being seventy feet long, it is forty feet wide, and forty feet high.

The house was built in the seventeenth century, and in the 1750s, James Gibbs remodelled and decorated the Great Hall. It is a classically symmetrical room: there are, for example, four doors all exactly the same. But one of them is a fake and is actually a

Littlecote House, near Hungerford, Berkshire. One of the most intriguing and beautifully appointed great houses in England, it is still comparatively unknown.

glorified cupboard. What lies behind it? A bar! It is a house of superlatives. There are no fewer than ten thousand leather-bound volumes in the library, exquisite furniture by Sheraton, Sèvres china along with the Spode and the Chelsea, Grinling Gibbons carvings, and, among the paintings, Franz Hals's 'Laughing Cavalier'. Each room seems more spectacular than the last. There is, for example, the menthol-cool Green Drawing Room, with its Chinese Chippendale mirrors, the aforesaid Library and Great Hall, the Dining Room, with table silver created in 1772, where twenty-four people can sit down comfortably for dinner. This is not just a preserve of the Hertfords: you can hire the room for functions and sit down to food fit for a duke, which you can, incidentally, also do at Harewood House, in Yorkshire.

There was consternation in the mid 1970s when, during repair work at Chawton House, Hampshire, where Jane Austen wrote her *Emma, Mansfield Park* and *Persuasion*, the famous squeak in the door of the drawing-room to which she referred in her books disappeared. There were attempts to reinstate the squeak, without much success. Ultimately, the curators had to admit defeat, but this is probably the only detail missing from a house which, in most important respects, is exactly as Jane Austen knew it. Due to the efforts of the Jane Austen Society, the house has been restored and reinstated to its original form after – a common phenomenon – having at one time been sub-divided into three separate workmen's cottages. The garden has been replanted as nearly as possible in the way it would have appeared 170 years ago, and downstairs and upstairs rooms are more or less completely intact.

Hardly enjoying the same degree of intimacy as Chawton, the great Tatton Hall, in Cheshire, is also dominated by an unseen figure – in this case Lord Egerton – who died in 1958 but whose life seems to belong to something out of the *Boys' Own Paper*. The Tenants' Hall he built behind the servants' quarters contains hundreds of often bizarre hunting trophies, including a tiger and tigress shot by Egerton at the age of eighty-one. Tatton stands in an estate of over a thousand acres and the lake in the grounds alone is over a mile long. This is at the top of the popularity league of houses owned by the National Trust and it invites many superlatives. There is a rare and vast collection of paintings, a priceless library, exquisite furniture.

Houses associated with well-known modern personalities include Shugborough Hall, on the northernmost edge of Cannock Chase, which is the ancestral home of society and fashion photographer, Patrick Lichfield, a cousin of the Queen. Lichfield's house would be much visited for its own sake (its fine grounds contain an unusual number of decorative summer-houses, temples and gazebos, including the Chinese House, built during the Chinoiserie craze in the mid-eighteenth century), but it also happens to contain the Staffordshire County Museum in a stable block, delightful in itself, dating from 1765. And right on the Staffordshire–Shropshire border, which divides its grounds, Weston Park is the family seat of the former Viscount Newport, now the Earl of Bradford, who in the 1970s made a big impact as a restaurateur on the London gastronomic scene. (His Caviar Bar was a great success.) Disraeli, incidentally, was a frequent visitor to Weston Park. He was a passionate admirer of the wife of the third Earl.

Weston's paintings alone are worth millions, especially the Van Dykes and the Stubbs. Each room has a powerful style of its own – the Tapestry Room, for example, has Gobelin and Aubusson tapestries, and in the same room is a priceless sketch, in crayon, of Anne Boleyn as Queen, by Hans Holbein. The house is one of the best examples in England of a Dutch style of architecture that marries brick and stone, and the colour of the house, which is pinkish orange, enhances its impact on the surrounding countryside. If it is close to perfection, however, it cannot hold a candle to The Vyne, near Basingstoke in Hampshire, which is a house for the connoisseur. It may not get as many visitors as some but *everybody* who visits it seems to count it as one of their favourites. It incorporates three outstanding architectural styles – Tudor, Stuart, and Georgian. It gets its name from a nearby Roman settlement known as Vindonis, house of wine. It is almost exactly the same age as Hampton Court Palace and it is a coincidence that Henry VIII, who wheedled Hampton Court out of Cardinal Wolsey, was especially fond of The Vyne. So was his daughter, Elizabeth, who was entertained here in 1569. The sixteenth-century building was transformed in about 1655 by many classical additions.

Inevitably the nicest country houses tend to be the ones that are overlooked and tucked away. Typical of the best of these, just a few minutes' drive from Woodbridge in

Little Moreton Hall, Cheshire. In some 'balloon game' in which only one English building might be allowed to survive, this almost entirely original example of an Elizabethan half-timbered mansion would get many votes.

Suffolk, is Glemham Hall, which you can see to your right, as you drive north on the A12, across parkland that sometimes has a herd of brown-and-white cattle to set it off to advantage. It is one of my favourite houses, and is totally unpretentious, though once it was very grand. Some of the faded furniture and paintings would not fetch three figures even in a Woodbridge antique shop, which is saying something, but it is the sort of place that would not require too much of a transition for most people who like that sort of thing, to be able to live there. You can even potter around the top floor servants' quarters, some of them with the original spartan furniture, and you can take your time in the kitchen garden that may be a curiosity now but was an essential cog in the running of the house during its early-nineteenth-century heyday.

The great man-made garden landscapes, that literally shaped the countryside as we know it, began as extensions to country houses. And the reason a house might have imposing doors at ground level, whether the front or the back, instead of at the top of a handsome flight of steps, was simply that this made it possible to walk out among the flower beds or shaded arbours. This was especially important at the beginning of the nineteenth century when entertaining on an often lavish scale became the norm. Added to all this, it was fashionable after the middle of the eighteenth century to travel abroad for the grand tour, and to bring back not just artefacts such as sculpture and archaeological relics (the ultimate oneupmanship being represented by the Elgin Marbles), but rare plants: there were no customs posts at Dover to check on whether what you imported might be dangerous because of any disease to indigenous plants.

People did not realise it at the time, but one great advantage of the English climate is that plants from all over the world can prosper. I have been corrected by more that one great house's custodian when assuming that such and such a famous architect was responsible for it. 'Oh no,' they say, 'so-and-so did the house, but the chap you are talking about just did the garden.' In twentieth-century England garden design is the poor relation of house design, but it never used to be so. During the second half of the seventeenth century, for example, many wealthy landowners tried to emulate what was being done in Europe, but the terrain just did not suit that, and the familiar English parkland became used to having other people's styles adapted to the lie of the land.

After 1689, however, and the accession of William and Mary, some Dutch influence made itself felt. The Dutch liked statues and lots of architectural detail in their gardens, and a good example of a Dutch garden inspired by that country's canals is at Westbury Court, which dates from about 1700, and at Dyrham Park – both in Gloucestershire. A hundred miles away, in rural Bedfordshire, Thomas Archer's Dutch canal at Wrest Park is one of the unexpected pleasures of one of the least-known attractions of a little-known county. At the end of a canalside walk is a domed pavilion: you can climb to its lofty chambers and look out over an exceptional survivor of eighteenth-century landscape that was *not* Capability Brown's. I don't think I know anybody who knows anybody else who has been to Wrest Park. And my own visit was an accident. I had been browsing for antiques in the nearby village of Ampthill, which if it is ever bypassed will be a delightful town, but at the moment keeps you on the lookout for juggernauts mounting the pavement. The nearest village to Wrest Park is Silsoe (pleasant enough, with one or two pastel-washed thatched cottages, and an old Georgian coaching inn, called the Old George). Just down a lane that runs at right angles from the village street is this superb example of how they landscaped a great park when money was no object. It is as impressive as a small Versailles. A rather gloomy big house, built in the 1830s, and not open to the public, overlooks grounds that were laid out by Thomas Archer at the very beginning of the eighteenth century. He was, incidentally, one of the people responsible for the landscaping of Chatsworth House, Derbyshire home of the Duke of Devonshire.

Questions were once asked in the Commons because of the huge amount of money spent on the upkeep of Wrest Park in proportion to its very small number of visitors. And even now you have a good chance to wander as lonely as a Wordsworth among its groves and beside its Long Water. Within the park three great periods of garden landscaping are represented: the early eighteenth century, the mid-eighteenth century, and the early nineteenth century. The Chinese Bridge, however, which looks as if it could have come straight off a Willow Pattern dinner plate, and which gets people reaching for their cameras, was built in 1874.

The creation of great rolling landscaped gardens was a major industry in the eighteenth century. One cannot go far without hearing how this or that garden was laid out by Northumberland-born Lancelot 'Capability' Brown. Inevitably, though, since Brown had only one pair of hands, much of the work with which he is credited was actually done by his pupils, mostly but not always under his instruction. An advantage of such gardens for the visitor is that they are usually enjoyable at virtually any time of the year. I remember first going to Sissinghurst in Kent, which Brown would probably have been very rude about, my head ringing with admonishments from people who knew better about such things and said 'It's absolutely the wrong time to go.' And while Sissinghurst's layout is interesting at any time of the year, and is shot through with all kinds of poignant memories of the people who laid it out, most gardeners would say that spring is the best time to see it, although rose lovers might disagree and would probably pick July and August. Incidentally, Sissinghurst happens to have one of the south of England's finest viewpoints: you can climb to the top of the famous tower in which Vita Sackville-West was wont to write her idiosyncratic essays and poems.

One of the reasons suburbanites warm so much to Sissinghurst's garden is the fact that it is on a human scale and is not so perfect as to be daunting. It has its little foibles and puzzles, and if it is occasionally unkempt here and there, this does not detract. The garden has been described as a series of open-air rooms, each planted with flowers of one colour or making a special effect at any particular time of the year. It is romantic rather than formal, and if you can succeed in arriving before everybody else, or if there is an unexpected lull in the number of visitors (Cup Final Day is a good day to choose, and so is Finals Day at Wimbledon) then you are in for a rare treat. It could almost be a corner of the Royal Horticultural Society's gardens at Wisley, Surrey.

I suspect the same people who told me I was wrong about Sissinghurst would be very particular about when I went to an arboretum, but every season has something to offer, and at Batsford, in the heart of the Cotswolds, or Westonbirt, on their edge, there is no need to follow the Bank Holiday crowd: better to steal a mundane Monday morning on a crisp December day ('Just have some Christmas shopping to do, dear'), than be a Bank Holiday lemming. Westonbirt is much enhanced for the non-specialist

The restored sixteenth-century tower at Sissinghurst Castle, Kent, in
which the poet and novelist Vita Sackville-West had a study.

visitor by a good museum that pays particular attention to the growth and care of the classic trees represented here.

I think my own greatest weakness is for topiary – not necessarily the rabbits and chickens made of yew that for most people represent the state of the art, but those lime green and golden-syrup-yellow boxes, cones and lozenges that turn a walk along a humble paved path into a stately promenade in which you feel you ought to discuss eighteenth-century philosophy rather than the price of video recordings. They render evening shadows sharp but unreal, as long as poplars, as rotund as cottage loaves. Quite a few stately homes – not necessarily the oldest – have impressive topiary. An outstanding example is at Great Dixter, in Sussex, in gardens designed by Edwin Lutyens. Chastleton, in Oxfordshire, a house which has admittedly seen better days, was once famous for its topiary. Perhaps top of the topiary tree is Levens Hall, in Cumbria, whose garden was laid out in 1699 by a pupil of Le Nôtre. He came directly from the formal tradition that created Versailles. Walking round the gardens of Levens Hall is like finding yourself in the pages of *Alice in Wonderland*: there are unlikely mushroom-shaped yews with what look like sombreros on the top, umbrellas, fanciful birds, recognisable domestic animals, cylinders, cones, all set off by formal flower beds and further relieved by hedges of different colours.

But I am also fond of those modest domestic bits of topiary that, even if sometimes a little threadbare-looking, add a bit of leavening to one's progress through any number of tucked-away country villages. Perhaps best of all is the Yorkshire village of Terrington. The Post Office announces its presence by every one of the ten letters of its name picked out in topiary, which is enough to make you go and buy a few first-class stamps simply in order to pay your respects. The best trees or bushes, incidentally, for the topiary gardener, are cypress, box, yew, privet and rosemary. Hatfield House, in Hertfordshire, has a maze of yew hedges, which must qualify it technically as a topiary garden, and Hever Castle also has a symmetrical square maze, though it has never achieved the fame of, say, Hampton Court. However, the world's largest, if not most famous, maze, is at Longleat House. There is over a mile and a half of paths flanked by over 16,000 yew trees. The *tallest* yew hedge in the world, incidentally, is at Earl Bathurst's park in Cirencester, Gloucestershire: planted in 1720 it runs for 170 yards, reaches a height of 36 feet and is 15 feet thick. The base alone takes twenty full working days for a man to trim.

When an Irish nobleman offered Capability Brown £1000 for merely landing in what was then a province, he replied, 'But I have not finished England yet.' He is said to have been a difficult man to live with, and at the height of his creative powers the great and good hung on his every dictatorial word. If he announced, after a tour of inspection of some noble estate, that he was prepared to take on a commission ('I see great capability here'), his clients would be able to look their neighbours in the eye. The fees he charged were seldom a problem. If you were rich and powerful enough to move a village because it did not fit in with your scheme of things and spoilt the view from your drawing-room, it was no hardship to dam a lake and damn the expense. By the same token, if you were rich and vain enough you could ensure your house looked as good from the outside as it did inside, and in so doing you made your contribution consciously or unconsciously to the look of the landscape.

The best of England, rural and metropolitan, is a happy balance. The view from the terrace may be divine, but it would never have been the same without Capability Brown, Humphrey Repton, Fred Streeter and many a few thousand Mr Browns, Humphreys and Freds ever since. As the vicar said one day as he strolled past a cottage garden which looked like the picture on a Carter's seed packet: 'Why, Jim, it's quite marvellous what you and the good Lord have managed to achieve with that lovely garden.' To which Jim replied, 'Yes vicar, but you should have seen it when the good Lord had it all to himself.'

The Old Palace, Hatfield, Hertfordshire, photographed in February.
Elizabeth I was born here: could this be her effigy out in the cold?

3. Mysterious England

I once overheard a senior television executive advising would-be playwrights. He was half serious: 'If you want our people to look twice at your manuscript, write about strange goings-on in rural Suffolk. Or, even better, Cornwall. Put in a couple of ordinary events that develop a nasty turn. Put in the landlord of a pub in which weird things happen after closing time. People like that sort of thing and it always has a ring of truth.'

Behind the smiling face of stone villages and remote hill farms, the passing of the years has left a trail of curious things. The Brothers Grimm would not feel too disorientated. There is more going on among those Wiltshire downs than Unidentified Flying Objects landing at dead of night for a little look around. There is more to the ancient ceremony of rolling the vicar down the hill than meets the eye, and innocent festivals that celebrate this or that solstice have an edge to them that is at least disconcerting and at most terrifying.

Up in them there windswept hills the twentieth century can seem a long way away. People have refused to enter Wayland's Smithy, a prehistoric burial place near White Horse Hill. And White Horse Hill is mysterious enough itself, with an abstract neolithic figure of a horse that is beautiful to us but must have been awesome to prehistoric man. It is well-documented that there are dogs that will not enter the grounds of Berkeley Castle, in Gloucestershire. This is where Edward II, after being incarcerated in the hope that foul smells from the cesspits and dungeons would kill him, was murdered in a manner so bizarre (in order to leave no outwardly visible marks on his body), that teenage boys giggle and elderly spinsters block their ears. The expectation that those unpleasant stenches would be the end of Edward were not so fanciful. In Windsor Castle, as comparatively recently as 1861, Prince Albert, consort of Victoria, contracted typhoid because his private rooms were over uncovered foul drains. The cell in which Edward was kept is, incidentally, still accessible to visitors.

Sometimes the spirit-of-the-place so haunts a sacred or mysterious site that the lack of tangible evidence of its past does not seem very important. The priceless treasure left at Sutton Hoo, for example, by the Vikings, and discovered at Woodbridge in Suffolk, in 1939, is now in the British Museum. If you go to Woodbridge, which is well worth a visit for its own sake, you can look across the River Deben to the low hill on the far side, and imagine the place without the yachts, without the famous tide mill, without the railway station, all under those vast East Anglian skies as it might have appeared when this was a holy place.

Also investing extra magic in a place that is haunting enough in its own right, is King John's treasure. Legend says that some time after John signed the Magna Carta in 1215, the King's jewels were dropped in the Wash, that great bite out of eastern England,

The Edward II room, Berkeley Castle, Gloucestershire. Open to visitors, this is thought to have been where Edward was incarcerated prior to his gruesome murder.

which many hundreds of years ago was not the massive bay we know today but a much less wet, windswept region of mudflats and sands, criss-crossed by dangerous currents and at the mercy of relentless tides, similar perhaps to Lancashire's Morecambe Bay, but writ larger. It is believed that quicksands were responsible for the loss of John's treasure and documents: the King would have travelled separately from his baggage train, which he would probably have dispatched by the quickest and most dangerous route which passed near Long Sutton. Like the treasure of Tobermory Bay, on the Isle of Mull, buried as it is in many fathoms of unyielding mud, the truth will probably never be known.

Not knowing for sure is, of course, all part of the fun, and half a truth is better than none. People say, for example, that those gargoyles that with hideous expressions adorn many a corner of a country church, are devils from hell. A medieval peasant would have known better, however, for these are effigies of pagan gods that – curiously, considering where they now repose – predated Christianity by many hundreds of years. Most of them date back to at least the fourteenth century, as they were rarely incorporated in church buildings after that, so it is not surprising that their features are, to say the least, weather-worn. Human sacrifice had been an everyday matter in Roman Britain, and you will sometimes see a gargoyle into whose mouth tiny human figures are being popped. More common, however, is a gargoyle surrounded by leaves and foliage, known as the Green Man or Jack o' the Green. A crown of leaves, frequently oak which was held by the druids to be holy, represented a symbol of divinity. The most remarkable set of gargoyles is at Kilpeck Church, in Herefordshire, whose entrance door has fortunately survived the effects of wind and weather. Many of the symbolic

The parish church of St Peter at Winchcombe, Gloucestershire, is famous for its gargoyles: there are nearly fifty of them.

medieval carvings are elaborately interlinked, and the pagan symbols set off by a Christian angel. But elsewhere on the exterior of the church are beak heads, serpents, female fertility figures.

If Kilpeck's gargoyles are the best you will find in any modest little parish church, York Minster has the best to be found in any cathedral. The Minster has a silvery grey beauty that, since the late 1970s, has looked almost exactly as it would have done soon after it was built. There is a collection of gargoyles so high up in the ceiling that they look tiny from the ground but are actually life size. They are best seen with binoculars or telescopes. Among them is a creature reminiscent of the Cerne Abbas Giant, who has been given wings to suggest that he is Lucifer, the fallen angel. The Cerne Abbas Giant is the archetypal Celtic god, whose most dramatic representation is at Cerne Abbas in Dorset, where a two-hundred-foot-high portrayal of him was carved deep into the chalk two thousand years ago. He is further represented at Cerne Abbas Church, less than half a mile away, where, in a series of gargoyles, we see the giant's mouth being held open by two small figures. In the last group these figures are helping the giant to swallow a third.

The Romans became absorbed and integrated with the local community only when the threat from outside – that is, from the Picts to the north – seemed to recede. They gradually picked up an agrarian way of life that was at odds with the clash of cold steel. However, the Romans were a religious people (superstitious, really, by today's standards), and their military forts reveal as much about the importance of keeping the gods satisfied as they do about military strategy and sophisticated engineering.

During their domination of Britain, though as you went about your normal business you would hardly have recognised it as domination, about nine-tenths of the country was still covered by forest. And even though only a tiny percentage of England's landscape, in comparison with what went before, is now covered by trees, forest legends have persisted. The second most common pub name in England after The Chequers is The Green Man, a friendly green forest giant, and you can't go far in Nottingham without coming up against a Robin Hood this or a Robin Hood that, another legend which adds extra flavour to a visit to Nottingham Forest.

Epping Forest is shot through with half-believable tales of Queen Boadicea and Dick Turpin; and the New Forest, for all the sun-dappled clearings where picnickers can spread themselves, or feed the forest ponies, is still strange – William Rufus is believed to have been murdered – not just killed accidentally – on 2 August 1100, in the heart of the forest near Minstead. In the same way that Fen people lived a separate existence in the Victorian era, forest dwellers were not as much a part of civilisation in England as people like to think. Even today, as you drive between, say, Ringwood, and Bournemouth, there are places where the forest rolls inexorably over the low hills to left and right of the road, dark and impenetrable – a far cry from those soft leafy glades around Beaulieu and Lyndhurst.

In the heart of Epping Forest, near where one of the most horrific battles in history is said to have taken place, are Ambresbury Banks. Ambresbury Camp was one of several Iron Age forts dating from around 300 BC, each one a tree-topped concave several hundred yards across, about half a mile in circumference, bounded by earthworks and a ditch. When Boudicca (or Boadicea), Queen of the Iceni, clashed with the Romans here under the command of Suetonius in AD 61, the success of the Roman occupation – at

Highgate Cemetery, London. The effect of the careworn tombs and
catacombs of England's most celebrated necropolis can be just as eerie on a
still summer's day as by night.

least in this part of England – actually hung in the balance. The Britons really almost
won, and this would have put back the Roman plans for several years, for it would have
given the indigenous population a chance to regroup and fight a war of attrition among
the endless woods and marshes of what was then an almost impenetrable part of
England. Hundreds of years later, in Ely, Hereward the Wake stood out against the
Normans mainly on account of the nearly impassable terrain.

For all its proximity to London, much of Essex remains an inward-looking secret
enclave of the country. In the parish of Great Stambridge, for example, on the banks of

the River Crouch, there was once a large copse known as Shrieking Boy Wood. The name derives from a long forgotten and probably quite spurious tale of horror fostered by smugglers who found it a useful way to keep the prying eyes of villagers away from their own nefarious nocturnal activities. They also fostered the idea of a ghost bus, said to have been the idea of one Old Moss, a smuggler, who muffled the sounds of a coach's wheels and put sponges on the horses' hoofs. Not only did this make its progress silent, but kept curious local people at bay if they happened to see it. In Canewdon's quite exceptional church, there is part of a whale's vertebra on display, which was thought by the villagers to have been a Viking's kneebone.

I knew there was something different about Canewdon when I sat at midday in a corner of the Anchor over a pint of Greene King and perused the Ordnance Survey map, listening at the same time to a conversation between an old man in baggy brown cord trousers and the barman. 'I always talk to my plants, especially the tulips. That's how I win so many prizes. When I was in hospital in Southend there was nobody to talk to them, and they nearly died.' The barman reached for his glass: 'Mrs Garner, at the end of the street, says hers like music.' 'What kind of music?' 'Classical music. Mantovani and Semprini, that sort of thing.'

The Danes brought rape and pillage to Canewdon and its environs. There is little pillage nowadays (perhaps a bit of housebreaking, and a friend who lives there had some of his apples scrumped), but plenty of rape, or rather oilseed rape, which farmers grow primarily for cattle fodder and which turns the fields canary yellow and makes old ladies on WI outings exclaim 'Ooh, look at all that mustard'.

If you get a kick from seeing bats flying across overgrown churchyards at dusk, the atmosphere of three-hundred-year-old pub snugs, where a log fire and a pint of hand-pumped ale keep the wind from across the marshes at bay (for *real* ambience, it should rattle the panes), you will like rural south-east Essex. But I have toasted my knees in front of the fire in quite a few white-weatherboarded country pubs in Kent and Sussex where I half expected mine host to be a hobgoblin. The Lion Hotel, Nyetimber, Pagham, Sussex, for example, has everything that a haunted inn should. It is an ancient, picturesque building, not far from the sea. It was built as three cottages in 1407 and was once a smugglers' rendezvous. It has a priest's hole – allegedly part of a secret passage – and, of course, a wandering ghost. This is of a tall lady, dressed in blue or grey, who passes through rooms numbers five and six 'with the sound of rustling silk robes' and always at three o'clock in the morning. There is some doubt about who she actually was – some believe that she was the live-in mistress of a former landlord, and that she was eventually murdered by the landlord's jealous wife. A tiny cottage-style staircase led up to my low-ceilinged, oak-beamed room (number six) where, after the glass of sherry laid out for my arrival, I could have been convinced I felt the silent welcome of a phantom, friendly despite her violent end. Over dinner I was told by a fellow guest that a mysterious bump I had noticed under the carpet between the front door and the staircase was probably the entrance to a smugglers' tunnel which is said to lead to the beach. It could be connected to nearby Barton Manor, they say, a house of Saxon origin believed once to have been a priory. The ghost has also been seen at the Manor but here she was dressed as a nun.

I once accompanied a friend who writes and lectures about witchcraft and folklore into darkest Bedfordshire, to a place that gave even him the shudders. This was

Priest's hiding hole, Harvington Hall, Kidderminster, Worcestershire.

Clophill, where, on what is called Dead Man's Hill, is a churchyard that positively reeks of stories of black magic. On Midsummer's Eve, 1969, there was an attempt to revive the black mass, and during this, the tomb of an eighteenth-century apothecary's wife was torn open and what remained of her bones arranged in a circle around the ruined nave of the church, open to the skies. It is an unkempt, cold, unfriendly place, entirely at odds with the semi-rural easy-going flavour of this part of the country.

If you get the chance to see the Wiltshire village of Avebury from the air, do not pass it up, because from above you see how the oldest part of the village is circumscribed by an almost perfect earthwork circle like an only slightly misshapen, grassed-over rubber tyre. This is generally not noticed by visitors confined to the ground, unless they are well versed in deciphering the mysteries of the neolithic age. Even if you have to climb into a small plane, a balloon or a glider it is worth the effort in order to appreciate how substantial it looks after four or five thousand years – just imagine the impression you would get approaching Avebury at around the time that the Romans were colonising the Cotswolds and driving north towards the Midlands, or, better still, two thousand years before that. The circumference of the earthworks encloses approximately thirty acres, which makes Avebury more than ten times as big as the territory occupied by Stonehenge.

It was John Aubrey, idiosyncratic author of *Brief Lives*, who came across Avebury's stone circle, the second most enduring mystery of prehistoric England, when he was out hunting on Christmas Eve, 1648. He found himself in the centre of a ring of great stones that local people had lived with quite uncomprehendingly. Aubrey later described these Sarsen, or Saracen, stones as monoliths that do 'much exceed Stonehenge in grandeur as a cathedral does an ordinary parish church'. For Stonehenge was already well documented, while Avebury, the Cinderella of archaeological sites, was hardly known. Not only had local people tried to make use of the stones, but at one point had even tried to bury them: when the countryside began to be more intensively farmed, it was not just fear of the stones that caused people to try to put them out of sight and out of mind, for they got in the way of even hand- or horse-drawn ploughs. It has been deduced that one man was actually crushed during the process of pulling the stones over before an intended interment, because his bones were found underneath. The idea was to dig pits beside the stones, fill the pits with wood, which was then set on fire. The fire was supposed to crack the stones and pickaxes did the rest.

During the Victorian era, most such sites, including Silbury Hill, were reckoned to have a religious significance. But they tend to be all things to all men. Soldiers wonder whether Avebury was a former military camp; sociologists assume it was a glorified market place to which people came from many miles around to trade cattle and other goods. Astronomers fancy it as an elaborate device for predicting cosmic events. It has even been said – because the Ridgeway passes only a mile or so away, and this was the most firmly established and regularly trodden trunk route of the prehistoric age, the M1 of its time – that this was actually the capital of neolithic England.

Grassy, cone-shaped Silbury Hill is within easy walking distance of Avebury's stone circle. Archaeologists used to think that Silbury too was a burial tomb, but although there were exhaustive explorations, nothing significant was ever found. The only thing that was established in due course, mundane though it seems now, was that Silbury was entirely man-made. It must have been built with antler picks and other laborious hand tools and the approximate period of construction was established around 3,000 to 2,500 BC. That is about as much as anybody knows, except that this remains one of the strangest man-made structures in the whole of Europe. It has been a puzzle for centuries. The hill is certainly pre-Roman because the west to east Roman road that runs nearby makes an uncharacteristic detour to avoid the obstruction. I wonder what the Roman infantry thought of it, and how many of them scrambled up it out of sheer curiosity. It is recorded that Charles II 'cast his eye on Silbury Hill, which he had the curiosity to see, and walked up to the top of it'. Perhaps in years to come Charles III will do the same.

Curiously, two of the geographical features most closely associated with King Arthur (about whom we know less than we know for certain about the people who toiled to build Silbury Hill), are reminiscent of the hill. These are Cadbury Camp, at the top of a great green hill in Somerset, one of the most memorable natural features in the West Country and Glastonbury Tor, in the same county. By rights Arthur should have been destined for a quiet corner of history, lost in the toffee-stained pages of a schoolboy's textbook along with Canute, Alfred, Ethelred the Unready and other such dignatories. Arthur lived, if he lived at all, in the late fifth or early sixth century, the so-called Dark Ages that spanned the period between the Roman withdrawal from Britain and the Saxon takeover. These ages were 'dark' not by dint of some climatic quirk – the way the Ice Age had made earlier times intensely cold – but because they were so poorly recorded by contemporary historians.

The Arthur we know is largely a product of romantic fantasies. Facts that may have lingered in memories were transmitted by bards, elaborated by chroniclers, embroidered by storytellers, revised and revitalised by nineteenth-century Romantics and, most recently, commercialised by twentieth-century Hollywood. From his very conception Arthur was dragged off the rails of truth.

Haytor, Dartmoor. Not quite Ayer's Rock, but probably eeriest of all Dartmoor's outcrops of granite.

The place was Tintagel, a hag-tooth of a castle perched on one of Cornwall's most beautiful rocky promontories. It stands at the very heart of the Arthurian romance and tourists have flocked there. But it doesn't take a mathematical genius to spot the apparent contradiction behind King Arthur being born fourteen centuries ago in a twelfth-century castle. While Tintagel does happen to be the site of a fifth- or sixth-century Celtic monastery, there is still no evidence to link the place with the man. Not that anyone setting off on a quest for Arthur's Britain will find a shortage of places to visit, particularly in the West Country, where the geographical links are fiercely advocated. Only the Devil apparently, has been more widely commemorated in place names. Geoffrey of Monmouth, a Welsh monk, insisted Arthur's court stood in Wales, at Caerleon. Thomas Malory, author of *Morte d'Arthur*, maintained that it was in Winchester, and others pointed to Castle Kilibury, near Camelford in Cornwall, to Cadbury Castle in Somerset, and, of course, to Tintagel.

Before and after the Romans, people really did live in caves. Of all the subterranean cathedrals in England, it must be the caves of Wookey Hole that are most worth a substantial detour. Wookey is to Cheddar Gorge what Avebury is to Stonehenge: it is much less well known, but altogether more impressive. Here, among the Mendips, the River Axe erupts straight out of the face of the rock from subterranean tunnels, created not by the hand of Stone Age man but by many thousands of years of erosion of the limestone by the force of water. As if in some phantasmagorical grotto, three huge chambers hung with stalactites like bizarre, rocky icicles, lead the visitor through to a spectacular underground lake. Of course, this would, without the floodlighting, be pitch dark (imagine its effect on the first people to come here in modern times, armed as they were only with oil lamps). The caves were occupied during the Iron Age and occasionally by the Romans. Fourteen human skulls, thought to be Roman, were found here between 1947 and 1949. Almost all of them had been under thirty, and it was thought at first they were trophies of war, but the fact that two of them were female, and therefore extremely unlikely to have been under arms, discounted this. So here may be further evidence of human sacrifice. The caves are wreathed around with legend. One of them features a thirty-foot conger eel hidden in the depths of the subterranean lake, too big ever to escape. There is also the story of a witch who lived in the caves with her familiars, a goat and its kid. Crossed in love, she hated the human race, and cast evil spells over the people of Wookey, who eventually appealed to the Abbot of Glastonbury to get rid of her. A monk was accordingly despatched on this errand. She had no defence against the holy water he sprinkled on her and turned to stone, and the huge stalagmite known as the Witch of Wookey, with her bonnet and nose in sharp detail, stands inside the cavern to this day. In 1912, they actually discovered the remains of a woman in the cave, close to which were the bones of a goat and its kid. Also among the relics were a round stalagmite which, to any fanciful eye, looks like a gypsy's crystal ball.

As dusk begins to fall at Wookey and Cheddar, the strange shapes of the rocks against the sky and perhaps the barking of a sheep dog echoing from a distant hillside seem to transport you back many hundreds of years. The twentieth century seems nothing more than an illusion. But these are interesting rather than exceptional places. Every third village in England, it seems, revels (sometimes literally) in some mists-of-time custom that defies comprehension but amuses tourists. If you talk tongue-in-cheek about the ancient ceremony of 'rolling the vicar down the hill' cynics will know what you mean. I was once caught up in the Hallaton Hare Pie scramble in Leicestershire, and knew a man who knew a man who had taken part in the Ashbourne Shrove Tuesday and Ash Wednesday football free-for-all, in which the goal posts are three miles apart. There are no holds barred. The event makes a clash between Wales and the All Blacks look like a game of tiddly-winks. Only one old custom has ever really made me genuinely uneasy, and that is the Abbots Bromley Horn Dance. It is eerie and unsettling, and has a lingering primeval strangeness about it. The dance, or 'running' as it is called, is performed by six deer men, three of whom carry white wooden replicas of reindeer heads, adorned with real horns; three others have the same in black. There is a fool, a hobby horse, a Maid Marion, a man-woman and bowman, and music from an accordion. The horse beats time with its snapping jaws, and the bowman twangs his bow string. The climax comes when the black and white deer men face each other, and with their horns lowered, act out a mock fight, their movements made deliberately cumbersome by the weight of the antlers, all as if in slow motion. Maybe it does not sound like a show that will 'run and run', but it is in fact one of the longest surviving customs of its kind in Europe. Nobody knows the reason it became so well-established, but even though it was adopted by the church, and legitimised in the Middle Ages, its origins are clearly pagan.

Up Helly Aa is the most impressive of all the New Year celebrations, and despite the comparative inaccessibility of Shetland, Lerwick is packed to the rafters with tourists every New Year's Eve. A scaled-down, still intriguing version, with probably the same pagan origins, is held in Allendale, near Hexham, Northumberland. Men in costume carry barrels of blazing tar on their heads through the streets in the market and the barrels are tossed on to a bonfire; then begins dancing in the streets until midnight, when 'first foot' takes place, better known north of the border but still surviving throughout Northumberland. In this ancient ceremony, taken as it is for granted by generations of northerners and Scots, a dark-haired man – the taller the better – must be the first to enter a house after midnight, carrying gifts of bread and coal, which bring good luck. If you are red-haired, and are carrying a copy of the evening paper, you will not be welcome.

Such activities are harmless and fun, and at least have the advantage of keeping ancient traditions alive. How we wish, for example, that five thousand or so years ago somebody had kept a diary about Stonehenge: there are enough enigmas as it is. It is easy to see how comparatively modern structures will, in hundreds of years' time, be the subject of intrigue and legend. What will they make, for example, of the bee-hive coke ovens on the edge of the Durham coal fields at Inkerman? Will they think they were connected in some way with the bee-hive huts of early Irish monks? Even as the Industrial Revolution was getting properly under way in the early years of the nineteenth century, these curious structures, like something out of a Doctor Who film, had been abandoned.

People will wonder, too, about village stocks, even though they are taken so much for granted today. Dogs wee on them unceremoniously and hikers hoist their weary limbs on them to do up their shoelaces. Parish councils argue about whether to get Rentokil in to have a look at the wet rot. In 1350 Edward III decreed that every town should have stocks, and sixteen years later another royal dictate determined that every village should have them too. They normally consisted of upright posts with a wooden board containing round holes where the feet of minor criminals were inserted and locked, but there were some interesting variations. One of the upright posts might be extended to make a whipping post – and, a rare find (there is one in Coles Hill, Warwickshire, last used in 1863), you might even happen across a combined whipping post and pillory. Among other places where you will find pillories are Saffron Walden, Waltham Abbey and Midhurst. The stocks at Bottesford, in Leicestershire, have room for two people side by side, making the chances of a direct hit with your pound of rotten tomatoes more likely – it was not only permissible, but even encouraged, to throw things at miscreants. Failure to go to church was one of the grounds for being put in the stocks, unless you had a very good reason – having a lie-in was not.

But stocks are not the only example of village paraphernalia. Headstones and epitaphs recall the past as poignantly as any parish register or marble tomb. In the churchyard of St Leonards in Bridgnorth, Shropshire, mystery still surrounds an old stone coffin. It is said to have been found several centuries ago beneath the cellar floor of a Bridgnorth house. Inside it was the embalmed body of a woman. The woman was hastily reburied and her coffin placed in the churchyard – her identity has never been proved, but it is believed she was murdered.

Village stocks at Bottesford, Leicestershire. Perhaps one reason for their universal appeal to visitors is that their original function is so obvious.

Condemned cell. Berwick upon Tweed jail: this is the sort of place to get
the imagination working.

Nothing quite beats the sight of village stocks illuminated by moonlight, or a gallows
silhouetted against an evening sky. And the atheist who half believes in God in the wee
small hours will shudder as he walks across a lonely country graveyard.

I once had a good shudder in the city of York, where there are lots of dark little
alleys, relics of medieval passageways that will work on the imagination of even the most
unimaginative visitor. I joined a party of ghost hunters, being guided with an
impressive air of stealth around some of York's most reliably haunted sites. The first
stop was the Cock and Bottle, where there was a landlady who could have made a living
as a model for the most typical English barmaid. She nervously retold – one suspects for
the umpteenth time – the story of small children upstairs in the pub who talk to friendly
apparitions, of a man in old-fashioned dress who touches her on the shoulder, of dogs
whose hair bristles, of keys that disappear only to turn up again months later.

I was one of a mixed bunch of visitors. Instead of wispy-haired academics of psychic
sensitives blinking in the warm spring sunshine, there was an amiable sprinkling of
Americans from an air-force base in Bedfordshire and a polite Asian man taking notes. I

York, and getting the wheels in motion for the York Mystery Plays, which
are held every four years. The part of Jesus is always played by a
professional, but the other actors are amateurs.

wondered aloud why he did, and who he was, but his English was poor and he merely
shook his head and smiled.

The Cock and Bottle was a bit of fun, a chance to extend Saturday night conviviality
for a couple of hours in a *gemütlich* wood-panelled pub that belied its new exterior.
People were visibly more moved when, on the Sunday afternoon, they trooped down to
the dark cellars of one of York's finest mansions, very close to the Minster. Here, below
the Treasurer's House, redolent by any standards with spooky stories, they heard Police
Constable Harry Martindale relate his vision many years before of a band of Roman
legionaries who had the ill manners to march peremptorily to the sound of trumpets
through the cellar where he was working. Harry's story was told to each group of
ghost-weekenders, and his apparent indifference to whether you believed him or not,
made it hard not to be impressed by the tale. York had been, after all, an important
Roman settlement.

The School of Dancing, the unlikeliest venue for ghost hunters, was a special treat.
Being joined by a coach load of dilettante spook-seekers from Sheffield – out, that is,
only for a day trip – gave the twenty-five strong group a carnival atmosphere. Between
impromptu displays of youthful dancing prowess by some of her pupils, the
proprietress told the assembled company about ghostly footsteps (not, surprisingly,

ghostly *dancing* steps), about coins that jingled and electronic equipment that refused to work when a visiting television camera crew tried to record some apparitions on film. Well, it was about as ghostly as you can get on a Saturday morning when York is full of shoppers.

When the wind howls across the marshes and the windows in the remote farmhouse you have rented for Christmas rattle all night, and when in late November the last leaves fall from skeletal trees on to a remote and desecrated graveyard and you are half convinced a headstone shifts, it is easy to conjure up witches and demons.

But beware the suffocatingly hot night in the haunted room of some four-hundred-year-old pub, when you tell yourself it is merely the lack of air that prevents you from sleeping. Be careful not to laugh too much at the antics of some lord of misrule lest he catches your eye, and do not completely disregard the tinker's curse: at Appleby in June, during the gypsy horse-fair, mind your p's and q's.

Postscript

There are probably two schools of thought among the people who give up on England and emigrate. Some say 'It's a morgue, it's boring, there's nothing going on. Let's try somewhere with a bit of life.' Others say 'What ever happened to England? It's noisy, aggressive, it's changed too much. Let's go somewhere where they still respect the old values.'

Between them, if you distil what they say, they have got it about right. If the doyen of English travel writers, H.V. Morton, were to return today to places he visited and wrote about in the 1930s, he would be astonished by the difference. He might also think that nothing had really changed. For just as the English are adaptable and able to absorb new ideas, so the towns and the countryside have survived more or less intact into the twenty-first century – or almost. You might almost imagine that the English wanted to prove they lose every battle except the last: just in time, the Victorian heart of an industrial town is saved from destruction; just in time, a bypass is diverted to save a patch of primeval woodland. Permission is given for a new supermarket in an eighteenth-century terrace, but it must have a facia that matches; a street is pedestrianised, a canal restored with local authority support.

There is not necessarily anything coy about the old man who says he has never been beyond the next parish but one. ('Well, there was the Sunday school outing to the seaside in 1925, but I was sick on Mrs MacFarlane's home-made fudge and I didn't take much notice of where I was.') And there is not necessarily anything twee about the little Victorian cottage where he lives – especially when, given a bidet and a solar heating system, modern developers are trying to reproduce it more or less exactly. Long live the bidets and the solar panels, but long live the weeds and the wilderness yet. Orwell's *1984* still touches a few nerves but Morton's reflections in *The Call of England* have the ring of truth instead of sounding old hat and precious.

'My mind went back over the road to York, to Whitby, to the abbeys of the north, to the gold sands of Lindisfarne, to the wild Border Marches, to the sudden beauty of the village and the energy of the city. I tried to penetrate the minds of people who live in England yet spend their leisure out of England. I can conceive no greater happiness than that of going out into England and finding it almost too English to be true: the little cottages, which vary from county to county, the churches with their naves in Norman England, the great houses, the castles, the incredible cathedrals, the strange little places which will, let us hope, never quite emerge from an earlier and, I believe, happier world. England is one of the easiest countries to see because it does not matter whether you set off north, south, east, or west. Whichever way you go, you will in the first mile meet something worth your attention and perhaps your respect.'

That, as they say, hits the spot.

Index

Page numbers in italics refer to photographs

The new county of Hereford and Worcester is referred to in this index, but the former (and still popularly used) county names of Herefordshire and Worcestershire are retained for the text.